ONE DAY IN HISTORY

The Days That Changed the World

DECEMBER 7, 1941

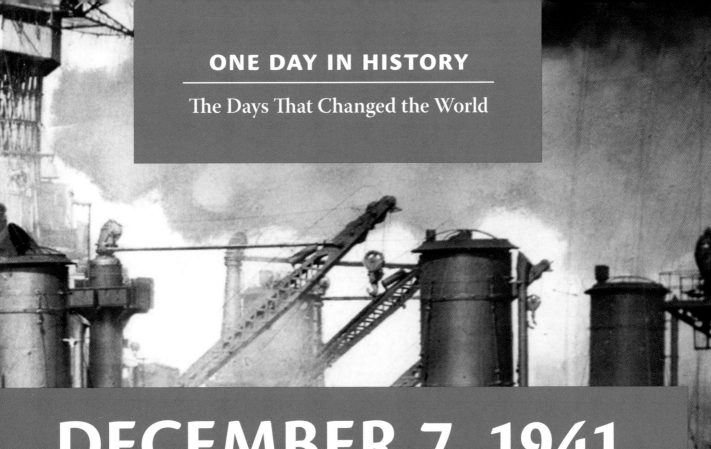

ONE DAY IN HISTORY

The Days That Changed the World

DECEMBER 7, 1941

Rodney P. Carlisle, Ph.D., General Editor

Collins

An Imprint of HarperCollinsPublishers

Special Thanks to:

Jennifer L. Jones from the National Museum of American History, Behring Center, Smithsonian Institution
and Dik Daso from the National Air and Space Museum, Smithsonian Institution

HarperCollins books may be purchased for educational, business, or sales promotional use. For information please write: Special Markets Department, HarperCollins Publishers, 10 East 53rd Street, New York, NY 10022.

FIRST EDITION

The name of the "Smithsonian," "Smithsonian Institution," and the sunburst logo are registered trademarks of the Smithsonian Institution.

Library of Congress Cataloging-in-Publication Data

One day in history: December 7, 1941 / Rodney P. Carlisle, general editor. — 1st ed.
 p. cm.
 Includes index.
 ISBN-13: 978-0-06-112034-3
 ISBN-10: 0-06-112034-0
 1. Pearl Harbor (Hawaii), Attack on, 1941. 2. World War, 1939-1945—Naval operations, Japanese. I. Carlisle, Rodney P. II. Title.

D767.92.054 2006
940.54'26693—dc22   2006049115

---

06 07 08 09 10 TPNJ 9 8 7 6 5 4 3 2 1

Photo Credits

National Archives and Records Administration: Pages iv left, v left, 2 right, 32, 36, 41, 43 top, 49 (Associated Press, right), 52 left/right, 62, 67 bottom, 81 left/right, 87 left/right, 100 top, 110, 112 left/right, 113 left/right, 117 left/right, 122 left/right, 134, 137, 138, 149, 157 (H.C. Fawcett), 158, 160 (UPI), 162, 165, 167, 168, 171, 173, 178, 180, 183, 185 left/right, 187 left, 194 left/right, 195, 200, 202, 211, 213, 216, 218 left/right, 220 bottom, 228, 230 left/right, 231, 233, 237, 240, 250 left/right, 255 left, 256, 258; Loretta Carlisle Photography: Pages 6, 11, 16, 19 top/upper middle, 28, 30, 34, 43 center right/left, 51 left/right, 60, 64, 74 right, 77, 79, 100 center/bottom, 115 top/bottom, 120 left/right, 123 top/bottom, 128, 143, 145, 147, 150, 151, 176 left/right, 187 right, 188, 199 top/bottom, 214, 244, 248 left/right, 255 right; ACME: Page iv right, 48; Corbis: Page 99 right; Getty Images: Page xvi, 2, 27, 124; Library of Congress: Pages ii-iii, v right, xvi, 8, 13, 20, 23, 40, 43, 46, 82, 90 top/bottom, 93 left, 94, 105, 126 left/right, 132, 141, 190, 209, 220 top, 221, 222, 224 left/right, 239, 242, 259; © 2006 Jupiterimages Corporation: Pages 15, 19 lower middle/bottom, 28, 29, 59, 67, 69, 74 left, 106, 108, 118, 155, 246. Department of Defense: Page 12; NSA: Page 38; www.snydertreasures.com: Page 239. U.S. Air Force: Page 82.

Golson Books, Ltd.

President and Editor	J. Geoffrey Golson
General Editor	Rodney P. Carlisle
Design Director	Kevin Hanek
Designer	Mary Jo Scibetta
Compositor and Editor	Linda C. Angér
Copyeditor	Martha Whitt
Proofreader	Barbara Paris
Indexer	JS Editorial, LLC

CONTENTS

Articles are presented in alphabetical order. Cross-references to other articles are in SMALL CAPS within the text.

Preface by Sir John Keegan	vii	Culture, 1941	42
Introduction	ix	Daily Life, 1941	47
Reader's Guide to Articles	xii	Damage, Memorial	50
December 7, 1941: Timeline	xiii	De Gaulle, Charles	52
		Declaration of War in Tokyo	53
Aircraft Carriers	1	Diplomatic Relations	54
Airplanes versus Ships	3	Doolittle, James	55
Allies on December 7, 1941	6	French Indochina	57
Arcadia Conference	9	G-2 and Army Intelligence	61
Arizona, USS	10	German Declaration of War	63
Arizona, USS Memorial	13	Germany	64
Axis Powers in 1941	16	Great Britain, Reaction in	68
Bloch, C.C.	21	Greater East Asia Co-Prosperity Sphere	69
British Commonwealth	22	Grew, Joseph	71
California, USS	31	Guam	71
Caroline Islands	33	Hawai'i to 1898	73
Churchill, Winston	34	Hawai'i, 1898 to 1942	76
Codes, Japanese	36	Hirohito, Emperor	80
Congressional Medal of Honor	39	Historians' Views	82
Congressional Reaction	40	Hitler, Adolf	87

Hong Kong	88	Pacific Fleet, U.S.	169
Honolulu	89	*Panay* Incident	174
Hull, Cordell	92	Panic	176
Intelligence, Pacific Theater	95	Pearl Harbor: Action Report	177
Investigations of Responsibility	97	*Pennsylvania*, USS	180
Isolationism	101	Philippines, Preparation for Attack	182
Isolationist Press	104	Philippines	183
Japan	107	Preparedness	184
Japanese Aircraft	111	Rankin, Jeannette	189
Japanese Fleet	114	Richardson, James O.	191
Japanese American Internment Camps	117	Roosevelt, Franklin D.	193
Kidd, Isaac	119	Russia–Japan Relations	197
Kimmel, Husband E.	121	Salvage Operations	201
Knox, Frank A.	122	Sanctions against Japan	204
Lend-Lease	125	Short, Walter C.	207
Literature and Films	127	Stalin, Josef	209
MacArthur, Douglas	133	Stark, Harold R.	211
Malaya and Singapore	134	Stimson, Henry L.	212
Marshall Islands	136	*Tennessee*, USS	215
Marshall, George C.	137	Tojo, Hideki	217
Maryland, USS	138	Toyoda, Teijiro	218
Matsuoka, Yosuke	139	Truman, Harry	219
Memoirs, American	140	United States	223
Memoirs, Japanese	144	WACs	229
Midget Submarines	147	Wake Island	231
Midway, Battle of	148	Wallace, Henry A.	232
Mussolini, Benito	151	WAVES	233
Neutrality Acts	153	*West Virginia*, USS	234
Nevada, USS	156	World War II, Causes of	236
Nimitz, Chester	158	World War II, Results of	242
Nomura, Kichisaburo	159	World War II	247
Oahu Airfields and Bases	161	Yamamoto, Isoroku	257
Oahu Forts	164		
Oklahoma, USS	166	*Index*	260

PREFACE

BY SIR JOHN KEEGAN

DECEMBER 7, 1941, a Sunday in the central Pacific: at Pearl Harbor in the Hawai'ian Islands, headquarters of the U.S. Pacific Fleet, the crews of the battleships were enjoying a longer than usual sleep. Many of the officers were ashore. The Army Air Corps base at Hickham Field was expecting an inward flight of B-17 bombers but very few of its aircraft were aloft or on patrol. There had been so many false alarms of a Japanese attack in the preceding weeks and months that the edge of alertness had been lost among the island's defenders. The only active surveillance was being staged by a British-delivered radar station located at the extreme north of the island. Its search was due to close down for the day at 7 A.M. Just before it did so, the operator detected aircraft approaching the island. The news was reported to headquarters at Pearl Harbor but the operators were told by the duty officer that they had probably picked up the incoming B-17s and to shut down as scheduled.

In fact the operators had detected the approach of the aircraft of the Japanese combined fleet, which were already flying off to attack Pearl Harbor. The fleet consisted of six large carriers, the *Akagi, Kaga, Hiryu, Soryu, Shokaku,* and *Zuikaku,* which embarked 460 torpedo bombers, dive bombers, high altitude bombers, and their escorting fighters. The carrier fleet was accompanied by large numbers of destroyers, cruisers, and battleships and presented a large target to a vigilant defender. The defenders were not vigilant. At 7:55 A.M., as the Pacific Fleet began to hoist colors for the start of the day, the Japanese attacking aircraft arrived overhead and began

to deliver ordnance against Battleship Row, where eight battleships were moored in pairs in the lee of Ford Island. The Japanese also attacked Hickham Field, barracks, and naval and military installations. The alarm was sounded, accompanied by the loudspeaker warning "This is no drill!" As ships began to sink, their shocked crews manned their guns and began to fire back at the attackers. Aircraft took off from Hickam Field. Some Japanese aircraft were hit, but at 8:50 A.M., a second wave of attackers appeared. Resistance was by then better organized and 20 of the attackers were shot down. Those losses were heavily outweighed by those suffered by American forces. Five of the eight battleships had been sunk and 188 out of 394 American aircraft destroyed and 159 damaged. Of the 94 warships in harbor, 18 had been sunk or seriously damaged. Almost the only consolation for the U.S. Navy was that none of its aircraft carriers were present at Pearl Harbor on December 7. They were either in the continental United States or delivering aircraft to U.S. island bases elsewhere in the Pacific.

In Washington, D.C., the staff of the Japanese embassy were hastening to prepare a presentable form of a message from the Tokyo government to Cordell Hull, the U.S. secretary of state, announcing the termination of discussions undertaken to preserve the increasingly fragile peace between the two countries. Ambassador Nomura had been instructed that he was to type the document himself, so secret was it. It was to be delivered to Cordell Hull by 1 P.M., just before the surprise attack on Pearl Harbor was to begin. Nomura was not a good typist and completed, with each retyping, the 14-part message too late to meet the deadline. When he arrived at the State Department to deliver the message, Hull was already receiving news of the Pearl Harbor sinkings.

Meanwhile Japanese attacks were also opening on American bases in the Philippines, on the British colony of Malaya, and on island outposts at Guam and Wake. Hong Kong had been invaded and Japanese forces were sailing to intercept the British fleet sent to defend Singapore. In London, Winston Churchill, who had based all his hope of a successful outcome to the war on "dragging the Yanks in" was, since Britain's expulsion from the European continent in 1940, almost the only person at a high level of government in any of the nations at war, to see a silver lining to the news. As he retired to bed on the evening of December 7, he confided to himself "so we had won after all."

That was one way in which December 7, 1941, changed history. By forcing the United States to enter World War II, Japan had ensured that the world's foremost economic power would set itself to become the foremost military power as well. Because Japan was allied to Adolf Hitler's Germany in the Tripartite Pact, America's intervention was not confined to the Pacific but included Europe as well. Hitler then ensured that the United States would fight Germany as well as Japan by declaring war on the United States on December 11. American intervention against Germany and its espousal of the cause of Germany's other enemies ensured the survival of Josef Stalin's Soviet Union near-defeat in 1941, because Soviet Russia then became eligible for United States lend-lease war supplies. December 7, 1941, changed almost every important international relationship in the world—to the disadvantage of the Axis (Germany-Japan-Italy) and to the advantage of the Allies (United States-United Kingdom-Soviet Union), which would dominate the world in subsequent years.

INTRODUCTION

T HE LIGHT OF DAWN was just touching the mountains of Oahu on a quiet Sunday morning that promised to be like any other on Hawai'i. This morning, December 7, was warm but with gentle off-shore breezes to break the humidity. Despite alerts that restricted sailors' leave, they anticipated another uneventful day, secure in their ships, moored next to Ford Island. In the galley of the USS *Arizona*, cooks busied themselves serving the crush of sailors lined up for coffee, flapjacks, oatmeal, bacon, and eggs. Breakfast odors wafted through the companionways of the ship and enticed the men; some had trouble stumbling out of their bunks even though they had been allowed to sleep late, until 6:30 A.M.

After breakfast, those sailors with no special duty assignments drifted out on the decks to enjoy the morning air. The ship's chronometer read 7:53 A.M., December 7, 1941.

High in the sky above Hawai'i, aircraft swept in, apparently another demonstration by navy flyers, most sailors thought. But distant thumps came closer quickly, and then direct hits shook the USS *Arizona*. As waves of aircraft came sweeping overhead and explosions rocked the harbor, the realization swept through the crews of all the American ships: this is not a drill.

The sudden and effective Japanese raid on Hawai'i took nearly 2,400 lives, about half of them aboard USS *Arizona*. As 19 ships burned or exploded in the harbor and over 120 aircraft were destroyed in the air and on the ground at airfields around Oahu, Americans reacted with shock, then with bitter determination.

The news swept the world. In Kuibyshev, Russia's wartime capital, American journalist C. L. Sulzberger lived across the hall in the Grand Hotel from three Japanese correspondents. Politely, they knocked on his door, smiled, and said how sorry they were that the American fleet had been demolished. Sulzberger remembered, "To my horror, I found that what they said was true."

Driving up the Henry Hudson Parkway in New York City to play golf that sunny Sunday afternoon, Frank Brandstetter, a young National Guard member with a real estate business in the city, noticed cars pulling off to the side of the road, for no apparent reason. He pulled over and turned on the car radio, and then he understood what was going on. The news from Pearl Harbor was on every station.

At 2:05 P.M. in Washington, D.C., the Japanese delegation of Saburo Kurusu and Ambassador Kichisaburo Nomura finally got in to see Secretary of State Cordell Hull. The attack had already begun in Hawai'i, and Hull knew it. Hull read the document offered by the two Japanese delegates, presenting suggestions for a Pacific settlement. Quietly, his eyes like steel, Hull said: "In all my fifty years of public service I have never seen a document that was more crowded with infamous falsehoods and distortions. I never imagined that any government on this planet was capable of uttering them." Nomura and Kurusu found the reaction rude.

American neutrality vanished. World War II in Europe had been going on for over two years since September 1, 1939, and war had been brewing for four years prior to that, but officially and emotionally,

Americans had stayed out of it. Through 1939 and 1940, Poland, Belgium, France, Denmark, and Norway had fallen to the Nazi onslaught. In June 1941, Hitler decided to attack the Soviet Union. The United States had remained aloof, neutral in policy but clearly sympathetic to the defeated countries of Europe and to Britain. It seemed by late 1941 that soon Britain, too, could face an invasion by German forces and all of Europe could fall under the control of the Fascist powers. The attack on Pearl Harbor on December 7, 1941, changed all that, hurtling the United States in one bloody morning from a nervously complacent neutral into the status of a full-fledged combatant in the greatest war the world had ever seen.

Americans wondered then, and over the coming months, why the Japanese had struck so suddenly—what lay behind the act that plunged the United States into war? The Japanese believed that the United States was setting out to oppose their plans for expansion in Southeast Asia, but few Americans, even those who had followed the details of diplomacy in that part of the world, expected the Japanese to react with an act of war. The Japanese doctrine, that of "Greater East Asia" was to replace European dominance and colonial controls in China, Southeast Asia, and the islands of the Pacific, with Japanese administration, and the Japanese move into Indochina with the permission of the Vichy French showed that Japan was willing to take from the Europeans whatever possessions might become available.

Japanese plans to supplant the European empires and influence in that region could be thwarted by the United States, and it seemed to Japanese leaders that was exactly what the United States was attempting to do. The Japanese decision for a preemptive strike was reasonable from their own strategic perspective. U.S. Ambassador to Japan Joseph Grew observed about the attack, "National sanity would dictate against such an event, but Japanese sanity cannot be measured by our own standards of logic." Editorialists took a stronger tone. The *Los Angeles Times* cried out: "It was the act of a mad dog."

The raid on Pearl Harbor, Schofield Barracks, and other bases on Oahu struck Americans as a "dastardly attack"—a "stab in the back." It seemed especially devious because on the date of the attack, U.S. and Japanese diplomats Nomura and Kurusu had continued discussions in Washington regarding Japanese moves in Southeast Asia, knowing full well that the attack was in preparation. The combination of polite diplomats and a secret fleet of aircraft carriers approaching their targets under radio silence seemed a grand deception, intended to trick the United States into complacency about American holdings in Hawai'i and the Philippines. The press and the public shared Secretary Hull's shock.

From San Francisco to Toledo to New York, Americans believed the next Japanese air raid would begin to devastate American cities before anti aircraft defenses and barrage balloons could be mounted. Eleanor Roosevelt was aboard an airplane with the mayor of New York, Fiorello La Guardia, headed for San Francisco on December 8, when the pilot reported a radio communique that San Francisco was under attack. She woke up La Guardia and told him the news. When the plane stopped to refuel, she called ahead to learn the rumor was false.

Within days, volunteers flooded into recruiting offices with the motto "Remember Pearl Harbor," as a song with that refrain played over radio stations. Brandstetter and thousands like him reported for duty. Sulzberger's reports from Russia now reflected admiration for a staunch ally.

Almost as soon as the smoke cleared and the salvage operations in Pearl Harbor began, controversies emerged. Aircraft carriers had been out to sea during the attack; Pearl Harbor and other military bases on the island of Oahu seemed unprepared; battleships were moored in harbor. Critics charged that someone was at fault. Some saw the American battleships, neatly paired in a double row next to Ford Island in Pearl Harbor, as sitting ducks, inviting attack.

Hostile critics charged that Roosevelt and the War Department had known the attack was coming and had not properly warned the local commanders, Admiral Husband Kimmel and General Walter Short, even after intelligence revealed an attack was about to begin. Worse yet, conspiracy theorists suggested that the attack provided the United States with a "back door to war," so that Roosevelt could achieve his ambition of aiding Britain by enticing the Japanese into an attack that would result in American entry into the World War. Such views were held by a small but persistent minority; most Americans, even die-hard neutralists, isolationists, and even most of the committed "America Firsters," tended to rally behind the war, precisely because it was a foreign attack, by a military power, upon U.S. military forces, on U.S. territory.

Never before nor since was there ever such a clear *casus belli* for America to go to war. Even so, the lack of preparedness seemed appalling; that failure to be prepared was viewed as a failure of individual commands and even more so, as a failure of intelligence. Investigations and courts-martial attempted to place blame. The post-war effort to provide a single coordinating central intelligence agency to prevent such surprises in the future can be traced to the shock of the surprise at Pearl Harbor on December 7.

Because of the surprise attack, the apparent duplicity of launching the attack while diplomacy went forward, and because the attack was on American territory, the U.S. public and leaders felt justified in waging a war for victory — a war without mercy, with a demand of unconditional surrender. Few other actions could have rallied U.S. opinion so solidly behind a vigorous campaign against an enemy.

Vast consequences beyond the damage and death of December 7 flowed from the events of that day. This encyclopedia sets out in 100 articles the details of the day in history, the causes and consequences of the day's events, and how December 7 impacted the lives of ordinary Americans.

—RODNEY P. CARLISLE
GENERAL EDITOR

READER'S GUIDE TO ARTICLES

This list is provided to assist readers in finding related articles by topic.

HISTORY & CULTURE

Allies on December 7, 1941
Arcadia Conference
Axis Powers in 1941
British Commonwealth
Congressional Reaction
Daily Life, 1941
Hawaiʻi to 1898
Hawaiʻi 1898 to 1942
Historians' Views
Isolationism
Isolationist Press
Japan
Literature and Films
Neutrality Acts
Panic
Preparedness
Russia-Japan Relations
Sanctions against Japan
United States

IN MEMORIAM

Arizona, USS Memorial
Congressional Medal of Honor
Damage, Memorial
Memoirs, American

INTELLIGENCE AND DECEMBER 7

Codes, Japanese
G-2 and Army Intelligence
Grew, Joseph
Historians' Views
Hull, Cordell
Intelligence, Pacific Theater
Investigations of Responsibility
Japanese Fleet

Roosevelt, Franklin D.
Short, Walter C.
Stimson, Henry L.

PEOPLE

Bloch, C.C.
De Gaulle, Charles
Doolittle, James
Grew, Joseph
Hirohito, Emperor
Hitler, Adolf
Hull, Cordell
Kidd, Isaac
Kimmel, Husband E.
Knox, Frank A.
MacArthur, Douglas
Marshall, George C.
Matsuoka, Yosuke
Memoirs, American
Memoirs, Japanese
Mussolini, Benito
Nimitz, Chester
Nomura, Kichisaburo
Rankin, Jeannette
Richardson, James O.
Roosevelt, Franklin D.
Short, Walter C.
Stalin, Josef
Stark, Harold R.
Stimson, Henry L.
Tojo, Hideki
Toyoda, Teijiro
Truman, Harry
WACs
Wallace, Henry A.
WAVES
Yamamoto, Isoroku

SHIPS & AIRCRAFT

Aircraft Carriers
Airplanes versus Ships
Arizona, USS
California, USS

Japanese Aircraft
Japanese Fleet
Midget Submarines
Nevada, USS
Oklahoma, USS
Pacific Fleet, U.S.
Panay Incident
Pennsylvania, USS
Salvage Operations
Tennessee, USS
West Virginia, USS

WORLD AT WAR

Allies on December 7, 1941
Axis Powers in 1941
British Commonwealth
Caroline Islands
December 7, 1941: *Timeline*
Declaration of War in Tokyo
Diplomatic Relations
French Indochina
German Declaration of War
Germany
Great Britain, Reaction in
Great East Asia Co-Prosperity Sphere
Guam
Hong Kong
Japan
Japanese American
    Internment Camps
Malaya and Singapore
Marshall Islands
Midway, Battle of
Oahu Airfields and Bases
Oahu Forts
Pearl Harbor: Action Report
Philippines
Russia-Japan Relations
United States
Wake Island
World War II, Causes of
World War II, Results of
World War II

DECEMBER 7, 1941: *TIMELINE*

Except where noted, all times are Hawai'ian.

7:55 A.M.

American sailors in Pearl Harbor notice lines of planes approaching.

7:56 A.M.

Japanese torpedo bombers swoop down on the American ships moored on the north side of Ford Island, slapping torpedoes into the light cruiser USS *Raleigh* and the target ship USS *Utah*, an old battleship, lying at Berth F-11, and Lt. Tsuyoshi Nagai's *Soryu* torpedo bomber puts a "fish" into the cruiser USS *Helena.* The concussion bursts the seams of the USS *Oglala* moored alongside.

8 A.M.

At Pacific Fleet headquarters, Cdr. Vincent Murphy radios Washington, the Chief of Naval Operations, and the C-in-C of the Atlantic and Asiatic Fleets: "Air raid on Pearl Harbor. This is no drill."

8 A.M. (1:30 P.M. IN WASHINGTON, D.C.)

Secretary of the Navy Frank Knox gets the message "Air raid on Pearl Harbor. This is no drill." Stunned, Knox says, "My God, this can't be true! This must mean the Philippines!" Adm. Harold "Betty" Stark, the Chief of Naval Operations, responds, "No, sir! This is Pearl!" Marshall gets the same message at the same time, while eating lunch.

8:01 A.M.

USS *Oklahoma* takes the first of five torpedoes. USS *West Virginia* takes the first of six. USS *Oklahoma*'s second hit punches out her electricity. The next three flood the ship.

9:02 A.M.

The Japanese second wave of attack swoops down on Pearl Harbor.

9:05 A.M.

High-level bombers from *Zuikaku* pound Hickam Field.

9:06 A.M.

Lt. Cdr. James Craig steps back on board USS *Pennsylvania* and is killed by a 500-lb. bomb that hits the starboard casemate just as Craig is passing through.

9:10 A.M.

USS *Curtiss*'s guns clip a dive-bomber flown by Lt. Mimori Suzuki of *Akagi*, which crashes into the ship's starboard seaplane crane, starting a fire. Battered by bombs, USS *Nevada* is grounded at Hospital Point after being warned that she cannot leave harbor—there are enemy submarines in the channel.

9:12 A.M.

USS *Shaw*, sitting in the floating drydock, takes a hit that ignites her forward magazine.

9:15 A.M.

Japanese dive-bombers attack Hickam Field again.

9:21 A.M.

Admiral Halsey's task force and all other U.S. ships at sea in the Pacific are ordered to search for the Japanese carriers.

9:30 A.M.

A massive explosion in USS *Shaw*'s forward magazine sends a ball of fire hurling into the air. Dive-bombers hit Kaneohe. Americans defend the area with machine guns mounted on water pipes and tail-wheel assemblies.

9:30 A.M.

One of 39 explosions in Honolulu caused by improperly set American anti aircraft shells tears the legs off fly-weight boxer Toy Tamanaha on Kukui Street.

9:30 A.M. (3 P.M. IN WASHINGTON, D.C.)

President Franklin Roosevelt, his secretaries of state, war, and the navy, listen to Rear Adm. Claude C. Bloch, on an unsecure phone from Hawai'i, giving a vague account of the attack.

9:31 A.M.

USS *St. Louis* backs out from her pier, the first cruiser under way in Pearl Harbor.

9:37 A.M.

A bomb hits USS *Cassin* and the destroyer sags on its starboard side and onto the USS *Downes*.

10 A.M.

With the aid of tugs, Cdr. Thomas hauls the USS *Nevada* off Hospital Point and releases the men from battle stations. USS *Oglala* rolls over on her port side and sinks.

10 A.M.

The first Japanese planes to return from Hawai'i start landing on their carriers. Of 353 sent to Hawai'i, 324 return. Twenty-nine planes and 55 men have been lost.

10:02 A.M.

With burning oil engulfing his ship's stern, Capt. J. W. Bunkley orders "abandon ship" on the USS *California*. So does the senior officer on the wreck of USS *Arizona*, Lt. Cdr. Sam Fuqua. Only 39 men on the USS *Arizona* are alive to obey the order.

10:15 A.M.

Wind blows burning oil clear, and Capt. Bunkley orders his crew back aboard USS *California* to douse the fires.

10:20 A.M. (3:40 A.M. IN SINGAPORE)

Japanese bombers attack Singapore, finding it fully lighted. At the same time, despite heavy casualties, Japanese troops finally gain their Kota Bharu beachhead.

10:30 A.M. (9 P.M. IN LONDON, 6 A.M. IN TOKYO)

Winston Churchill learns of the attack on Pearl Harbor. The Japanese War Ministry releases the Imperial Rescript declaring war on Britain and America.

10:30 A.M. (5 A.M. IN MANILA)

American generals in the Philippines delay launching a B-17 raid on Formosa.

11 A.M.

Lt. Yoshio Hasegawa of the Honolulu Police Department and two carloads of men arrive at the Japanese consulate, to find the staff burning documents and vehemently insisting they do not know about the attack that has just ended.

11 A.M.

Fuchida does a last sweep over Pearl Harbor to check on damage and look for stray planes. He finds two *Zuikaku* fighters and shepherds them home back to the rendezvous point 20 miles northwest of Kaena Point.

11:30 A.M. (8 A.M. IN GUAM)

The Japanese bomb Guam, sinking a U.S. Navy gunboat.

11:45 A.M.

Tadao Fuchikami arrives on his two-cylinder Indian Scout motorcycle at Fort Shafter's main gate, having battled traffic jams and police checkpoints. The sentry waves Fuchikami right in. He delivers his telegram to the message center.

11:50 A.M. (7:20 A.M. IN TOKYO)

Tojo tells his cabinet that the attack on Hawai'i is a success. Ten minutes later Togo presents the declaration to Grew.

12 NOON

The army and navy begin evacuating dependents from Pearl Harbor and Hickam. Ensign Kazuo Sakamaki's midget submarine damages the second of its torpedoes on a reef. The midget sub works clear, but has no weapons left.

12:14 P.M.

Fuchida slaps his plane down on the deck of *Akagi*, the last to return home. On the flag bridge, Vice Adm. Nagumo and his staff are discussing whether or not to launch a third wave. But Nagumo will not push his luck.

12:30 P.M. (MIDNIGHT IN BERLIN)

Hitler learns of the Pearl Harbor attack. "The turning point!" he shouts, delighted. "Now it is impossible for us to lose the war: we now have an ally who has never been vanquished in 3,000 years."

1:30 P.M. (8 A.M. IN HONG KONG AND MANILA)

Japanese bombers attack Kai Tak airport. Other Japanese planes attack Davao in the Philippines. The American bombers circle over their bases, awaiting orders that never come. The fog lifts over Formosa, and the Japanese bombers headed for Luzon take off.

2:30 P.M. (8 P.M. IN WASHINGTON)

Hawai'i's army defenders deploy around Oahu to protect the island from potential invasion. In Washington, FDR briefs his shocked cabinet on the Pearl Harbor details and shows them his draft declaration of war.

2:30 P.M. (1 P.M. ON WAKE ISLAND)

Japanese bombers pulverize the American defenses.

2:45 P.M. (7:45 A.M. IN BANGKOK)

Facing Japanese invasion by land and sea, Thailand agrees to permit the passage of Japanese troops through the nation.

2:58 P.M.

Fuchikami's telegram is decoded and delivered to the Fort Shafter adjutant, who turns it over to Short. The message is from the chief of staff, Gen. George C. Marshall, telling Short that Japanese diplomats in Washington are to present an ultimatum to Secretary of State Cordell Hull at 1 P.M. Eastern (7:30 A.M. in Hawai'i), and Short should be on the alert accordingly. Short is furious, but sends a copy to Kimmel, who reads it and tosses it angrily in the wastebasket.

3:30 P.M. (10 A.M. IN MANILA)

Brereton orders his circling fighters and bombers, all short on fuel, to land, so the pilots can eat lunch, and the B-17s can be readied for the attack on Formosa.

4:30 P.M. (NOON IN TOKYO)

The Imperial Rescript declaring war on the United States and Britain is read on Japan's national radio.

5:30 P.M. (NOON IN MANILA)

Radar and observer reports of Japanese bombers headed for the U.S. Army Air Force's main base at Clark Field go unread because the teletype operator has gone to lunch. So have all the pilots and aircrews, and the planes are lined up wingtip to wingtip, for ease in servicing. This enables the Japanese to blast the American aircraft at Iba Field with ease.

6:15 P.M. (12:45 P.M. IN MANILA)

The Japanese pounce on Clark Field, wrecking 48 fighters and bombers on the ground. American 3-inch AA guns are unable to answer back; their 9-year-old corroded fuses fail to explode. In all, the Americans lose 85 fighters and 17 B-17 bombers.

6:30 P.M. (9 P.M. IN SAN FRANCISCO)

Panic-stricken authorities in San Francisco hit alarms and hurl searchlight beams into the night sky to find nonexistent Japanese planes.

7:30 P.M.

Lt. Fritz Hebel leads six USS *Enterprise* fighters toward Ford Island, after a fruitless search for Japanese carriers. They are greeted by a barrage of "friendly fire" that kills three American pilots.

9:30 P.M. (9 A.M. IN ROME)

Mussolini expresses delight over Pearl Harbor, saying it clarifies the position between the Americans and the Axis.

9:30 P.M.

With rumors and false reports of Japanese aircraft, paratroopers, spies, and Fifth Columnists menacing Oahu, the island's defenders spend a sleepless night firing on imaginary enemies, which include kites in trees, the planet Venus, palm fronds waving in front of lights, and each other.

10:30 P.M. (3:40 A.M. IN SINGAPORE)

Japanese troops seize Kota Bharu airfield and start preparing it to accept their own aircraft. The British have no effective air support left in Malaya.

11:30 P.M. (11 A.M. IN BERLIN)

Hitler tells his aides that he will declare war on America. "If we don't stand on the side of Japan," he says, the alliance with Japan "is politically dead."

NEAR MIDNIGHT

Ensign Kazuo Sakamaki surfaces his unmaneuverable submarine and climbs out of the hatch into the cool night air. He is completely lost. In Washington, an exhausted FDR is awake before sunrise to put the finishing touches on a speech about a "Day of Infamy."

—**DAVID H. LIPPMAN**

A

Aircraft Carriers

The weapon that won the day at Pearl Harbor for JAPAN never sailed within sight of the Hawai'ian Islands. When Vice Admiral Chuichi Nagumo launched the first of 353 planes on the morning of December 7, it represented the apotheosis of Japanese naval power and the triumph of 30 years of naval design and experimentation.

The idea of launching and recovering aircraft from ships dates back to 1910, when American aviator Eugene Ely's 50-horsepower Curtiss biplane took off from a temporary 57-foot platform on the light cruiser USS *Birmingham*, lying at anchor in Hampton Roads, Virginia. On January 18, 1911, Ely became the first man to land on a warship when his biplane slapped down on a 102-foot platform on the armored cruiser USS *Pennsylvania*, in San Francisco Bay.

The French, British, German, and American navies preferred seaplanes, which could be stored in protected hangars, shot from catapults, or lowered by cranes into the water before take-off. The Germans also preferred their massive Zeppelins, with vast ranges.

The Royal Navy shot Short biplanes from battleships in 1912, mounting guns and radio sets on them, and on July 28, 1914, Squadron Commander Arthur Longmore launched the first aerial torpedo.

The British converted three fast cross-channel steamers into seaplane tenders, and on Christmas Day 1914 their Short biplanes launched the first aircraft-carrier attack in history, raiding the German bases at Cuxhaven and Wilhelmshaven. The following year, the converted steamer HMS *Ben-my-Chree*'s seaplanes torpedoed and sank a Turkish transport in the Gallipoli campaign.

In 1915, the Royal Navy converted the Isle of Man packet USS *Vindex* to carry two Bristol Scout fighters. They saw their first action in 1916, when the pilot dropped Ranken incendiary darts on a Zeppelin. As World War I droned on, the Royal Navy kept trying by converting the cruiser USS *Yarmouth* to accommodate the Sopwith Pup fighter. One of USS *Yarmouth*'s Pups was the first to shoot down an enemy aircraft, incinerating the Zeppelin *L-22* on August 21, 1917, with incendiary bullets.

Success in hand, the Royal Navy converted the battle cruiser HMS *Furious* into the aircraft carrier role, removing her forward 18-inch gun turret and replacing it with a flight deck and a hangar. She hurled six Sopwith Camels at the Tondern Zeppe-

lin base on July 18, 1918. Still, the Royal Navy was not through with aircraft carriers. They converted a liner into the carrier HMS *Argus*, the first carrier with a full-length unobstructed flight deck. The carrier made her trials in October 1918, and was operational before the Armistice.

The HMS *Argus* was the first modern carrier, replete with arresting ropes and a hangar deck below the flight deck, but funnel gases spewing over the stern still made deck landings a tricky affair. The Royal Navy's answer was deck-landing trials with a temporary superstructure erected on HMS *Argus*'s starboard flight deck, representing masts, bridge, and funnel. Pilots reported no problem landing with this design, and the standard look of aircraft carriers was born.

The success of British carriers inspired the Americans and the Japanese. The Americans converted

FROM FIRST FLIGHT TO LEGEND
AT RIGHT AND ABOVE LEFT *A B-25B takes off from the USS* Hornet, *on its way to the first U.S. air raid on Japan, April 1942. The USS* Hornet, *the USS* Yorktown, *and the USS* Enterprise *were authorized in 1934 as part of President* FRANKLIN D. ROOSEVELT's *Works Progress Administration. The ships displaced 20,000 tons, contained three elevators, geared turbines, handled 85 aircraft, and cut the waves at 34 knots. The three carriers would become legendary.*

the collier USS *Jupiter* into the small carrier USS *Langley*. She looked like USS *Argus*, and her funnels were on hinges, so they could flip down during flight operations.

The Japanese, however, beat everybody. Their Naval Air Service had begun training in 1912 and operated seaplanes from the tender *Wakamiya* against the German colony of Tsingtao. They launched the first carrier built from the keel up, the *Hosho*, on November 13, 1921, putting her in operation the following year, beating Britain's HMS *Hermes* into service. At 7,420 tons displacement, with a flight deck 500 feet, *Hosho* had horizontal funnels and no bridge. She also used mirrors and lights to assist landings—a forerunner of the system the British developed in 1954.

Nations that had carriers operated them singly, usually with an escort of battleships, cruisers, and destroyers. Initially, the British carriers covered convoys and hunted down German warships. The carrier HMS *Victorious* was the first to attack an enemy ship at sea, hurling nine Swordfish torpedo bombers at the German battleship *Bismarck* as she fled to France. The attacks did no damage, but HMS *Ark Royal*'s Swordfish punched out the battleship's propellers and rudder, sending the dreadnought helplessly to the waiting guns of the British Home Fleet.

Nevertheless, armchair strategists did not take carriers seriously. Despite maneuvers and wartime operations that showed carriers could deliver tremendous long-range punches and slip away, they were seen merely as reconnaissance arms of the fleet. Pre-war American and Japanese naval planning called for a tremendous dreadnought duel to decide the fate of the Pacific Ocean, with battleships slugging it out in best Trafalgar style, and carriers taking a backseat, operating singly.

Those ideas changed when Japan's Admiral ISOROKU YAMAMOTO ordered his staff to plan an air attack on Pearl Harbor, to cripple the U.S. Fleet at the outbreak of war. One of the officers assigned to develop the plan was the brilliant Minoru Genda, who was the navy's greatest advocate of aviation.

Sometime in November 1940, while working on the Pearl Harbor plan, Genda watched a newsreel that included footage of four American carriers sailing in a majestic single column. Genda did not think much of it until a few days later, when, while jumping off a streetcar, he considered, "Why should we have trouble in gathering planes in the air if we concentrate our carriers?"

He wrote that the task force being sent to Pearl Harbor should consist of Japan's six fleet carriers, with the aircraft massed in "two big attack waves," each of about 80 bombers with 30 fighters for protection, the planes all pooled for a greater punch.

The idea was accepted. When Japan's task force sailed for Hawai'i a year later, it was the first multicarrier task force in history. (See also AIRPLANES VERSUS SHIPS.)

Further Reading: Chris Bishop and Christopher Chant, *Aircraft Carriers* (MBI Publishing, 2004); Donald M. Goldstein, Katherine V. Dillon, and J. Michael Wenger, *The Way It Was: Pearl Harbor* (Brassey's, 1991); Bernard Ireland, *Aircraft Carriers* (Anness Publishing, 2006); John Keegan, *The Price of Admiralty* (Penguin, 1988).

—DAVID H. LIPPMAN

Airplanes versus Ships

The period from World War I to the outbreak of WORLD WAR II witnessed a sweeping change in naval doctrine, as airplanes evolved from their role in support of surface groups to become the offensive arm of naval fleets.

World War I saw some of the earliest uses of airpower in combat. Airplanes offered nations the ability to extend the range of their sea-power projection. By the 1920s, Britain, JAPAN, and the UNITED STATES each had a prototype aircraft carrier. Despite the investment in naval aviation, the experience with airplanes in World War I failed to convince naval officers that carriers would eventually replace battleships as the main offensive arm of the surface fleet.

One U.S. Air Service officer, William Mitchell, believed that the airplane had made the battleship obsolete. Mitchell was an early enthusiast of the airplane, and the army assigned him to the Signal Corps.

In 1917, Mitchell went to Europe to learn about European equipment and air operations, which enabled him to lay the foundation for coordinating American air operations. He served in World War I as the air commander of the American Expeditionary Force of I Corps and was the first American pilot to fly over enemy lines.

Following World War I, Mitchell returned to the United States and served as the deputy chief of the U.S. Air Service. In his writings and speeches, Mitchell offered several reasons why the airplane would make the battleship obsolete. First, battleships were limited by geography—they could only project their power from the sea. Airplanes could go anywhere and attack anything. Second, airpower was inherently offensive, despite naval claims of the opposite. In order to prove his assertions, Mitchell set up an aerial demonstration over the Chesapeake Bay.

The demonstration began on June 2, 1921, when three flying boats of the Naval Air Service attacked an ex-German submarine, *U-117*. Each aircraft dropped three 180-pound bombs, sending the submarine to the bottom of the bay. Over the course of the next month aerial forces sank an ex-German torpedo destroyer, several other vessels, and the German battleship *Ostfriesland*, which many considered unsinkable. Mitchell's bombers struck the battleship with two 2,000-pound bombs. The *Ostfriesland* sank within 20 minutes. Mitchell flew over observers on the USS *Henderson*, rocking his wings in victory.

The Japanese conducted similar tests throughout the 1920s. In the United States, Lieutenant Commander Frank D. Wagner, leading a flight of Curtiss F6C Hawks, developed the aerial maneuver that was eventually labeled dive-bombing. Wagner's flight started their attacks from 12,000 feet against a fleet sailing out from San Pedro. The fleet had prior knowledge of the attacks but did not detect Wagner and his flight of Hawks until they were close to the deck of the ships. The surprise left the ships' crews little time to reach their battle stations. The unanimous opinion was that this type of attack could succeed over any defense—barring opposing aircraft to defend the ship. Demonstrations such as Wagner's convinced the navy of the need to procure and field a light bomber capable of overcoming the g-forces involved when pulling out of high-degree dives.

The Japanese realized the importance of bombing in any attack on Pearl Harbor. Although they relied heavily on torpedoes, they knew that torpedo nets would protect the outer ships. Horizontal bombing and dive-bombing offered the Japanese forces the only way to strike ships on the inside of Battleship Row. The Japanese had to devise a tactic that would allow a coordinated attack using all forms of offensive airpower. This was their solution: while horizontal bombers released their bombs from 13,000 feet above the water, dive-bombers started their attacks from 10,000 feet, and torpedo planes launched their weapons from 300 feet. Such a complex opera-

Japanese Aircraft Carriers

THE SIX carriers that delivered Japan's Sunday attack on Hawai'i were among the most powerful ships the Imperial Navy ever sent into battle.

The flagship of the task force was the venerable carrier *Akagi* (Red Castle), Japan's second flattop and first large carrier. Originally designed as a battle cruiser, she was converted into an aircraft carrier after the 1922 Washington Naval Treaty. *Akagi* was completed in 1927, displaced 41,300 tons, steamed at 31 knots, and carried 91 aircraft.

Akagi was unique. She was one of only two aircraft carriers in the world with her "island" on the port side, the other being the later *Hiryu*. Her captains included Isoroku Yamamoto and Chuichi Nagumo, both future admirals.

The battle cruiser *Kaga* (Increased Joy) was finished in 1928 and was the mammoth of the six carriers, displacing 42,541 tons. She operated 91 aircraft, had a top speed of 28 knots, and also had side-venting funnels.

Both carriers served in the war with China, flying air support in the invasions of Chinese ports. Their success propelled Japan to lay down two more flattops, *Hiryu* and *Soryu*. *Soryu* (Blue Dragon) had her island on the starboard side, displaced 18,880 tons, topped out at 34 knots, and carried 71 aircraft. She was completed in 1937.

Hiryu (Flying Dragon), finished in 1939, displaced 20,250 tons, steamed at 34 knots, and carried 73 aircraft. However, her island was on the port side and had four feet greater of beam than her sister. Neither of these carriers had enormous range, and they sailed to Pearl Harbor with additional fuel tanks lashed to their hangar decks.

The final two carriers, *Shokaku* and *Zuikaku* (Flying Crane and Glorious Crane, respectively), were almost identical. Both were finished in 1941, could do 34 knots, and each carried 84 aircraft. They had enormous range, able to sail to Hawai'i and back without refueling.

The attack on Pearl Harbor was the only time all six carriers sailed to battle together. The group was broken on June 4, 1942, when the *Akagi*, *Kaga*, *Hiryu*, and *Soryu* were battered by American dive-bombers at Midway (see MIDWAY, BATTLE OF).

tion required precise planning, timing, and coordination, which the Japanese practiced going into the Pearl Harbor attack.

On December 7, 1941, the Japanese proved that airplanes could significantly damage an opposing nation's fleet. Unknown to the Americans, the Japanese had developed a torpedo that would operate in the shallow waters of Pearl Harbor. Moreover, the dive-bombers employed an armor-piercing bomb that wreaked havoc on the decks of the American battleships. By the end of the attack, Japanese naval aviation had seriously damaged or sunk 19 American vessels, including eight battleships, three cruisers, and three destroyers. Much like Mitchell's exhibition 20 years earlier, Japanese forces showed the vulnerability of battleships to airpower.

Further Reading: Tom Clancy, *Carrier: A Guided Tour of an Aircraft Carrier* (Penguin Group, 1999); James J. Cooke, *Billy Mitchell* (Lynne Rienner Publishers, 2002); DeWitt S. Coop, *A Few Great Captains: The Men and Events that Shaped the Development of U.S. Air Power* (EPM Publications, 1980); Alfred Lord, *Day of Infamy* (Owl Books, 2001); William Mitchell, *Winged Defense: The Development and Possibilities of Modern Air Power Economic and Military* (Dover Edition, 1988); Mark R. Peattie, *Sunburst: The Rise of Japanese Naval Air Power, 1909–1941* (Naval Institute Press, 2001); Mark Stille and Tony Bryan, *Imperial Japanese Aircraft Carriers, 1921–1945* (Osprey Publishing, 2005); Mark Stille and Tony Bryan, *U.S. Navy Aircraft*

Carriers, 1922–1945 (Osprey Publishing, 2005); Thomas Wildenberg, *Destined for Glory: Dive Bombing, Midway, and the Evolution of Carrier Airpower* (Naval Institute Press, 1998).

—MELVIN DEAILE

Allies on December 7, 1941

All across the Pacific the war began emphatically. Japanese ships and planes attacked GUAM, WAKE ISLAND, and Midway; 24,000 troops invaded Malaya. Japanese bombers smacked Singapore that night. (see MALAYA AND SINGAPORE). At HONG KONG, Japanese bombers swooped down on Kai Tak Airport and destroyed all five Royal Air Force planes on the ground.

Stern 16-inch guns, such as those in the photo BELOW, *were mounted on the* USS Arizona.

In Shanghai, the Anglo-American-ruled International Settlement, surrounded by Japanese forces, fell quickly. The British gunboat HMS *Peterel*, commanded by New Zealand Lieutenant Steve Polkinghorn, was scuttled. However, the U.S. gunboat USS *Wake*, after a stiff fight, was captured and pressed into Japanese service. U.S. Marines in Tientsin were swiftly arrested by Japanese troops.

In Peking (Beijing), the U.S. Marine Legation Guard defending the American embassy and interests, surrounded by Japanese troops, was ordered to surrender rather than die in a pointless bloodbath. For the Leathernecks, it was a day of despair.

THE SOVIET UNION VERSUS GERMANY

The outbreak of war in Asia did not affect the Soviet Union, which had a neutrality treaty with JAPAN. However, the Soviets launched attacks at Tikhvin, near Leningrad. There, the Soviets had just opened a 200-mile road across the empty terrain from the railhead at Zaborie to the edge of the frozen Lake Ladoga the previous morning. Thousands of Soviet citizens had died to build the road, and many of their frozen corpses were holding it up. The road was mostly cut between embankments of snow and ice, surfaced with felled tree branches. Trucks tackling this dreadful route could do little better than 20 miles a day. In some places, the road was one lane wide. More than 300 of the trucks sent along the road could not get through at all, defeated by blizzards, huge gradients, and breakdowns.

GERMANY's advance on the Soviet capital had come to a halt. Cold weather, snow, a long logistics thread, and determined Soviet defense had halted the Wehrmacht. On December 5, ADOLF HITLER abandoned the Moscow offensive for the winter, and his Army Group Center pulled back. At its closest point, the Germans were 12 miles from the Kremlin. Hitler's troops, having held their ground, began a slow, organized retreat.

The following day, three Soviet "Fronts" smashed into the German forces. While the Soviets lacked a numerical edge, they had one in contending with the elements: the temperature was minus 45 degrees. Snow stood a meter deep. The sun rose as a fog-shrouded ball at 9 A.M. and set at 3 P.M. The Germans had gone into the Soviet Union unequipped for winter warfare. Now the temperatures were so cold that tank engines could not run, gun recoil mechanisms were frozen solid, and even mines did not work. Some German troops only had their cloth caps as winter wear. One German rifle company battalion had only 16 greatcoats and 16 pairs of boots for 800 men.

Backed by intelligence reports that Japan would not attack Siberia, the Soviets had been able to scrape up fresh reserves. Some were trained in winter warfare, others were just used to the ghastly conditions. Nearly all wore thick, fleece-lined greatcoats and fur caps. The Soviet artillery included the deadly Katyusha mobile rocket, and the Soviets also hurled a tougher air force at the Germans, including the IL-2 Sturmovik attack bomber, with great success.

The Soviets attacked along a 500-mile front before Moscow, hurling white-clad ski troops and Siberians in furs against the shivering Germans. Panzer tanks and antitank guns were trapped in the snow, unable to move or fire. In one battle, the Germans left 70 tanks behind. The Germans began a 50-mile retreat from Moscow to avoid annihilation.

THE BRITISH IN AFRICA

The British 8th Army was locked in mortal combat with the German Afrika Korps under General Erwin Rommel and its associated Italian forces in the barren Libyan sands. The British objective was to relieve the siege of Tobruk, where the British 70th Infantry Division and the Polish Carpathian Brigade were dug in.

On December 6, Rommel, facing critical shortages of fuel and ammunition, decided to retreat. The following day, the British 8th Army broke through the Axis ring and lifted the siege of Tobruk. The relieving forces, consisting of the 1st Durhams of the 23rd Brigade, pushed aside the Italian Trento and Pavia Divisions, with the help of 32nd Tank Brigade's armor. The Durhams lost 11 dead and 245 wounded, but took 150 Italians prisoner, which added little to the Italian fighting reputation.

PACIFIC REPERCUSSIONS

The war's expansion bounced across the Pacific. American ocean liner and cargo ship crews at sea started painting over their portholes to enforce blackout, and painted battleship gray on their ships' sides, to reduce the chances of being detected. Such measures did not help the freighter USS *Cynthia Olsen*, carrying a cargo of lumber near Hawai'i. The Japanese submarine *I-26* had been stalking her through the night, waiting for the hour of attack. At the right time, *I-26* surfaced and fired over the freighter's bow. The crew took to the boats, and two Long Lance torpedoes sent the USS *Cynthia Olsen* to the bottom of the sea. The Japanese were so busy with this small target, they missed the large and nearby liner USS *Lurline*, heading from Hawai'i to San Francisco.

THE U.S. REACTION

In the UNITED STATES, the news of Japan's attack flooded across the country like a shock wave (see PANIC). John F. Kennedy was at a football game in Washington, D.C., when he learned of the attack. Richard Nixon found out as he was leaving a movie theater with his wife, Patricia. General Dwight D. Eisenhower, just off maneuvers in San Antonio, Texas, got the call from his boss, General Walter Krueger, and told his wife, "I have to go to headquarters. I don't know when I'll be back." It was four years.

New York Mayor Fiorello La Guardia ordered his city blacked-out and warned his citizens to stay calm, though the city might be attacked. CBS radio reacted by canceling a performance of Gilbert and Sullivan's *The Mikado* and replacing it with *HMS Pinafore*, "in honor of the Royal Navy." In Washington, D.C., a super patriot chopped down four Japanese cherry trees in the Tidal Basin.

In Norfolk, Virginia, news that the United States was in the war was greeted aboard the new battleship USS *Washington* with excitement. Commander Hank Seely, gun boss, a China veteran, told his shipmates that he has seen the Japanese in action and that "these guys are really tough." The radio played

the "Star-Spangled Banner," and all stood and sang the anthem. Then, without word from the bridge, the battleship's crewmen went calmly to their battle stations to check their ship's equipment.

America's isolationists were a little slower on the uptake. North Dakota Senator Gerald Nye, the keynote speaker at an America First rally in Pittsburgh, went ahead with his anti-Roosevelt speech well after a newsman handed him a note of the Pearl Harbor attack. By the time Nye got to his next appearance that evening, serving as a lay preacher at a Baptist church (also an America First stalwart), he had the full story. With defeat in his voice, Nye said that America First was finished, and "the only thing now is to declare war and jump into it with everything we have and bring it to a victorious conclusion."

Most Americans got their news from familiar sources: Eric Sevareid's broadcasts on CBS radio, the *New York Times* ticker in Times Square, immense headlines on extra editions of daily newspapers on street corners. In Dallas's Majestic Theater, the news was flashed on the screen during the second daily showing of the movie *Sergeant York*. The Texan

ABOVE LEFT AND RIGHT *Recruiting posters encouraged women to join the armed services and work in factories to support the war effort.*

audience roared and cheered. York himself, living in Tennessee, told reporters that the Japanese should "be given a lickin' right away. We should take care of the Japs first and then take on the Germans."

The men of the American Volunteer Group, training in Toungoo, Burma, to fly P-40 fighters for China's Chiang Kai-shek, received the word from the Royal Air Force in Rangoon, in the middle of the night. They were told to take off as soon as possible, but their planes were not warmed up; engines sputtered and landing gear collapsed on the muddy strip. The "Flying Tigers" figured they were better off not damaging their irreplaceable planes any further.

FRANKLIN D. ROOSEVELT held what he called the most important cabinet meeting since Fort Sumter. Outside, people were standing by the White House fence, singing "God Bless America." On top of the White House, troops were setting up antiaircraft guns. Not until V-J Day would they discover that their guns had the wrong caliber of ammunition.

Roosevelt told his cabinet the harsh facts of the Pearl Harbor attack—most of the details would be censored—and read his draft Declaration of War message. Roosevelt wanted something that his envoy to Great Britain, Harry Hopkins, described as "an understatement and nothing too explosive." The cabinet accepted the draft.

Later, Roosevelt met with the congressional leadership, to ask them to receive him in joint session the following day (see CONGRESSIONAL REACTION). Roosevelt did not read his speech to them, but he admitted to heavy losses. He asked House Foreign Affairs Committee Chairman Sol Bloom to introduce the resolution for war. Bloom declined. He was a Jew from New York City's Washington Heights, and did not want to expose "the Jews of a future generation to the possible charge that this war had been set in motion by a Jew." The isolationist forces were rife with anti-Semitism. Bloom checked with the House parliamentarian, Lew Deschler, and worked out a way to have a clerk read the resolution.

Earlier in the evening, Roosevelt dictated the draft message to his secretary, Grace Tully, who quickly typed the 500-word draft. Roosevelt went over it with Hopkins and Tully during a quick supper. He made changes in every sentence, starting with the first. Among the changes, he crossed out the words *world history* and penned in the word *infamy*.

Further Reading: Winston S. Churchill, *The Second World War* (Houghton Mifflin, 1986); Jon Meacham, *Franklin and Winston: An Intimate Portrait of an Epic Friendship* (Random House, 2004); Bradley F. Smith, *Sharing Secrets with Stalin: How the Allies Traded Intelligence, 1941–1945* (University Press of Kansas, 1996).

—DAVID H. LIPPMAN

Arcadia Conference

Two days after the Japanese attack, British Prime Minister WINSTON CHURCHILL cabled President FRANKLIN D. ROOSEVELT, indicating his readiness to leave for Washington, D.C., with key members of his staff on short notice. The meeting, Churchill felt, should be held "on the highest executive level" to review decisions made at their first meeting in August 1941 at Argentia, Newfoundland, in light of the changed situation brought about by Pearl Harbor.

Although reluctant to undertake a major meeting before his military staffs had the opportunity to conduct in-depth wartime planning, Roosevelt agreed, and the British delegation boarded the battleship HMS *Duke of York* on December 13, 1941, for the eight-day voyage to the UNITED STATES. While at sea, the British staff prepared an agenda covering the main points it wanted discussed, and forwarded it to the United States for approval. General GEORGE C. MARSHALL, chief of staff of the U.S. Army and point-man for the American delegation in the forthcoming meetings, put his staff to work to develop position papers on the British proposals, which were then submitted to the Navy Department and White House for comment and approval.

Arcadia was the cover name given to the series of Anglo-American staff meetings held between December 24, 1941, and January 14, 1942.

The main achievement of Arcadia was the agreement on a sound structure for future strategic planning and direction of the war. Marshall urged that there must be a single commander in each area with authority over all forces: army, navy, and air. In what was termed Post-Arcadia Collaboration, a series of combined Anglo-American staffs were developed. National staffs, consisting of the military service representatives at each level, were to be known as joint staffs. Washington, D.C., was selected as the location of the Combined Chiefs of Staff Committee (CCS), consisting of the British Chiefs of Staff and a new American organization called the Joint Chiefs of Staff.

All the British proposals were examined in detail, often with some debate, but generally American views prevailed and, as Churchill's physician Sir Charles Wilson noted, "the war will be run from Washington."

Further Reading: David J. Bercuson and Holger H. Herwig, *One Christmas in Washington: The Secret Meeting between Roosevelt and Churchill That Changed the World* (Overlook Press, 2005).

—**ALAN HARRIS BATH, PH.D.**

Arizona, USS

Approximately half of the American lives lost on December 7, 1941, were those of men on the battleship USS *Arizona.* Today, the USS ARIZONA MEMORIAL is built over the sunken hull. Droplets of oil from the sunken ship can still be seen bubbling up to the surface beneath the memorial, leaving a rainbow sheen on the harbor water. Legend has it that when the last surviving veteran of the ship dies, the tears will stop.

Construction of the USS *Arizona* began March 16, 1914, at the New York Navy Yard, and the ship was launched June 19, 1915. After a shakedown cruise and post-shakedown repairs, the USS *Arizona* joined the U.S. Fleet April 2, 1917, four days before the UNITED STATES declared war on GERMANY to enter World War I. During that war, the USS *Arizona* patrolled the U.S. east coast. Powered by oil-burning steam engines, the ship was not sent to Great Britain because of the severe shortage of oil there.

At the end of World War I, the battleship steamed to Europe to accompany the USS *George Washington,* the ship that carried President Woodrow Wilson to the Paris Peace Conference. While the conference was in session, the USS *Arizona* was dispatched to Turkey to protect American lives in Smyrna during the brief Greco-Turkish war. After picking up American citizens in Smyrna, the USS *Arizona* proceeded through the Dardanelles to Constantinople, and then returned to the United States in June 1919.

The ship received the alphanumeric designation *BB39* on July 17, 1920. During the following 19 years, the USS *Arizona* saw service in the Caribbean, the Atlantic, and off the coast of California, transiting the Panama Canal several times. From 1929 to 1931, she was extensively remodeled with more armor protection, modernized fire-control tops on the masts, and new 5-inch antiaircraft guns. In 1931, the battleship hosted President Herbert Hoover on a trip to Puerto Rico and the Virgin Islands. In September 1938, she became the flagship of Battleship Division 1, based in Pearl Harbor, under the command of Admiral CHESTER NIMITZ. Nimitz later became commander in chief of the Pacific Fleet (see PACIFIC FLEET, U.S.) during WORLD WAR II. The last change of command ceremony for the USS *Arizona* occurred in January 1941, when Rear Admiral ISAAC KIDD took command.

From July until December 6, 1941, the USS *Arizona* continued with exercises and tactical maneuvers in the Pacific. After practices in October with the USS *Nevada* and USS *Oklahoma* (see NEVADA, USS; OKLAHOMA, USS), the three battleships were moored in Battleship Row along the quay of Ford Island in Pearl Harbor. The three battleships were anchored in the protected harbor with their sister ships, the USS *California*, USS *Maryland*, USS *West Virginia*, and USS *Tennessee* (see CALIFORNIA, USS; MARYLAND, USS; WEST VIRGINIA, USS; TENNESSEE, USS). The eighth battleship of the Pacific Fleet, the USS *Utah*, now a training vessel, was also in the harbor, but not tied up in the row at the Ford Island quay. The repair ship USS *Vestal* was moored alongside USS *Arizona* on December 6. The USS *Arizona* was one of 185 ships of the U.S. Pacific Fleet in the harbor that evening. Admiral Kidd and the ship's captain, Franklin Van Valkenburgh, spent the night aboard the battleship.

Early on the morning of December 7, the Japanese attack fleet of 33 warships and auxiliaries arrived at their launch position after following a northern route out of normal shipping lanes. The JAPANESE FLEET, which included six aircraft car-

THE REQUEST FOR WAR *On December 8, 1941, U.S. President Franklin D. Roosevelt addressed members of Congress, asking the legislature to declare war on Japan. Congress passed the resolution, and the official declaration of war was signed by Roosevelt later that day.*

One Survivor's Story: In His Words

Donald Gay Stratton, SEA1c

THE USS *Arizona* was dockside, being worked on by shipyard workers. We stood a lot of fire watch on board, as welders and yard workers were working 24 hours a day.

December 7, 1941, was a Sunday morning like any other. I picked up a few oranges to take to sickbay, where my incinerator partner had gone the day before. His name was Harl Nelson from Rouston, Arkansas. He did not survive.

I went to my locker and came out on deck via No. 2 casement to the forecastle deck. Some sailors on the bow were shouting and pointing to planes that were bombing Ford Island. I thought I saw the water tower on Ford Island topple over.

I went immediately to my battle station as a sight setter in the Port AA director. General Quarters sounded: THIS IS NO DRILL—MAN YOUR BATTLE STATIONS! We were strafed, torpedoed, dive-bombed, and hit by high-altitude bombers. We started firing immediately at dive-bombers and later at the high-altitude bombers. Our Director Officer Ensign Lomax went to see if he could speed up ammunition supply. I never saw him again.

About that time, the ship was hit. It could have been a 2,000-lb. bomb hitting the starboard-side right aft of the No. 2 turret, or a torpedo, as from my vantage point I saw two torpedo wakes headed right for the USS *Arizona*. A horrendous explosion blew about 110 feet of the bow off, with a fireball that went 400–500 feet in the air, engulfing the forward half of the ship.

The bomb set off ammunition powder, 180,000 gallons of aviation gasoline, and of course fuel oil. Some below decks did not know what hit them. The worst tragedy is, of course, the young American lives, but did we learn anything? Let us keep America alert, for they say history has a way of repeating itself.

I guess being inside the director saved some of our lives as it took 40 to 50 men to man sky control, plus the observation personnel and plane spotters. I do not know what happened to most of them as only six of us went across a line to the USS *Vestal*.

The USS *Vestal* was tied up outboard, her crew working on the USS *Arizona*. We could not go down the ladders as everything was burning. As the flames died down, we were out on the platform with nowhere to go.

A sailor named Joe George was out on the afterdeck of the USS *Vestal*. He threw us a heaving line and attached a heavier line, which we pulled across and tied to the sky-control platform. We came across the line, hand over hand, after we were burned very badly. The line was about 45 feet in the air, over lots of fire and water. Six of us went across, and only three are alive today, Lauren Bruner, Russell Lott, and myself. I was burned over 50 to 60 percent of my body. We were aboard the USS *Vestal* a while, then taken to the landing where we were driven to the U.S. Naval Hospital in Pearl Harbor.

ABOVE *Navy Cmdr. Mark Manfredi welcomes an unnamed Pearl Harbor survivor and crewmember of the USS* Ward *aboard the USS* Crommelin *in Pearl Harbor on December 5, 2005. The USS* Ward *sank a Japanese submarine at the entrance to Pearl Harbor one hour before the Japanese air attack on the island of Oahu.*

riers, had secretly steamed from Japan on November 26, and paused some 230 nautical miles north of the island of Oahu.

The first wave of Japanese attack aircraft arrived just before 7:55 A.M., and the leader of the raid, Commander Mitsuo Fuchida, sent the coded message, *"Tora! Tora! Tora!"* indicating that the aircraft had reached their target without being detected.

The USS *Arizona* suffered eight bomb hits, one hitting forward of gun turret II. The 1,760-pound armor-piercing bomb smashed through the deck and exploded inside the black-powder magazine. That magazine blew up, igniting other, smokeless-powder magazines. An explosion of cataclysmic proportions ripped open the forward part of the ship, touching off fires that burned for two days. Debris from the explosion scattered across Ford Island. The ship sank within nine minutes, taking with her Admiral Kidd and Captain Van Valkenburgh, both of whom earned posthumous CONGRESSIONAL MEDALS OF HONOR. One of the survivors was Lieutenant Commander Samuel G. Fuqua, who served as the ship's damage-control officer. His attempts to put out the fires and to ensure that survivors got off the ship earned him a Congressional Medal of Honor. Of the 2,390 Americans killed that day at Pearl Harbor, 1,171 died aboard *Arizona*.

The USS *Arizona* Memorial was dedicated in 1962. A flagpole is attached to the severed mainmast of the sunken ship, and the flag of the United States flies as a tribute to the lost crew and the ship. In 1979, the Department of Interior's National Park Service assumed control of the memorial. The memorial can only be reached by a special navy shuttle boat from a visitor center on the mainland.

The names of those killed on December 7, 1941, are engraved in marble at one end of the memorial structure. Sometimes unnoticed by the thousands of international visitors, in a smaller group at the lower left of the wall are the names of USS *Arizona* crewmen who survived the attack and asked that their ashes be buried with the comrades who lie entombed in the ship below.

Further Reading: Adolph A. Hoehling, *Ships That Changed History* (Rowman & Littlefield, 1992); Joy Waldron Jasper, et al., *The USS Arizona: The Ship, the Men, the Pearl Harbor Attack and the Symbol That Aroused America* (St. Martin's Press, 2003); National Park Service, www.nps.gov/usar (cited March 2006); Michael Slackman, *Remembering Pearl Harbor: The Story of the USS Arizona Memorial* (Arizona Memorial Museum Association, 1996); USS Arizona.org, "Donald Gray Stratton, SEA 1C (Survivor)," www.ussarizona.org (cited March 2006).

—RODNEY P. CARLISLE
—DAVID W. MCBRIDE

Arizona, USS Memorial

The destruction of the battleship USS *Arizona* (see ARIZONA, USS) was one of the iconic images of the attack on Pearl Harbor. The image was used again and again on propaganda posters reminding the American public of why they were fighting. Even decades after the attack, histories of December 7 frequently bear that photograph of the battleship engulfed in smoke, her masts tilted and sagging from the heat that was literally sufficient to soften steel.

However, the USS *Arizona* did not long remain in that condition. Almost as soon as she had cooled enough to be handled, salvage crews came aboard to retrieve anything that might be useful. The two aft gun turrets, largely undamaged by the blast, were dismantled and taken away to become shore batteries against an invasion that never came. The twisted and charred superstructure was cut away and taken

The USS Arizona *Memorial at Pearl Harbor, Hawai'i, was erected over the stricken battle-ship. The flagpole holding the U.S. flag is attached to the mainmast of the sunken ship.*

back to the mainland as scrap to be melted down and forged anew for a war industry hungry for steel. Soon only the submerged hull remained, a slender oval whose ghostly form lay just beneath the clear tropical waters of the harbor as a bitter reminder of the events of that disastrous day.

Yet already there was a sense that the wreck was somehow special. She was the tomb of over 1,000 American servicemen, slain together in one catastrophic event. As such, she was owed due respect, and each year throughout the war, a wreath was laid upon the wreck on December 7.

On December 7, 1946, a HONOLULU businessman, Tucker Gratz, did the honors and noticed that the wreath he had laid there the previous year had remained undisturbed. He began to consider the possibility of a more permanent memorial and to lobby for its construction. Within five years, the U.S. Navy had erected a flagstaff, although not without opposition from those who thought a memorial would draw too much attention to a defeat when it might

be better to remember America's victories. Even Fleet Admiral CHESTER NIMITZ publicly expressed his regret that Pearl Harbor Day was becoming a nationally important memorial, on the basis that it was one of the country's great defeats.

Naval opinions could not stand in the way of public sentiment, and soon a wooden platform was constructed over the wreck, so that people could come and gaze down into the waters. A ten-foot stone obelisk was soon added, but even that seemed insufficient to honor the sheer magnitude of the USS *Arizona* and her destruction. A movement began to construct a permanent memorial.

In order to create a memorial of the size Gratz and other like-minded individuals considered suitable for the USS *Arizona* tragedy, it was necessary to seek congressional approval. Instead of being merely a tribute to the dead, it became tied in with the ongoing efforts to keep the Cold War and the peril of communism in the forefront of the minds of the American public. As a result, the attack on Pearl Harbor was soon spun into a perpetual warning against the perils of lack of preparedness in the face of Soviet aggression, leading to a perception common among Americans through the later decades of the Cold War that a nuclear attack would come as a bolt from the blue.

Some members of Congress saw the planned memorial primarily as a tourist attraction that would help bring revenue to Hawai'i. Congressman Mendel Rivers of South Carolina saw it as a way to honor the dead on the cheap, noting that the total cost of the planned memorial was less than the burial allowances that would have been granted had the men been buried individually in a military cemetery.

In addition to the federal money authorized by Congress, a sizeable portion of the money to build the memorial was raised by public donations. The senior surviving officer of the USS *Arizona*, Samuel G. Fuqua, who had by that time attained flag rank, appeared on the popular television show *This Is Your Life*. Although Fuqua maintained proper military decorum throughout his appearance, it was clear that remembering his dead shipmates, many of them friends, caused him emotional distress. The show was used openly to raise funds for the memorial.

By 1961, the Pacific War Memorial Commission (PWMC) was still running short of the funds necessary to construct the memorial and decided more extreme measures were needed. At that time Elvis Presley was in Hawai'i filming *Blue Hawai'i*. When he heard about the PWMC's struggle to raise funds for the memorial, he volunteered to do a benefit concert. Bringing the teen idol into the fund-raising operation was seen as lessening the gravity of the matter, perhaps even as diminishing the magnitude of the valor of the dead. However, it did raise a significant amount of cash toward the memorial's construction.

Architect Alfred Preis originally proposed a design that would have brought visitors face to face with the reality of the battleship's destruction, involving a submerged tank into which visitors would descend. There, under the blue tropical sky, they would have peered through glass portholes into the world of the sailors entombed within. The idea was to impress the horror of the sailors' last moments, particularly the terror of being trapped underwater. The navy immediately rejected that design as excessively morbid.

Preis then went back to the navy's earlier idea of a bridge across the wreck. Although the navy had suggested an open structure, he decided to enclose portions of it, creating a structure that sags in the middle, to recall the defeat of December 7, and rises at its ends to symbolize the ultimate victory at the end of the war. A shrine room, in which was mounted a plaque with the names of all the men who perished aboard USS *Arizona*, is illuminated by stained-glass windows in abstract patterns. The idea was to create a serene yet friendly place that would encourage visitors to pause and reflect upon the events that had occurred in this place on that bright Sunday morning in 1941.

Some critics point out that the very sense of friendliness and welcome may have actually ended up lessening the sense of reverence owed to the dead.

For decades, all salvage diving activities related to the battleship USS *Arizona* were kept to the exterior of the ship, lest they desecrate the final resting places of the slain servicemen. However, in the 1990s, evidence of the impending collapse of critical parts of the ship's deck and the possibility that such an event might crush the ship's fuel tanks raised serious environmental concerns. In order to determine how much danger the fuel oil within the tanks might pose to the harbor, it was decided to permit a special mission to investigate the situation.

AT LEFT *The USS Arizona's* Gun Turret *#3 stands as part of the memorial. The oil slicks (lower right) that rise up from the ship below are called the "Tears of Arizona." Lore has it that when the last surviving veteran of the ship dies, the tears will stop.*

The team of divers was chosen with the utmost care, and those who were chosen had to have two qualifications. First, they had to bring a special skill to the team that was not duplicated elsewhere. Second, they must hold the firm belief that the wreck of the USS *Arizona* was a sacred place, not to be treated casually.

The divers performed a careful survey in the early part of 2000 and discovered that the very marine organisms that fouled the old ship's hull, and that are usually a bane to maritime activities, may actually be forming a protective casing around the ship. This casing may be helping to keep the remaining fuel oil in place so that it does not seep out faster than normal organic processes in the harbor can deal with it. (See also DAMAGE, MEMORIAL.)

Further Reading: Arizona Memorial Museum Association, www.arizonamemorial.org (cited January 2006); Thurston Clarke, *Pearl Harbor Ghosts: A Journey to Hawai'i Then and Now* (William Morrow, 1991); Joy Waldron Jasper, James. P. Delgado, and Jim Adams, *The USS Arizona: The Ship, the Men, the Pearl Harbor Attack, and the Symbol that Aroused America* (St. Martin's Press, 2003); Paul Stilwell, *Battleship Arizona: An Illustrated History* (Naval Institute Press, 1991).

—**LEIGH KIMMEL**

Axis Powers in 1941

The road that led to WORLD WAR II began in the 1930s as GERMANY, Italy, and JAPAN each sought to extend their power through conquest and diplomacy.

ADOLF HITLER had come to power in Germany in 1933 and shortly thereafter violated the terms of the Versailles Treaty as he advocated German rearmament.

By 1936 he had Nazi soldiers stationed in the Rhineland and in 1938, had annexed Austria and portions of Czechoslovakia.

While Hitler sought to expand Nazi power throughout Europe, BENITO MUSSOLINI, the Italian leader and head of the Fascist Party, invaded Ethiopia in 1935. The Japanese sought to extend their control over China, fearing that China would eventually rise up against the Japanese.

Such thinking prompted the Japanese to invade Manchuria in 1931 and with the start of the Sino-Japanese War in 1937, Japan attacked the city of Nanking, massacring nearly 300,000 Chinese civilians and prisoners of war.

AMERICAN ISOLATIONISM

In the midst of these actions, America had firmly adopted a policy of ISOLATIONISM due to both the Great Depression and American bitterness following World War I. The American public wanted the UNITED STATES to stay out of foreign affairs, a belief that Congress fully adopted throughout the decade. The Munich Agreement of 1938, which recognized Hitler's "right" to the Sudetenland in Czechoslovakia, was initially thought to be a victory for France and Britain, as Hitler had supposedly agreed to peace. However, Hitler and Mussolini both interpreted appeasement as an acknowledgment that the Western democracies were incapable of opposing their Fascist regimes.

War in Europe broke out in September 1939. Three major occurrences sent shockwaves throughout the Western world. On August 23, the Soviet Union signed a nonaggression pact with Nazi Germany in Moscow. The leaders of France, Britain, and the United States disliked JOSEF STALIN, the Soviet Communist premier, but the agreement was nevertheless a surprise as Stalin was known to hate the Nazis. Following the nonaggression pact, Hitler launched an invasion of Poland, thus breaking his promise at the Munich conference. When this occurred, France and Britain declared war on Germany to protect Poland's borders, as they had previously sworn to do in March 1939.

BIRTH OF THE AXIS POWERS

By June 1940, Hitler controlled Belgium, the Netherlands, Poland, and Scandinavia. Later that month his forces took Paris, effectively knocking France out of the war. Britain was left to stand alone and its plight took an even worse turn in September 1940, when Germany signed the Tripartite Pact with Italy and Japan.

The pact stated that if any one of the signatories were attacked, the other two would come to its aid and was the official military formation of the Axis powers. Later the Axis would include Bulgaria, Finland, Hungary, Romania, and the puppet states established in Croatia and Slovakia. Neither the Germans nor the Japanese viewed the Tripartite Pact as an aggressive treaty, but rather thought they were acting defensively, especially with regard to the United States. The agreement sent a definite message to the United States: do not become involved in the situations in Europe or Asia. The threat of having to face all three nations if the United States did become involved was hoped to be enough of a deterrent to keep it at bay.

The United States, however, saw the agreement as an aggressive act intended to limit American power. The United States continuously demanded that the Japanese remove themselves from the agreement. However, the Japanese, at the start of 1941, clearly believed that the Germans would be victorious in the war and that it was only a matter of time before Britain fell. YOSUKE MATSUOKA, the Japanese foreign minister, believed that being on the victorious side of the war would enable the Japanese to share the victor's spoils and that they could also finally claim legitimacy in China.

BRITAIN CONTINUES TO STAND ALONE

While the Axis military alliance formed, Roosevelt observed anxiously from Washington, D.C. He knew that Britain needed help but he also knew that the American public and Congress remained opposed to intervention. Important public figures such as Charles Lindbergh and Henry Ford spoke up for keeping America out of the war. British officials believed that Roosevelt, after he had won an unprecedented third term in office in 1940, would finally be able to overcome the isolationists and supply Britain with much-needed aid. However, Prime Minister WINSTON CHURCHILL expressed disappointment that aid was not immediate. Roosevelt was finally able to provide some help early in 1941, but the Germans had already begun bombing British cities by that point. Roosevelt was able to pass the LEND-LEASE Act on March 11, 1941. Knowing that he had to appear "neutral" to appease the public, the Lend-Lease simply allowed the United States to supply Britain with goods and weapons that Britain would repay after the war. Roosevelt began to aid both Britain and China as he searched for a way to break America out of its isolationist mindset.

Meanwhile, the Nazis continued to conquer more of Europe. Besides having begun bombing British cities during the winter, Germany invaded Yugoslavia in the spring of 1941. The Yugoslav government was forced to sign the Tripartite Pact on March 25, but a political coup replaced the Yugoslav government with an anti-Fascist government just two days later. In response the Nazis invaded both Yugoslavia and Greece in April. When the Nazis invaded Greece, Mussolini had already sent forces there, but Hitler feared that his inferior counterpart could not defeat the Allied forces alone (see ALLIES ON DECEMBER 7, 1941). On May 20, 1941, the Battle of Crete took place with a German airborne invasion. The Germans successfully took control of the island, beating back Allied forces comprised of Greek, British, Australian, and New Zealand troops. However, the Germans suffered large losses and would never again attempt an airborne invasion.

HITLER BREAKS THE NONAGGRESSION AGREEMENT

Once a major British stronghold, the eastern Mediterranean continued to fall into the grip of the Nazis, and under the direction of the "Desert Fox" Erwin Rommel, the Nazis proved too powerful for the British in northern Africa. Still, though, Roosevelt was unable to bring America into the war in Europe, even as the British situation grew dire by the end of May. Amid all of these successes, Hitler decided to break his nonaggression pact with the Soviet Union and with nearly 3,000,000 German troops invaded that country. Hitler also brought 3,600 tanks and 2,500 combat aircraft into the Soviet Union.

This initiative was called Operation Barbarossa and was launched on June 22, 1941. Hitler believed that he would have quick success against the Soviets; his mistake in underestimating the tenacity of the Soviet army would eventually lead to the turning point in the war for the Allied powers, when the Germans surrendered at Stalingrad in January of 1943. When the Germans first attacked, Stalin was surprised that they had broken their nonaggression pact. He had earlier suggested that Hitler would not launch a second front into Russia because the Nazi leader was no "idiot." Hitler, however, believed that he could take Moscow before the Russian winter came, but instead would watch as the resilient Red Army eventually broke the backbone of his army.

While Roosevelt appeared hesitant in entering the European war, in the Pacific he proved to be much more aggressive. In 1941 he ordered an embargo on the Japanese (see SANCTIONS AGAINST JAPAN). This was essentially a form of economic war, as the embargo was placed on the export of oil and scrap metal to Japan and was potentially crippling for the Japanese economy. Many American and Japanese officials were surprised that Roosevelt placed such a restrictive embargo on oil. Japan had approximately two years' worth of oil in reserve, and most of its oil came directly from the United States. With the world at war, oil had become extremely scarce, and Japan could not find a viable alternative supplier. The American embargo further added to the already existing tension between the two nations.

A POORLY COORDINATED AXIS

When America entered World War II in December 1941, Roosevelt and Churchill would plan out the war together. The United States and Britain were in constant contact and both militaries were organized together. The same closeness could not be said of the Axis countries; the Axis powers failed to replicate such a close working relationship. Hitler never liked Mussolini and thought that the Italian leader was weak and not very intelligent. With the Japanese, Hitler never totally confided his plans to Japanese leaders.

In the spring of 1941, Hitler assured Foreign Minister Matsuoka that the Nazis had no intention of invading the Soviet Union. Meanwhile, this was exactly what Hitler had planned. Matsuoka next visited Russia and in April 1941 signed a nonaggression pact with the Soviets (see RUSSIA–JAPAN RELATIONS).

Hitler had not consulted with his Japanese allies about the attack on the Soviet Union, but once the Nazis had penetrated the Soviet border, Hitler urged the Japanese to attack the Soviets. Hitler thought that the war in Russia would be a relatively short campaign. The Japanese decided to wait and see what would transpire in the Soviet Union.

The relationship between Japan and Germany throughout 1941 was far from close, and both sides did not always appear to be following the same war plan. While American and Japanese officials struggled to find a diplomatic solution to their differences in the Pacific, the Germans warned the Japanese that they were violating the Tripartite Pact. Hitler

WEAPONS OF WAR *World War II weaponry included the 101 Alpha-One* ABOVE LEFT, *60mm M2 mortar* ABOVE RIGHT, *guns such as this German MP40 .40 cal submachine gun* BELOW RIGHT, *and land mine kits* BELOW LEFT.

also assured the Japanese that if they would go to war against the United States, then the Germans would also go to war against the United States.

DECLARATIONS OF WAR

By the fall of 1941 it was clearly apparent that the tensions between the United States and Japan could not be rectified. A message was sent to Washington, D.C., as the Japanese neared Pearl Harbor. The message stated that the Japanese were breaking off all negotiations. This ultimately signaled a declaration of war. By the time U.S. officials had decoded the message, the Pearl Harbor attack had already occurred (see CODES, JAPANESE).

On December 8, 1941, the U.S. Congress voted to go to war with Japan. There was no such declaration to enter the war in Europe. On December 11, however, Hitler came through on his promise to the Japanese and declared war on the United States. Some have argued that this decision was another of Hitler's egregious mistakes; however, Hitler had already come to the understanding that the Americans would find a way to enter the European war. Others assumed that Hitler believed the Japanese would so tie up the American military in the Pacific that it would prevent any American assistance to the Allies in Europe. For Roosevelt and Churchill, the German decision to declare war on the United States came as a relief, for now the United States had every grounds for bringing aid to the battered British military.

Further Reading: Peter Calvocoressi, Guy Wint, and John Pritchard, *The Penguin History of the Second World War* (Penguin Books, 1999); John Costello, *The Pacific War* (Quil, 1981); John Keegan, *The Second World War* (Hutchinson, 1989); Henry Kissinger, *Diplomacy* (Simon and Schuster, 1994); Walter LaFeber, *The American Age: United States Foreign Policy at Home and Abroad: 1750 to the Present* (W.W. Norton, 1994); Francis MacDonnell, *Insidious Foes: The Axis Fifth Column and the American Home Front* (Lyons Press, 2004); David Reynolds, *From Munich to Pearl Harbor: Roosevelt's America and the Origins of the Second World War* (Ivan R. Dee, 2001).

—DAVID W. MCBRIDE

B

Bloch, C.C. (1878–1967)

In January 1940, Admiral Claude C. Bloch was replaced as the commander in chief of the U.S. Fleet by Admiral JAMES O. RICHARDSON. Bloch became the commander of the Fourteenth Naval District, responsible for commanding the naval forces that provided air surveillance of the waters around Pearl Harbor with a force of 72 patrol planes. In the early morning hours of December 7, a single naval plane was patrolling the air over Pearl Harbor.

A year before the attack occurred, Bloch submitted a memorandum to address military concerns following a British attack by torpedo bombers on an Italian harbor on November 22, 1940. Military officials realized that American forces were not sufficiently prepared to prevent a similar attack on the U.S. Fleet at Pearl Harbor. In response to Bloch's memorandum, Rear Admiral Richmond K. Turner advised Secretary of War HENRY L. STIMSON that the Pacific Fleet (see PACIFIC FLEET, U.S.) at Pearl Harbor was a prime target for a Japanese attack.

Bloch's responsibilities were basically administrative; however, he was included in various meetings geared toward planning for the defense of Pearl Harbor, especially as it appeared more likely the UNITED STATES would enter the war. On March 21, Bloch joined General WALTER C. SHORT in signing off on a joint agreement to coordinate efforts to protect the U.S. Fleet at Pearl Harbor. Under the agreement, the army took command of defensive air operations, while the navy was responsible for directing operations during a joint attack on enemy ships.

AT LEFT *"Führer and Duce in München." Hitler and Mussolini in Munich, Germany, ca. June 1940. The German and Italian alliance formed the Tripartite Pact, which included Japan.*

Bloch was also present at meetings to plan reinforcements of American military bases at Wake, Midway, and Canton Islands. There is no record that the whereabouts of the Japanese navy was discussed at any of these meetings. During the subsequent investigations into the Pearl Harbor attack, both Short and Bloch expressed their belief that the War Department was at fault for not classifying the situation at Pearl Harbor as a "Cat E," which would have alerted officials that "in all probability" an attack on the Pacific Fleet would occur.

On December 2, 1941, Admiral Husband Kimmel and Bloch were notified that the Japanese had ordered all communication code systems destroyed except one, a move indicative of war preparations. No move was made to place military personnel at Pearl Harbor on emergency alert. Neither Kimmel nor Bloch discussed this information with Short. Kimmel later stated that he assumed the War Department would pass the information on to Short.

During investigations into the attack on Pearl Harbor, the Navy Court found the U.S. government responsible for the lack of preparedness at Pearl Harbor, and censured Admiral Harold R. Stark, its chief of operations. Stark's failures included neglecting to inform navy officials of a Japanese concentration in the MARSHALL ISLANDS, and failing to report the presence of a Japanese submarine near the entrance to Pearl Harbor only an hour before the attack of the Pacific Fleet took place.

Further Reading: Charles R. Anderson, *Day of Lightning, Years of Scorn: Walter C. Short and the Attack on Pearl Harbor* (Naval Institute Press, 2005); Edward L. Beach, *Scapegoats: A Defense of Kimmel and Short at Pearl Harbor* (Naval Institute Press, 1995); Henry C. Clausen and Bruce Lee, *Pearl Harbor: Final Judgement* (Da Capo Press, 2001).

—ELIZABETH PURDY, PH.D.

British Commonwealth

One of the supreme ironies of the outbreak of WORLD WAR II in the Pacific was that the British were attacked before the Japanese bombed Pearl Harbor—yet because of the International Date Line, the Japanese blow fell upon the British Empire a day later, on December 8, 1941.

However, while the first Japanese bombs did not fall on British territory until December 8, JAPAN did attack the British Empire on December 7, 1941, at about 7:40 P.M., when the Japanese minelayer *Tatsumiya Maru* began laying 456 mines in British territorial waters between Tioman Island and the Malay coast, just above Singapore (see MALAYA AND SINGAPORE).

JAPANESE "INVASION IMMINENT"

At that moment, 19 Japanese transports, carrying Japan's 5th and 18th Infantry Divisions, were steering for Singora and Patani in Thailand and Kota Bharu in Malaya. They had been seen by Royal Air Force (RAF) air reconnaissance; however, British defenses in the Far East were at the bottom of the empire's list. Most of the empire's best troops were fighting in the North African desert against Erwin Rommel's legendary Afrika Korps.

The major British military forces in the Far East in Malaya totaled 86,000 men in 31 battalions. Their air cover consisted of 158 outdated aircraft, far below the 582 pre-war planners estimated Malaya would need.

The trump card was Force Z, which had arrived in Malaya on December 1, 1941, the new battleship HMS *Prince of Wales* and the battle cruiser HMS *Repulse*. Both were powerful, well-armed, fast ships and were intended as a deterrent against Japanese aggression. But this bristling mass of guns had a flaw: the aircraft carrier HMS *Indomitable* had run aground in Jamaica and never made it to Singapore. This denied Force Z commander Admiral Sir Tom Phillips of fighter cover.

The British commander in chief, Air Chief Marshal Sir Robert Brooke-Popham, put his troops on alert and pondered whether or not to launch his deterrent, Operation Matador. Under this plan, a British brigade group called Krohcol would race north into Thailand and deploy on the Singora and Patani beaches ahead of the Japanese convoys. The 11th Indian Division would follow Krohcol.

RESPONSE IN LONDON

Officials in London, where it was still December 6, were not idle. At 5 P.M. General Sir Alan Brooke, the chief of the Imperial General Staff, met with the First Sea Lord Admiral, Sir Dudley Pound, and top officials. They could not tell whether the Japanese were heading for Malaya, Thailand, or just bluffing. They informed Churchill of the situation, discussed what to do if Japan attacked holdings in the Far East, and decided the hard part would be finding a way to bring the UNITED STATES into the conflict, if the Americans were not attacked.

Their decision was made by a telegram from Sir Josiah Crosby, British minister in Thailand, which read, "For God's sake do not allow British forces to occupy one inch of Thai territory unless and until Japan has struck the first blow at Thailand." Brooke-Popham cancelled Operation Matador. Just after midnight on December 8, the Japanese began landing at Kota Bharu on Malaya's east coast. Midnight in Malaya was dawn in Hawai'i.

Japanese Major General Takumi's 5,300-man force was to seize the port primarily to divert British attention from Singora and Patani. The heavily loaded Japanese infantry came ashore and immediately came

ABOVE *Prime Minister Churchill salutes troops as he walks from the aircraft in which he flew to the Middle East to meet with Allied war chiefs. August 1942.*

under machine-gun fire from Brigadier Billy Key's 11th Indian Brigade. Japanese naval guns shot back, forcing the Indian defenders to withdraw. News of the Japanese invasion rocketed up the British chain of command to Sir Shenton Thomas, governor of the Straits Settlements, the top civilian, who was contacted by General Arthur Percival, who commanded Brooke-Popham's ground forces. Thomas's reaction to Percival's call showed the civilian disconnection

Army–Navy Cooperation

WHILE ASSURING government officials of full cooperation between army and navy forces at Pearl Harbor in 1941, navy officers secretly blamed the army for not protecting the U.S. Fleet. Members of the Army Pearl Harbor Board included Major General Henry D. Russell, General George Grunert, and Major General Walter H. Frank. Their report supported the navy's contentions, finding General GEORGE C. MARSHALL guilty of neglect for not preparing Pearl Harbor for an attack even though reliable information had been received that an attack was likely. Russell's personal notes on the investigation were locked in a vault until the mid-1990s. They were published in 2001 as *Pearl Harbor Story.*

from the reality of war. Thomas said, "Well, I suppose you'll shove the little men off!"

At 2:15 A.M. on December 8, Admiral Phillips, known as "Tom Thumb" for his short stature, met with Thomas, Brooke-Popham, and others to discuss the situation. Brooke-Popham could only offer a cliché: "Once he is in a fight, the only way to get a Jap out of it is to kill him!" Air Vice-Marshal C. W. H. Pulford warned that his aircraft had limited range. And Thomas, still not facing reality, suggested that the Kota Bharu attack might be a feint.

Then the governor suddenly switched his views and realized the gravity of the situation, saying Malaya was in "a regular pot-mess and no mistake." Seconds after that, the air-raid sirens began warbling. Everyone hit the floor under the conference table. It was a false alarm, but when the "All Clear" sounded, the meeting broke up quickly.

REPORTS OF PEARL HARBOR ATTACK

By now Britain's diplomats in Washington, D.C., were getting the word. Lord Halifax, Britain's lean, fox-hunting ambassador to the United States, was about to go riding, while his first secretary, William Hayter, was going to take his wife for a drive in the country. Both were about to leave when President FRANKLIN D. ROOSEVELT phoned from the White House to say that Pearl Harbor had been bombed.

The Britons were stunned—they expected attacks on Hong Kong and Singapore, but not Hawai'i. Hayter suggested Halifax phone London, and they got through to a sleepy Foreign Office resident clerk, who asked Halifax, "What was that place? Could you spell it?"

In Malaya, Indian troops struggled to hold bunkers against determined Japanese attacks. The Japanese had been told the Indian defenders had poor morale

The Fall of Hong Kong

SUNDAY, DECEMBER 7, began in the British Crown Colony of Hong Kong with a parade at the Fortress Headquarters in the city center. General Christopher Maltby, the British commander, read from the Book of Matthew.

Meanwhile, 60,000 Japanese attackers north of the border with occupied China moved into position. A patrol of Punjabis on the frontier spotted the Japanese and reported it up the chain of command to Maltby in his pew. By 5 P.M. every one of Hong Kong's 14,000 defenders—8,919 Britons and Canadians, 4,402 Indians, and 660 Chinese—was at his post. Beyond the ground troops, Maltby's other forces were slim.

While hundreds of British, Canadian, and Indian troops yanked on khaki uniforms and ran to their stations, 48 Japanese attack bombers roared over the New Territories. The Japanese swooped down on Kai Tak, defended by four machine-guns, and blasted the airfield, wrecking the planes. The remaining Japanese bombers turned on Sham Shui Po Barracks. Most of the Canadian troops were gone.

Hong Kong would fall in 18 days, a brutal siege that cost the British defenders about 4,500 casualties, with the rest "going in the bag," enduring starvation and torture for three years in captivity. The great irony of the short campaign was that Canada had been at war with GERMANY for three years. Yet when Canadian troops took the brunt of the Japanese assault on Hong Kong Island, it was the first time that nation's ground forces went into action during the entire war, doing so against Japan, and it was the only time the two nations clashed on the ground during the entire war.

and training. Instead the Japanese suffered 329 dead and 538 wounded, ultimately taking the pillboxes with the favorite Japanese tactic, bayonet charges.

At 3:20 A.M. twin-engine "Nell" bombers of Rear Admiral Sadaichi Matsunaga's 22nd Air Flotilla, which had managed to battle through heavy rain and winds by flying low, were approaching Singapore. The RAF ordered a blackout, but the chief warden had gone to an all-night movie theater, and only he had the keys for the air-raid siren switch. Efforts to locate the engineer with the master keys to shut off electricity and enforce a blackout were equally fruitless. That would not have mattered anyway: most of Singapore's streets were still gas-lit, and that required men with long poles to walk around and extinguish them, one at a time. When the Japanese bombers roared over Singapore at 4:15 A.M., the city was fully lighted.

Meanwhile, London was grappling with the worst. A steady stream of frightening reports from Malaya, Washington, D.C., and Hong Kong had landed in the Cabinet War Rooms, beneath Horse Guards Parade. The chiefs of staff met in Room 67, using *The Times*'s "Map of the Far East" to decipher complex Asian geography. When the messages came in reporting the attack on Pearl Harbor, General Brooke realized there would be no problems with how to bring the United States into the war. "All our work of the last 48 hours wasted; the Japs themselves have now ensured that the U.S.A. are in the war!" Brooke wrote in his diary.

There was not much the top officers could do on a practical level. The empire's defenders had already been given their orders. All that was left was for the admiralty to send a message to its ships across the globe, saying, "To: All Concerned Home and Abroad

From: Admiralty: Commence hostilities against Japan repeat Japan at once." During this flurry of activity, nobody had yet alerted Prime Minister Churchill. The BBC's Alvar Liddell announced the attack in his 9 P.M. news broadcast.

"WE ARE ALL IN IT TOGETHER"

At that moment, Churchill was dining with his daughter, Pamela Churchill, American Ambassador John Winant and fellow diplomat Averell Harriman, and Harriman's wife, Kathleen, at Chequers. Also present were Churchill's military aide, General Hastings "Pug" Ismay, and his naval aide, Commander C. R. "Tommy" Thompson.

Butler-valet Frank Sawyers brought in a $15 portable radio, so all could listen to the 9 P.M. news. By the time Sawyers set up the radio and returned to the kitchen, Churchill had missed the opening items, and only caught Liddell mention the "Hawai'ian islands," before the broadcaster launched into a report on the battle raging south of Tobruk in Libya. Then Liddell moved on to the battle raging between German and Soviet forces outside Moscow. According to Churchill's memoirs, he sat bolt upright in his chair and asked, "Didn't he say there has been an attack on American bases?"

As if in answer to Churchill's request, Liddell repeated his first item, saying "Japanese aircraft have raided Pearl Harbor, the American base in Hawai'i." Churchill rose from his chair and said, "We will declare war on Japan." Actually, his forces had been in battle for three hours, but he had not yet been informed. Then Churchill said, "We are all in it together."

At this time, the admiralty finally reached Churchill, and the service chiefs briefed the prime minister. Winant then called the White House and got Roosevelt on the phone.

Now came Hayter's reports from Washington, D.C., admiralty messages from Malaya. Churchill ordered Britain's ambassador in Tokyo, Sir Robert Craigie, to inform the Japanese that a state of war existed "between our two countries." Craigie did not get the telegram. The Japanese withheld it. It did not matter. At 7:45 A.M. in Tokyo, Craigie took a phone call from the Foreign Ministry, summoning him to be there by 8 A.M. Craigie, a senior ambassador, had repeatedly warned London that war was coming. Now he arrived at the Foreign Ministry to receive from Principal Secretary Toshikazu Kase a memorandum identical to one Kase had just given U.S. Ambassador JOSEPH GREW: it said that Japan had broken off negotiations with Washington, D.C. It did not mention Britain or war.

When Craigie returned to the British embassy, his American-born wife, Pleasant, told him that Japanese radio had announced "warlike operations against Britain and the United States had commenced." Pleasant Craigie and Embassy Counselor Paul Gore-Booth showed initiative by burning the embassy's confidential papers and codes and phoned staff members who lived outside the compound to bring their bedding and clothes to the embassy.

Singapore was now waking up to war, learning that Hawai'i, Hong Kong, and the PHILIPPINES had been attacked. The *Singapore Free Press* put out a single-sheet extra with the news. Troops deployed mobile antiaircraft guns in appropriate places. The new official British communiqué reported that Japanese troops on the Kota Bharu beaches were being heavily machine-gunned and the Japanese ships were retiring to sea.

MALAYA CAPTURED

In actuality, the Japanese were now bombing RAF bases in north Malaya, blasting 21 Squadron's

Buffaloes while they were on the ground. The pilots who took off found that their aircraft could not reach the bombers' altitude and their guns did not work, either. The Japanese used small-scale 150-pound bombs, which would rip up airplanes, but not damage the runways. The Japanese intended to use the airstrips when they captured them.

In Malaya, it was 9:30 A.M. when the Japanese air force began pounding the RAF 1 Squadron's base at Kota Bharu again, strafing the Hudson bombers on the ground as they refueled. At 10:45 A.M., the Japanese hit the British base at Sungei Pattani and were intercepted by Brewster Buffalo fighters. The Japanese made short work of the Buffaloes and shorter work of the base, hitting the aviation fuel tanks, incinerating 200,000 gallons of gas. The Japanese had control of northern Malaya's skies.

By 11:30 A.M., Percival realized that Operation Matador was dead. His men went over to the defensive just over the Thai border. On the battleship HMS *Prince of Wales*, Admiral Phillips convened his staff to discuss what Force Z should do. Options were limited, and Phillips summed them up. "We can stay in Singapore. We can sail away to the East—Australia. Or we can go out and fight. Gentlemen, we sail at five o'clock."

Phillips informed the RAF that he intended to hit the Japanese off Kota Bharu on the morning of the 10th and requested air cover off the port at that date and time. With that, working parties on the two battleships and their four escorting destroyers loaded fuel, food, and ammunition.

Phillips did not inform London, so Whitehall did not know Force Z was heading to sea. Churchill suggested to Ismay that the big ships should vanish into the open sea like "rogue elephants" or hook up with the U.S. Pacific Fleet (see PACIFIC FLEET, U.S.).

FEBRUARY 1942: *Women and children being herded together by Japanese soldiers after the fall of Singapore.*

From Churchill's Journal

CHURCHILL PUT the seal on the long day, writing, "I do not pretend to have measured accurately the martial might of Japan, but at this very moment I knew the United States was in the war, up to the neck and in to the death. So we had won after all! Saturated and satiated with emotion and sensation, I went to bed and slept the sleep of the saved and thankful."

again bombing Singapore, and Japanese troops were forcing British defenders to retreat from their positions north of the Thai border. They would keep retreating all the way to Singapore—one of the greatest defeats in British history.

Churchill put the seal on the long day, writing, "I do not pretend to have measured accurately the martial might of Japan, but at this very moment I knew the United States was in the war, up to the neck and in to the death. So we had won after all! Saturated and satiated with emotion and sensation, I went to bed and slept the sleep of the saved and thankful." Even so, it was a long time before Churchill slept. He stayed awake, talking with Winant, until 5 A.M. (See also GREAT BRITAIN, REACTION IN.)

Further Reading: Krishnan Scinivasan, *Rise, Decline and Future of the British Commonwealth* (Palgrave Macmillan, 2006); Philip Snow, *The Fall of Hong Kong* (Yale University Press, 2003); Christopher Somerville, *Our War: How the British Commonwealth Fought the Second World War* (Orion Publishing Group, 1998); Stanley Weintraub, *Long Day's Journey into War* (Dutton, 1991).

—DAVID H. LIPPMAN

Around 5 P.M., Force Z stood out to sea. As the ships sailed past Changi Signal Station, Phillips received a radiogram from the RAF, "Regret fighter protection impossible." Phillips shrugged. "Well, we must get on with it." Neither of the two battleships, nor their admiral, nor 840 of their crewmen would return.

At the same time, Kota Bharu's airfield was no longer tenable. With the airfield damaged by bombing and rain, the Japanese troops were now moving inland and on the field. The British evacuated what they could but did not have time to crater the field or destroy the remaining fuel or bombs. When the Japanese moved in at 6:15 P.M., they found it intact.

By nightfall, half of the RAF's Buffalo fighter strength had been destroyed, the Japanese were

ABOVE *The B-17 bomber was used extensively during World War II, with the American Air Force operating from seven airfields in Northamptonshire, England.*

Australia

THE OUTBREAK of war in the Pacific was an additional shock to Australia, as the nation was still stunned by a bizarre naval battle on November 30, 1941. That day, the disguised German raider *Kormoran* met up with the Australian light cruiser HMS *Sydney*. Both ships sank, but while a number of *Kormoran* crewmen survived to enter captivity, the *Sydney* went down with all hands.

The incident was a national calamity and reminded Australians that despite their distance from the battles in North Africa, the war was coming to their doorstep. Proof of that point came in the editorial in the *Sydney Morning Herald* on December 8, 1941—the exact time Japanese bombers were attacking Pearl Harbor. It was entitled, "Twilight of Peace in the Pacific."

At 5:30 A.M. an aide woke Australian Prime Minister John Curtin in Melbourne's Victoria Palace Hotel, on his way home for a Christmas holiday. With Japanese ships heading for Malaya, where Australian troops and airmen were deployed, Curtin stayed at the hotel, holding conferences, and taking time out to tell reporters that Australia faced "a new war." Australians arriving at work heard Curtin call Japan "an assassin in the night" and call for courage and determination. By noon, the War Cabinet was reviewing the situation, which mostly consisted of increasingly frightening telegrams and radio reports from the Department of Information's round-the-clock monitoring of shortwave radio. Curtin told his cabinet that "the situation should be accepted as involving a state of war with Japan."

Curtin and his staff reviewed Australia's situation: there were labor disputes on the piers; Japanese citizens in Australia had to be interned; war production had to be intensified; Christmas leave for servicemen and munitions workers had to be cancelled. Darwin, at the top of Australia's Northern Territory, was now the nation's front line, and Australia had to man its defenses. Those defenses did not amount to much. Australia had three tough infantry divisions committed to North Africa, part of the British Eighth Army. Two brigades of another understrength division were in Malaya. Australia's best airmen and most modern planes were in North Africa and England. Australia had fewer than 100 serviceable planes at home, mostly Wirraway and Gypsy Moth trainers. The latter were biplanes with fabric-covered wings, whose propellers were wound by hand. Australia's defenses were wafer-thin.

But Australia responded with courage and determination. Recruiting depots had their busiest day of the war. In Perth, hundreds of people lined up at dawn, having heard Curtin's broadcast, to enlist. One man said, "I've been meaning to join up for some time, but the war has come so close that a man must get in it now."

At 3 P.M., the Australian War Cabinet recalled Parliament, then adjourned. Curtin finally broadcast to the nation. "We are at war with Japan," he began. "The hands of the democracies are clean."

ABOVE *An historical world map shows the extensive lands of the British Commonwealth in red, circa 1920.*

C

California, USS

When the Japanese attacked Pearl Harbor on the morning of December 7, the USS *California* was situated among six other battleships in Battleship Row. The USS *California* had been the flagship of the Pacific Fleet (see PACIFIC FLEET, U.S.) since 1921, and had an illustrious career leading up to Pearl Harbor, winning the Battle Efficiency Pennant in 1921 and 1922, and leading a goodwill cruise to Australia and New Zealand in 1925.

The first bomb to hit the USS *California* occurred just after 8 A.M. A second bomb started her sinking into the harbor. Though the sailors of Battleship Row were caught off-guard as the Japanese attacked, the crew of the USS *California* responded with great courage. Four sailors aboard the USS *California* were awarded CONGRESSIONAL MEDALS OF HONOR for their brave actions on that fateful morning and no other ship would be given as many medals.

Herbert Jones, a 23-year-old ensign and a native of Los Angeles, California, organized his crew to pass ammunition up to the antiaircraft guns. When the ship was struck, the mechanisms that lifted ammunition to her guns were destroyed. As the Japanese dropped bombs on the USS *California*, Jones was determined to make sure the ship's guns were supplied.

While leading his crew, Jones was fatally wounded when a Japanese bomb struck the ship. His last act of heroism was that he ordered his men to evacuate the ship before the deadly smoke caused by the

AT LEFT, *the American flag is raised over the USS* Arizona *Memorial. The 184-foot-long memorial structure spans the mid-portion of the sunken battleship and consists of the entry/ assembly room, an observation/ ceremonial room, and the shrine room, where the names of those who lost their lives are engraved in marble.*

bomb's fire killed them. For his bravery Jones received the Medal of Honor posthumously and had a ship named in his honor.

Thomas Reeves from Connecticut was chief radioman on the ship. When a torpedo stopped the flow of ammunition to the aircraft guns, Reeves began to manually carry ammunition to the guns. Reeves refused to evacuate and risk leaving the ship defenseless against the Japanese. His bravery ultimately cost him his life. He too received the Medal of Honor and had a ship dedicated to him.

Robert Scott of Massillon, Ohio, received a Medal of Honor after he died making sure that the ship's guns remained active. Machinists Mate First Class Scott was responsible for ensuring that the ship's air compressors remained operational. As the ship was being struck, the room containing the compressors began to flood. While other members of the crew fled, Scott stayed behind to work the compressors.

Lieutenant Jackson Pharris was the fourth member of the USS *California* to receive a Medal of Honor. Pharris was wounded by the first blast to the ship, but still helped to pass ammunition to the ship's guns. When it became clear that the USS *California* was going to sink and the crew began to evacuate, Pharris carried off unconscious sailors, often placing his own life at risk.

Further Reading: California State Military Department, "USS California, (BB-44)," www.militarymuseum.org/usscalif.html (cited February 2006); Daniel Madsen, *Resurrection: Salvaging the Battle Fleet at Pearl Harbor* (Naval Institute Press, 2003); William Manchester, *Goodbye, Darkness: A Memoir of the Pacific War* (Little, Brown and Company, 2002); Oliver North and Joe Musser, *War Stories II: Heroism in the Pacific* (Regnery Publishing, 2004).

—DAVID W. MCBRIDE

WHY THE USS CALIFORNIA WAS UNPREPARED: *Because the ship was due for inspection, not all her protective features were in place. Watertight mechanisms to prevent flooding had been left open. The Japanese torpedoes ripped into the ship and she flooded rapidly. The extent of the damage was a shock to her crew, who thought she had been built to better withstand such attacks.* **AT RIGHT,** *the crew of the USS* California *abandon ship.*

Caroline Islands

For Americans, one of the most shocking aspects of JAPAN's attack on Pearl Harbor was not just that it had been a "sneak" attack, but that it had happened at all. Prior to December 7, 1941, nobody had imagined that the powerful Pacific Fleet (see PACIFIC FLEET, U.S.) could be destroyed within the confines of its own safe harbor.

Then, in 1944, the Americans pulled off their own sneak attack on a complacent, powerful Japanese fleet—an attack that would come to be called "Japan's Pearl Harbor."

The Caroline Islands are an archipelago curving for 850 square miles out into the Pacific Ocean, west of GUAM and just north of the equator. The main islands are Truk, Yap, Ponape, Palau, and Kosrae. Micronesian and Polynesian settlers had populated the islands for many centuries when the first Westerners arrived in 1526. But until the end of the 19th century, the islands were mostly left to themselves.

Spain, which had named the islands the Carolines in honor of King Charles V in the 16th century, began to exert control over the islands in 1886, but at the end of the Spanish-American War in 1899, they sold them to Germany for around £1 million. During World War I, Japan stepped in and seized the territory. Over the next 30 years, the Japanese built military fortifications on all the major islands.

Just after the entry of the UNITED STATES into WORLD WAR II in January 1942, the Australians launched reconnaissance flights to survey the fortifications at Truk, which they believed the Japanese could be using as a forward station for attacks on New Guinea. Poor weather prevented the Australians from getting a complete picture of the lagoon. They requested that a B-17 Flying Fortress be sent to bomb the island, but the Americans did not feel it was worth the effort. On January 15, the Australians launched a limited attack on their own, inflicting little damage.

Beginning in July 1942, the Japanese Combined Fleet made their home in and around Truk. This would be their chief forward operating base for attacks throughout the Pacific until February 1944. At the height of the war, over 1,000 ships were moored at Truk, the atolls monitored by submarines and patrol boats, the skies defended by more than 500 aircraft flying out of five separate airbases. Its seeming impenetrability won Truk the nickname "The Gibraltar of the Pacific."

It was not until 1944 that Allied forces were in a position to move against Truk and the Caroline Islands. Task Force 58, a powerful fleet of nine aircraft carriers, 10 submarines, 45 warships, and almost 600 planes, set out for Truk early in February. The operation was given the code name Hailstone.

The Japanese pulled several of their ships out of the area on February 10, sensing an attack was on the horizon. But there were still dozens of ships at anchor and hundreds of planes on the airfield when Operation Hailstone began on the morning of February 16, 1944. Over the next two-and-a-half days, Task Force 58 destroyed over 200,000 tons of Japanese military steel—the largest loss the Japanese would suffer in a single action during the war. Losses included 45 ships and 275 planes. By comparison, the American force lost 25 aircraft and had one carrier damaged by a torpedo. About 30 pilots died, along with 11 crewmembers on the carrier. Japanese losses were likely in the thousands.

In March and April, American bombers finished destroying the fortifications on Truk, assuring the Japanese would not be able to use it as a base again. They unloaded hundreds of tons of bombs on enemy positions on the nearby islands of Ponape and Yap. By the end of 1944, the archipelago was becoming the peaceful backwater it had been before the war.

The destruction of the Japanese bases at Truk and the liberation of the Caroline Islands was one of the swiftest and most decisive battles of the Pacific war, and while the Japanese military fought on until August 1945, it never again had control of the waters or the skies. In 1986, the Caroline Islands became part of the independent Federated States of Micronesia.

Further Reading: John W. Dower, *War Without Mercy: Race and Power in the Pacific War* (Pantheon, 1987); William Manchester, *Goodbye Darkness: A Memoir of the Pacific War* (Little, Brown, 2002); Floyd W. Radike, *Across the Dark Islands: The War in the Pacific* (Random House, 2003).

—HEATHER K. MICHON

Churchill, Winston (1874–1965)

Barely a day after hearing of the Japanese attack on Pearl Harbor, Winston Churchill proclaimed the following during his radio message to the British people on December 8, 1941: "We have at least four-fifths of the population of the globe on our side. We are responsible for their safety and their future. In the past we have had a light which flickered, in the present we have a light which flames, and in the future there will be a light which shines over all the land and sea." In fact, supplies for lamps, heating, and cooking were running out. The British people were stretched to their maximum, as they held out almost alone against the Germans.

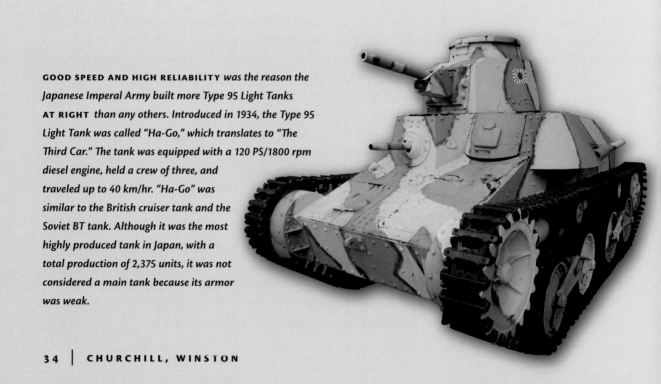

GOOD SPEED AND HIGH RELIABILITY *was the reason the Japanese Imperial Army built more Type 95 Light Tanks* **AT RIGHT** *than any others. Introduced in 1934, the Type 95 Light Tank was called "Ha-Go," which translates to "The Third Car." The tank was equipped with a 120 PS/1800 rpm diesel engine, held a crew of three, and traveled up to 40 km/hr. "Ha-Go" was similar to the British cruiser tank and the Soviet BT tank. Although it was the most highly produced tank in Japan, with a total production of 2,375 units, it was not considered a main tank because its armor was weak.*

Rations were so low that some in Churchill's political circle were ready to formally suggest a substantial reduction. Churchill refused, saying that to reduce the rations would "savour of panic" and that the British people should know that their position had "immeasurably improved." Churchill knew that the fires and lamps in Britain in December 1941 would not flicker away. America was now fully and openly on their side.

Churchill heard about the attack on Pearl Harbor on the radio on the evening of December 7. He immediately made plans to visit America, and arranged for cipher staff to accompany him on his trip. He was especially concerned about the progress of the North African war theater. A telegram from FRANKLIN ROOSEVELT shows that he was initially concerned for Churchill's safety "on security grounds" as the British leader traveled across the Atlantic. But Churchill doggedly insisted on the need to meet Roosevelt and review the war plan as a whole. Writing to the King of England, Churchill explained that there was a need to be certain that British aid "does not suffer more than is, I fear, inevitable." It was clearly in British interests to coordinate fully with America. First, however, he would need to address Parliament and the nation, and, indirectly, his audience across the seas.

SOLIDARITY WITH GREAT BRITAIN

In his now-famous address to Parliament, Churchill described how he had "pledged the word of Great Britain" a month previously, "that should the United States be involved in a war with JAPAN, a British declaration of war would follow within the hour." Churchill had spoken with Roosevelt on the night of the 7th and had arranged to declare war immediately after the American declaration was to be made by Congress. However, it was soon discovered

that Pearl Harbor was not Britain's only, or even primary, concern. On December 7, Japanese forces also attacked British territory, landing in Malaya and bombing Singapore and Hong Kong (see HONG KONG; MALAYA AND SINGAPORE). The Japanese had already declared war against Britain. Churchill did not need to wait for a declaration by Congress. At 12:30 P.M. BST on December 8, the cabinet called for "an immediate declaration of war upon Japan."

The Home Office, similar to the Justice Department in the UNITED STATES, began to take almost immediate "action against Japanese nationals" living in Britain. In his address to Parliament, Churchill had described the "Japanese treachery" upon "the English-speaking world." The Japanese had clearly violated international norms, as signed under the League of Nations. It was only natural, in Churchill's view, that Japanese nationals in Britain should be seen as a threat. Although not as well known as the Japanese internment camps in the United States, Britain also detained many Japanese nationals under Churchill's orders.

The Netherlands and the United States also "marked their solidarity with Great Britain." Churchill in addition expressed his full and open solidarity with the nationalist Chiang Kai-shek of China and his struggle against the Japanese. Thus, even as Britain faced a new and powerful enemy in the Japanese, it also attracted forceful allies. In the conclusion of his remarks to Parliament, repeated in a radio address, Churchill spoke, with his particular rhetorical genius, a genius that demanded more from his people, and rallied his new allies to prepare for more struggles ahead. Churchill included a special plea to munitions manufacturers in his speech to "make a further effort proportionate to the magnitude of our perils and the magnitude of our cause."

Further Reading: Winston Churchill, *The Unrelenting Struggle: War Speeches*, compiled by Charles Eade (Cassell and Company, 1943); Winston Churchill, *The Second World War* (Cassell and Company, 1948–54); Martin Gilbert, *Winston S. Churchill: Road to Victory*, (Heinemann, 1986).

—ALLEN FROMHERZ

Codes, Japanese

On December 3, 1941, a group of men stood in the Signal Intelligence Service (SIS) office at U.S. Army headquarters in Washington, D.C., poring over a dispatch intercepted and decoded that morning. The message told the Japanese embassy staff to burn their codebooks and destroy one of their precious cipher machines.

It made no sense to them: how would the Japanese ambassadors communicate with their government without their codebooks and machines? Finally, Colonel Otis Sadtler put it together. "Do you know what this means?" he said to senior cryptan-

alyst Frank Rowlett. "It means Japan is about to go to war with the United States!" And with that he took off at a run down the corridor of the Munitions Building to notify his superiors.

As the UNITED STATES took its place on the world stage in the first quarter of the 20th century, it became clear that the military needed to recruit analysts who could make and break codes. The SIS of the U.S. Army and OP-20-G of the U.S. Navy were set up with little fanfare and small budgets. Few people within the government knew or cared what these early cryptanalysts did.

In the mid-1920s, much of their effort was being put toward breaking codes used by JAPAN, which was growing more aggressive toward the United States. Japanese cryptography was not particularly sophisticated. Because they had been isolated for a large portion of their history, it wasn't something they had needed to develop. Their language was complex and not understood by many Westerners.

Japanese was commonly written in *kanji*, a series of about 2,000 ideograms representing whole words and concepts. But words could also be written using *kana*, a series of 48 characters that stood for individual syllables. Using *kana* as a basis, the Japanese had developed their own form of Morse code for use in sending information by telegraph. In the 1920s, a modest program was begun by the U.S. Navy to teach more staff members Japanese Morse, and eventually developed a typewriter that could be used to quickly and easily translate the dots and dashes as they came across the wire. That system worked well enough for regular traffic intercepted from overseas telegraph and radio. But encoded messages—the documents that traveled between embassies or the military—were a whole different matter.

Japan used a common method of encryption. First, individual words and syllables were given a numerical value. The message would be then translated into this series of numbers. A code clerk would give the message a second layer of encryption using a book of additives—a random series of numbers assigned to each group of meaningful numbers that would, in theory, hide the real words being transmitted.

Embedded somewhere in the message was a code that told the recipient what page of the additive book had been used in this second encryption. They could then strip out the meaningless numbers and find the original string. American cryptanalysts understood the principles of this method, but that did not mean it was easy to decipher the code. In trying to separate the gibberish from the actual information, forward-thinking officers in both the army and navy cryptography departments turned to a new technology—the computer.

The huge IBM tabulating machines used by the military in this period had been around for a while, and the government had been using them for statistical work since the 1890s. But technological advances in the 1920s and 1930s made them more robust in their ability to find hidden patterns in seemingly random bits of information. Cryptanalysts took thousands of intercepted messages and painstakingly copied them onto paper punch cards. They were loaded into the IBM machines, where they could be analyzed in countless ways. The patterns were finally clear in 1941.

In the end, it was a combination of mechanical tabulation and careful human analysis that broke the most critical Japanese codes, PURPLE and JN-25.

PURPLE

PURPLE, the code used to pass messages between the Japanese government and its embassies, was the first to fall. PURPLE had appeared without warning in June 1939, superseding a much simpler code called RED, which the Americans had already broken in the 1920s. PURPLE used a cipher machine to encode and decode messages. The physical machine was made up of two typewriters connected to a box filled with relays or step-switches that could, in theory, create millions of variations of a code. Cipher machines were not new, but each machine was different. To break the code, American cryptanalysts realized they would have to build their own PURPLE machine.

William Friedman, head of the Signal Intelligence Service, assigned the task of cracking PURPLE to Frank Rowlett, a young mathematician on his staff. Asked later what he felt was his greatest contribution to the project, Rowlett replied: "I was the one who believed it could be done." He and his team figured out the basic patterns of the code relatively quickly, but it took a year of poring over every bit of data to find the deeper patterns.

One day, they unlocked the last key. When they told Friedman, he was so overcome with emotion that they thought he might faint. "The recovery of this machine will go down as a milestone in cryptanalytic history," he told them. "Without a doubt we are now experiencing one of the greatest moments of the Signal Intelligence Service."

Once the framework of PURPLE was uncovered, it was relatively easy to mimic the random sequencing. Working with a new recruit named Leo Rosen, an electrical engineer just out of MIT, the team hit on the idea of using a simple telephone-switchboard stepping switch to create the proper sequences. As it happened, the Japanese had used an identical stepping switch in building their machine.

When Rosen's machine was plugged in on September 25, 1940, it worked perfectly, and the United States had the power to decipher Japanese diplomatic traffic. The cryptanalysts nicknamed the

Women Cryptanalysts

AGNES MEYER Driscoll graduated from Ohio State University with a major in mathematics, music, physics, and foreign languages. She was assigned to the Code and Signal section of the Director of Naval Communications. Agnes helped break Japan's RED diplomatic code in the 1920s, the BLUE BOOK code in the 1930s, and the JN-25 code in 1940.

Two of the top staffers at the Signal Intelligence Service were Genevieve Grotjan and Delia Taylor. Grotjan figured out one of the most complicated patterns in PURPLE, a discovery that made the construction of MAGIC possible. Taylor helped crack a German diplomatic code known as "Keyword."

By 1944, about 60 percent of the army's Signal Intelligence Service staff and 75 percent of the navy's OP-20-G staff were female.

AT LEFT *Elizebeth S. Friedman, wife of cryptanalyst William Friedman, enjoyed many successes in cryptology in her own right and was dubbed "America's first female cryptanalyst." (See "The Friedmans" page 96.)*

device MAGIC, and became so proficient in its use that by 1941, they were able to decipher messages faster than the embassy staff.

The secrecy of MAGIC was vital. If the Japanese learned that PURPLE had been compromised, they would change their codes. Only 13 people outside SIS were permitted to know about MAGIC. The Japanese didn't learn about it until after the war.

JN-25

Cracking PURPLE was such a triumph that after the birth of MAGIC, many within the U.S. government ignored the need to keep working on other Japanese codes. PURPLE carried mainly diplomatic traffic. If a war was coming, the code-breakers would need to crack the codes used by the Japanese military, particularly the Imperial Navy.

On June 1, 1939, the Imperial Navy switched to a new code, which the Americans called JN-25. The OP-20-G handed the task to Captain Joseph J. Rochefort, a Japanese language expert with almost 15 years in cryptanalysis. Early in 1941, he was sent to Pearl Harbor, Hawai'i, to set up Station Hypo.

His hand-selected team included cryptanalysts, linguists, and technical experts. They would spend most of 1941 working up to 22 hours a day, seven days a week. Taking messages picked up from an intercept station set up about 30 miles from the base, Rochefort's team compiled more than 3,000,000 punch cards per month to feed into their IBM machines. No sooner would they begin to separate out the real codes from the additives than the Japanese would change the additives, putting them back where they started.

The Station Hypo team was still working on the morning of December 7, 1941. Rochefort was devastated. "I can offer a lot of excuses, but we failed in our job," he said later. "An intelligence officer has one job, one task, one mission—to tell his commander, his superior, today what the Japanese are going to do tomorrow."

By May 1942, cryptanalysts were deciphering up to 140 intercepts per day. Their greatest triumph came when they handed the navy enough information to defeat the Japanese at the Battle of Midway in the spring of 1942, a victory many historians consider the turning point of the Pacific war.

In the years after WORLD WAR II, investigations were launched into whether cryptanalysts had known the attack on Pearl Harbor was coming and had not given warning for fear of signaling to the Japanese that their codes had been cracked. This probably was not the case. On the whole, the men and women of SIS and OP-20-G did a remarkable job under tremendous pressure.

Further Reading: Stephen Budiansky, *Battle of Wits: The Complete Story of Codebreaking in World War II* (The Free Press, 2000); Hervie Haufler, *Codebreakers' Victory: How the Allied Cryptograhers Won World War II* (NAL Trade, 2003); David Kahn, *The Codebreakers* (Signet, 1973).

—HEATHER K. MICHON

Congressional Medal of Honor

There is a military saying that heroes happen when someone blunders. The catastrophic blunder that allowed the Japanese to surprise the U.S. Pacific Fleet (see PACIFIC FLEET, U.S.) in Pearl Harbor on December 7, 1941, created many heroes.

The Congressional Medal of Honor is the highest award to a member of the U.S. military and is given, often posthumously, only for conspicuous valor above and beyond the call of duty. Ten of the 15 Medals of Honor awarded for actions at Pearl Harbor were posthumous. The recipients represented all ranks, from enlisted men to an admiral.

The destruction of the battleship USS *Arizona* (see ARIZONA, USS) was so catastrophic that there was no way to recognize every act of bravery on that ship. Three examples of bravery were singled out for public acclaim. Two, given to Rear Admiral Isaac C. Kidd and Captain Franklin Van Valkenburgh, were posthumous awards. Those most senior officers hurried to their battle stations and began the effort to direct the response of their commands, but it was only moments before the entire forward half of the ship exploded in a tremendous fireball. Both men were killed. Their scorched and melted naval academy class rings, inscribed with their names, were pulled from the wreckage.

A third naval Medal of Honor was awarded to the senior surviving officer of the USS *Arizona*, Lieutenant Commander Samuel G. Fuqua. When the first bombs dropped, he was belowdecks and came topside onto the quarterdeck. As a damage-control officer, his first response was to organize his firefighting teams, but it soon became obvious that nothing could be done except to rescue survivors. Fuqua finally give the order to abandon ship. As senior surviving officer aboard, he did not leave the quarterdeck until everyone else was safely ashore.

All around the harbor others put their lives on the line to salvage a disastrous situation. There was Donald Kirby Ross aboard the USS *Nevada* (see NEVADA, USS), who shut down the ship's generators after it ran aground, then spent two-and-a-half days organizing rescue crews, all the time refusing medical treatment for his injured eyes. Edwin Joseph Hill, also of the USS *Nevada*, swam back from safety to help keep his ship from sinking in the channel and was killed

The Two Careers of Samuel G. Fuqua

LIEUTENANT COMMANDER Fuqua gained fame as the senior surviving officer of the battleship USS *Arizona*. After Pearl Harbor, he was sent to the training base in Newport, Rhode Island, then returned to the Pacific for a second tour of duty. He was awarded the Congressional Medal of Honor for his heroics at Pearl Harbor, and remained in the

Cold War navy through the end of the Korean War, by which time he had attained the rank of rear admiral. In 1953 he retired and went to Stanford University, earning a degree in mathematics. He spent the next two decades teaching high school math. He retired for a second time in 1970, and died on January 27, 1978.

ABOVE *The Congressional Medal of Honor*

the boilers. When it came time to present his posthumous Medal of Honor, no relative could be found. A new destroyer was named for him, and the ship's commanding officer accepted the award on Tomich's behalf. In 1947, the governor of Utah declared him an honorary citizen of the state.

The Congressional Medal of Honor was also awarded to the following: Captain Mervyn Sharp Bennion, U.S. Navy, who died on the bridge of the battleship USS *West Virginia*; Lt. John William Finn, U.S. Navy, Naval Air Station at Kaneohe Bay, who kept firing at the strafing attackers after being shot five times; Ensign Herbert Charpoit Jones, U.S. Navy, who died passing shells by hand to keep the guns of the battleship USS *California* firing; Lt. Jackson Charles Pharris, U.S. Navy, who, while already badly wounded, organized a human chain to transport ammunition to the guns of the USS *California*; and Commander Cassin Young, U.S. Navy, who saved the repair ship USS *Vestal*.

Further Reading: Peter Collier, *Medal of Honor: Portraits of Valor Beyond the Call of Duty* (Artisan, 2003); Edward F. Murphy, *Heroes of World War II* (Presidio Press, 1990).

—LEIGH KIMMEL

in the process. Aboard the USS *California* (see CAL-IFORNIA, USS), Robert Scott kept the air compressors running to power antiaircraft guns until he drowned, while Thomas Reeves kept passing ammunition up to the guns until he died of toxic fumes. Aboard the capsized USS *Oklahoma* (see OKLAHOMA, USS), Francis Flaherty and James Ward helped their shipmates escape until their compartment flooded.

But the most poignant story was that of Peter Tomich, a water tender aboard the target ship USS *Utah*. When the ship capsized, he ordered everyone out of the engine room and remained to secure

Congressional Reaction

The bitter divisions that had split Congress ended almost instantly as word was received of the attack on Pearl Harbor. With but one notable dissent, isolationists quickly lined up in full support of the president's war effort. Though fearing that President FRANKLIN D. ROOSEVELT was provoking an attack from JAPAN in order to draw the UNITED STATES into war with Nazi GERMANY, the isolationists had never mounted a major campaign to avert war with Japan. Their concerns focused exclusively on the war in Europe.

The congressional leadership met with Roosevelt in the White House on Sunday night, eight hours after the attack. The president opened the meeting by passing out Cuban cigars. It was agreed that Roosevelt would address a joint session of Congress the following afternoon and ask for a formal declaration of war. Capitol Hill was under unprecedented guard as the session approached. Reporters entering the building were confronted by bayonet-wielding Marines. Roosevelt himself arrived in formal mourning attire, complete with a silk top hat.

For the first time since he took office, Roosevelt received applause—even cheers—from most Republicans as he spoke. After the president's historic speech, the two bodies separated to consider the war resolution. The Senate passed the measure with no dissent or debate; in the House, the final vote was 388–1. The sole opponent was JEANNETTE RANKIN, who had also voted against America's entry into World War I. Some isolationists pursued an investigation into the Pearl Harbor attacks in hope of proving that Roosevelt had known of the impending Japanese strike.

Further Reading: Conrad Black, *Franklin Delano Roosevelt: Champion of Freedom* (Basic Books, 2003); Garet Garett, *Defend America First: The Antiwar Editorials of the* Saturday Evening Post, *1939–1942* (Caxton Press, 2003); "War Is Declared against Japanese," *New York Times* (December 9, 1941).

—ERIC FETTMANN

"A DAY THAT WILL LIVE IN INFAMY" *On December 8, 1941, U.S. President Franklin D. Roosevelt signs the declaration of war against Japan as members of his cabinet look on.*

Culture, 1941

The movies, literature, radio broadcasts, and music in 1941 all suggest that Americans felt that their eventual involvement in the war was inevitable. Caught between the Depression and war, American culture was a blend of social criticism, anxiety, and growing patriotism. The military draft, started in October 1940, added to the sense of the inevitability of conflict.

The economic collapse of the Depression that began in 1929 and caused millions of Americans to lose jobs, homes, and families had challenged people's faith in capitalism. Americans during the Depression criticized their failed economic system, while searching for a replacement. The wholesale support of the voting public for FRANKLIN D. ROOSEVELT's New Deal signaled the willingness of everyday Americans to abandon traditional *laissez-faire* policies in favor of more regulation in economic affairs.

But by 1941, the ominous reverberations of the war in Europe caused some to rally in support of capitalism and individualism, in opposition to the bleakness and aggressive terror of fascist Italy and Nazi GERMANY. Americans found themselves simultaneously preparing to defend their country while continuing their Depression-era reevaluation of American institutions. Yet with Roosevelt's aid program to England, including Cash and Carry in 1939 and Lend-Lease in 1941, lots of money was being made in the war industry.

MOVIES

In 1941, Judy Garland sang "I'm Always Chasing Rainbows" in the sparkling musical *Ziegfeld Girl*. Cary Grant and Irene Dunne struggled in the melodrama *Penny Serenade*, and Greta Garbo's *Two-Faced Woman* was called "immoral" by the National Legion of Decency and pulled from theaters. The most significant films of the year were those that presented the struggle of average Americans to make sense of life in the midst of the great moral challenges of economic depression and war. Orson Welles's *Citizen Kane* gave audiences a fully realized portrait of a man undone by his own narcissism. Bette Davis's ruthless Regina in *The Little Foxes* scandalized audiences with her immoral greed. The struggle of Welsh coal miners to unionize, told in John Ford's *How Green Was My Valley*, reflected the desires of many Americans to create protections for the working classes that were so strongly hit by the Depression, while also anticipating the sentimental visions of home and family that would be evident in American culture after the UNITED STATES entered the war.

The most blatant film that pitted good against evil was *Sergeant York*, starring Gary Cooper. *Sergeant York* metaphorically illustrated the battle between those who desired to stay out of the European war and those who believed that America had a moral responsibility to join the conflict. The debate is told through the story of real-life conscientious-objector-turned-war-hero Alvin C. York, who during World War I abandoned his pacifism.

Films such as *Sergeant York* led many to believe that the motion picture industry was a propaganda outlet for interventionists. The cumulative effect of films that urged American involvement in the European war was so powerful that two isolationist senators called for hearings in Washington, D.C., to investigate whether Hollywood was actively producing interventionist propaganda. Though the hearings began in August 1941, nothing was resolved before the events of Pearl Harbor.

The Stuff that Dreams Are Made of: *The Maltese Falcon*

THE MALTESE FALCON packed people into the theaters and captured the imagination of millions. The movie centered on the complex mystery surrounding a legendary, jewel-encrusted gold statuette of a falcon and the intricate, murderous relationships of the people who sought to own it. The film starred Humphrey Bogart as world-weary detective Sam Spade, who unwittingly becomes part of the dangerous plot surrounding the infamous "Black Bird," and Mary Astor as Brigid O'Shaughnessy, the sexy and manipulative *femme fatale*. Rounding out the cast was Peter Lorre as the flamboyantly effeminate criminal Joel Cairo, first-time film actor Sydney Greenstreet as the scheming Casper Gutman, and Elisha Cook Jr. as Gutman's gunsel, Wilmer Cook.

The Maltese Falcon was screenwriter John Huston's first assignment as a director. The film emphasized pessimism, suspicion, and the less honorable aspects of human nature as the main characteristics of modern life. With the war already under way in Europe threatening to engulf the United States, *The Maltese Falcon* perfectly captured the anxious mood of Americans in December 1941. (See also DAILY LIFE, 1941.)

ABOVE TOP *Leopold Stokowski conducts the orchestra during a live-action filming of* Fantasia, *on Disney's largest sound stage.* **ABOVE BOTTOM** *Women in Florida, attended vocational schools to learn war work, allowing men to serve in the fighting forces.* **AT LEFT** *Popular foods included Campbell's Soup and Spam.*

LITERATURE

The greatest literary work of social criticism of 1941 was James Agee's documentary novel *Let Us Now Praise Famous Men*, in which the author's lyrical prose and the stark photographs of Walker Evans laid bare the painful lives of tenant farmers in depressed rural America.

Such brutal indictments of American life existed in glaring contrast to Franklin Roosevelt's glorification of traditional American values. Many writers took up Roosevelt's theme in their own work and clarified the American ideals worth fighting for. In *Illinois Poems*, Edgar Lee Masters conjured the small-town ways of life that Roosevelt championed, while in *The Ground We Stand On*, John Dos Passos used biographies of American heroes to remind readers of the nation's historic role as defender of liberty. Lillian Hellman's *Watch on the Rhine* zeal-

ously promoted opposition to the Nazis and was one of the 11 plays that ran on Broadway in the 1940–41 season that dealt with war-related topics.

Historian William Graebner has argued that author Robert McCloskey's beloved 1941 children's book, *Make Way for Ducklings*, which told the story of a mother duck shepherding her children to safety, was in effect intellectual preparation for children whose fathers would soon leave home to fight in the war.

Two of the most popular books in December 1941 were A. J. Cronin's account of a young priest's spiritual crisis, *The Keys of the Kingdom*, a story of faith and courage that gave many Americans comfort at an anxious time, and William Shirer's *Berlin Diary, 1934–41*, the CBS correspondent's first-person chronicle of the Nazi consolidation of power. Shirer had to smuggle his diaries out of

Let Us Now Praise Famous Men

FORTUNE MAGAZINE sent writer James Agee and photographer Walker Evans to Alabama in 1936 to investigate the lives of tenant farmers in New Deal America. They were charged with creating a literary and visual account of, according to Agee, "the daily living and environment of an average white family of tenant farmer." The resulting book, *Let Us Now Praise Famous Men*, was a revolutionary new form of social criticism. Agee and Walker exposed the grinding poverty and desolation of a forgotten segment of American life in episodic portrayals of the limited education, clothing, shelter, and work lives of three families. Agee's passionate and poetic prose, along with Evans's forceful black-and-white photos, angrily indicted modern industrial capital-

ism and its class system for exploiting and oppressing the human spirit, forcing powerless men and women into lives of great suffering and crippling limitations.

What made Agee's prose so different was his self-conscious expression of concern about his intrusion into the lives of the three families. He worried that his "prying" into their lives was "obscene" and that he was contributing to their exploitation. But his respect for each family was also evident in the care he took to maintain the human dignity of his subjects. Though it did not receive favorable reviews when it was first published in 1941, *Let Us Now Praise Famous Men* is now considered one of the more influential books of the 20th century.

Germany when he learned the Gestapo was investigating him.

RADIO

Shirer was already a well-known figure to most Americans when *Berlin Diary* was published. In the 1941 *Mayflower* decision, the Federal Communications Commission (FCC) ruled that radio broadcasters could not act as advocates for any specific point of view, but intelligent and forceful radio news personalities were instrumental in bringing the real effect of the European war directly into the homes of Americans through the first overseas radio broadcasts in 1938. Their coverage of the war in Europe greatly increased the importance and popularity of the radio as a news source. More Americans owned radios than telephones in the 1930s, and the radio brought opinion as well as news in its broadcasts.

In addition to news and sports shows, Americans listened to quiz shows, domestic radio dramas, and variety shows offered by entertainers such as Jack Benny and George Burns. On May 6, 1941, comedian Bob Hope broadcast his first variety show from a military installation, inaugurating his long career as entertainer to America's troops. More and more, Americans routinely settled in front of their sets to share in nationally broadcast programs.

MUSIC

The radio also became the medium through which most Americans were exposed to music. Americans increased their knowledge of classical music, often broadcast live from symphony halls, and popular country stars such as Gene Autry joined the Grand Ole Opry. The new "swing" music, though, rapidly eclipsed both genres in popularity. Though radio stations often practiced musical segregation, limiting broadcasts of innovative black blues and jazz musicians to specially appointed times, those white bandleaders that adopted jazz music into the swing form, including Artie Shaw, Jimmy Dorsey, and Harry James, dominated the popular-song playlists. The enormous success of Benny Goodman helped him to defy the restrictive racism of the era and include in his band important black musicians, such as Lionel Hampton and Teddy Wilson. Chart toppers in 1941 included "Boogie Woogie Bugle Boy " and "I'll Be with You in Apple Blossom Time," the hits of the popular vocal group the Andrews Sisters that addressed the fears of war and separation held by average Americans.

Those fears became reality on December 7, 1941, and the most popular radio shows of that day were those that told Americans of the horrifying attack on Pearl Harbor. At that moment, the culture of Americans would break away completely from the fractured combination of the Depression's earnest criticism and the anxious concern about world affairs that characterized the year. Instead, after December 7, the war would bring a whole new theme to American culture, a wholesale support for the war aims of the American government, united by sentimentality, patriotism, and sacrifice.

Further Reading: Gregory D. Black and Clayton R. Koppes, *Hollywood Goes to War: How Politics, Profits and Propaganda Shaped World War II Movies* (The Free Press, 1987); John Morton Blum, *V Was for Victory: Politics and American Culture During World War II* (Harcourt Brace Jovanovich, 1976); Susan J. Douglas, *Listening In: Radio and the American Imagination* (Times Books, 1999); Doris Kearns Goodwin, *No Ordinary Time: Franklin and Eleanor Roosevelt: The Home Front in World War II* (Simon and Schuster, 1995); William Graebner, Library of Congress, *"Bob Hope and American Variety,"* www.loc.gov/exhibits (cited January 2006); Richard R. Lingeman, *Don't You Know There's A War On? The American Home Front, 1941–45* (G. P. Putnam's Sons, 1970); Robert S. McElvaine, *The Great Depression: America 1929–41* (Random House, 1985).

—JILL SILOS, PH.D.

WAR GARDENS

FOR VICTORY

GROW VITAMINS AT YOUR KITCHEN DOOR

D

Daily Life, 1941

As America emerged from the Great Depression, most families earned at least $40 a week, despite the fact that some 4,000,000 men were unemployed.

In 1941, families tended to live near one another, and many Americans lived and died within a few miles of where they were raised. Others, particularly African Americans, migrated to large cities. Electrification was common in areas such as New England, where 79 percent of homes had electricity. In Mississippi, however, 90 percent of the population still depended on primitive methods of illumination. Some 23,521 Americans had telephones, but only 5,000 or so had access to the two television stations that were available.

Much of the news of 1941 was concerned with war and politics. There were four national radio stations, broadcasting to hundreds of affiliates. *Life* magazine discovered its niche by publishing pictorial accounts of the war, and CBS sent Edward R. Murrow to furnish an eyewitness account of the London blitz of 1940–41. Accounts of the horrors experienced by the Allies were integral in developing scorn for ADOLF HITLER and in rousing support for the Allies (see ALLIES ON DECEMBER 7, 1941). President FRANKLIN D. ROOSEVELT continued to prepare for the eventuality of American entry into WORLD WAR II.

On January 6, 1941, in his weekly radio address, Roosevelt announced plans for a LEND-LEASE program aimed at furnishing military equipment to the Allies in exchange for American military

"WAR GARDENS FOR VICTORY." *Many Americans grew their own vegetables in small Victory Gardens to reduce the pressure on the public food supply brought on by the war effort.*

bases. On May 27, the address in which Roosevelt proclaimed a national state of emergency drew an audience share of 65 million people. Following a secret meeting in August with British Prime Minister WINSTON CHURCHILL, Roosevelt announced his Four Freedoms, the basic human rights that became the foundation for the charter of the United Nations. In the fall, Roosevelt ordered American troops to open fire on all German ships after an American destroyer, the USS *Reuben James*, clashed with a German submarine.

Labor union activity continued to be a major news item in 1941, but tensions that had heightened after a Harlan County, Kentucky, coal-mining strike in the spring eased after companies began signing contracts with unions. Several unions signed no-strike agreements for the duration of the war. The Grand Coulee Dam on the Columbia River opened on March 22, and the Rainbow Bridge at Niagara Falls opened on November 1. After the attack on Pearl Harbor, much of the news focused on how Americans could contribute to the war effort through conservation, recycling, and participation in civil defense programs.

Many of the teenage boys who would eventually die on the battlefields of World War II were living normal lives in 1941. Smoking and drinking were seen as sophisticated because adolescents saw favorite movie and sports figures doing the same. Square dancing was a popular form of entertainment in rural areas, and urban couples swayed to the music of big bands.

In 1941, some 80 million people attended movies at an average cost of 25 cents a ticket. Popular movies included *Life with Henry*, starring Henry Aldrich and the Aldrich Family; *The Philadelphia Story*, featuring Katharine Hepburn, Jimmy Stewart, and Cary Grant; and Disney's animated feature, *Dumbo*. Popular songs of the year included "Chattanooga Choo-Choo," "Deep in the Heart of Texas," and "The White Cliffs of Dover." Jack Benny, Bob Hope, Edgar Bergen, and Red Skelton were favorite radio personalities. *For Whom the Bell Tolls* by Ernest Hemingway and *Blood, Sweat, and Tears* by Winston Churchill were among the top books of the year. Superman was the number one superhero, regularly appearing in two magazines and 230 newspapers.

Popular entertainers such as Jimmy Durante earned $62,500 a week for appearing at the Copacabana. Traveling road shows and carnivals were a major form of entertainment in small towns. Whirlaway won the Triple Crown, New York beat Brooklyn 4 to 1 in the World Series, Joe DiMaggio's batting streak came to an end, and Lou Gehrig died of the rare disease that would be named after him. Heavyweight boxing champ Joe Louis successfully defended his title 14 times, and golfer Craig Woods won the Masters Tournament. The Boston Bruins won the National Hockey League championship, and Mauri Rose and Floyd Davis won the Indianapolis 500.

ABOVE LEFT *Mrs. Imo Sansom fills vaporproof bags with blanched peas in preparation for freezing.*
ABOVE RIGHT *Custards and cookies made with dried egg powder.*

While most respectable females refrained from wearing form-fitting clothes, the more daring saw such clothing as a fashion statement. One-piece bathing suits appeared and some women began wearing shorts in public, even though they were considered risqué in many communities and illegal in others. Women's skirts were narrow and short or gored, and jackets sported padded shoulders. Ruffles and lace were common accessories. Skirts and cardigan sweaters matched, and women wore sheath evening gowns for formal occasions. Shoe designers created footwear of reptile skins and mesh with cork soles.

Once the UNITED STATES entered the war, women's fashions tended to mirror the somber mood of the country, with subdued colors and simple lines. Brooks Brothers offered olive drab serge suits at $75 apiece.

A study by *Ladies Home Journal* (1940–41) revealed that the average American consumed 2,500 calories a day in 1941. A typical breakfast included orange juice, oatmeal, and milk. Twice a week, a family might vary the menu with bacon and eggs. Typical lunches included soup, bread and butter, and raw celery or carrots. Milk and fruit were staples for children. Sandwiches were rarely consumed. Dinner fare was simple, such as macaroni and cheese, or vegetable beef soup. Chicken or pot roast might be on the Sunday menu, or when guests were present. Farm families tended to eat better since menus were based on home-grown products.

In 1941, after years of deprivation during the worst of the Depression, retail sales in the United States were rebounding, and retailers boasted an average increase of $10,000 over the previous year. By the end of 1941, Americans had spent $82.3 billion on various products. Families could purchase staples at reasonable prices: flour, 22 cents per pound;

ABOVE LEFT *POST–1942 classic suits and a summer uniform.* **ABOVE RIGHT** *LaMoyne Porter, Laura Conner and Bettye Tiner vie for Sportfishing Queen in Long Beach, California.*

bread, 39 cents a loaf; butter, 41 cents per pound; sugar, 28 cents for five pounds; and potatoes, 23 cents for a ten-pound bag. Milk was delivered for 13 cents a quart. Women entered the work world in order to free males for service or essential jobs, and various products were designed to make domestic life less time-consuming.

Advertisers had discovered the benefits of using celebrities to hawk products. Joe DiMaggio of the New York Yankees became one of a long line of athletes to promote Wheaties cereal. Kirby Hughes of the Brooklyn Dodgers promoted Camel cigarettes. The "Big Three" automobile companies, General Motors, Chrysler, and Ford, which controlled 90 percent of the automobile market, used sex appeal to promote sales. Twenty-one makes of cars and 20 kinds of trucks were on the market, and the trend was toward large, heavy vehicles with rounded and smoothed-out body styles. The first automatic transmissions were made available in 1941; other inventions included General Motors' concealed running board and Studebaker's concave windshield. (See also CULTURE, 1941.)

Further Reading: Kristin Anderson, *While They're at War: The True Story of American Families on the Homefront* (Houghton Mifflin, 2006); Tom Brokaw, *The Greatest Generation* (Dell, 2001); Alistair Cooke, *American Home Front: 1941–1942* (Grove/Atlantic, 2006); "How America Lives," "History of Fashion," www.vintageblues.com (cited March 2006); Richard R. Lingeman, *Don't You Know There's A War On: The American Home Front, 1941–1945* (Putnam, 1980); W. A. Mattice, "The Weather of 1941 in the United States," *Monthly Weather Review* (December 1941); Judith E. Smith, *Visions of Belonging: Family Stories, Popular Culture, and Postwar Democracy, 1940–1960* (Columbia University Press, 2004); Ruth Tabrah, *Hawai'i: A Bicentennial History* (W. W. Norton, 1980).

—**ELIZABETH PURDY, PH.D.**

Weather Report

ON NOVEMBER 2, the Japanese fleet left JAPAN and sailed northeast to avoid the harsh wintry Pacific weather. By November, the fleet was just north of Hawai'i, outside military radar. On December 7, as Japanese fighter planes honed in on the Pacific Fleet at Pearl Harbor, the clouds broke up. December 7 was a typically balmy Hawai'ian winter day, with winds from the north at 10 miles per hour. At 7:30 A.M., early golfers spotted planes overhead and noticed the Rising Sun insignia on their wings. The attack began at 7:55 A.M.

The weather played a role in INTELLIGENCE reports for some time. Three days before the attack, a Tokyo weather report had mysteriously inserted the words "east wind rain" that were purportedly a message to Japanese diplomats that an attack on the United States was imminent (see CODES, JAPANESE). When officials at the Japanese embassy heard the fake weather report, they began destroying all sensitive materials.

Damage, Memorial

The Japanese air raid on Pearl Harbor was the second time that a foreign power directly attacked the UNITED STATES. The first time was when the British burned the White House during the War of 1812.

Around the island of Oahu on December 7, much of the damage was soon repaired. But as time wore on, military authorities began to realize that the damage itself might serve as a memorial of the day if left unrepaired. Of course, the most famous and most institutionalized damage-as-memorial was the wreck of the USS *Arizona* (see *ARIZONA*, USS), visited informally for years before the memorial itself was built over the remains of her sunken hull.

However, other sites on Ford Island, Hickam Air Force Base, Schofield Barracks, Kaneohe Bay Naval Air Station, and elsewhere on Oahu all bore marks of that day's attack, many of them now preserved and displayed to visitors to demonstrate the shock of the surprise attack on American territory. Leaking oil from the USS *Arizona* marks the sunken ship, giving rise to the legend of the "tears of the *Arizona*." When the last veteran of the attack dies, the legend holds, the oil sheen will disappear. Not far from the USS *Arizona* Memorial the concrete docking quay for the USS *Vestal* still bears the marks of machine-gun hits. On Ford Island, in hangars now used for storage and soon to be converted to an air museum, several panes of glass bear bullet holes from attacking aircraft.

On the runways on Ford Island, and on the concrete ramps where once the amphibious PBY aircraft pulled out from the harbor, chipped "stitchmarks" mark the spots where the lines of machine-gun slugs tore through aircraft and personnel. The wavering lines of hits in the concrete bear mute testimony, decades later, to the fact that the Japanese pilots were being tossed about by explosions and in attempts to evade ground fire.

At Schofield Barracks, U.S. Army troops rushed outside to see aircraft sweeping in from the west. Immediately, the legend grew that the craft had come in through Kolekole Pass, a low saddle in the mountains separating Schofield from a naval munitions depot over the hills. Later study revealed that the planes had approached from the North Shore of Oahu, not crossing through Kolekole. Across from McComb Gate at Schofield, the Keemoo Tavern still serves beer, and the proprietor there will tell you how the lake behind the bar was used as a landmark for Japanese low-flying aircraft. The scene in *From Here to Eternity* in which Montgomery Clift plays the bugle was filmed in the Keemoo Tavern. Nearby in Wahiawa, a modest house at 711 Neal Avenue was rebuilt after a Japanese aircraft crashed there, shot down on December 7 by Lieutenant George Welch.

At Hickam Air Force Base, the main barracks building was severely damaged by bombs and machine-guns (see photos at right). The base, which prides itself on its amenities, clean streets, and well-maintained buildings, has preserved the damage, both on an interior courtyard of the barracks and on the outside corner of "G" wing. In the Courtyard of Heroes, a small plaque memorializes those who gave their lives that day. The Art Deco–style water tower is unmarked, as the Japanese assumed it was some sort of religious shrine. Nevertheless, they used the tower as a guiding landmark as they strafed the field.

At Kaneohe Bay, then a naval air station and today a Marine Corps base, a concrete and stone marker on the hill below the Kansas Tower marks the spot where Lieutenant Fusata Iida crashed his plane. Legend has it that, knowing his plane was fatally damaged, he hoped to smash it into the fully occupied Bachelor Officers' Quarters a few hundred feet farther up the hill. Lieutenant Iida was the highest-ranking Japanese pilot killed on that day. Off nearby Bellows Air Force Base, one of three U.S. aircraft that got into the air from Bellows was shot down into the bay. On the reef that shelters the scenic windward-side beaches of Wailua and Lanikai, one Japanese midget submarine was wrecked, later towed and beached on the Bellows Air Force Base shore.

While the USS *Arizona* Memorial draws hundreds of thousands of visitors a year, these and other mostly unheralded remnants of damage across the island also stand as quiet physical witnesses to that one day in history.

Further Reading: Hawai'i War Records Depository, http://libweb .hawai'i.edu/digicoll/hwrd/HWRD_html/ HWRD41.html (cited December 2005); Susan Wels, *Pearl Harbor: America's Darkest Day* (Time-Life, 2001).

—RODNEY CARLISLE

ABOVE LEFT *Machine-gun damage to the barracks at Hickam Air Force Base.* **ABOVE RIGHT** *Stitch marks on the runways on Ford Island show the line of machine-gun slugs from the Japanese aircraft.*

De Gaulle, Charles (1890–1970)

Born in Lille, France, Charles de Gaulle graduated from the Ecole Militaire of Saint-Cyr in 1912 and promptly joined the infantry. Captured during the World War I Verdun campaign in March 1916, while imprisoned he wrote *The Enemy's House Divided*, an explanation of the German defeat, later published in 1924. Between 1919 and 1940 he served in various military capacities and authored several books on military affairs and leadership, but the political leadership in France rejected his ideas as far too militaristic.

Premier Paul Reynaud appointed him undersecretary of state for war, his first foray into politics. When de Gaulle's old mentor, Marshal Philippe Pétain, became leader of the Vichy government as a puppet of the Nazis, de Gaulle left France for London. On June 18, 1940, he made an impassioned plea on the radio for the French to continue the struggle. De Gaulle vowed to lead the Fighting French by leading the resistance against the German occupiers.

In December 1941, Colonel André Dewarin, chief of intelligence and operations (code named "Passy" after the Paris Metro stop), met de Gaulle at his home at Berkhamsted, 30 miles from London, where the two took a long walk and discussed the Resistance and its slow progress. Passy offered to resign his post and accept reassignment to a fighting unit, but de Gaulle refused. French historian and biographer Jean Lacouture records Passy's account of De-Gaulle's reaction to the Japanese attack:

> We came back from our long walk and the general switched on the radio. The Japanese had attacked Pearl Harbor. The general turned it off and sank into a deep meditation. Hours seemed to pass. Then the general said roughly this: "Now the war is certainly won! And the future has two phases for us: the first will be the salvage of Germany by the Allies; as for the second, I am afraid it may turn out to be a war between the Russians and Americans and the Americans run a great risk of losing that war if they do not take the necessary steps in time!"

Critics note that de Gaulle often confused his will with that of France; nevertheless, he stated in his memoirs: "On December 7 the attack on Pearl Harbor hurled America into the war. One might have thought that, from that moment, American policy would treat as allies the Free French who were fighting its own enemies. Nothing of the sort happened, however."

De Gaulle spent much of the war in England but in 1943 moved his headquarters to Algiers. By 1944 he was the recognized leader of France, and entered Paris on August 25. In November 1945, he

ABOVE LEFT *De Gaulle arriving at his office in London.* **ABOVE RIGHT** *De Gaulle speaking during a visit to the French port city of Cherbourg, August 20, 1944.*

became president of France, but resigned in January 1946 because his political opponents would not permit a strong executive. De Gaulle formed the Rassemblement du Peuple Français (Rally of the French People), a coalition designed to unite the nation, in 1947. When the effort failed, de Gaulle retreated to his home. France called upon him to lead again and elected him president in December 1958 by an overwhelming margin, and he held that office until his resignation in 1969. He died the following year.

Further Reading: Donald Cook, *Charles De Gaulle: A Biography* (G.P. Putman, 1983); Charles de Gaulle, *The Complete War Memoirs of Charles de Gaulle* (Carroll and Graf, 1998); Jean Lacouture, *De Gaulle: The Rebel, 1890–1944* (W. W. Norton, 1990).

—JAMES S. BAUGESS

Declaration of War in Tokyo

At the meeting of the Privy Council of Japan on December 1, 1941, Japanese leaders considered an address to the emperor stating, "We declare war against the United States and Great Britain." The premier, HIDEKI TOJO, declared that hostilities against England, America, and the Netherlands existed.

At a Committee of Advisement meeting on December 8, 1941, at 7:40 A.M. in the Imperial Palace, all cabinet ministers gathered, except the minister of foreign affairs, who was holding interviews with the U.S. and British ambassadors. All members of the Advisory Council or *Komonkan* attended, and Tojo explained the reasons for declaring war. The declaration was unanimously approved.

The Congressional hearings into the Pearl Harbor attack revealed that the Japanese had not written or delivered a declaration of war until after they had confirmed that the attack on Pearl Harbor had been successful. They delivered the two-line declaration of war to U.S. Ambassador JOSEPH GREW in Tokyo 10 hours after the Pearl Harbor attack was over. Grew received a telegram from the Japanese Ministry of Foreign Affairs in Tokyo dated December 8, 1941. The telegram said, "Excellency I have the honor to inform Your Excellency that there has arisen a state of war between Your Excellency's country and Japan beginning today. I avail, et cetera. Signed Shigenori Togo. Minister for Foreign Affairs."

Grew sent the telegram to Washington, D.C., from Tokyo after the embassy had been placed incommunicado. It arrived in Washington, D.C., late Monday afternoon, December 8.

On September 27, 1940, Japan, GERMANY, and Italy had signed the Tripartite Pact, formalizing their partnership and agreeing to assist each other if any of them were attacked. The pact solidified the breech between the United States and Japan.

By July 1941, the Western powers had effectively stopped trade with Japan and by late November 1941 peace negotiations between the United States and Japan had snarled (see DIPLOMATIC RELATIONS). U.S. officials had deciphered the Japanese diplomatic codes (see CODES, JAPANESE) and predicted that the Japanese would attack the East Indies and the Philippines.

In the final week of November 1941, Hull and Japanese special envoy Saburo Kurusu were meeting in Washington, D.C., to attempt to resolve the serious differences between Japan and the United States over East Asia. The United States demanded that Japan withdraw its troops from China, give up its plan to forcibly incorporate countries into its proposed GREATER EAST ASIA CO-PROSPERITY SPHERE, and withdraw from the Tripartite Pact. Tojo rejected the demands and warned Britain and the United States that Japan would vigorously repel U.S. and British power in East Asia. The *New York Herald Tribune* printed Tojo's threat on the front page on Sunday, November 30, 1941, seven days before the Japanese fleet arrived at Pearl Harbor.

Further Reading: Edwin Hoyt, *Warlord: Tojo Against the World* (Cooper Square Press, 2001); Saburo Ienaga, Frank Baldwin, translator, *The Pacific War, 1931–1945: A Critical Perspective on Japan's Role in World War II* (Random House, 1979); Ronald H. Spector, *Eagle Against the Sun: The American War with Japan* (Random House, 1985).

—KATHY WARNES

Diplomatic Relations

On July 25, 1941, the UNITED STATES froze Japanese assets in response to Tokyo's ongoing occupation of southern FRENCH INDOCHINA. The decision, which the British and Dutch empires quickly embraced, meant that JAPAN now faced a near-total trade embargo. Confronted with Japan's economic ruin, Prime Minister Fumimaro Konoe initiated a series of talks with the U.S. government that continued until the efforts to avoid conflict all but ended in late November 1941.

EARLIER SUMMIT ATTEMPTS

Konoe determined that in order to avoid war and end the crippling embargoes, he needed to meet with Roosevelt. The president's senior advisors, however, opposed a Konoe-Roosevelt summit.

From mid-August until mid-October, when Konoe finally stepped down, Japanese and American officials conducted preliminary talks in advance of the supposed Konoe-Roosevelt conference, but failed to bring about a summit. In early September, Secretary of State Hull demanded that negotiators reach preliminary agreements on such issues as Japan's relation to its Axis partners (see AXIS POWERS IN 1941), the ongoing war in China, and the stationing of Japanese troops in postwar China.

Tokyo refused to either abrogate its membership in the Axis or remove all its forces from China following the end of the war. Konoe's government turned a blind eye to the undeclared German-American naval war under way in the Atlantic, and deepened American suspicions when it demanded that Washington, D.C., suspend aid to China during the Sino-Japanese negotiations. Given these unbridgeable differences, the summit did not take place. Konoe, unable to meet Roosevelt and unwilling to lead Japan to war, resigned on October 16.

Konoe's successor, Hideki Tojo, selected the veteran diplomat Shigenori Togo as foreign minister. An opponent of the coming war, Togo wanted assurances from Tojo that he would pursue diplomacy, and that the army would make sufficient concessions to achieve an agreement with the United States. The emperor had already smoothed the way for Tojo and Togo with his command to "wipe the slate clean." This order instructed Tojo's government to reexamine the decisions of the September 6 Imperial Conference.

TWO PLANS FAIL

Tojo and Togo managed to secure backing for a plan where Japan would pursue diplomacy until November 30, while simultaneously preparing for war. The foreign ministry prepared two proposals in advance of the conference. Plan A sought a comprehensive settlement, but had deep flaws. Tokyo pledged only a partial withdrawal from China, and envisioned the complete withdrawal of Japanese forces from French Indochina "upon the settlement of the China Incident or upon the establishment of a just peace in the Far East." The plan flatly rejected abrogating the Axis Pact.

Togo knew the plan held little promise, and introduced a second proposal. Plan B called for the United States to resume normal trade relations with Japan and help Tokyo secure raw materials in the Dutch East Indies, in return for a Japanese pledge to withdraw troops from southern French Indochina and forsake attacks on Dutch, British, American, or Soviet targets. Shidehara Kijuro and Yoshida Shigeru reviewed the plan with Joseph Grew and British Ambassador to Japan Sir Robert Craigie. Both diplomats approved Plan B. On November 7, KICHISABURO NOMURA, Japan's ambassador to the United States, presented Plan A to Cordell Hull.

In Tokyo, authorities desperately sought to conclude the talks. Nomura and Saburo Kurusu submitted Plan B on November 20. Two days earlier, Kurusu informally proposed that Japan withdraw its forces from southern Indochina in return for a relaxation of trade restrictions. Hull respond that quite possibly "the troops you withdraw from Indo-China will be diverted to some equally objectionable movement elsewhere."

Public opinion leaned away from any deal that smacked of appeasement. Rather than rejecting Plan B outright, Hull agreed on November 22 that the United States should offer a plan for a temporary agreement on *modus vivendi*. Four days later, perhaps influenced by what he perceived as lackluster British and Dutch support and outright Chinese hostility, Hull decided to drop the proposal. Instead, the secretary submitted a 10-point proposal that focused on the issues left over from the preliminary summit talks, as well as Japan's Plan A. The Tojo cabinet found the proposal that Japan withdraw from China and render moot their alliance with GERMANY unacceptable. Meaningful efforts to avoid war in the Pacific had ended. On December 1, an Imperial Conference endorsed the decision to initiate hostilities against the United States as well as the British and Dutch empires. The following day, Admiral Yamamoto signaled his attack force to strike Pearl Harbor on December 7, 1941.

Further Reading: Dorothy Borg and Shumpei Okamoto, eds., *Pearl Harbor as History* (Columbia University Press, 1973); Nobutaka Ike, ed., *Japan's Decision for War: Records of the 1941 Policy Conferences* (Stanford University Press, 1967); William Morley, *Japan's Road to the Pacific War: The Final Confrontation* (Columbia University Press, 1994); Jonathan G. Utley, *Going to War with Japan, 1937–41* (University of Tennessee Press, 1985).

—SIDNEY PASH

Doolittle, James (1896–1993)

James H. Doolittle's raid on Tokyo after Japan's bombing of Pearl Harbor was simply one event in an illustrious life. Called "the master of the calculated risk," Doolittle was famous for his contributions to the development of aviation. Doolittle helped show America that Japan was vulnerable after the tragic attack on Hawai'i.

Born in Alameda, California, on December 14, 1896, he was educated in Alaska, Los Angeles Junior College, and the University of California School of Mines. After enlisting in the Signal Corps Reserve in 1917, he trained at the School of Military Aeronautics at the University of California and Rockwell Field.

In 1920, Doolittle received a promotion to first lieutenant. In 1925, he earned a Ph.D. in aeronautics. By 1930 he was commissioned a major in the Specialist Reserve Corps. In 1934 he became a member of the army board to study Air Corps organization and was transferred to the Air Corps Reserve.

In the year leading up to December 7, 1941, Doolittle was assigned to a post in Detroit, where he served as a liaison between the Air Corps and the Automotive Committee for Air Defense. In the summer of 1941, he visited England to study British methods of operation, maintenance, and repair of aircraft.

When the Japanese attacked Pearl Harbor, Doolittle immediately wrote a letter to his commanding general, requesting transfer to a combat unit. His initial request was denied, but by December 24, 1941, he had been assigned to Washington, D.C., with the rank of lieutenant colonel.

After the raid on Japan, which earned him the Medal of Honor, Doolittle was promoted to the rank of brigadier general and later to lieutenant general. He commanded the Twelfth and Fifteenth Air Forces in the North African and Mediterranean theaters in 1942–43. During 1944–45, he led the Eighth Air Force in both the European and Pacific theaters.

On May 10, 1946, he reverted to inactive reserve status and retired. During his military career, in addition to the numerous flying awards he won, he was awarded two Distinguished Service Medals, the Silver Star, Bronze Star, three Distinguished Flying Crosses, and four Air Medals. He died September 27, 1993, and is buried in Arlington Cemetery, in section 7-A.

Further Reading: Dik Alan Daso, *Doolittle: Aerospace Visionary* (Potomac Books, 2003); Craig Nelson, *The First Heroes: The Extraordinary Story of the Doolittle Raid—America's First World War II Victory* (Viking Books, 2002); Duane Schultz, *The Doolittle Raid* (St. Martin's Press, 1988).

—JAMES E. SEELYE JR.

Doolittle's Raid

AFTER THE Japanese bombing of Pearl Harbor, President FRANKLIN D. ROOSEVELT pressed his advisors for a plan to strike back. However, there were no Allied air bases close to Japan. An aircraft carrier would have to approach very close to Japan, creating great safety risks. However, the need for a plan persisted, and by January 16, 1942, an idea was in place. B-25 medium-range bombers would take off from carriers and land in China. Two ships, the USS *Enterprise* and the USS *Hornet*, sailed to Japan in April. On the 18th, 16 planes took off toward Japan. Unfortunately, they had to take off earlier than planned because Japanese ships were spotted. James Doolittle's own plane was the first to launch. At around noon Tokyo time, the bombers struck, to the great humiliation and despair of Japanese leaders, who thought their nation was impervious to attacks. After the raid, one plane turned north and landed safely in Russia. The remaining 15 planes either crashed or ditched in China. Of the 80 pilots and crewmen who took part in the raid, four were killed during the actual raid, eight were captured upon landing, three were executed by the Japanese, and another died in captivity. Although the damage inflicted by the raid was slight, it was a tremendous boost to American morale and a psychological blow to the Japanese.

French Indochina

The Japanese use of South Vietnam in French Indochina for air-fields and naval bases concerned Franklin Roosevelt and it was a leading cause for American protests to Japan over the summer and fall of 1941. On November 26, 1941, U.S. Secretary of State Cordell Hull proposed that Japan withdraw from French Indochina. While offering to consider the proposal, the same day, Japan launched its fleet toward Pearl Harbor.

French Indochina consisted of what are now Vietnam, Laos, and Cambodia. The French colonial regime provided few opportunities for native populations to attain leadership positions and by the 1930s, a resistance movement had developed among the Vietnamese and Cambodians. In 1939, the French had about 50,000 troops, including auxiliary forces, stationed in Indochina to retain control of the area.

The old order collapsed after the fall of France to the Germans in 1940. The Germans allowed a French government to continue in the south of France, with its capital at Vichy. The Vichy government essentially was impotent, including in its control of overseas territories and colonies. Japan, taking advantage both of its alliance with Germany and France's weakness, demanded that the French cede basing rights to them in Indochina.

On September 22, 1940, the Japanese reached an agreement with the French colonial government in Indochina, giving the Japanese the right to use three air bases and permission to station 6,000 troops north of the Red River in northern Indochina. They also could use northern Indochina as a transit area to move up to 25,000 troops at a time into China. During the Japanese movement into the area, there were a handful of military incidents, particularly around Haiphong, but no serious overall French resistance.

On July 28, 1941, the Japanese completed the occupation of the remainder of French Indochina. Despite the Japanese occupation, they left the French colonial regime in nominal control of the area. French security units continued some military operations against Vietnamese nationalists even under the Japanese occupation. Relations between the French in Indochina and the Japanese initially were correct if not especially cordial. The Japanese occupiers seemed to try to make the French colonial officials more independent of the Vichy government in France. The Japanese strategy for dealing with Indochina made considerable sense because it enabled them to have the advantages of controlling the area without having to tie up large numbers of troops.

As the war progressed, more French resistance developed to the Japanese overlords. French resistance activities reflected the larger conflict between supporters of Vichy and members of the Free French forces of CHARLES DE GAULLE. De Gaulle became involved in opposition to the Japanese earlier and more actively than did the Vichy officials. Allied forces provided support, with airdrops of men and equipment averaging twice a week. However, the level of French resistance activities in Indochina never represented a significant threat to the Japanese.

Native Vietnamese—many of whom were also involved in anti-French activities—were more active in their opposition. The principal Vietnamese opposition, the Viet Minh, publicly called for French cooperation against the Japanese, but were rebuffed.

Indochina served two principal purposes for the Japanese. First, during the early part of the war it provided an excellent rear base for supporting operations elsewhere in the Pacific and China. By late 1944, the series of Japanese territorial losses in the Pacific began increasing the importance of Indochina in the Japanese defensive strategy, making it key to retaining their presence in territory around Japan. Second, Tokyo viewed the natural resources available from Indochina as critical to the Japanese economy and war effort. Throughout the war, the Japanese government extracted large quantities of foodstuffs and other material from the area.

In March 1945, the Japanese decided to remove the French colonial government. Japanese forces quickly occupied critical facilities with only scattered French resistance. Most French forces were interned by the Japanese. One group of 6,000 French soldiers in northern Indochina refused to surrender and conducted a fighting retreat toward China. These units marched some 600 miles, with the last elements crossing the border in May. After the Japanese took formal control of Indochina, they granted its components nominal independence.

Although no major military campaigns took place in Indochina during the war, the Japanese occupation had a major long-term impact on the region. Vietnamese nationalist groups, both communist and noncommunist, had been active for a number of years before the war. The pressures imposed on them within Indochina by both the French and Japanese resulted in most Vietnamese political groups seeking refuge in southern China. This enabled them to regroup and reorganize. The most significant organizational effort led to the formation in May 1941 of the League for the Independence of Vietnam, better known as the Viet Minh. Its leader was Nguyen Ai Quoc, who took the name of Ho Chi

Minh. Although communist-dominated, the Viet Minh were able to portray themselves as nationalists whose aims were solely to end French and Japanese occupation. Viet Minh operations against both occupiers during the war gave the group important nationalist credentials for its struggle against the French after the war. It also should be noted that the Viet Minh received some support from both the Americans and the Nationalist Chinese during the war. Also, the ease with which the Japanese occupied the area discredited the French in the eyes of many of the native population, making it more likely that they would support resistance to the colonial power after the war.

Finally, the complications that ensued in the area at the end of the war almost guaranteed problems for further French colonial rule. The internment of French troops led to a power vacuum in Indochina. At the time of the Japanese surrender, no organized foreign units were available to reoccupy Indochina. Japanese troops were used for a while after the end of the war to maintain order in the region. After a brief gap—in which the Viet Minh took control of parts of Vietnam—British troops occupied the south of the region and the Chinese the north. It took French troops until 1946 to restore some semblance of control. Despite the French return to Indochina, the security situation continued to worsen, with the ultimate results of the French loss of Vietnam to the Viet Minh and the later Vietnam War. (See DIPLOMATIC RELATIONS.)

Further Reading: Jacques Dalloz, *The War in Indo-China, 1945–54* (Gill and Macmillan, 1990); Takashi Shiraishi and Motoo Furuta, eds., *Indochina in the 1940s and 1950s* (Cornell University Press, 1992); Jennifer Yee, *France and "Indochina": Cultural Representations* (Rowman & Littlefield, 2005).

—LAWRENCE E. CLINE, PH.D.

Thailand

THAILAND PLAYED a significant role in developments in Indochina. The Thai government, loosely allied with the Japanese, had several border demands involving French-controlled territory. Border clashes broke out between the Thai army and the French in January 1941. The Thais advanced into Cambodia, with their ground campaign succeeding well against French units. On January 17, the French fleet in Indochina fought the Thai fleet in the Gulf of Siam. In about two hours, the French put about 40 percent of the Thai ships out of commission. Following this setback, the Thais agreed to negotiate their differences with the French. They selected the Japanese as the mediators. Tokyo engaged in what might best be described as coercive mediation. As a result, the French were forced to cede three provinces in Cambodia, amounting to almost a third of its territory, and some parts of Laos to the Thais.

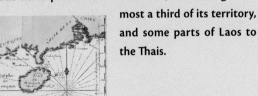

AT LEFT *An early and colorful French cartograph of Indochina.*

G

G-2 and Army Intelligence

As the war in Europe began in 1939, the Military Intelligence Division (MID) assigned to the G-2 (Military/Ground Intelligence) in Washington, D.C., consisted of only 20 officers, three soldiers, and 46 civilians. Most of their work involved processing reports from military attachés. The Signal Intelligence Service, a branch of the Signal Corps, had one officer and 14 civilians on its national staff. Counterintelligence support to the entire army was provided by only 16 Corps of Intelligence Police agents. In 1941, the Corps of Intelligence Police was increased to over 500, and the MID reached a strength of 200 officers and 848 civilians.

The overall quality of the MID and other army intelligence units was not aided by this rapid expansion; most army officers considered intelligence to be a dead end to their careers. As General Omar Bradley noted in his memoirs, *A Soldier's Story*, "In some stations, the G-2 became the dumping ground for officers ill-suited for command. I recall how scrupulously I avoided the branding that came with an intelligence assignment in my own career." Even purported intelligence professionals were not necessarily prepared for their roles. Some 573 officers from the Military Intelligence Officers Reserve Corps were called to active duty, but many of these officers were public-affairs specialists rather than intelligence analysts. Also, although there were schools to train counterintelligence and signal intelligence personnel, there were no formalized training programs for other intelligence officers or troops.

AT LEFT, *Burt Lancaster and Deborah Kerr played out the famous beach scene in* From Here to Eternity *on this little, unnamed beach near Mokapu Point. The film told the stories of military personnel from the Schofield Barracks in the days leading up to the attack on Pearl Harbor. The beach looks exactly the same today as it did in December 1941.* From Here to Eternity *was released by Columbia Pictures in 1953.*

The Warning Message

THROUGH THE MAGIC intercept system, the G-2 had access to Japanese diplomatic traffic. Based on these intercepts, the G-2 had issued a warning to field units in November 1941 regarding possible Japanese military moves. After U.S demands for changes in Japanese policy, the Japanese responded with a 14-part coded message to its embassy in Washington, D.C. It was clear to the MID that this response would be critical. Thirteen parts of the message were received by the MID the evening of December 6 and passed to the State Department.

The critical 14th part—which instructed the Japanese ambassador to deliver the Japanese response to the U.S. secretary of state at 1:00 P.M. on December 7—was received slightly before 9:00 A.M. on the 7th. Being a Sunday, it took some time for the G-2 and its staff to track down Army Chief of Staff General GEORGE C. MARSHALL, who was out horseback riding. Marshall recognized the importance of the decrypted message. He consulted with Admiral HAROLD R. STARK, the chief of naval operations,

who initially did not want to send a warning to naval forces in the Pacific. After some conversation, both agreed that a warning message should be sent to all Pacific units.

The alert message was quickly drafted, and in fact to save time, Marshall's handwritten draft was used, rather than taking additional time to have the message typed. All units were to receive the warning, with priority being given to the Philippines. G-2 personnel took the message to the army's message center, with instructions to send it by the "fastest possible safe means." Since there were problems with the army's communications circuits, the Signal Corps officer on duty decided to send the warning message by commercial telegraph.

The timeline of the message is best viewed through using Hawai'i time. The message was filed at the War Department Message Center at 6:30 A.M. It was transmitted via Western Union at 6:47 and received in the RCA office in HONOLULU at 7:33 A.M. It was delivered to the army's signal officer in Hawai'i at 11:45 A.M., who then delivered it to his headquarters at 2:58 P.M. By then, of course, it was much too late.

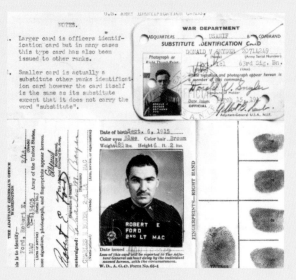

AT LEFT *Samples of American identification cards made for Force G-2 instructional purposes. The larger card was issued to officers, but was also issued to other ranks. The smaller card at the top is a substitute card. The original card would have looked the same, but lacked the word "substitute." Although the American military had schools to train counterintelligence and signal intelligence personnel, there were no formalized training programs for other intelligence officers or troops.*

The MID was responsible for providing intelligence to the army and the State Department. Naval intelligence was responsible for reporting to the White House.

According to MID officers, there was good coordination with their counterparts at the Office of Naval Intelligence. The two services took turns translating and processing intercepted messages. At the same time, most of the coordination appears to have been rather informal, with few channels for assessing the overall intelligence picture. Even within the army, coordination and cooperation between the MID and G-2 personnel was minimal. In MID itself, decrypted Japanese traffic was "close hold," with only some officers authorized to see it (see CODES, JAPANESE).

By late 1941, many intelligence officers in MID began viewing Japanese military operations in the Pacific as increasingly likely. At the same time, according to one MID officer, an attack on Pearl Harbor was considered as a "remote possibility." Most attention was focused on threats to southeast Asia, the Dutch Indies, and the PHILIPPINES. The War Department sent a general alert to commanders in the Pacific on November 27, 1941, stressing the possibility of Japanese operations against targets other than Pearl Harbor. As with many other elements of the prewar military intelligence system, the G-2 and MID had neither the capabilities nor credibility to provide actionable intelligence to the army.

Further Reading: John Patrick Finnegan and Romana Danysh, *Army Lineage Series: Military Intelligence* (Center of Military History, 1998); John Keegan, *Intelligence in War: The Value—and Limitations—of What the Military Can Learn about the Enemy* (Knopf Publishing Group, 2004); Edwin M. Nakasone, *The Nisei Soldier: Historical Essays on World War II and the Korean War* (J-Press Publishing, 1999); Abram N. Shulsky and Gary James Schmitt, *Silent Warfare: Understanding the World of Intelligence* (Potomac Books, 2002).

—LAWRENCE E. CLINE, PH.D.

German Declaration of War

On the night of December 7, 1941, ADOLF HITLER instructed his minister of propaganda to summon the Reichstag for a December 10 meeting. Having just been informed of the Japanese attack on Pearl Harbor, Hitler made the unilateral decision to declare war on the UNITED STATES. He would use the Reichstag meeting to announce the decision.

The meeting and declaration of war were ultimately postponed until December 11. Hitler, under pressure from the Japanese to declare war immediately, was nervous that FRANKLIN D. ROOSEVELT might beat him to the draw. But time was needed to convene the Reichstag and Hitler had to travel from his headquarters to Berlin. He was also eager to conclude a pact with Italy and JAPAN before making a formal declaration of war. The treaty, signed on the morning of the 11th, ensured that Japan would not withdraw from the war before victory had been won in Europe.

Many historians characterize Hitler's decision to declare war on the United States as an act of extreme folly. Why, when Germany was already fighting a war on two fronts and faring so poorly in the east, would Hitler willingly take on another foe? Hitler believed it was only a matter of time before Roosevelt declared war on Germany. Both for strategic reasons and for the sake of German morale, Hitler wanted to retain the initiative and control the timing of the conflict. If war with the United States was inevitable, as Hitler believed that it was, then he would rather it took place while American troops and resources were engaged in the Pacific.

Foreign Minister Joachim von Ribbentrop read Germany's declaration of war to the American chargé d'affaires in Berlin on December 11, 1941. Later that morning, an identical copy of the statement was delivered to the State Department in Washington. The following is an excerpt:

Although Germany on her part has strictly adhered to the rules of international law in her relations with the United States during every period of the present war, the Government of the United States from initial violations of neutrality has finally proceeded to open acts of war against Germany. The Government of the United States has thereby virtually created a state of war. The German Government, consequently, discontinues diplomatic relations with the United States of America and declares that under these circumstances brought about by President Roosevelt Germany too, as from today, considers herself as being in a state of war with the United States of America.

Further Reading: The Avalon Project, "German Declaration of War with the United States: December 11, 1941," John Lukacs, *The Hitler of History* (Alfred A. Knopf, 1997) www.yale.edu/lawweb/avalon/wwii (cited December 2005).

—**KATHLEEN RUPPERT, PH.D.**

Germany

When informed that the Japanese had bombed Pearl Harbor, German Foreign Minister Joachim von Ribbentrop believed the report to be mere propaganda. News of the December 7 attack took Ribbentrop—and all of Germany—completely by surprise. The Japanese had purposely kept the Germans in the dark regarding their plans in order to ensure absolute secrecy. Nevertheless, the Japa-

Hitler's Speech

IN HIS December 11 speech to the Reichstag, Hitler accused President Franklin Roosevelt of leading a "continuously augmented campaign of hatred and agitation" and consciously sabotaging all possibilities for peace. After enumerating Roosevelt's allegedly belligerent actions against the German Reich, he expressed his satisfaction at the events of December 7, 1941:

First, this man agitates for war, then he falsifies the causes, makes arbitrary declarations, and later disgustingly hides behind a cloud of Christian hypocrisy. Slowly but surely, he leads mankind toward war. ...I think that all of you felt relieved that now finally one state has protested, as the first, against this historically unique and brazen abuse of truth and law. This man asked for it and, therefore, he should not be surprised by it. It fills all of us—the German Volk and, I think, all decent people of the world—with

profound satisfaction that the Japanese government, after negotiating with this falsifier for years, has finally had enough of being derided in so dishonorable a manner.

ABOVE *The 2-wheel drive German Kuebelwagen was produced by Volkswagen from 1939–1945 and used as a Wehrmacht staff car during World War II.*

nese decision to bomb Pearl Harbor was connected to the course of events in Germany over the previous several years. Germany, like JAPAN, pursued an aggressive and expansionist foreign policy. Germany's dealings with Japan doubtless played a role in the decision to launch the December 7 attack.

EVENTS LEADING TO GERMANY'S INVASION OF POLAND

By December 1941 ADOLF HITLER had been in power for nearly nine years. Central to Hitler's foreign policy objectives were the conquest of more living space (*Lebensraum*) for the German *Volk* and the reversal of perceived injustices resulting from the 1919 peace settlement. Among the Versailles provisions that rankled the most was the cession of German territory to Poland. According to the terms of the treaty, Germany had been forced to cede Posen and part of West Prussia to the Poles, while the port city of Danzig was made a free city controlled by the League of Nations.

Faced with mounting criticism over the failure of appeasement, British Prime Minister Neville Chamberlain agreed to support the Polish government in the event of any threat to Polish independence. The guarantee was formalized as a treaty on August 25, 1939. Four days earlier, Hitler had informed the army high command of his intention to invade Poland. Although he doubted whether Britain and France would intervene, Hitler was more than willing to risk going to war. "Our enemies are small fry. I saw them in Munich," he said. As he told his army commanders, "I am only afraid that at the last moment some swine or other will yet submit to me a plan for mediation."

Using fabricated reports of Polish aggression along the border, Hitler ordered a September 1 attack on Poland. Just before dawn, without warning and without a declaration of war, 1.5 million troops invaded Poland while German planes bombed Polish cities. Great Britain honored its commitment to Poland by declaring war against Germany on September 3. France followed suit the same afternoon. WORLD WAR II—which would reach truly global proportions following December 7, 1941—had begun.

On the same day that war broke out in Europe, President FRANKLIN D. ROOSEVELT announced that his administration would make every effort to maintain American neutrality. Roosevelt knew that public opinion opposed American involvement in another European conflict. While offering assurances that a declaration of neutrality was forthcoming, the president reminded the American public that their own national security could be affected by events in Europe: "You must master at the outset a simple but unalterable fact in modern foreign relations. When peace has been broken anywhere, peace of all countries everywhere is in danger."

U.S. RESPONSE TO THE WAR IN EUROPE

In accordance with the Neutrality Act of 1935 (see NEUTRALITY ACTS)—Roosevelt placed an embargo on the shipment of arms and munitions to belligerent nations. Had the embargo remained in effect, Germany would have benefited greatly. Hitler had been rapidly rearming Germany. In order to catch up, Britain and France had turned to the U.S. munitions industry to supply them with arms and aircraft. Once war broke out, the embargo made it impossible for the United States to fulfill its role as a supplier. Congress amended the law to allow for the purchase of arms by any nation able to pay cash and transport the material in its own ships.

Following the fall of France in the spring of 1940, Roosevelt stepped up efforts to assist Britain, while still refusing to commit American troops. On September 2, 1940, the United States gave the British 50 naval destroyers in exchange for a 99-year lease to build and operate military bases on British colonies in the Western Hemisphere. The president assured Congress that the destroyers-for-bases deal was "not inconsistent in any sense with our status for peace. Still less is it a threat against any nation." From the German perspective, however, the United States appeared dangerously close to violating its neutrality—both with the destroyers-for-bases deal and later with its policy of LEND-LEASE, which enabled the United States to provide war material to the Allies (see ALLIES ON DECEMBER 7, 1941).

Over the course of the next several months, the United States increasingly aligned itself against Nazi Germany. In April 1941 the United States agreed to defend Greenland against Nazi aggression. Three months later, American troops entered Iceland to take over the defense of that country as well. Hitler was anxious to avoid drawing the United States into the European conflict. He ordered the German Admiralty to exercise restraint and avoid provoking an American declaration of war. At least while Germany was entangled in the conflict with the Soviet Union, Hitler could not afford to face the United States alone.

Recognizing that the United States might enter the war at any time, Hitler grew increasingly responsive to Japanese overtures for closer relations. Already in 1936 Germany and Japan had concluded an Anti-Comintern Pact, in which neither party would assist the Soviet Union if it were to attack the other party. The agreement served as notice that German-Japanese relations were growing closer. In August 1939, Hitler shocked the Japanese by sending Ribbentrop to sign a nonaggression pact with the Soviet foreign minister, Vyacheslav Mikhailovich Molotov.

THE TRIPARTITE PACT

The Molotov-Ribbentrop pact would be short-lived, with Nazi Germany attacking the Soviet Union on June 22, 1941. In the meantime, a new Japanese government under Prime Minister Fumimaro Konoe had aggressively pursued strengthening relations with the Axis powers (see AXIS POWERS IN 1941). On September 27, 1940, Germany, Italy, and Japan signed the Tripartite Pact. The agreement recognized the leadership of Germany and Italy in establishing a "new order" in Europe and of Japan in doing the same in greater East Asia. The three powers pledged to come to one another's aid in the event that one of them was attacked by a power not involved in the European war or the Sino-Japanese conflict—in other words, by the United States. Hitler was willing to sign the pact because, as he explained in a letter to BENITO MUSSOLINI, he believed "a close cooperation with Japan is the best way either to keep America entirely out of the picture or to render her entry into the war ineffective." The Tripartite Pact did not obligate Germany to come to Japan's assistance in the event of a war caused by Japanese aggression.

Hoping to cut off Britain's lifeline and divert American interest to the Pacific, Hitler repeatedly urged the Japanese to attack Singapore or other British possessions in East Asia. When Japan failed to heed Hitler's advice, he offered Japan a verbal commitment that went beyond the terms of the Tripartite Pact. When Japanese Foreign Minister YOSUKE MATSUOKA visited Germany in early April 1941, Hitler pledged to join Japan immediately and unconditionally in the event of a war with the United States. At this point Hitler hoped merely to galvanize the Japanese to attack Singapore.

In a November meeting with the Japanese ambassador to Berlin, Ribbentrop repeated Hitler's pledge of support. When Japan requested a formal agreement

The Nazi Rise to Power

1918: WORLD WAR I ends in defeat for Germany. An armistice is signed in November, and Kaiser Wilhelm II abdicates power. On November 9, a coalition government declares Germany a republic.

1919: ELECTIONS are held in January for a National Assembly, which drafts a constitution for the new Weimar Republic. The Treaty of Versailles is signed in June. In August, Adolf Hitler joins the German Workers' Party (DAP), the forerunner of the Nazi Party.

1920: THE DAP changes its name to the National Socialist German Workers' Party (NSDAP), called the Nazi Party for short.

1921: HITLER becomes the official leader, or *Führer*, of the Nazi Party.

1923: IN NOVEMBER Hitler attempts to overthrow the local authorities in Munich. The failed coup, known as the Beer Hall Putsch, is easily suppressed by the military. The Nazi Party is outlawed, and a number of party leaders, including Hitler, are arrested.

1924: HITLER is sentenced to five years in prison for his role in the Beer Hall Putsch, but is released after nine months. While in prison, Hitler spells out his ideological beliefs in *Mein Kampf* [My Struggle].

1925: HITLER resurrects the Nazi Party and begins turning it into a mass movement. Conservative Paul Hindenburg is elected president and Germany is, for a time, stabilized.

1928: THE Nazi Party wins only 2.6 percent of the total vote in the Reichstag elections.

1929: THE onset of the Great Depression contributes to massive unemployment in Germany and to the collapse of the coalition government. Hindenburg invokes emergency presidential powers and restructures the government, placing authority in the hands of a chancellor and cabinet ministers.

1930: WHEN the first chancellor, Heinrich Brüning, fails to unify the government, new elections are held in September. The Nazi Party wins 18 percent of the vote, making it the second-largest party in the Reichstag.

1932: HINDENBURG is reelected, but Hitler wins 37 percent of the vote, making the Nazi Party the largest party in the Reichstag.

1933: HINDENBURG names Hitler chancellor in January. In February, the Reichstag building is destroyed by fire and the Nazis blame their Communist opponents. Hitler uses the fire (which was almost certainly planned by the Nazis) as a pretext for assuming police-state powers. Political opponents of the Nazis are rounded up and placed in concentration camps. An Enabling Act passed in March empowers Hitler and his cabinet to rule by decree for four years, thus paving the way for a complete Nazi dictatorship. Hitler bans all other political parties in Germany.

1934: AT the end of June, Hitler orders the arrest and execution of leaders of his private army, the *Sturm Abteilung* (SA), on the Night of the Long Knives. Hindenburg dies in August, Hitler declares himself *Führer*.

ABOVE *Thousands of books smolder in a huge bonfire as Germans give the Nazi salute during the wave of book-burnings that spread throughout Germany. 1933.*

to that effect on the evening of December 1, however, Ribbentrop replied that there would be a few days' delay. Hitler was traveling and waylaid by bad weather, and would be unavailable for consultation until December 4 or 5. In the early hours of December 5, Germany and Italy agreed to what was essentially a new tripartite pact, stipulating that if any of the three partners were to enter a war with the United States, the other two would at once consider themselves at war with the United States. The agreement had not yet been finalized, however, when, on the morning of December 7, Japanese planes bombed Pearl Harbor.

Further Reading: Ian Kershaw, *Hitler, 1936–45: Nemesis* (W. W. Norton, 2000); William K. Klingaman, *1941: Our Lives in a World on the Edge* (Harper and Row, 1988); William R. Shirer, *The Rise and Fall of the Third Reich* (Simon & Schuster, 1990).

—KATHLEEN RUPPERT, PH.D.

Great Britain, Reaction in

News of the attack on Pearl Harbor met with a mixed reaction in Great Britain. A sense of relief and renewed optimism at the prospect of the UNITED STATES finally entering the war was tempered by concerns that, at least in the short term, American resources—considered vital to Allied success in Europe—would be diverted to the campaign in the Pacific (see ALLIES ON DECEMBER 7, 1941). In addition, the bombing of the American naval base at Pearl Harbor was not an isolated assault. Rather, it was part of a coordinated attack that included among its targets British territory in the Pacific (see BRITISH COMMONWEALTH; HONG KONG; MALAYA AND SINGAPORE). On the whole, however, there was confidence that the events of December 7, 1941, would ensure ultimate victory for the Allies.

For quite some time—and especially since the fall of France in 1940—Great Britain had been looking to the United States for help in defeating the Axis powers (see AXIS POWERS IN 1941). While American assistance in the form of LEND-LEASE material had enabled the British to hold out against Germany for as long as they had, it seemed increasingly clear that nothing short of American entry into the war would truly tip the balance in Britain's favor. On Saturday, December 6, the British Chiefs of Staff had sat in continuous session with representatives of the Foreign Office discussing how the United States might be brought into the war. Now, at last, the Japanese attack on Pearl Harbor seemed to ensure such an outcome. When British Prime Minister WINSTON CHURCHILL heard the news on the evening of December 7, his initial thought was "So we had won after all."

At a special meeting of Parliament the next day, Churchill's announcement that Great Britain had declared war on Japan was greeted with unanimous approval. Both in Parliament and in the British press, the sentiment was widely expressed that the Japanese attacks were part of Hitler's grand strategy for domination but that, with the United States entering the war, Hitler was sure to be defeated. Along with renewed confidence in ultimate Allied success, however, came the realization that the Lend-Lease supplies might now be held back and American attention diverted to the war in the Pacific. Munitions workers were therefore called upon to redouble their efforts, and many war-weary Britons realized that the road ahead would not be easy.

During World War II, English novelist Mollie Panter-Downes served as the London correspondent for *New Yorker* magazine. Panter-Downes wrote to the *New Yorker* on December 14, 1941:

On Monday, December 8, London felt as it did at the beginning of the war. Newsdealers stood on the corners handing out papers as steadily and automatically as if they were husking corn; people bought copies on the way out to lunch and again on the way back, just in case a late edition might have sneaked up on them with some fresher news. Suddenly and soberly, this little island was remembering its vast and sprawling possessions of Empire. It seemed as though every person one met had a son in Singapore or a daughter in Rangoon; every post office was jammed with anxious crowds finding out about cable rates to Hong Kong, Kuala Lumpur, or Penang.

Further Reading: Winston S. Churchill, *The Second World War: The Grand Alliance* (Houghton Mifflin, 1950); Richard Collier, *The Road to Pearl Harbor: 1941* (Bonanza Books, 1981); Warren F. Kimball, *Forged in War: Roosevelt, Churchill, and the Second World War* (William Morrow, 1997); William K. Klingaman, *1941: Our Lives in a World on the Edge* (Harper and Row, 1988).

—KATHLEEN RUPPERT, PH.D.

ABOVE TOP *London, England, 1941: Vegetables grown in the United States and dehydrated for economical shipment across the Atlantic provide a meal for little evacuees from London's East End.* **ABOVE BOTTOM** *Meeting the first American food ship to arrive in England in 1941 under the Lend-Lease program. Right to Left: Kathleen Harriman; Lord Woolton, minister of food; Averill Harriman, U.S. Lend-Lease representative; Robert H. Hinkley, U.S. assistant secretary of commerce.*

Greater East Asia Co-Prosperity Sphere

The Greater East Asia Co-Prosperity Sphere refers to JAPAN's empire and expansionist foreign policy both before and during WORLD WAR II. In theory, it was to be liberating and economically beneficial for the people of Asia and the Pacific, but in reality colonial exploitation simply shifted from European to Japanese domination.

Japan sought to emulate, and eventually to surpass the West economically, socially, and militarily.

Japanese victory in the First Sino-Japanese War (1894–95) and the Russo-Japanese War (1904–05), the annexation of Korea in 1910, and participation in World War I on the side of the *Entente* demonstrated that Japan's reforms had been successful.

Japanese attitudes toward the West soured after the peace treaties of World War I and the Washington Naval Conference of 1921–22. Japanese leaders criticized Western hypocrisy and called for a return to traditional values. Japan argued that as the chosen Yamato race, it had the responsibility of *Hakko Ichiu*, gathering the eight corners of the world under one roof. This idea was the Asian version of ADOLF HITLER's theory of the Aryan master race.

In 1931, Japan invaded Manchuria in China, securing control of the Manchurian railroad and a base from which to launch an invasion of the rest of China, which occurred in 1937. In response, the UNITED STATES placed embargoes on steel, oil, and other military necessities. Japan used the embargoes to justify further expansion to make up for the loss of supplies.

With the outbreak of World War II in Europe in 1939 and the fall of France in 1940, Japan seized the opportunity to invade the former French possessions in Indochina (see FRENCH INDOCHINA). Under the slogan "Asia for the Asians," Japan promised to liberate the nations of Southeast Asia from the tyranny of Western colonialism. With few exceptions the "liberated" nations were treated no better under Japanese rule. In some countries native culture was outlawed or forced to conform to Japanese standards.

As Japan conquered more territory, it needed more troops and supplies to manage them. As the military grew, more land was needed to provide the necessary resources. Japan targeted the PHILIPPINES as the next area of conquest. One major obstacle stood in the way: the U.S. Pacific Fleet was anchored at PEARL HARBOR on the island of Oahu (see

The Rape of Nanking

THE JAPANESE invasion of China in 1937 included one of the largest atrocities of any war. After conquering Nanking, the capital of Nationalist China, the Japanese unleashed a seven-week rampage of pillaging, murder, and rape. Death toll estimates range from 100,000 to over 300,000. Victims were often killed in truly brutal ways. Some victims were burned alive; others were buried up to their chests and then set upon by attack dogs. Japanese officers lined up people in rows and using sabers held decapitation contests. The Japanese subjected enemies, prisoners, and civilians to extremely brutal treatment, enslavement, and execution. These atrocities were reported, but the focus of the world was on the situation in Europe. Controversy over the death toll, Japanese accountability, and even the veracity of the entire event are still debated today. Although the Japanese had a long history of conflict with China, and the atrocities committed at Nanking did not occur in every conquered territory on the same scale, individual atrocities of a similar nature occurred throughout the empire and were outward manifestations of Japanese racial attitudes of the time.

PACIFIC FLEET, U.S.). The Philippines were an American possession and any attack was certain to bring America into the war. Japan's solution was to destroy the American fleet in one quick stroke. The naval attack coincided with numerous land-based attacks throughout the entire Pacific in an effort to remove American, British, and Dutch influence.

On December 7, 1941, Japan launched its massive Pacific offensive. By February 1942, Japan had successfully extended its borders to include Malaya, the Philippines, Burma, and Indonesia. At its peak, the Greater East Asia Co-Prosperity Sphere stretched from India to the MARSHALL ISLANDS, from Siberia to Australia, and encompassed over 150 million people. It collapsed with Japan's defeat in 1945.

Further Reading: Iris Chang, *The Rape of Nanking: The Forgotten Holocaust of World War II* (Penguin, 1998); Joyce Lebra, *Japan's Greater East Asia Co-Prosperity Sphere in World War II: Selected Readings and Documents* (Oxford University Press, 1975).

—CHRISTOPHER THOMAS

Grew, Joseph (1880–1965)

Joseph Grew's political career began in 1920 when he served as U.S. minister to Denmark. He was U.S. minister to Switzerland from 1921 to 1924 and undersecretary of state from 1924 to 1927. For the next five years he served as U.S. ambassador to Turkey before becoming U.S. ambassador to JAPAN from 1932 until 1942.

In January 1941 Grew sent a message to Washington, D.C. He had been informed that if U.S. relations with Japan continued to sour, not only would Japan be forced to militarily confront the UNITED STATES, but also that Pearl Harbor could be a realistic target of attack. Negotiations between the two powers proved fruitless throughout the summer of 1941; by autumn war seemed likely. In November Grew warned Secretary of State CORDELL HULL that Japan could strike the United States in the very near future.

In the days prior to the attack, Roosevelt wrote a final message to EMPEROR HIROHITO to see if the two nations could make peace. Roosevelt wanted Grew to deliver the message, but Grew did not receive the message until December 6 and thus never had a chance to meet with the emperor before the attack on Pearl Harbor.

Grew was openly critical of Roosevelt's errors and miscalculations leading up to Pearl Harbor. He claimed that had Roosevelt sat down face-to-face with Emperor Hirohito in August 1941, the two sides could have found a resolution, and that had Roosevelt eased the U.S. economic embargo on Japan, Pearl Harbor could have been avoided. Grew was one of the few American officials who believed that the use of the atomic bombs against Japan could have been avoided. His was a minority opinion.

Further Reading: Peter Calvocoressi, Guy Wint, and John Pritchard, *The Penguin History of the Second World War* (Penguin Books, 1999); Robert Stinnett, *Day of Deceit: The Truth about FDR and Pearl Harbor* (Touchstone Press, 2001).

—DAVID MCBRIDE

Guam

For centuries, the tiny island of Guam served as the crossroads of the Pacific. First contact with the West came when Ferdinand Magellan landed in 1521. Spain ruled the island for 333 years, until the UNITED STATES took control of Spanish possessions in 1898. The United States installed a military governor and a few troops. Guam remained a peaceful, placid tropical island until 8:27 A.M. on December 8, 1941, when Japanese bombers appeared in the skies. With less than 400 American troops and a handful of poorly equipped local militia, the island could not be held. Governor George J. McMillin surrendered to JAPAN on December 10, 1941.

The Last Soldier

ON JANUARY 24, 1972, two fishermen in southern Guam came upon a ragged man checking shrimp traps. The man lunged at them, but the fishermen overpowered him and took him to the local police, where he related a remarkable story. His name was Shoichi Yokoi, formerly a sergeant in the 38th Regiment of Japan's Imperial Army. He had been in hiding for 28 years.

Yokoi's unit had been posted along the upper Talofofo River when the Americans landed on July 21, 1944. He and two other soldiers had fallen behind. They dug a cave in a bamboo thicket to hide. When their supplies ran out, his companions moved to another part of the river. In 1964, he found them dead of starvation.

Yokoi wove clothing of wild hibiscus bark. His diet was breadfruit, coconuts, papaya, and fish. On February 2, 1972, Yokoi was flown home to Japan. He greeted the press saying he was "sorry I did not serve his majesty to my satisfaction." He died of heart failure on September 22, 1997 at the age of 82.

For the next 31 months, the people of Guam lived under harsh military occupation. The Japanese renamed it Omiya-jima, or Great Shrine Island, and seized both public and private property. Among other indignities, the native Chamorros were forced to bow to their captors, to parrot imperial propaganda, and to build military fortifications along the coastline. Beheadings and rapes were not uncommon during these dark years.

U.S. military planners had not forgotten Guam. Aside from the humanitarian desire to liberate more than 20,000 Guamanians—all of whom were U.S. citizens—was the island's strategic importance. It had at least one deep harbor suitable for small warships, and two airstrips that could be used for bombing runs against Japan just 1,500 miles away.

Less than 10 miles of the coastline could be used for amphibious landings. The entire island was ringed by coral reefs with only a few channels for landing craft. Once ashore, troops would be confronted with tall cliffs and dense tropical terrain. Japanese troop-level estimates in Guam in the spring of 1944 were as high as 36,000 men.

"W Day" was scheduled for July 21, with "H Hour" set for 8:30 A.M. The III Amphibious Corps, made up of marine and army units under the command of Major General Roy Geiger, was assigned to the task. The 3rd Marine Division made landing at Asan Beach, with their 1st Provisional Marine Brigade coming ashore seven miles away at Agat. They met fierce resistance from Japanese troops entrenched in the surrounding hills. The marines expanded their beachhead over the next four days. Joined by the army, they had control of the vital Orote Peninsula, with its airfield and harbor, by July 29.

Fighting continued for the next several days, but on August 10, General Geiger announced that the last Japanese positions had fallen. In 20 days of fighting, over 1,000 American soldiers died and 7,000 were wounded. Over 17,500 Japanese were killed. Guam became a critical forward operating base for Pacific operations until the war ended in August 1945. And July 21—Liberation Day—is still celebrated every year by the citizens of Guam.

Further Reading: Robert F. Rogers, *Destiny's Landfall: A History of Guam* (University of Hawai'i Press, 1995); Gordon L. Rottman, *Guam 1941/1944: Loss and Reconquest* (Osprey Publishing, 2004).

—HEATHER K. MICHON

H

Hawai'i to 1898

When humans first set foot on the volcanic islands of Hawai'i is not known, but native legend and song describe events that occurred as early as the year 300, after the arrival of the first Polynesian settlers. According to those songs and chants, travel between Hawai'i and Tahiti, 2,600 miles away, was frequent.

Hawai'ian society underwent an abrupt change sometime between 1000 and 1100 with the visit of the Tahitian priest Pa'ao, who apparently was alarmed at what he perceived as a lack of piety among Hawai'ians. He returned to Tahiti, then sailed back to Hawai'i with sufficient resources to enforce the strict religious laws and formal caste barriers that endured until the 1820s.

Some anthropologists say before the year 300, Hawai'i may have been used as a base for peoples with trans-Pacific contact between Asia and the northwest coast of South America. Hawai'i is about 2,400 miles from the nearest continent and more than 2,000 from the nearest neighboring island chain.

The oldest stone walls that survive today were built on the island of Hawai'i around 500 C.E. By 900, all the main islands were occupied. It is believed that around 1100, Tahitians arrived, conquered the descendants of the Marquesians, and enslaved them. The Tahitian priest Pa'ao enforced the stringent *kapu* religious laws, which included reverence of *kahuna nui* or the divinely ordained high-priest line from which the ruling king or *moi* for each island was descended. From

Tahiti, Pa'ao brought Pili, who was the father of the royal line leading to Kamehameha I, who 28 generations later forcibly united all of the islands.

Travel between Tahiti and Hawai'i apparently ceased or diminished around the year 1200, resulting in 500 years of near-isolation in which the Hawai'ian culture and language developed without significant exposure to the outside world.

In January 1778, explorer Captain Cook, the British commander of HMS *Resolution* and HMS *Discovery*, landed on Kauai. He was thought by the Hawai'ians to be the reincarnation of Lonoiki, one of their two principal gods. Cook returned to Hawai'i a year later, and was killed there on February 13, 1779, by a group of natives who, during a scuffle over a rowboat, heard him gasp from exertion, realized that he was not a god, and angrily killed him for his deception.

In 1782, Kamehameha I became the ruler of the Big Island and by 1792 had conquered Maui, Lanai, Molokai, and Oahu by military force. In 1810, he unified the islands after negotiating a peace with Kauai, and proclaimed the entire island chain to be the Kingdom of Hawai'i. He believed he was destined by prophecy to unify the islands and shrewdly promoted trade with Europe and the UNITED STATES. He died in 1819 in Kona on the Big Island.

His son and successor, Kamehameha II, did not convert to Christianity, yet ordered the destruction of all pagan temples and idols and the end to the *kapu* (taboo) system. He formed a dual rulership with his wife, Kamamalu. They visited England and both died of measles on July 14, 1824.

His successor, Kamehameha III, proclaimed the first Hawai'ian Constitution, which included freedom of worship. U.S. President John Tyler recognized the Kingdom of Hawai'i in 1842. On February 10, 1843, Lord George Paulet of the British Royal

AT LEFT ABOVE *Kamehameha the Great united the islands into the Kingdom of Hawai'i in 1810.* AT RIGHT ABOVE *A rainbow over Waikiki Beach. Rainbows are a frequent occurrence in Hawai'i as light showers blow in while the sun is still shining.*

Navy warship HMS *Carysfort* entered HONOLULU Harbor, captured the Honolulu fort, and effectively gained control of the town. Paulet then demanded Kamehameha III abdicate and that the islands be ceded to the British Crown. Under the guns of the frigate, Kamehameha stepped down, but lobbied a formal protest with both the British government and Paulet's superior, Admiral Richard Thomas, who repudiated Paulet's actions, and on July 31, 1843, the Hawai'ian government was restored. In his restoration speech, Kamehameha declared, "The life of the land is perpetuated in righteousness," which is today the motto of the State of Hawai'i.

In 1845 Kamehameha III proclaimed the Great Mehele, changing the concept of land ownership to deeds, ending Hawai'ian tradition in which land use was granted by each king but reverted to the throne at the death of that king to be redistributed by his successor. Foreigners were permitted to purchase land and private estates were established. By 1893 Europeans controlled 90 percent of Hawai'ian real estate. By 1840 the forests of Hawai'i, Oahu, Molokai, and Kauai had been stripped of mountain sandalwood trees, one of the world's most valuable woods at that time.

Upon Kamehameha's death in 1854, Kamehameha IV ascended to the throne. He and his wife, Emma, were responsible for establishing Queen's Hospital for sick and destitute Hawai'ians. He translated the English *Book of Common Prayer* into his native language. Kamehameha IV and his queen ruled from 1855 to 1863 and were succeeded by his brother, Kamehameha V, who died in 1872, and in whose reign a third constitution went into effect in 1864 by royal proclamation.

MISSIONARIES

In the late 1700s, King Kamehameha was the official guardian of the war god Kukailimoku and paid it special attention. He appointed priests to attend to the ceremonies due to the other gods—and barred missionaries from preaching in Hawai'i.

The *kapu* laws instituted so many years before by Pa'ao were carefully observed. Kamehameha sentenced several persons to death for *kapu* violations as late as 1817. *Kapu*, translated in English as *taboo*, was barbaric. Violators were publicly strangled or clubbed to death. No commoner dared allow his shadow to be cast on a high chief on penalty of execution. All had to be quick to kneel or lie down in the presence of royalty. Birth, death, faulty behavior, the building of a canoe, and many other activities were regulated. *Kapu* permeated all aspects of Hawai'ian life.

Kamehameha proclaimed that the ancient gods had empowered him to conquer the entire island chain and that he owed them his loyalty. Before his death Kamehameha appointed his son Liholiho to succeed him as king. Liholiho announced that upon ascending the throne, he would take the title of Kamehameha II. An amiable prince, he possessed considerable shrewdness and was a skilled diplomat.

Upon his father's death, he set in motion the abolition of the *kapu* laws and repudiation of the ancient gods—although he did not publicly embrace Christianity. Kamehameha had reveled in the ceremonial execution of his captured foes on *heiau* altars. The elimination of rival leaders had ensured his rule over all the islands—and demonstrated the fate of any who would dare lead a revolt. Liholiho viewed such tactics as barbaric.

His first public repudiation of the *kapu* laws was to overturn the prohibition of men and women eating together. For centuries, women were barred from eating pork, bananas, coconuts, and certain kinds of fish. The young king met with his father's two favorite wives. Both of them, Kaahumanu and Keopuolani, agreed that the whole *kapu* system should be abolished as soon as the young king was assured of support from his island chieftains.

In August 1819, a French warship visited Hawai'i and the Christian commander of the ship was consulted on board about the new king's plans. He let it be known that he would support the king. At this time Kamehameha II's chief advisor, Kalanimoku, and his brother Boki, governor of Oahu, were publicly baptized by the chaplain of the French ship with Kamehameha looking on. It was a very public demonstration that the ban on Christianity had been lifted.

Kamehameha II privately professed to the captain that he also would be baptized if it were not for the political turmoil it might cause. Instead, a great feast was prepared and the young king sat down and ate with the women. When the assembled nobles, chieftains, and common people saw that no harm came to him, they shouted, "The *kapus* are at an end, and the gods are a lie!"

This action was referred to as the *Ai Noa* (free eating), and orders were sent to all the islands to destroy the pagan temples and burn the idols. Today only one ancient idol exists—a statue of Lonoiki, housed at the Bishop Museum in Honolulu.

Meanwhile, Congregationalist and Catholic missionaries began to arrive. On October 15, 1819, the Sandwich Islands Mission was organized in Boston with Reverend Hiram Bingham and Reverend Asa Thurston signing on as preachers. On March 30, 1820, after a voyage of five months, the passengers of the *Thaddeus* spotted the Big Island's snow-covered volcano Mauna Kea looming above the clouds. Messengers were sent ashore and brought back astonishing news. "Kamehameha is dead," they were told. "Kamehameha II is king, the *kapus* are abolished, the *heiau* temples have been destroyed, idols burned, supporters of the old order overthrown in battle."

The leaders of the mission went ashore, paid their respects to Kamehameha II and his chiefs, stated their purpose in coming to Hawai'i, and requested permission to begin missionary work. Cautiously, Kamehameha II agreed, but required certain conditions. He asked that the physician and two of the native youths remain at his court. Some of the missionary group were granted permission to begin work, and on April 12, 1820, they established the first mission station at Kailua on the Big Island. Others went on to Honolulu and Kauai, where they were welcomed and assisted by the authorities.

From 1837 to 1840, nearly 20,000 Hawai'ians accepted Christianity as their new religion. The missionaries who came to Hawai'i in the earliest years were from Puritan backgrounds, which explains their insistence that the Hawai'ian women cover their breasts. Men, who generally wore only a small loincloth, were encouraged to adopt Western dress. Swimming, fishing, and surfing nude had been prac-ticed by both genders for thousands of years. Children wore little or nothing. This shocked the missionaries, who introduced the *muumuu*, a floor-length, loose-fitting dress that is comfortable in tropical weather and continues to be popular among tourists.

The missionaries established an alphabet for the Hawai'ian language, enabling the Hawai'ian people to read and write in their own language. Schools were established throughout the islands. By 1831, only 11 years after the missionaries' arrival, some 52,000 pupils had been enrolled. The missionaries introduced Western medicine and undertook the kingdom's first modern census. (See also HAWAI'I, 1898 TO 1942.)

Further Reading: Gavan Daws, *Shoal of Time: A History of the Hawai'ian Islands* (University of Hawai'i Press, 1989); Boyd Dixon and Michael J. Kolb, "Landscapes of War: Rules and Conventions of Conflict in Ancient Hawai'i" *American Antiquity* (v.67/3, 2002); Nathaniel Emerson, *Unwritten Literature of Hawai'i: The Sacred Songs of the Hula* (Charles E. Tuttle Publishing, 1965); Herb Kawainui Kane, *Ancient Hawai'i* (Kawainui Press, 1997); Kathleen D. Mellen, *An Island Kingdom Passes: Hawai'i Becomes American* (Hastings House, 1958); James A. Michener, *Hawai'i* (Random House, 1994); William Shaw, *Golden Dreams and Waking Realities: The Far Western Frontier* (Arno Press, 1973).

—ROB KERBY

Hawai'i, 1898 to 1942

The Territory of Hawai'i was created on July 7, 1898, with Congressional passage of the Newlands Resolution that annexed the islands to the United States. The laws of the Republic of Hawai'i were to remain in effect unless they were contrary to the U.S. Constitution.

President William McKinley appointed five commissioners to report on laws Congress should

FRUITS AND FLOWERS *Hawai'i grows some of the most popular and beautiful fruits and flowers in the world.* **AT LEFT,** *bananas ripen on a thick vine.* **ABOVE LEFT AND MIDDLE** *is the achiote tree and its seed. Imported to Hawai'i from the Philippines, the achiote was traditionally used as a cosmetic ingredient for rouge and lipstick.* **ABOVE RIGHT,** *bright yellow hibiscus flowers in full bloom.*

pass for Hawai'i. Their findings were debated by Congress for over a year, but the major issue was that Congress was afraid of the possibility of new states entering the Union that were not predominantly European in ancestry. Hawai'i was even more unsettling: a proposed state in which Polynesians and Asians outnumbered whites. In the 1900 U.S. Census, Hawai'i's population was 154,001, of which 39,656 were native Hawai'ians and another 40,000 or so were Japanese or Chinese, leaving whites as the largest ethnic group with about 75,000 citizens, but outnumbered by non-Europeans 52 percent to 48 percent.

In 1900 Congress passed An Act to Provide a Government for the Territory of Hawai'i, referred to as the Organic Act. The Organic Act established the Office of the Territorial Governor, appointed by the president of the United States. He served at the pleasure of the president and could be replaced at any time.

The first Hawai'ian territorial governor was the former president of the Republic of Hawai'i, Sanford B. Dole. Born in HONOLULU of American missionary parents, Dole had been a leader of the revolution that in 1887 denied King David Kalakaua absolute power and secured the "Bayonet Constitution," which the king signed at gunpoint and which empowered Hawai'ian citizens of American and European ancestry to take control of the government of the Kingdom of Hawai'i while denying Asians and Hawai'ian-born non-landowners the vote.

Dole served as a justice of the Hawai'ian Supreme Court and opposed the white-led revolution of 1893 that overthrew Queen Liliuokalani. He then accepted the office of president of the Republic of Hawai'i.

The application of the revolutionists for annexation to the United States was at first refused by President Grover Cleveland, who demanded the restoration of the queen. Dole defended the revolution and refused to reverse the course of events. The Republic of Hawai'i was created.

However, with the Spanish-American War and America's taking of the PHILIPPINES from Spain, Hawai'i's location in the mid-Pacific became very attractive to the United States—particularly with JAPAN asserting itself in the region. With annexation, the United States saw Hawai'i as its most strategic military asset. President William McKinley and his successor, Theodore Roosevelt, expanded the military presence in Hawai'i and established several key bases. By 1906, the entire island of Oahu was fortified at the coastlines with gun batteries mounted in coastal hills and mountains.

SUGAR PLANTATIONS

The first commercially viable sugar plantation, Ladd and Co., was started at Koloa, Kauai, in 1835. Its first harvest in 1837 produced two tons of raw sugar, which sold for $200. Early sugar planters shared many problems: shortages of water and labor, trade barriers, and the lack of markets for their sugar.

Beginning in 1856, sugar planters solved the water shortages in the drier area of the island by building aqueducts, digging artesian wells, and erecting irrigation systems that enabled the planters to grow on more than 100,000 acres of arid land. Hawai'i's sugar exports to California soared during the U.S. Civil War, but the end of hostilities in 1865 also meant the end of the sugar boom.

The major trade barrier to Hawai'i's closest and major market for its raw sugar was eliminated by the 1876 Treaty of Reciprocity between the United States and the Kingdom of Hawai'i. Through the treaty, the United States was allowed to establish a coal station for its warships at Pearl Harbor. In return, Hawai'i's sugar planters received duty-free entry into U.S. markets for their sugar.

Sugar interests helped elect King Kalakaua to the Hawai'ian throne in February 1874, and Kalakaua immediately sought the treaty that allowed duty-free sales of Hawai'ian sugar. Sugar exports from Hawai'i to the United States soared from 21,000,000 pounds in 1876 to 114,000,000 pounds in 1883 to 224,500,000 pounds in 1890. At one point, 254,563 acres were planted with sugarcane.

Local politics and the islands' economy became dominated by the sugar corporations, particularly Castle & Cooke, Alexander & Baldwin, C. Brewer & Co., Amfac, and Theo H. Davies & Co., referred to as the "Big Five."

For nearly a century, agriculture was Hawai'i's leading economic activity, providing the major sources of employment and tax revenues. With statehood in 1959 and the almost simultaneous introduction of passenger jet airplanes, the tourism industry began to grow rapidly, and within a decade became the state's largest economic activity.

DOLE PINEAPPLE

The territory's first governor's cousin, James Drummond Dole, arrived in Hawai'i in 1899 and purchased land in Wahiawa, where he established Hawai'i's first large pineapple plantation. Believing that pineapples could become a popular food substance outside Hawai'i, Dole built a cannery near his first plantation in 1901.

Actually, John Ackerman and Waldemar Muller had canned pineapple commercially in Kona around 1882. In 1885, Captain John Kidwell began crop development trials when he planted in Manoa, Oahu. At that point, pineapples were about a fourth to a third the size of modern-day pineapples. Kidwell is credited with experimenting with hybrids that increased the size of the fruit. His revolutionary Smooth Cayenne pineapple was planted near Pearl Harbor in the early 1890s.

As the fruit gained popularity on the U.S. mainland, in 1895 Kidwell and John Emmeluth built a pineapple cannery in Waipahu. In 1897, 150,000 pecks of pineapple were exported at a value of $14,000. A year later, Alfred W. Eames arrived in Hawai'i to begin pineapple cultivation. His company eventually became Del Monte Fresh Produce, Inc.

But it was James Dole who would win the title of "Pineapple King." In 1899, he purchased 61 acres in Wahiawa and began experimenting with pineapple. By 1905, Dole's company was packing 125,000 cases of pineapple per year. In 1911, the pineapple industry was revolutionized when Dole worked with mechanical engineer Henry Ginaca to invent a machine that could core, peel, and slice pineapple—eliminating the need for thousands of workers. Demand for his pineapple rose, and in 1922, he purchased and transformed the arid and largely unpopulated island of Lanai into the world's largest pineapple plantation. For years, Lanai produced 75 percent of the world's pineapple.

By 1930, Hawai'i had become the pineapple capital of the world. In 1935 and 1937, Congress again deliberated over whether or not Hawai'i should be granted statehood. Debate centered on racial issues with Congress still uneasy with the idea of a state that was predominantly nonwhite. Statehood was finally granted August 21, 1959.

Further Reading: John Chambers, *On the Road History: Hawai'i* (Interlink Publishing Group, 2006); Tom Coffman, *Island Edge of America: A Political History of Hawai'i* (University of Hawai'i Press, 2003); J. Sullivan and John Schlegel, *Hawai'i* (Capstone Press, 2003).

—ROB KERBY

ABOVE TOP *In 1922, Dole purchased the island of Lanai and turned it into the world's largest pineapple plantation.* **ABOVE MIDDLE** *A saimin shop. Saimin is a common Hawai'ian noodle dish.* **ABOVE BOTTOM** *The Hawai'ian ti plant is believed to bring good luck to residents.*

Hirohito, Emperor (1901–89)

American scholars have disagreed on the extent to which Emperor Hirohito was involved in the decision making that led to the Japanese attack on America's Pacific Fleet (see PACIFIC FLEET, U.S.). A minority accepted General DOUGLAS MACARTHUR's assessment that Hirohito, who became emperor of JAPAN in 1926, was basically a peace-loving figurehead who had little to do with waging war against the Allied countries (see ALLIES ON DECEMBER 7, 1941) in WORLD WAR II. Most scholars agree that Hirohito was an active decision maker in addition to serving as Japan's symbolic leader.

There is little doubt that Hirohito saw Japanese expansion as a way to honor his imperial ancestors. According to the Japanese constitution, however, military officials were responsible for policy and military decisions. Prime Minister HIDEKI TOJO was one of the strongest advocates for Japanese imperialism. He endorsed the concept of *kodutai*, which was based on promoting Japanese interests by purging Japan and all of Asia of Western influences, thus providing a justification for waging "holy war" against the Allies in World War II. Hirohito participated in *kodutai* until 1945.

Although a number of Japanese records were destroyed before the invasion in 1945, remaining records reveal that Hirohito was actively involved in planning the Pearl Harbor attack, and that he maintained a close eye on military activities, frequently ordering commanders to take specific actions. Ultimately, it was Hirohito who made the decision to surrender on August 15, 1945, after atomic bombs were dropped on Hiroshima and Nagasaki. A number of military leaders committed suicide after Hirohito announced the surrender to the Japanese people via radio.

For decades, scholars have attempted to understand *why* the Japanese were able to surprise America on December 7, 1941 (see also HISTORIANS' VIEWS). Proponents of the "back door to war theory" argue that President FRANKLIN D. ROOSEVELT provoked the Japanese into attacking the United States in order to push Congress and the American public into supporting entry into World War II. However, most evidence indicates that the United States simply underestimated Japan's military might and the dedication of the Japanese military. Although American cryptanalysts had broken Japanese codes (see CODES, JAPANESE), Hirohito and his advisors also had excellent intelligence resources, including the Japanese embassy in HONOLULU, which closely observed schedules and activities at Pearl Harbor.

In the months immediately after Pearl Harbor, the Japanese military appeared unbeatable. Once the Allies rallied their offense teams, however, the Japanese failed to muster well-planned responses. From December 1941 to February 1943, the Japanese lost 26,006 warplanes, one-third of their navy, thousands of experienced pilots, hundreds of thousands of tons of fighting ships, and massive amounts of merchant and naval transports. Hirohito was convinced that the Soviet Union would come to his aid, not knowing that the Allies had made concessions to the Soviets to prevent such an outcome.

When MacArthur read "Operation Olympic," the War Department's plan to invade Japan, he believed that Washington, D.C., had vastly underestimated Japan's ability to defend its homeland and that the invasion planned for November 1, 1945, would result in massive Allied casualties. Indeed, the Japanese had vowed to fight to the death. Opting to save American lives, President HARRY TRUMAN scrapped "Operation Olympic" in favor of dropping atomic bombs on Japan.

Chronology of Japanese Activities

SEPTEMBER 1940: During a meeting in the Imperial Conference Room of the palace, the Japanese lay out plans for an attack on the United States and Great Britain.

SEPTEMBER–OCTOBER 1940: The Japanese implement plans to tighten internal security, position Japanese troops in strategic locations, and enhance diplomatic maneuvers to lull the United States into believing the Japanese want to prevent war.

SUMMER 1941: The Japanese conduct simulated attacks on Pearl Harbor. A plaster model of Pearl Harbor is used as a teaching tool at the Japanese War College to pinpoint the locations of battleships, planes, hangars, and other targets. A Sunday morning is chosen for the attack to exploit the fact that American military personnel are likely to have been out late the night before.

SEPTEMBER–OCTOBER 1941: Diplomatic negotiations with the United States continue (see DIPLOMATIC RELATIONS).

NOVEMBER 2, 1941: The JAPANESE FLEET begins its journey to Hawai'i.

DECEMBER 4, 1941: Clerks and diplomats attend a party at the Japanese embassy.

DECEMBER 5, 1941: Japanese officials in Washington, D.C., are ordered to break diplomatic ties with the United States as of 3 A.M. on December 8. As a result of the party the night before, decoding of the message is delayed.

DECEMBER 7, 1941: After launching from 200 miles away, the Japanese make their way to Pearl Harbor. On the way, they listen to the G.I. radio station, following its beam. At 7:55 A.M., the Japanese attack Pearl Harbor, successfully taking out much of the Pacific fleet. They are successful in large part because all nine battleships have been brought into the harbor to await an inspection planned for December 8. However, they are unable to take out American aircraft carriers as planned because the carriers have been removed from Pearl Harbor in case of an attack.

DECEMBER 8, 1941: At 8 A.M., Secretary of State CORDELL HULL receives the message that Japan is severing diplomatic ties with the United States.

AUGUST 6, 1941: The United States drops an atomic bomb on the Japanese city of Hiroshima.

AUGUST 8, 1945: The United States drops a second atomic bomb on the Japanese city of Nagasaki.

AUGUST 15, 1945: At noon, the Japanese surrender unconditionally.

On August 6, 1945, the *Enola Gay* dropped an atomic bomb on Hiroshima, killing some 80,000 people and damaging 80 percent of the city. Still, Hirohito continued to delay his decision on accepting the terms of surrender. Consequently, on August 8, the *Bock's Car* dropped a second bomb on Nagasaki, killing 70,000 people and destroying much of that city. Hirohito surrendered one week later to keep Japan from being totally destroyed.

ABOVE LEFT *Emperor Hirohito reviews Japanese troops prior to the outbreak of the war.* **ABOVE RIGHT** *Full-length portrait of the emperor.*

Further Reading: Edward Behr, *Hirohito: Behind the Myth* (Villard, 1989); Herbert P. Bix, *Hirohito and the Making of Modern Japan* (HarperCollins, 2000); Daikichi Irokawa, *The Age of Hirohito: In Search of Modern Japan* (Free Press, 1995); Peter Wetzler, *Hirohito and War: Imperial Tradition of Military Decision-Making in Prewar Japan* (University of Hawai'i Press, 1998).

—ELIZABETH PURDY, PH.D.

ABOVE *Col. Paul W. Tibbets, Jr., poses in front of his B-29 "The Enola Gay" (named for his mother). The Enola Gay dropped an atomic bomb on Hiroshima, killing some 80,000 people and damaging 80 percent of the city.*

Historians' Views

In the decades that followed Pearl Harbor, historians have attempted to come to terms with that "infamous" day, choosing to focus on why the attack was such a surprise, what could and should have been done differently, and what lessons could be learned.

CHARLES TANSILL

In nearly all of the literature written by U.S. Army and Navy officers stationed at Pearl Harbor in December 1941, the blame is placed clearly on government officials in Washington, D.C., particularly President FRANKLIN D. ROOSEVELT. In *The Final Secret of Pearl Harbor: The Washington Contribution to the Japanese Attack*, which contains a forward by Rear Admiral HUSBAND E. KIMMEL, Robert Theobold argues that the president's military buildup, his exchange of 50 World War I destroyers for locating American military bases in British territory, and various other decisions of the Roosevelt administration provide positive proof that the government was *orchestrating* rather than *preparing for* American entry into the war.

Theobold was mirroring arguments laid out two years earlier by revisionist historian Charles Tansill in *Back Door to War: The Roosevelt Foreign Policy, 1933–41*. Tansill insists that the anti-Hitler bias of the American press helped to create an environment that made American entry into World War II inevitable. He places the blame for the timing of that entry squarely on the shoulders of Roosevelt who, according to Tansill, had begun the military buildup as early as 1933, six years before Germany invaded Poland and launched World War II. Tansill levels blame not only at Roosevelt but at the entire American government for making the preservation of the

British Empire the primary objective of American foreign policy from 1900 onward.

Tansill notes a November 25, 1941, entry from the diary of Secretary of War HENRY L. STIMSON, in which Stimson ruminated on how the UNITED STATES could maneuver JAPAN into an attack while minimizing danger to Americans. He argues that when Secretary of State CORDELL HULL issued an ultimatum to Japan the day following Stimson's diary entry, he knew that it would not be accepted. Tansill contends that examination of confidential files and the correspondence of Roosevelt's advisors indicates that the president focused on provoking Japan to attack the United States only because GERMANY had rejected his bait.

Tansill suggests that Japan was the chosen aggressor because Roosevelt had received word that a Japanese-German alliance was in the works. In response to this information, Roosevelt levied an embargo blocking delivery of all iron and steel scraps to Japan. According to Tansill, this move was irrelevant because Japan had stockpiles of such material. Furthermore, he believes the Germans were using Japan not as a means of propelling the United States into World War II but as a means of keeping America out of the war.

On September 27, 1940, Japan, Germany, and Italy pledged to defend one another in case of attack. Tansill believes that Japanese officials saw the move as a means of deterring the United States from entering World War II. Some two weeks later, Roosevelt began planning economic sanctions against Japan (see SANCTIONS AGAINST JAPAN) and reaffirmed American support for Europe.

Tansill implies that the secret meeting between Roosevelt and WINSTON CHURCHILL on August 9 that led to the signing of the Atlantic Charter, which in turn provided a basis for the establishment of the United Nations, was chiefly responsible for Japan's subsequent behavior. On August 17, 1940, Roosevelt presented the Japanese ambassador with a statement that made it clear that a declaration of war would follow any act of aggression, stating unequivocally that the United States would take "any and all steps necessary toward safeguarding the legitimate rights and interests" of American property, citizens, and nationals. In Tansill's view, Japan's only option at that point was to attack the United States. He contends that on December 4 Roosevelt received evidence of when the attack would take place when a coded message, "east wind rain," was irrelevantly inserted into a Tokyo news broadcast (CODES, JAPANESE). Tansill maintains that Roosevelt went to bed on the night of December 6, 1941, without notifying officials at American military bases in the Pacific that an attack would take place the following day.

ROBERTA WOHLSTETTER

In *Pearl Harbor: Warning and Decision*, noted historian Roberta Wohlstetter provides a thorough examination of the INTELLIGENCE operations concerning Pearl Harbor and details the chain of events that took place on December 7, 1941. Wohlstetter carefully studied the 39 volumes generated by the Congressional hearings on Pearl Harbor, memoirs of both American and Japanese military leaders, the unpublished private papers of Roosevelt, and secondary accounts by other historians before drawing her own conclusions about the attack. Wohlstetter examined how intelligence and communication operations failed and the implications of those failures on Pearl Harbor and in considering the possibility of future surprise attacks on the United States. In light of the events of September 11, 2001, her examination of Pearl Harbor takes on new meaning.

Wohlstetter concluded that the U.S. government was, indeed, expecting an attack in 1941; but it "just expected wrong." She also contends that the plethora of available intelligence made it difficult to extract essential information. The government, according to Wohlstetter, forgot that the Pacific fleet (see PACIFIC FLEET, U.S.), which was intended to serve as a deterrent to would-be attackers, could also serve as a prime target. She dismisses the theory of revisionist historians that "east wind rain" was a code for the attack, noting that contradictory signals always accompanied messages that seemed to signify an attack on Pearl Harbor. Wohlstetter suggests that because the focus at Pearl Harbor was on training rather than on military preparedness, officials did not correctly interpret information that was available.

Most scholars agree that a lack of communication between the army and navy at Pearl Harbor set the stage for disaster. The line of communication was established, with information directed first to the Hawai'i air force headquarters, then to the Department of the Army, and finally to the Department of the Navy. The line of communication was not used on December 7, and no patrols operated directly over Pearl Harbor. Furthermore, the Air Warning System in use at Pearl Harbor was only able to detect planes flying at a range of 30 to 130 miles. According to Wohlstetter, the military discovered a blank sector after the attack.

If the radar operator at Pearl Harbor noted relevant information, he was supposed to transmit it by commercial telephone lines. Operators were not on duty at all times, and there was no designated supervisor responsible for the operation. Wohlstetter faults Admiral C.C. BLOCH, the commander of the 14th Naval District, for observing such a rigid schedule that the Japanese could have predicted that radar operators were only on duty from 4 A.M. to 7 A.M., which was considered the likeliest time for an attack. General WALTER C. SHORT, the army official in charge of defending Pearl Harbor, believed that the base needed only 30 to 35 minutes' warning to react in case of an attack, and he was sure that no attack would occur without that warning. As a result, he chose not to keep the army patrol planes in the air at all times, determining that it was wiser to save them for a time when war was a reality rather than a possibility.

Testimony from various individuals connected with Pearl Harbor indicates that neither the army nor the navy believed the Japanese would attack Pearl Harbor. Fanny Halsey, the wife of Admiral William F. Halsey, reportedly told Admiral Kimmel, the commander in chief of United States Naval Forces, at a dinner party on the night of December 6 that she felt sure the Japanese would attack the base. Kimmel replied that such an attack was "remote." Reports written by a number of military officials stationed at Pearl Harbor suggest that military officials were certain that Japan was simply too weak to take on the U.S. military.

Wohlstetter writes that on December 7, Private Joseph L. Lockard was operating the radar at Pearl Harbor, and Private George E. Elliott was operating the plotter. The two men remained at the radar station after their shift was over. At 7:02, Elliott noticed something unusual, recording the information that a plane was 137 miles north of Oahu. He reported it to the switchboard at the information center. Subsequently, Lieutenant Kermit Tyler, who was convinced the plane was "friendly," told the operators to ignore it. Elliott plotted the plane until it was 30 minutes from Oahu. If officials had acted on his information, Wohlstetter believes that the army and navy would have had 45 minutes' advance warning.

"Back Door to War" Theory

BY 1941, Europe had been at war for over two years, and the Allies had already suffered devastating losses. President Roosevelt had made it clear that he wanted to throw the military might of the United States into winning the war. However, isolationists were adamant about letting Europe fight its own battles. Consequently, Roosevelt did all that he could to help the Allies without a declaration of war. Proponents of the "back door to war" theory insist that since Roosevelt could not legitimately enter the war, he did so by forcing Japan into a situation where they were obligated to attack the United States.

According to the theory, once an attack occurred, opposition to America's entry into World War II would evaporate. Revisionists believe that Roosevelt knew the Japanese were going to attack Pearl Harbor on December 7, and did nothing to warn army and navy officials.

During a Congressional hearing and in interviews with various executive and military commissions, Admiral JAMES O. RICHARDSON insisted that he had been relieved of his role as commander in chief of the U.S. Fleet after informing the president in January 1940 that the fleet was vulnerable at Pearl Harbor. Subsequently, revisionist historians such as Charles Tansill, Robert B. Stinnett, and George Morgenstern joined the military in offering what they say is irrefutable proof of Roosevelt's prior knowledge of the attack on Pearl Harbor. They insist that the fleet was in Hawai'i to entice Japan into an attack. Stinnett perused government documents and concluded that an eight-point plan for provoking Japan, generated by the Roosevelt administration, was responsible for the attack on Pearl Harbor.

She notes that the navy already had patrol planes carrying live charges in the area and that the USS *Ward*, a destroyer, was nearby. With the necessary warning, the planes and the destroyer could have been redirected to Pearl Harbor. Instead, the time was lost.

Shortly before 4 A.M., according to Wohlstetter, the USS *Condor*, a minesweeper patrolling the entrance to Pearl Harbor, notified the USS *Ward* that a submerged submarine had been spotted. Neither ship forwarded the information to the Harbor Control Post. At 6:30 A.M., Lieutenant Harold Kaminski, the duty officer on the USS *Condor*, received a message from the USS *Ward* that the conning tower of a submarine had been spotted near the USS *Antares*. The records reveal that 15 minutes

later, Captain Outerbridge ordered his men to open fire and reported his actions to the proper officials. Outerbridge repeated the message at 6:53 A.M. but was unable to reach the commandant's aide. On his own, Outerbridge began relaying orders to the ships involved. The USS *Ward* sent word that it was bringing a sampan into HONOLULU. At that point, the Coast Guard was called in, and the War Planes Office contacted department heads. Admiral Kimmel was told about the submarine at 7:40 A.M. At no point was the army apprised of the situation, ostensibly because the navy did not believe the base was under attack. Within 15 minutes, the Japanese began dropping bombs on Pearl Harbor.

The clearest evidence that military officials at Pearl Harbor had the necessary information to defend the base from a Japanese attack came from a memorandum of November 2, 1941, written by Admiral HAROLD R. STARK, the chief of Naval Operations in Washington, D.C., to Admiral Kimmel. Beginning with the warning that the dispatch was "to be considered a war warning," the memorandum stated unequivocally that negotiations with Japan had stalled (see DIPLOMATIC RELATIONS) and that an attack was to be expected within days. Guam was considered the likeliest target.

GORDON PRANGE

In *Pearl Harbor: The Verdict of History* and to a lesser extent in *At Dawn We Slept: The Untold Story of Pearl Harbor*, Gordon Prange, a veteran of World War II and one of the foremost scholars on the history of the attack on Pearl Harbor, responds to the "back door to war" theory, which blamed Roosevelt for precipitating the Japanese attack on Pearl Harbor. Prange suggests that the Roberts Commission, which issued its report in early 1942, was convened so close to the attack on Pearl Harbor that it lacked historical perspective (see INVESTIGATIONS OF RESPONSIBILITY). Rather than laying all the blame on either the government or the military, Prange concludes that all parties involved were at fault. He identifies four major factors that came into play on December 7, 1941: a vast number of human errors, a plethora of false assumptions, the fallacious views of a number of individuals, and poor handling of intelligence data.

Prange notes that the Japanese government was determined to go to war, and nothing Roosevelt did could have changed that fact. He identifies a number of factors that assured that Japan's attack on Pearl Harbor would be successful, ranging from precise planning and tireless training to courage and pure luck. Because the Japanese were willing to expend as many lives and as much money as necessary on both research and procurement, they were fully prepared to make war, while the United States was not expecting it to come without a formal declaration of war.

Prange suggests that Roosevelt made a major blunder in not closing the Japanese embassy in Honolulu where most of the Japanese intelligence on Pearl Harbor originated. He criticizes Roosevelt's cabinet for giving the president faulty advice and blames Congress for coming within one vote of abolishing the draft just a few months before Pearl Harbor. Prange states that a close examination of historical evidence reveals repeated efforts on the part of the United States to maintain peace with Japan and that the focus of the American government was always on aiding the Allies and defeating ADOLF HITLER. In Prange's view, the lion's share of the blame must be placed with the United States naval officials in charge of Pearl Harbor on December 7, 1941. He faults both Admiral Kimmel and Admiral Bloch. Prange feels that Bloch should shoulder most of the blame for failing to provide long-range air patrol of Pearl Harbor in light of the warning of a potential Japanese attack.

Prange, Wohlstetter, and numerous other scholars have expressed astonishment that even when the actual attack occurred, American response was delayed. The Japanese surprised the Americans on December 7. The military failed to sound an alert even after planes were spotted over Pearl Harbor. The warning did not go out until the first bomb exploded. Even after Pearl Harbor had suffered a surprise attack and information had been dispatched in intelligence reports around the globe, the Japanese managed to launch a second surprise attack on the Philippines where they found the patrol planes on the ground rather than in the air, where they should have been.

Further Reading: Edward L. Beach, *Scapegoats: A Defense of Kimmel and Short at Pearl Harbor* (Naval Institute Press, 1995); Gordon W. Prange, *At Dawn We Slept: The Untold Story of Pearl Harbor* (Penguin, 1991); Gordon W. Prange, *Pearl Harbor: The Verdict of History* (McGraw-Hill, 1986); James O. Richardson, *On the Treadmill to Pearl Harbor: The Memoirs of Admiral James O. Richardson* (Department of the Navy, Naval History Department, 1973); Robert B. Stinnett, *Day of Deceit: The Truth about FDR and Pearl Harbor* (The Free Press, 2000); Charles Callan Tansill, *Back Door to War: The Roosevelt Foreign Policy, 1933–41* (Regnery, 1952); Robert A. Theobold, *The Final Secret of Pearl Harbor: The Washington Contribution to the Japanese Attack* (Devin-Adair, 1954); Roberta Wohlstetter, *Pearl Harbor: Warning and Decision* (Stanford University Press, 1962).

—**ELIZABETH PURDY, PH.D.**

Hitler, Adolf (1889–1945)

On the evening of December 7, 1941, Adolf Hitler sat pensively at the *Führer* Headquarters in East Prussia. Earlier that day, Hitler had issued his infamous "night and fog decree" intended to suppress the rising unrest within German-occupied territories. Resisters would thenceforth be executed or secretly deported to GERMANY. Transports had also begun that day to Chelmo, the first death camp established in the Nazis' systematic effort to exterminate the Jews. Also on December 7, Field Marshal Walther von Brauchitsch, commander in chief of the German army, had offered his resignation. Hitler would postpone his

ABOVE LEFT *Hitler at a Nazi Party rally, Nuremberg, Germany, ca. 1928.* **ABOVE RIGHT** *Hitler grimly inspects bomb damage in a German city.*

Night and Fog Decree

IN AN effort to quell resistance within German-occupied territories, Hitler issued the following directives on December 7, 1941:

I. WITHIN the occupied territories, the adequate punishment for offences committed against the German State or the occupying power which endanger their security or a state of readiness is on principle the death penalty.

II. THE offences listed in paragraph I as a rule are to be dealt with in the occupied countries only if it is probable that sentence of death will be passed upon the offender, at least the principal offender, and if the trial and the execution can be completed in a very short time. Otherwise the offenders, at least the principal offenders, are to be taken to Germany.

III. PRISONERS taken to Germany are subjected to military procedure only if particular military interests require this. In case German or foreign authorities inquire about such prisoners, they are to be told that they were arrested, but that the proceedings do not allow any further information.

response to Brauchitsch for nearly two weeks before declaring himself the new commander in chief of the German armed forces.

Hitler's prospects for victory had diminished considerably in recent weeks. Operation Barbarossa, launched against the Soviet Union in June 1941, was not progressing as anticipated. The *Blitzkrieg* was intended to last a matter of weeks. Instead, Soviet resistance, strategic reversals, and the superiority of Soviet panzer production had led one of Hitler's most trusted ministers to inform him that the war could no longer be won militarily. On December 5, two days before JAPAN attacked Pearl Harbor, the German offensive on Moscow had broken down and Soviet armed forces had begun a major counterattack. The German army, unprepared to wage a winter war in Moscow, faced very bleak prospects.

Confronted with such discouraging news from the east, Hitler responded to the Japanese attack on Pearl Harbor with renewed optimism. When handed a telegram informing him of the attack, Hitler was apparently delighted by the news: "We now have an ally which has never been conquered in 3,000 years," he exclaimed. Hitler immediately telephoned Minister of Propaganda Joseph Goebbels and ordered him to convene the Reichstag. Hitler would use the occasion of the Reichstag meeting on December 11 to announce a declaration of war on the UNITED STATES. Goebbels later recorded Hitler's delight at "such a happy turn of events." With the expansion of the war, Goebbels remarked that Hitler felt as if "a ton weight has been taken off him."

Further Reading: The Avalon Project, "Nazi Conspiracy and Aggression, Volume 7, Document No. L-90 [Night and Fog Decree]," www.yale.edu/lawweb/avalon/imt/document/l-90.htm (cited December 2005); Max Domarus, *Hitler: Speeches and Proclamations, 1932–45* (Bolchazy-Carducci Publishers, 2004); Adolf Hitler, *Secret*

Conversations: 1941–44, translated by Norman Cameron and R.H. Stevens (Octagon Books, 1972); Ian Kershaw, *Hitler, 1936–45: Nemesis* (W. W. Norton, 2000).

—KATHLEEN RUPPERT, PH.D.

Hong Kong

By late 1941, the British government became more convinced that the Japanese advance in China would eventually target the British colony of Hong Kong. The garrison consisted of four battalions of British and Indian troops. London requested more troops from Canada, and two Canadian battalions—largely untrained and officially rated as "unfit for combat"—arrived on November 16. Even with the reinforcements, the Commonwealth forces clearly were inadequate to defend against a determined Japanese attack.

The Japanese assault on Hong Kong began about eight hours after their attack on Pearl Harbor, involving over a division of soldiers. Japanese bombers quickly destroyed the colony's minuscule air force, and Japanese troops began to advance. The Commonwealth troops initially established their defensive line, called the Gin Drinkers Line, on the mainland (Kowloon) of Hong Kong. Although the British intended this line to hold for weeks, a Japanese unit seized a key position in the line and the British retreated even before all the Japanese forces had reached the line.

By December 13, Commonwealth forces were driven back to defensive positions on the island of Hong Kong. The Japanese forces began a five-day artillery bombardment of Hong Kong, and then their infantry crossed to the island on boats the night

Sergeant-Major John Osborn

DURING THE defense of Hong Kong, Sergeant Major John Osborn, of Manitoba, Canada, a member of the Winnipeg Grenadiers, won Britain's highest award for bravery, the Victoria Cross. Excerpts of his citation:

At Hong Kong on the morning of the 19th of December, 1941, a company of the Winnipeg Grenadiers to which Company Sergeant-Major Osborn belonged, became divided during an attack on Mount Butler. A part of the company led by Company Sergeant-Major Osborn captured the hill at the point of the bayonet and held it for three hours when the position became untenable. Company Sergeant-Major Osborn and a small group covered the withdrawal, and when their turn came to fall back Osborn, single-handed, engaged the enemy while the remainder successfully joined the company. With no consideration for his own safety he assisted and directed stragglers to the new company position, exposing himself to heavy enemy fire to cover their retirement.

During the afternoon the company was cut off from the battalion and completely surrounded by the enemy. Several enemy grenades were thrown which Company Sergeant-Major Osborn picked up and threw back. The enemy threw a grenade which landed in a position where it was impossible to pick it up and return it in time. Shouting a warning to his comrades this gallant warrant officer threw himself on the grenade which exploded, killing him instantly.

A statue of Sergeant-Major Osborn was erected in Hong Kong Park after the war.

of December 18. Brutal fighting occurred in the mountain pass of Wong Ne Chong Gap, in which the Japanese troops suffered some 800 casualties in a series of suicide attacks. Despite the sometimes intense fighting, however, the Commonwealth forces clearly were unable to stop the Japanese, and the governor of Hong Kong surrendered to the Japanese on Christmas Day. The surviving troops were shipped out to Japanese prison camps. Japanese commanders also declared all the Chinese women in Hong Kong to be prostitutes, and there were reportedly thousands of rapes by Japanese troops, together with widespread looting.

Further Reading: Philip Snow, *The Fall of Hong Kong: Britain, China, and the Japanese Occupation* (Yale University Press, 2003); Steve Yui-Sang Tsang, *A Modern History of Hong Kong* (St. Martin's Press, 2004); Veterans Affairs Canada, "Sergeant Major Osborn," www.vac-acc.gc.ca/general/sub.cfm?source=history/secondwar/citations/osborn (cited December 2005).

—LAWRENCE E. CLINE, PH.D.

Honolulu

The beautiful city of Honolulu, Hawai'i, is forever identified in the collective memory of Americans in connection with the Japanese attack. In contemporary times, the city symbolizes the island paradise that is Hawai'i, which serves as the commercial capital of the Pacific. However, signs of Honolulu's past are evident in landmarks and memorials to the 2,403 persons killed at Pearl Harbor on December 7 (see ARIZONA, USS MEMORIAL; DAMAGE, MEMORIAL).

Honolulu became the unofficial capital of the Hawai'ian Islands in February 1845 when King Kamehameha III relocated his permanent residence to the city. Five years later, the Privy Council officially designated Honolulu as the capital of Hawai'i. In 1959, the state constitution mandated Honolulu as the capital of the 50th state.

In the late 18th century when Captain William Brown arrived in the Hawai'ian Islands, Honolulu was only a sleepy little fishing village. However, Brown took note of the protected harbor that made entry into Honolulu difficult. Because it was the only deep water port in the mid-Pacific, Honolulu quickly became a supply center and a base for repairing and maintaining ships. Furs from the Pacific Northwest were traded for Hawai'ian sandalwood, which was traded for Chinese tea. The tea was then traded for furs, initiating a repeat of the trading route.

AMERICA IN THE PACIFIC

In the 1860s the whaling industry collapsed, and Hawai'ian trade began to dry up. In order to revive the sagging economy, the government negotiated a Reciprocity Treaty with the United States, granting American vessels access to Hawai'ian harbors in exchange for an exemption from high American tariffs on sugar and for improved harbor facilities. The United States annexed Hawai'i as a territory in 1898 in direct response to the outbreak of the Spanish-American War. The first American troops were dispatched to Fort McKinley near Diamond Head in August of that year. In 1900, Honolulu was home to 39,306 residents. Within two decades, the population had swelled to 127,000. Subsequently, Honolulu surfaced as a major tourist attraction.

The first permanent American military post was established in 1908 at Fort Shafter just outside Honolulu. Naval Station Honolulu, at Pearl Harbor, was ready for occupation the following year. Approximately 1,000 servicemen served at Pearl Harbor during World War I. After the war, the United States continued to upgrade harbor facilities,

ultimately erecting three harbors and five wharves. In 1938, well aware of Hawai'i's significance in the Pacific, the U.S. Army enacted the Defense Mobilization Plan that placed Hawai'i under martial law in the event of an attack and began readying for war. Production of structural steel was placed under military control, blackout drills began, and cages were constructed to hold prisoners of war.

After the Germans invaded Poland and forced Britain, France, Australia, and New Zealand to reciprocate by declaring war on September 3, 1939, the United States further beefed up military power

ABOVE TOP *The beaches, hotels, and history of Honolulu attract international tourists year-round.*
ABOVE BOTTOM *An aerial view of downtown Honolulu.*

at Pearl Harbor. In May 1940, President FRANKLIN D. ROOSEVELT moved the Pacific Fleet (see PACIFIC FLEET, U.S.) to Pearl Harbor and decided to leave it there as a deterrent to enemy aggression. The following year, after staging a mock battle, navy officials announced that the defenses of Pearl Harbor were complete and that the base was prepared to repel enemy attacks. They were wrong.

HONOLULU, DECEMBER 7, 1941

With Pearl Harbor at their doorstep, the majority of Honolulu's residents assumed that the city would be a prime target for enemy forces. The blackout already in practice in Honolulu was extended to the rest of Hawai'i. Those who were cognizant of Japanese history knew that Japan had a history of surprise attacks. They also knew that the Roosevelt administration would not back down from its position of supporting the Chinese against Japanese imperialism, nor would Roosevelt veer from his course of aiding the Allies against the tyrannies of GERMANY and Italy.

Honolulu's newspapers had carried the news when Japan signed an alliance with the aggressor nations on September 27, 1940. Even so, Japan and the United States had continued to hold diplomatic talks (see DIPLOMATIC RELATIONS), and the Hawai'i chapter of the Institute of Pacific Relations was working frantically to develop a plan allowing the United States and Japan to avert war. The newest version, with the institute's recommendations, was scheduled to be delivered to President Roosevelt on Monday, December 8, 1941.

Like other American citizens and nationals, Hawai'ians were aware that American INTELLIGENCE was keeping a close watch on the movement of the JAPANESE FLEET, even though they would not know until later about the decoding program MAGIC and realize that the U.S. government had

deciphered Japan's latest top-secret code during the fall of the previous year (see CODES, JAPANESE). Hawai'ians did know that with General HIDEKI TOJO as prime minister of Japan, the time for an attack was ripe. In Honolulu, the City Council had already established a Major Disaster Council and enacted an Emergency Disaster Plan to prepare for civilian responses if war came to Hawai'i. On November 30, 1941, a bold headline in the *Honolulu Advertiser* announced: "The Japanese May Attack over the Weekend." However, military officials at Pearl Harbor were not expecting an attack.

At dawn on December 7, a low cloud cover hovered over the island of Oahu. At 7:30 A.M., Hawa'ians playing on Honolulu's golf courses observed that planes with the rising sun insignia on their wings had emerged as the clouds dispersed. They wondered if the planes were part of another mock battle staged by officials at Pearl Harbor.

The attack began at 7:55 A.M., and locals observed smoke over Pearl Harbor. They also saw planes spitting fire as they dived. Nearby, Lunalilo School was hit, convincing the crowd that Pearl Harbor was truly under attack.

In Honolulu, damage assessments revealed that most of the damage done to the city occurred when debris from spent American antiaircraft shells fell back to earth. Some damage occurred near Iolani Palace, and more extensive damage took place at Washington Palace where the governor resided. The heaviest damage in Honolulu occurred in the Japanese section of the city. Overall, 60 civilians in Honolulu were killed by falling debris and by fires resulting from explosions. Of those who were killed, 20 were of Japanese descent. Three hundred other residents of Honolulu were wounded. On the night of December 7, grocery stores were closed. For three days, only families with babies could buy milk and poi. All bars, liquor stores, arcades, dance halls, and brothels were closed, and gas was rationed. The military began burning acres of food to prevent its acquisition by Japanese invaders.

Backed by local, state, and national law, General WALTER C. SHORT accepted authority for governing Hawai'i. In the days following the attack on Pearl Harbor, the whole of Hawai'i was placed under mandatory nightly blackouts and curfews. Censorship was invoked, and the government monitored all mail, cables, and telephone calls. Air-raid sirens were readied for service, and gas masks were issued to residents of Honolulu.

Honolulu's beaches took on barbed-wire barricades and gun emplacements, and all navigational aids were removed from the coasts. Evacuation centers were organized, and 3,000 Hawai'ians reported for first-aid training, although no money had been allocated to support a training program. Hawai'ian women began making camouflage nettings and artificial shrubbery. It became clear that the Japanese had not forgotten Hawai'i when an army transport, the *Royal T. Frank*, was torpedoed on January 28, 1942, at a cost of 29 lives. Despite the military's precautions, nature took a hand and illuminated the entire area surrounding Honolulu in April when Mauna Loa erupted.

Even in wartime, Hawai'i was entertaining for the American military who regularly visited bars, honky-tonks, dances, and shows at the USO. The Black Cat on Hotel Street in Honolulu was a favorite for Americans because they could buy hotcakes for 10 cents, oyster omelets for 35 cents, or turkey and dressing for 50 cents. Americans also attended churches, concerts, the Honolulu Academy of the Arts, and free performances at the Honolulu Theatre.

Hawai'i's financial contribution to the overall war effort was estimated at $200 million. Because sugar and pineapple were designated as essential war crops, the agricultural contribution of Hawai'i was enormous. When casualties for WORLD WAR II were totaled, 80 percent of Hawai'ians killed in service were of Japanese ancestry. Over the next year, the population of Honolulu nearly doubled as the city became the base of American operations in the Pacific.

Today, Honolulu is home to the National Memorial Cemetery of the Pacific, locally known as the "Punchbowl Cemetery," which means *Puwaina* or "Hill of Sacrifice" in Hawai'ian. The cemetery serves as the burial grounds for some 13,000 soldiers and sailors killed in World War II.

Further Reading: Edward D. Beechert, *Honolulu: Crossroads of the Pacific* (University of South Carolina Press, 1991); George Chaplin, *Presstime in Paradise: The Life and Times of the Honolulu Advertiser* (University of Hawai'i Press, 1998); Gavan Daws, *Shoal of Time: A History of the Hawai'ian Islands* (University of Hawai'i Press, 1968); Kathy E. Ferguson and Phyllis Turnbell, *Oh, Say Can You See: The Semiotics of the Military in Hawai'i* (University of Minnesota Press, 1999).

—**ELIZABETH PURDY, PH.D.**

Hull, Cordell (1871–1955)

Called "the father of the United Nations" by President FRANKLIN D. ROOSEVELT, Cordell Hull was elected to the Tennessee House of Representatives in 1893. Resigning his office to take part in the Spanish-American War, Hull was a captain in the Fourth Regiment of the Tennessee Volunteer Infantry. His stay in Cuba during the conflict influenced his approach to foreign policy in Latin America after he became a member of Roosevelt's cabinet.

In 1907, Hull was elected to the U.S. House of Representatives, where he served until 1931. A major supporter of Woodrow Wilson and a prominent voice among southern Democrats, Hull authored the first Federal Income Tax Bill in 1913. In 1930 he was elected to represent Tennessee in the U.S. Senate, but his service to his state was cut short when President Roosevelt appointed him secretary of state. The appointment raised many eyebrows in Washington, D.C., but it was the result of the president's solid political calculations. Hull was a staunch Roosevelt supporter, but he was also a powerful figure among southern Democrats, whom the president was eager to court.

Hull had the longest tenure of any secretary of state in U.S. history, occupying the office for almost 12 years from 1933 to 1944. Though often overshadowed and sometimes even ignored by Roosevelt, Hull was strong in his convictions. He promoted good relations with Latin America and viewed the expansion of reciprocal world trade as a means of avoiding economic and political conflict between nations. He also envisioned early on a worldwide peacekeeping organization based in accordance with international law. Sensing danger as WORLD WAR II approached, Hull warned the American military—well in advance of December 7, 1941—to be on guard for a direct assault on American military installations around the world.

The war strengthened Hull's resolve to create an international peacekeeping concern and by 1943 his State Department had drafted documents related to the Charter of the United Nations, which became the basis for American efforts to form the organization. Although Hull resigned as secretary of state because of ill health in 1944, he continued to use his influence to make the United Nations a reality. Roosevelt praised him as "the one person in all the world who has done his most to make this great plan for peace an effective fact."

In recognition of his efforts, Hull was awarded the Nobel Peace Prize in 1945. Despite continued bouts with poor health, Hull lived another decade, long enough to see the United Nations become an institution. He died on July 23, 1955, in Bethesda Naval Hospital and was interred in the National Cathedral in Washington, D.C.

Further Reading: Michael A. Butler, *Cautious Visionary: Cordell Hull and Trade Reform, 1933–37* (Kent State University Press, 1998); Cordell Hull, *The Memoirs of Cordell Hull* (Reprint Services, 1993); Julius W. Pratt, *Cordell Hull* (Cooper Square Publishers, 1964).

—BEN WYNNE, PH.D.

ABOVE *Cordell Hull, 1936. Had Hull accepted Roosevelt's offer to run as his vice president, it would have been he rather than Harry Truman who became president upon Roosevelt's death.*

BUY WAR BONDS

I

Intelligence, Pacific Theater

In the world of operational intelligence, the UNITED STATES had certain key organizations in place and staffed with experienced and capable personnel. These would provide an important and occasionally critical advantage in the Pacific war.

The real heroes were those men and women who labored in windowless rooms, intercepting and breaking Japan's encoded messages. Intelligence analysts would then piece together Japanese intentions, capabilities, and operational plans. Finally, operational commanders, such as Admiral CHESTER NIMITZ, would act—when able, taking into account strength of forces, logistics requirements, and weather—on the offered intelligence.

The United States had developed a capable code-breaking apparatus in the years following World War I. The army's Signal Intelligence Service was headed by Colonel William F. Friedman. One of the greatest cryptanalysts of all time, Friedman was able to break the Japanese diplomatic code, named PURPLE (see CODES, JAPANESE). Similarly, the U.S. Navy had established a dedicated effort under Commander Laurence Stafford in 1924 to concentrate on communications intelligence.

The intelligence failure at Pearl Harbor on December 7 was so complete that it has spawned conspiracy theories. Some have surmised that President FRANKLIN D. ROOSEVELT and perhaps WINSTON CHURCHILL knew of the impending attack, but deliberately withheld

FINANCING THE WAR *Throughout World War II, posters such as the one shown at left were common, encouraging Americans to purchase war bonds, recycle paper, rubber, scrap metal, and nylon stockings.*

95

the information to ensure America's entry into the war. In the six months prior to the Japanese attack, the United States had intercepted and translated over 7,000 messages. When, on that fateful Sunday, Japanese diplomats delivered to Secretary of State CORDELL HULL an announcement that a state of war was now in existence, he already knew the contents of their diplomatic note and had prepared and rehearsed a righteously angry oral reply.

The inability to discern Japanese intentions, or at least deliver suitable warnings to Admiral HUSBAND E. KIMMEL and General WALTER C. SHORT in Hawai'i, is obvious. Certain facts concerning events of December 6 and 7 are indisputable.

Saturday, December 6: President Roosevelt made a final appeal to EMPEROR HIROHITO of JAPAN for peace. There was no reply. Late this same day, the U.S. code-breaking service begins intercepting a 14-part Japanese message and deciphers the first 13 parts, passing them on to the president and secretary of state. The analysis is that a Japanese attack is imminent, probably in Southeast Asia.

Sunday, December 7: The last part of the message, stating that diplomatic relations with the United States were to be broken off, reached Washington in the morning and was decoded around 9:00 A.M. About an hour later, another message is intercepted, instructing the Japanese embassy to deliver the main message to the Americans at 1:00 P.M.

The U.S. War Department then sends out an alert to commanders in Hawai'i, but uses a commercial telegraph because radio contact with Hawai'i is temporarily broken. Delays prevent the alert from arriving at headquarters in Oahu until four hours after the attack has already begun.

Pearl Harbor had not been in a state of high alert. Commanders Kimmel and Short believed that no attack was immediately forthcoming. Perhaps the most

objective and fair evaluation is in Roberta Wohlstetter's *Pearl Harbor: Warning and Decision* (1962). Wohlstetter deemed the problem one of separating signal from noise. There was contradictory evidence of other targets, as indeed there were (Southeast Asia, the East Indies, the PHILIPPINES). There were purely administrative signals. There was also cognitive dissonance, in that people had a tendency, then as now,

The Friedmans

IT IS probably safe to say the greatest codebreaking husband-and-wife team in all history is William and Elizabeth Friedman. As William Friedman broke the Japanese diplomatic code in the years prior to World War II, in early 1943, working with the highly classified U.S. Coast Guard Unit 382, Elizabeth Friedman broke the *Abwehr* (German intelligence service) code (see "Women Cryptanalysts" page 38). Colonel Friedman had headed a joint army-navy team (no frequent occurrence in those times) in actually rebuilding the Japanese encoding machine. He suffered a nervous breakdown in 1941, from which he probably never fully recovered. However, four individuals from his team visited the British Government Code and Cipher School at Bletchley Park as America was entering the war. In exchange for a PURPLE (Japanese code) machine, the United States was given access to the Enigma (German code) apparatus, which was the Nazi encoding machine smuggled out of Poland. This paved the way for an intelligence alliance between the United States and England that is unique in history and that continues to this day.

to find that which they wished to believe. There were also mistakes of priority and messages in Washington, D.C., that were either not delivered to the right people or, if they were delivered, not read until too late.

Seldom did a translation of a complete Japanese operational plan fall into Allied hands. High-frequency radio intercepts were not always possible because of locations and atmospherics. Those that were intercepted were often incomplete, and the texts often dealt with logistics issues, material casualties, weather, movements of various units, personnel issues, and items of no immediate importance.

OP-20-G AND FRUPAC

The U.S. Navy had a high degree of sophistication in code breaking prior to WORLD WAR II. OP-20-G, (a Navy code-breaking group) in Washington, D.C., was a mature industry by the outbreak of World War II. Certain officers had been brought up in the culture of naval intelligence and were sailors, cryptanalysts, Japanese linguists, and analysts all in one, and some of the best were stationed at Pearl Harbor. Fleet Radio Unit Pacific (FRUPAC) was commanded by Joseph Rochefort, a straight-talking Texan. A Japanese linguist, he was an excellent code-breaker and analyst. He had once broken the U.S State Department code just to show that it was too easy to do ("They were mad as hell").

FRUPAC, through equal parts hard work and genius, assembled the entire Japanese order of battle for Midway (see MIDWAY, BATTLE OF). Six months after Pearl Harbor, they made possible a major victory by enabling an American ambush. Throughout World War II, FRUPAC would provide invaluable intelligence for submarine operations, the great central Pacific offensive of 1944, and attacks upon the home islands of Japan.

Further Reading: Richard Aldrich, *Intelligence and the War against Japan* (Cambridge University Press, 2000); W. J. Holmes, *Double Edged Secrets: U.S. Navy Intelligence Operations in the Pacific during World War II* (Naval Institute Press, 1978); Edwin T. Layton, *And I Was There: Pearl Harbor and Midway, Breaking the Secrets* (Naval Institute Press, 1985); Gordon W. Prange, *At Dawn We Slept: The Untold Story of Pearl Harbor* (McGraw-Hill, 1981); Roberta Wohlstetter, *Pearl Harbor: Warning and Decision* (Stanford University Press, 1962).

—RAY BROWN

Investigations of Responsibility

Almost as soon as the bombs stopped falling on Pearl Harbor, the process of assigning blame began. Although television had not yet made its mark on the American cultural landscape, radio brought news of the attack into the living rooms of Americans within hours, and many newspapers printed special editions covering the attack.

Thus there was a hue and cry to know how the U.S. Navy could have been caught by surprise by a nation that was largely considered to be racially inferior. The obvious scapegoats for the systemic INTELLIGENCE failure were the two commanders in Hawai'i, Admiral HUSBAND E. KIMMEL and General WALTER C. SHORT. As a result of the rush to judgment, there has long been serious question of whether truth was sacrificed for the sake of political expediency.

THE INITIAL INVESTIGATION

The first investigation took place two days after the attack. On December 9, Secretary of the Navy FRANK A. KNOX took a plane to Pearl Harbor to see first-hand the scope of the disaster. There was no unified Department of Defense at that time, and the army and navy were separate cabinet-level departments. Critics would later point to the lack of administrative unity as a contributing factor in the failure to share intelligence. This awareness led first to the creation of the Joint Chiefs of Staff and ultimately the postwar reorganization of the military into a unified command structure.

The chaos and confusion Knox found left him with a very negative impression. It was particularly embarrassing because the situation stood in stark contrast to the public statement he had made only days before the attack, that the U.S. Navy was ready for any opponent and could casually beat the Japanese. He was convinced that the commanders must be dismissed from their posts. He returned to Washington, D.C., with a lengthy typed report, which he presented to President FRANKLIN D. ROOSEVELT.

ROBERTS COMMISSION INVESTIGATION

The next investigation, by the Roberts Commission, was held in a more deliberate manner. However, there has subsequently been extensive criticism of it on the grounds that it was tainted by political bias, and used methodologies that were inherently hostile toward the commanders in Hawai'i (see HISTO-RIANS' VIEWS). For instance, while the portion of the investigation that was held in Washington, D.C., treated senior officers with considerable respect and solicitude, during the portion held in Hawai'i neither Kimmel nor Short was permitted to retain legal counsel while giving testimony, a restriction that was in breach of military law as well as civilian law. Furthermore, neither was notified that he might be considered a defendant in a court-martial. Instead, they were both told that the investigation was purely a fact-finding commission. Finally, the manner of

questioning was actively hostile toward both men. Several times they were required to answer complicated multipart questions with a yes or no, a constraint guaranteed to make them look bad no matter what they said.

The final slap came at the end, when Justice Owen Roberts presented his findings to the president. Roosevelt ordered the commission's report published immediately. Suddenly the public was fed an account that portrayed the commanders in Hawai'i as culpable for the success of the Japanese attack. After having been given a solemn reassurance that they could testify freely because it was only a fact-finding commission, this report could only come as a blow to these two men who had endured the death of many friends and associates, as well as the ruin of their careers. Both men immediately demanded a full court-martial to attempt to clear their names.

NAVY, ARMY, AND OTHER INVESTIGATIONS

As questions arose about the impartiality of the Roberts Commission, the Navy Judge Advocate General's office suggested that another investigation be held. Admiral Thomas Hart, formerly commander in chief, Asiatic Fleet, was chosen to head the new investigation. Hart made a particular point of making sure that Kimmel was notified of all the meetings of the investigative committee; however, Kimmel never attended any of them. In his memoirs, Kimmel stated that he considered the restrictions under which his participation would be permitted to be prejudicial against him, but some historians have suggested that this decision was a major mistake on his part.

Shortly after Hart's investigation concluded, the army put together a board of inquiry to investigate Short's performance and culpability. This investigation's report was particularly critical of Army Chief of Staff GEORGE C. MARSHALL. As a result, the report was quickly covered up, with the rationale that it would damage the war effort by raising questions about the fitness for command of men still in critical positions, particularly Marshall.

Even as the army's board of inquiry was investigating Marshall's failure to keep Short apprised of the shifting situation before December 7, the navy was conducting a parallel board of inquiry. Publishing the inquiry's findings was problematic because of the necessity to keep secret the results of the effort to break the Japanese military code, known as MAGIC (see CODES, JAPANESE). The first and longest section of the navy report had to be classified top secret and not published in any way, while the second section, which completely exonerated Kimmel, asserted he had been deprived of vital intelligence

that would have enabled him to better assess and respond to the situation—but the section could not specify just what information Kimmel had been denied. As a result, the case made by the portion that was disseminated was not as persuasive as it might have been.

As the Navy Board of Inquiry was finishing its work, the Clarke Investigation was being rushed through. Colonel Carter W. Clarke, working on oral instructions from Marshall, examined the way in which top-secret intelligence materials were handled in the weeks leading up to the attack. The winds message, a coded diplomatic message disguised to look like an innocent weather report, was a critical bone of contention in this investigation. It would later become a subject of major interest for revisionist historians, due to suspicion that such a message

JAPANESE AIRCRAFT DEPLOYMENT *The first wave of the Japanese attack on Pearl Harbor consisted of 51 dive-bombers, 49 horizontal bombers, 40 torpedo bombers, and 43 fighters. The second attack consisted of 79 dive-bombers, 54 horizontal bombers, and 36 fighters.*

was indeed transmitted and that records of it were subsequently suppressed and even destroyed.

As a result of the critical report delivered by the Army Board of Inquiry, Secretary of War HENRY L. STIMSON detailed Colonel Henry C. Clausen to do yet another investigation. There is ample evidence that the purpose of this investigation was to outright destroy the credibility of any witness whose account disagreed with the line that Stimson wanted for of-

THE ARIZONA LIVES ON *The USS* Arizona, **ABOVE TOP,** *on the East River in New York City, on her way to sea trials in 1918. Note the "bird cage" towers.* **ABOVE BOTTOM** *The* Arizona's *docking quay in Pearl Harbor.*

ficial consumption. Only the necessities of war allowed him to get away with what he did, for in any other time he would have most likely faced charges for witness tampering and perhaps even suborning perjury. Nearly 40 years later, Clausen published a lengthy book, *Pearl Harbor: Final Judgement,* in which it was clear he had remained loyal to his former commander. From a historical perspective, it is slanted to the extreme, but is of interest in understanding the psychology that allowed blatant, willful blindness to evidence. One of the book's claims is that both Marshall and DOUGLAS MACARTHUR should be exonerated of any possible fault.

Parallel to the Clausen investigation, Knox conducted his own investigation. He originally intended to tap Admiral JAMES O. RICHARDSON for the job. Richardson declined on the basis that the foremost qualification was to have no fixed ideas regarding the matter. His firm belief that much of the responsibility could be traced directly to the Oval Office was an immediate disqualification. Knox finally approached Admiral Henry K. Hewitt. Kimmel freely lambasted Hewitt's proceedings as a star-chamber investigation in which he was given no opportunity to defend himself. Furthermore, Hewitt is known to have been close friends with Clausen, and there is ample evidence that they shared opinions on the importance of protecting the leaders in Washington, D.C., and ensuring that the commanders in Hawai'i took the blame for the disaster.

JOINT CONGRESSIONAL COMMITTEE INVESTIGATION

The final investigation was that of the Joint Congressional Committee, convened between November 1945 and May 1946. In theory, it should have been free to conduct an investigation unhampered by the wartime secrecy that had hobbled several of the earlier investigations. In practice, several major factors distorted the investigation almost beyond recognition. First, the death of Roosevelt made many of the participants uncomfortable about being overly critical of the administration's role in Pearl Harbor. Second, with congressional elections coming up in November 1946, every politician was keenly aware of the necessity of having the investigation play well in their home states.

To give the Joint Congressional Committee its due, it was a substantial undertaking that spanned months of hearings. The proceedings and findings were published in a series of thick books, which have become an important source for historians seeking the truth about the proper apportionment of blame for the Pearl Harbor attack. The committee was made up of five senators and five representatives, two of each were Republicans and the other three Democrats. As a result, the administration being investigated enjoyed a comfortable majority of party loyalists.

Even with these handicaps, the Republican members of the committee strove to carry out a thorough investigation. They sought to examine Roosevelt's personal files to confirm suspicions that the late president had deliberately set the Pacific Fleet (see PACIFIC FLEET, U.S.) up for a fall in order to get the UNITED STATES into the war. Committee members also questioned the whereabouts of disputed documents and paid special attention to the situation of Captain Alwin Kramer, a former intelligence officer who was being held in the lockdown mental ward of Bethesda Naval Hospital, and who was believed to have been deliberately driven to madness by systematic persecution in order to get him to change key testimony.

Once the formal hearings began, over 100 witnesses were called to testify, including the aging and ailing CORDELL HULL, former secretary of state, who had to be carried into the hearing chambers. In lieu of verbal testimony he brought a 20,000-word statement for the members to read and examine. Kimmel and Short were each given an opportunity to testify at length, although neither was satisfied that their cases had been presented accurately. In the end, the committee returned a report stating that significant errors of judgment had been made at all levels, but which soft-pedaled those of the administration and of the high command in Washington, D.C. Exoneration of the commanders in Hawai'i was lost in the verbiage.

Further Reading: Edward L. Beach, *Scapegoats: A Defense of Kimmel and Short at Pearl Harbor* (Naval Institute Press, 1995); Henry C. Clausen and Bruce Lee, *Pearl Harbor: Final Judgement* (Crown Publishers, 1992); Gordon W. Prange, *Pearl Harbor: The Verdict of History* (McGraw Hill, 1986); John Toland, *Infamy: Pearl Harbor and Its Aftermath* (Doubleday, 1982).

—LEIGH KIMMEL

Isolationism

*I*solationism refers to the preference of the American people, and some U.S. presidential administrations, for keeping out of the business of other nations. In the 20th century, isolationism developed a negative connotation, but George Washington regarded it as a good idea, advocating in his Farewell Address that the United States "steer clear of permanent alliances."

The assumption behind the isolationist view was that the UNITED STATES had different, possibly superior, interests and values to those held by Europeans. Rather than exercising military or diplomatic involvement, the United States would serve as the example to lead the world in the direction of freedom and democracy. Isolationism was never total; some isolationists had no objection to American expansion, as long as it was in the Western Hemisphere or in the Pacific and East Asia.

Isolationism dated to the colonial settlers who came to avoid religious persecution, economic dislocation, war, and other difficulties in Europe. They either assumed or hoped that America would be the shining beacon lighting the way for the world. Alliances such as the one with France during the Revolution were entered into with reluctance and abandoned as soon as practicable.

During the 19th century, the United States completed its expansion across North America and established economic and political influence, if not territorial control, in much of the Caribbean, the Pacific, and Asia. Wars with Britain, Mexico, and Spain occurred against a backdrop of expansion at the expense of Native Americans. At the same time that the U.S. was employing an expansionist foreign policy from an isolationist perspective, entanglements with Europe were increasing as the American economy became more complex and involved with the world economy, and communications and transportation progress brought news and immigrants. By the time of World War I, it seemed to many that national security depended on a peaceful world. Foreign entanglements made it hard for the United States to remain aloof.

Woodrow Wilson wanted to make the world safe for democracy. That meant that the United States would have to take a broader and more consistent role in the world. Not all American leaders agreed. Western agrarian progressives such as William Jennings Bryan of Nebraska and Robert M. LaFollette of Wisconsin were strongly opposed to America's meddling in irrelevant European affairs. Even when the United States entered the war, it entered not as an ally but as an associate power. After the war the United States rejected the Versailles Treaty and the League of Nations, signing a separate peace in the 1920s.

Although tired of war and suspicious of crusades abroad, the American people could not indulge their desire for "normalcy," a withdrawal from the world. In 1925 President Calvin Coolidge admitted, "The people have had all the war, all the taxation, and all the military service they want." But the world did not go away. Diplomacy continued, and in 1921 nine Asian and European nations sent representatives to the Washington, D.C., conference that established a 10-year moratorium on the construction of battleships. The Washington Conference also set the relative sizes of the major navies: for each five British or American naval vessels, JAPAN got three, while Italy and France could have one and three-fourths. Japan and Italy were not totally satisfied, but they bided their time.

As if stopping the naval arms race were not enough, in 1928 Secretary of State Frank B. Kellogg and French Foreign Minister Aristide Briand agreed to the Kellogg-Briand Pact that renounced war as a tool of diplomacy. Eventually, Kellogg-Briand had 61 signatories. Unfortunately, it lacked any means of enforcement. Legally, according to critics, it was an "international kiss," a meaningless action.

In the 1920s and 1930s *isolationism* was a term of opprobrium but that did not stop isolationist sentiment from being widespread. After all, the Great War had proved not so great after all. At least that is what the people understood from the 1934–36 Senate investigations of the munitions companies during the war.

Students opposed the war, but they were not alone. So did veterans: in April 1935, on the 18th anniversary of America's entry into the war, 50,000 veterans marched for peace in Washington, D.C. A 1935 poll reported that 70 percent agreed that American involvement in World War I was a mistake. For the public, obscene profiteers had started a war and killed millions for no more than private gain.

Politicians recognized the "writing on the wall" of the voting booth and enacted the NEUTRALITY ACTS of 1935, 1936, and 1937. These laws embargoed sales of arms to belligerents, barred American ships from entering war zones, outlawed the arming of American ships, and prohibited Americans from being passengers on belligerent ships. Congress had no intention of allowing the rise of conditions that had given cause to enter the Great War.

President FRANKLIN D. ROOSEVELT was a practical politician who declined to expend much political capital in fighting the isolationist tide. He made token objections to the provisions of the Neutrality Acts but signed them into law.

Isolationism was stronger among Republicans than Democrats, and its strongest areas were the Midwest and Great Plains. Agrarian populists blamed the eastern business, financial, and intellectual elites for getting the United States entangled in European matters.

As early as 1938, modernized Japan was taking raw materials and territory on the Asian mainland, GERMANY was militarizing and making one bloodless conquest after another, and Italy was seeking a new Roman empire in Africa. Roosevelt read the changes and began small steps in bringing assistance to the Allies. Isolationist sentiment remained strong.

By 1940, in Europe, Britain stood alone against the Axis, and Japan's conquest of East Asia was largely accomplished. Isolationists might have dreamed of a "Fortress America," economically and politically

America First Committee

BEGUN BY R. Douglas Stuart Jr. and other students, including Gerald Ford and Potter Stewart, the America First Committee (AFC, as it came to be called in August 1940) opposed President Franklin Roosevelt's increasing violations of neutrality—beginning with the removal of the arms embargo in 1939 after the invasion of Poland. The AFC called for an impregnable America. "Fortress America" could withstand foreign assault and would preserve democracy. Rooseveltian "aid short of war" would weaken national defense and increase America's risk of being drawn into war. The AFC tried to exclude communists, fascists, and others who were not committed to America's self interest above all.

AFC supporters included Charles Lindbergh, actress Lillian Gish, and leaders of business, the arts, politics, and other walks of American life. The AFC attracted the attention of Roosevelt and the FBI, and some members claimed they were blacklisted for membership. An important member was John T. Flynn, a muckraking journalist who had made his career attacking the New Deal and its similarities to European fascism. Through a speakers' bureau the AFC opposed LEND-LEASE, destroyers-for-bases, bases in Iceland, the Atlantic Charter, aid to Russia, and the extension of the draft. The AFC dwindled to insignificance after Pearl Harbor.

barring all intruders from Asia and Europe, but the reality was that America was too dependent on the rest of the world. The Axis must be stopped, even if it meant war—so agreed a majority of Americans in the fall of 1940.

That did not mean that the isolationists retreated. In 1940 and 1941 many prominent and not so prominent Americans backed the America First Committee. Although the isolationists were unable to stop Roosevelt's various aid programs for the Allies, 80 percent of Americans did not want the United States to declare war. Only the attack by Japanese on Pearl Harbor finally broke the isolationist sentiment. (See also ISOLATIONIST PRESS.)

Further Reading: Wayne S. Cole, *Roosevelt and the Isolationists, 1932–45* (University of Nebraska Press, 1983); Robert Dallek, *Franklin D. Roosevelt and American Foreign Policy, 1932–45* (Oxford University Press, 1998); Justus D. Doenecke, *In Danger Undaunted: The Anti-Interventionist Movement of 1940–41 as Revealed in the Papers of the America First Committee* (Hoover Institution Press, 1990).

—JOHN H. BARNHILL, PH.D.

Isolationist Press

Few Americans were as unsurprised by the attack on Pearl Harbor as those who ran the nation's isolationist newspapers. For though they had fought FRANKLIN D. ROOSEVELT's interventionism at every turn, all were convinced that he was intent on provoking America's entry into a global conflict and would undoubtedly succeed.

Yet when the Japanese attacked Pearl Harbor, the isolationist press fell right in line behind the war effort. Some did it with an "I told you so" attitude—but none were reluctant in their all-out backing of the war effort. These publishers considered themselves

to be ardent patriots for whom supporting a president during wartime was unquestioned. But it is also true that war with JAPAN was not the isolationist movement's great concern. Two of the most important isolationist publishers—William Randolph Hearst and Robert McCormick—had been warning of Japan's war-mongering. Hearst, in fact, had been preaching against the Japanese threat to U.S. long-term security for 40 years before Pearl Harbor.

There were three major publishers in the isolationist movement. Norman Chandler ran the *Los Angeles Times*, which held sway in California. The *Times* first post–Pearl Harbor editorial, headlined "Death Sentence of a Mad Dog," utterly repudiated the isolationist movement. It warned: "Let there be an end of internal dissension and an end to the foolish, if well-meant, isolationist obstructionists. It is time to sink without a trace not only the enemy abroad but also the enemies within."

Second was Hearst, who controlled the nation's largest newspaper chain. His concern was over what he perceived as Roosevelt's determination to bring America into the war against Nazi GERMANY; war with Japan, he believed, was inevitable—which is why Hearst continually pressed Roosevelt to bolster the Pacific defense. Still, Hearst faulted Roosevelt for having refused to accept Japan's bid to broaden its sphere of influence in Asia, asserting that "We have only to treat Japan in a fair and friendly fashion to establish firm peace between Japan and the U.S."

When war finally came, Hearst was unstinting in his support—a decision made easier by the fact that the initial enemy was Japan, against whom he had been militating since the turn of the century.

But the publishers who enraged Roosevelt the most constituted what he acidly labeled "the McCormick-Patterson axis." It consisted of McCormick, publisher of the *Chicago Tribune*, his cousin

Joseph Patterson, publisher of the the tabloid *New York Daily News*, Patterson's sister Cissy, publisher of the *Washington Times-Herald*, and his daughter Alicia Guggenheim, publisher of the fledgling Long Island newspaper, *Newsday*.

Like Hearst, McCormick had seen war with Japan as inevitable. Still, he blamed Roosevelt for forcing Japan to ally itself with Germany and blithely predicted that the presence of the U.S. Pacific fleet (see PACIFIC FLEET, U.S.) at Pearl Harbor would preclude any Japanese attack on Hawai'i.

Like other isolationists, McCormick and the *Tribune* quickly got behind the war effort. A front-page editorial on December 8 declared that "War has been forced on America by an insane clique of Japanese militarists." Still, it was only a matter of days before the *Tribune* was pressing for a full investigation of Pearl Harbor, and it soon became a persistent critic of Roosevelt's conduct of the war.

McCormick's cousin, Patterson, may have been almost the last American to learn about the Japanese attack. On December 6, he and his wife had gone to a South Carolina retreat belonging to his son-in-law, Harry Guggenheim—a home which, quite deliberately, had no telephones or radios. Not until the morning of December 8 did the Patterson chauffeur turn on a car radio and shout: "I think you'd better come and listen. I think we're at war."

The *Daily News* publisher headed home, but decided to stop off first in Washington, D.C. White House Press Secretary Steve Early thought it would be a good idea to reconcile the president and the *Daily News* publisher, a onetime Roosevelt loyalist who had broken away the previous year over what he termed Roosevelt's increasing pursuit of "dictatorial" powers to push the United States into war.

When they met on December 10, Patterson volunteered to provide "what aid I can be in the war effort." Roosevelt's acid reply: "There is one thing you can do, Joe, and that is to go back and read some of the editorials you have written during the past year." For the next 15 minutes, Patterson wrote in a private memorandum, "he gave me a pretty severe criticism of the way the *News* had conducted itself. ...He likewise said that as a result of our conduct we had delayed 'the effort' by from 60 to 90 days."

Rather than reconciling the two men, the confrontation only intensified the bitterness between them. When Roosevelt, at one of his press conferences, showed off a captured German Iron Cross medal, he told one reporter to give it to John O'Donnell, Patterson's Washington correspondent, saying he had earned it. (See also ISOLATIONISM.)

Further Reading: Robert Gottlieb and Irene Wolt, *Thinking Big: The Story of the* Los Angeles Times (G.P. Putnam's Sons, 1977); Leo E. McGivena, *The News* (News Syndicate, 1969); David Nasaw, *The Chief: The Life of William Randolph Hearst* (Houghton Mifflin, 2000); Richard Norton Smith, *The Colonel* (Houghton Mifflin, 1997); Frank C. Waldrop, *McCormick of Chicago* (Prentice-Hall, 1966).

—ERIC FETTMANN

AT RIGHT *William Randolph Hearst, who controlled the nation's largest newspaper chain, argued against U.S. involvement in the war until December 7, 1941, when he changed his position and whole-heartedly supported the war.*

J

Japan

The bombs that fell on Pearl Harbor on December 7, 1941, were the culmination of one of the most rapid military and economic expansions in history. In less than 50 years, JAPAN moved from obscurity to international power. Yet at the same time, the traditions that hurled Japan with such rapidity onto the world stage were older than those of the great European powers.

The samurai traditions that defined Japan's warrior elite were the modern incarnations of ancient forms of behavior and warfare that dated back to the nation's internal civil wars between feuding shoguns and warlords and external battles against Chinese, Mongol, and Korean enemies. The contempt Japan showed for enemies with greater power, like the Americans and the British, was in turn based on Japan's slamming shut her door to foreigners in the 1600s, and only grudgingly tolerating them in the decades that followed Commodore Matthew C. Perry's epic voyage to Japan in 1853.

Once the door opened, the Japanese were eager to take advantage of the West's advanced technology, feverishly modeling available sources. In some areas, they succeeded—patterning their battle fleet after Britain's Royal Navy, for example. In other areas, they were less successful—they modeled their constitution after GERMANY's, which made the minister of war a serving general and directly accountable to the emperor, not the civilian ministers. At the same time, Japan maintained many of its medieval traditions, such as the divinity of the emperor.

Japan's modernization was done at breakneck pace. Railways, factories, hospitals, and schools were built. Between 1860 and 1895 Japan went from being a nearly illiterate nation to one with 95 percent literacy.

SINO-JAPANESE CONFLICT

When Japan entered the European-led scramble for chunks of Asia in the late 1890s, they moved fast. They defeated China in 1895 and the Russians in 1905, seizing Formosa and Korea. In defeating the Russians, an Asian nation had for the first time vanquished a European power. Japan's warships now dominated the Pacific.

Still, Japan signed an alliance with Britain, and under this treaty, entered World War I on the Allied side—a fact often forgotten today. But after seizing German holdings in China and New Guinea, and the MARSHALL ISLANDS and CAROLINE ISLANDS in 1914, Japan limited her activities mainly to making territorial claims and imposing demands upon a fellow Allied power, China.

In the 1920s, droughts, earthquakes, and bank failures crippled the nation. Japan lacked oil, resources, and arable land. In addition, the British did not renew their alliance, and America put a halt on Japanese immigration to the UNITED STATES. And the disarmament treaties that put lids on construction of new battleships by Britain, the United States, and Japan created a 5:5:3 ratio, with Japan held at three.

During this period, the Japanese army, which did not answer to the politicians or the electorate, became increasingly politicized, with senior and ju-

A FEAT OF MODERN ENGINEERING *Japan rose from the ashes of World War II to be a major economic power at the end of the 20th century. In 1998, Japanese engineers completed the construction of the Akashi-Kaikyo Bridge, the longest spanning suspension bridge in the world. Linking the city of Kobe with Awaji-shima Island, the bridge spans 12,828 feet—equal to the Sears Tower laid end-to-end eight times. The unique design of the bridge allows it to stand against 180-mile-per-hour winds, and earthquakes with a magnitude of 8.5 on the Richter scale. The bridge holds records as the longest, tallest, and most expensive ($4.3 billion) suspension bridge ever built.* **AT RIGHT,** *the Akashi-Kaikyo Bridge at sunset.*

nior officers calling for *hakko isshiu*, the "eight corners of the world under one roof."

The hotbed of expansionism was the Kwantung Army in Manchuria, ostensibly there to protect Japanese interests, but in actuality, an autonomous force that often disobeyed orders from Tokyo. Army officers allied with extremist nationalistic societies and occasionally assassinated moderate civilians. Between 1912 and 1941, six Japanese prime ministers were murdered.

When the Great Depression occurred in 1929, the Japanese economy was devastated further. Army officers as high as the minister of war argued that expansion in Asia and conquest of China would give Japan needed resources to prosper and Japanese residents frontiers to develop. Japanese troops attacked local Chinese army units across Manchuria and took control of the Chinese province from its rightful owners. After the coup, Tokyo ratified the actions of the insubordinate generals and proclaimed the independent state of Manchukuo, setting up a puppet government.

THE RISE OF MILITARISM

With Manchuria swallowed up, the Japanese turned it into an industrial powerhouse, relying on forced labor and ruthlessness. The militarists were gaining control in Japan, and the government could not stop them. Instead, they played into the army's hands. To eliminate dissent, the government set up a military police force, the Kempei Tai, which functioned as a "thought-control police" to weed out anything not considered "Japanese." All political thought except extreme nationalism was banned.

In this climate, the army tried to make their power official in January 1936, by launching a coup in Tokyo. The 1st Infantry Division took over key government buildings and Japan was frozen for four days. Then it collapsed, and 1,483 conspirators faced courts-martial. While the ringleaders got the firing squad, the army was able to protect its most skilled officers and operators.

The generals even forced the government to give the army and navy the right to appoint the war and navy ministers. This gave the armed forces the power to make governments dissolve or not take power, by simply refusing to appoint a war or navy minister.

The drive into China was marked by appalling acts of violence. In Nanking, Japanese troops went on a three-month orgy of murder and terror, butchering nearly 500,000 people. Japanese bombers attacked and sank the American gunboat USS *Panay* (see *PANAY* INCIDENT). Both atrocities angered U.S. President FRANKLIN D. ROOSEVELT, who called for and got a voluntary American embargo on arms sales to Japan (see SANCTIONS AGAINST JAPAN).

By November 1938, the Japanese invasion of China was a stalemate. Chiang Kai-shek's government, such as it was, was still operational in Chungking, his armies in the field. Mao Zedong's Communist forces had launched a massive guerrilla war behind Japanese lines. The Soviets supplied Chiang with tanks, guns, planes, and airmen, which enabled the Chinese to inflict 16,000 casualties on the invaders in a battle.

ALIGNMENT WITH GERMANY

The army's solution was alliance with Germany against the Soviet Union and the Western powers. The Japanese were already signatories to the Anti-Comintern Pact and had tangled with Soviet forces on the Manchurian border.

Another idea the army had was to create the GREATER EAST ASIA CO-PROSPERITY SPHERE, which would be a group of Japanese-ruled puppet nations whose manpower and resources would fuel Japan's prosperity. Japanese planners and politicians now sought the conquest of the British, Dutch, French, and American possessions in the Pacific.

The new powers in the Japanese cabinet, Foreign Minister YOSUKE MATSUOKA and War Minister HIDEKI TOJO, beat the drum for aggression with great energy once WORLD WAR II broke out in Europe. With the major Western powers locked in mortal combat in Europe, they would not be able to put up any kind of resistance in Asia.

When France collapsed to ADOLF HITLER in 1940, the Japanese pressured the French colonial government in Indochina to stop sending supplies to Chiang Kai-shek and admit Japanese troops and airmen. The French yielded on August 30, 1940 (see FRENCH INDOCHINA).

But Japan's continued aggression in Asia, combined with her German alliance and arms production, earned American anger. In July 1940, the United States slapped an embargo on iron and other sales to Japan—a knife thrust at the heart of Japan's economy and war-making ability. The Japanese were enraged.

On September 27, Japan agreed to sign the Tripartite Pact with Germany and Italy, making Japan the third Axis power. The treaty recognized and respected "the leadership of Japan in the establishment of a new order in East Asia." Hoping to turn the Tripartite Pact into a four-way alliance, Matsuoka prevailed upon the Soviet Union to sign a nonaggression pact with Japan in April 1941, which ended the border tension in Manchuria (see RUSSIA–JAPAN RELATIONS).

In July, the Japanese landed 50,000 troops in French Indochina, turning the occupied area into a springboard for attack into Indonesia. The Americans, British, and Dutch retaliated by freezing Japan's

ABOVE *Leathernecks of the U.S. veteran Fourth Marine Regiment photographed during their occupation of the Japanese naval base of Yokusuka.*

assets and canceling all remaining commercial agreements. Japan's oil imports were cut by 90 percent.

THE DECISION TO ATTACK THE UNITED STATES

Either Japan gave up her war in China or she seized Indonesia's oilfields. To do so would almost certainly result in war with the United States. An attack would have to be launched by the end of 1941. Civilian oil supplies would be exhausted by mid-1942.

The Japanese believed that a quick victory over the Western powers in Asia would also lead to a quickly negotiated and victorious peace. On October 14, Prime Minister Fumimaro Konoe begged Tojo to accept withdrawal from China. Tojo refused. Two days later Konoe resigned. Tojo became prime minister, and Japan was in the hands of the army and the secret police. Shortly after that, the Japanese navy adopted Admiral ISOROKU YAMAMOTO's plan for the attack on Pearl Harbor.

Yet negotiations continued (see DIPLOMATIC RELATIONS), which kept pushing the deadline for war back, through September, October, and into

November. The Japanese set a deadline of November 29, then pushed it back to December 7—December 8 in Japan.

On November 20, Japan offered the Americans a promise not to seize the oil islands, if America would not interfere in any settlement of the Chinese war and would supply Japan with oil. In return, Japan would begin gradual withdrawal from French Indochina.

U.S. Secretary of State CORDELL HULL responded on the 26th, with a four-point note calling for Japanese withdrawal from China and Indochina, recognition of Chiang Kai-shek's government, Japan's nullification of the alliance with Hitler, and a Japanese nonaggression pact with the Western powers, including the Soviet Union.

The Japanese considered the demands a threat to their national existence. On December 1, the Japanese Imperial Conference faced the question of war or peace before the emperor. Tojo told the conferees that "in the circumstances our Empire has no alternative but to go to war." After the meeting, Hirohito quietly remarked that regrettable though the decision was, war was the lesser evil.

With the decision taken, the military men began cutting orders and sending radio messages to the emperor's far-flung armies and navies, all deploying for battle across the Pacific. Among the forces that received the coded message, "Climb Mount Niitaka: 1208," was the First Air Fleet, under Vice Admiral Chuichi Nagumo, which had been at sea since November 26. The force's destination was Pearl Harbor.

Further Reading: Herbert P. Bix, *Hirohito and the Making of Modern Japan* (HarperCollins, 2001); Haruko Taya Cook and Theodore F. Cook, *Japan at War: An Oral History* (The New Press, 1993); W. Scott Morton, Charlton Lewis, J. Kenneth Olenik, *Japan: Its History and Culture* (McGraw Hill, 2004).

—DAVID H. LIPPMAN

Japanese Aircraft

On the morning of December 7, 1941, Japanese commander Mitsuo Fuchida led his fleet of fighter airplanes and bombers in the predawn gloom north of Pearl Harbor. Six Japanese aircraft carriers, the *Akagi*, *Kaga*, *Soryu*, *Hiryu*, *Shokaku*, and *Zuikaku*, had transported a total of 387 Mitsubishi A6M2 Zero-sens, often called "Zeros," Nakajima B5N2s that the Allies named Kate, and Aichi D3A1 Model Hs that the Allies later named Val. After the planes left the carriers, they flew steadily for one hour and 40 minutes.

Fuchida scanned the horizon for the first sight of their target. A long white line of breaking surf appeared directly beneath his plane and the northern shore of Oahu appeared through the surf.

The 183 Japanese planes that made up the first wave of the attack veered right toward the west coast of Oahu and Fuchida noted that the skies over Pearl Harbor were clear. Soon he spotted Pearl Harbor across the central Oahu plain, covered by a film of hovering morning mist. "I peered intently through my binoculars at the ships riding peacefully at anchor. One by one I counted them. Yes, the battleships were there all right, eight of them! But our last lingering hope of finding any carriers present was now gone. Not one was to be seen."

Fuchida ordered his radioman to send the attack command. Lieutenant Commander Murata's torpedo bombers headed to lower altitudes to launch their torpedoes. Lieutenant Commander Itaya's fighters raced ahead to drive American fighters from the air. Takahashi's dive-bomber group climbed out of sight for altitude and Fuchida's bombers made a circuit toward Barbers Point. He didn't see any American fighters or American fire.

The first Japanese bomb in the attack fell on Wheeler Field, and then Japanese planes dive-bombed Hickam Field and the bases at Ford Island. Murata feared that the smoke from the bombing attacks would hide his targets, so he shortened his torpedo bombers' approach toward Battleship Row and released his torpedoes. Soon waterspouts dotted the harbor.

Itaya's fighters controlled the airspace over Pearl Harbor. His men shot down the four American fighters that managed to get aloft and by 8 A.M. there were no American planes in the air. The Japanese fighters began strafing the airfields.

Lieutenant Zenji Abe left the deck of the Japanese aircraft carrier *Akagi* and approached Pearl Harbor in his Aichi dive-bomber. He was the commander of a company of nine bombers and he and his crew members had trained without rest in several aerodomes at Kyushu. All the airplanes of six carriers had been assembled there and had used a naval vessel for target practice. "When I think of the hard training of the torpedo planes that flew every day over Kagoshima City, almost touching the rooftops and having the practice of dropping torpedoes at low altitude, I must conclude that our higher command headquarters had already begun to plan the raid for Pearl Harbor."

Abe proved to be an accurate prophet. One day in October 1941 all of the officers above the grade of company commander in Abe's task force were assembled at the Kasanohara Aerodrome in the southern part of Kyushu. Commander Minoru Genda, the operation staff officer, walked into the conference room and opened the curtain on the front wall. Behind it were models of Pearl Harbor and Oahu Island constructed all across the wall. And now Abe was really at Pearl Harbor and everything was proceeding "just like an exercise."

Fuchida's level bombing group began its bombing run toward the battleships moored along Ford Island. Fuchida himself missed on his first pass and others made as many as three runs before releasing their bombs. Fuchida was about to start his second bombing run when a shattering explosion sent out shock waves as far as Fuchida's plane several miles away from the harbor. A huge column of dark red smoke billowed hundreds of feet into the air. The bombs rained on the USS *Arizona* (see ARIZONA, USS) had exploded her powder magazine.

By now the Japanese bombers were encountering fierce antiaircraft fire, but they made several more successful runs and hit two more battleships. Fuchida believed one of them to be the USS *Maryland* (see MARYLAND, USS). The strafings and bombings had left Pearl Harbor in smoke and flames and devastated the ships, planes, and airfields that had stood in an impressive array an hour before. American antiaircraft fire grew more intense, but Fuchida did not see any

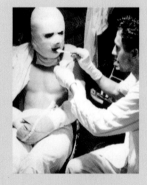

ABOVE LEFT *U.S. military forces view a Japanese plane shot down at Pearl Harbor.* **ABOVE RIGHT** *Pressure bandaged after they suffered burns when their ship was hit by a Kamikaze attack, men are fed aboard the USS Solace, 1945.*

Airplanes from the Sea

THE JAPANESE expertly operated the carrier-based airplanes that took off from their carriers. The Aichi D3A1, Model II (code-named Val by the Allies), the plane that Lieutenant Abe flew at Pearl Harbor, was a two-seated, carrier-based dive-bomber powered by a 1,000-horsepower Mitsubishi MK8 Kinsei 44 engine. The Val could climb to 31,200 feet and fly at 242 miles an hour at 7,500 feet. It had a range of 1,130 miles. Its armament was two 7.7 mm forward-firing machine-guns, and it could carry up to 700 pounds of bombs. The dive-bombing Val accumulated an 80 percent accuracy record during the first years of WORLD WAR II.

The Japanese began to produce the Nakajima B5N2 (Type 97), code-named Kate, in the early 1930s. Kate was powered by a 1,000-horsepower Nakajima Sakae II engine and it could climb to 10,000 feet fully loaded in less than eight minutes. Its normal range extended 634 miles and its overloaded range could stretch to 1,200 miles. The Kate carried one flexible 7.7 mm machine-gun in the rear cockpit and either one 1,764-pound torpedo or three 551-pound bombs. The Japanese used 40 of the new Kates against the American Pacific Fleet (see PACIFIC FLEET, U.S.) at Pearl Harbor with an accuracy rate of at least 50 percent.

The Mitsubishi Zero-sen fighter (Mitsubishi A6M2 Zero-sen, code-named Zeke) outperformed almost anything in the skies and the Japanese began to consider it invincible. The Zero was powered by a 940-horsepower Nakajima Sakae engine and it could climb at nearly 3,000 feet per minute to 20,000 feet. The Zeke had a top ceiling of 32,810 feet and a range of 1,160 miles. It could achieve a top speed of 335 miles per hour. The Zeke's armament was two 7.7 mm forward-mounted machine-guns, two 20 mm Mark 3 cannon, and two 132-pound bombs.

ABOVE LEFT *Japanese planes ready for takeoff to Pearl Harbor.* **ABOVE RIGHT** *Front view of two Japanese duck boats found at Kumamoto.*

enemy fighter planes. "Our command of the air was unchallenged," he marveled.

The first-wave attack planes made their way back to their carriers, but Fuchida remained over Pearl Harbor to assess damage and observe the second wave attack. At 8:54 A.M., 25 minutes after the first wave had left Pearl Harbor, the 167 airplanes of the second wave, led by Commander Shigekazu Shimazaki, joined the attack. This fleet consisted of 54 Kate high-level bombers heading for the airfields, 78

Val dive-bombers aiming at battleship targets, and 35 Zeke escort fighters.

Despite spirited American resistance, the second-wave bombing at Hickam Field took a heavy toll of aircraft, hangars, and barracks. The combined effects of both waves of aircraft attacks left Kaneohe Naval Air Station ruined. Gunfire peppered Ewa Marine Corps Air Station. Hidden by smoke, Wheeler Field and Ford Island escaped relatively unscathed although Wheeler Field lost more than half its aircraft during the attacks. Three airplanes at Bellows Field on the southeast windward coast of Oahu were destroyed. Five defending airplanes from Haleiwa Field on the northern coast of Oahu and five from Wheeler Field managed to get into the air and claimed eight victories between them.

The second-wave assault lasted for about an hour. At 10:00 A.M., Fuchida left Pearl Harbor. When he returned to the *Akagi*, Fuchida informed Vice Admiral Chuichi Nagumo that the American air and sea defenses had been destroyed. He and Genda pressed for another strike against the repair facilities and fuel-storage tanks. If these were destroyed the Americans could not use Pearl Harbor and they would be forced to retreat 2,000 miles across the sea to the west coast of the UNITED STATES. Nagumo believed that the Japanese force had accomplished its mission and he did not want to endanger the fleet any longer. He waited until all of the second-wave airplanes had been recovered, then the Japanese fleet withdrew as swiftly and silently as it had come. (See also PEARL HARBOR: ACTION REPORT.)

Further Reading: "Attack at Pearl Harbor, 1941: The Japanese View," www.eyewitnesstohistory.com/pearl2.htm (cited February 2006); Walter Lord, *Day of Infamy* (Holt, 2001); Nathan Miller, *War at Sea: A Naval History of World War II* (Scribner, 1995); Scott C.S. Stone, *The Way It Was: December 7, 1941* (Island Heritage Publishing, 1995).

—**KATHY WARNES**

Japanese Fleet

A Japanese task force of six aircraft carriers, *Akagi, Kaga, Hiryu, Soryu, Shokaku,* and *Zuikaku,* two battleships, *Hiei and Kirishima,* heavy cruisers *Tone* and *Chikuma,* light cruiser *Abukuma,* and nine destroyers glided like ghost ships on a northern Pacific route toward Hawai'i. The *Kido Butai,* or task force, was the largest number of aircraft carriers ever to operate together.

Two other destroyers, the *Ushio* and *Sazanami,* were detached to bombard Midway Island. Oil tankers for refueling in mid-ocean, an operation that caused Admiral ISOROKU YAMAMOTO some concern because it had never before been attempted, and several submarines completed the force. The submarines carried two-man MIDGET SUBMARINES, which were supposed to enter Pearl Harbor.

Yamamoto, commander in chief of the Japanese fleet since 1939, had originated the Japanese plan to attack Pearl Harbor, calling for a surprise aircraft strike against the American fleet. Powerful and battle-worthy Japanese ships and superb oxygen-driven Long Lance torpedoes made the Japanese a formidable force. The Japanese navy's planes outranked most American naval aircraft and the Mitsubishi A6M2 Zero fighter would soon become legendary. The Japanese navy also had substantial land forces as well as carrier-based aircraft, and JAPAN had only one ocean to consider compared to the U.S. Navy's two-ocean front. Japanese soldiers, sailors, and airmen were skilled fighters imbued with the centuries-old tradition of the Samurai.

The Japanese had precedents for a surprise attack. They had launched such attacks in victorious wars against China and Russia. Ironically, as early as 1928, American Rear Admiral William A.

Fate of the Japanese Ships

AIRCRAFT CARRIERS

AKAGI. In June 1942, the *Akagi* was set on fire by planes from the USS *Enterprise*, the carrier that had not been in Pearl Harbor during the attack.

KAGA. The *Kaga* was set on fire by planes from the USS *Enterprise* and sunk on June 4, 1942.

SORYU. The *Soryu* was set on fire and blown up by planes from the USS *Yorktown* on June 4, 1942.

HIRYU. The *Hiryu* was set on fire by planes from the USS *Yorktown* and USS *Enterprise* on June 4, 1942.

ZUIKAKU. The *Zuikaku* was struck by six torpedoes and seven bombs from aircraft from the USS *Essex* and USS *Lexington* and sunk on October 25, 1944.

SHOKAKU. The *Shokaku* was sunk by three torpedoes fired from the USS *Cavalla* on June 19, 1944.

BATTLESHIPS

HIEI. The *Hiei* was sunk by airplanes from the USS *Enterprise* on November 13, 1942.

KIRISHIMA. The *Kirishima* was disabled by gunfire from the USS *Washington* on November 15, 1942.

HEAVY CRUISERS

TONE. The *Tone* was sunk by airplanes from Task Force 38 on July 24, 1945.

CHICKUMA. Airplanes from Task Force 77.4.2 and torpedoes from the USS *Nowake* scuttled the *Chickuma* on October 25, 1944.

SCOUTING FORCE

ABUKUMA. U.S. Army Air Force airplanes sank the *Abukuma* on October 26, 1944.

DESTROYERS

TANIKAZE. The *Tanikaze* was torpedoed and sunk by the USS *Harder* on June 9, 1944.

ABOVE TOP *Site of bomb damage on Ford Island.* **ABOVE BOTTOM** *540 Wright Avenue, Wheeler Field, Hawai'i, after a Japanese plane crashed on the property.*

HAMAKAZE. Airplanes from the USS *Hornet* and USS *Cabot* sank the *Hamakaze* on April 7, 1945.

URAKAZE. The USS *Sealion* torpedoed and sank the *Urakaze* on November 21, 1944.

KASUMI. Badly damaged by airplanes from Task Force 58, the *Kasumi* was scuttled on April 7, 1945.

ARARE. The USS *Growler* torpedoed and sank the *Arare* on July 5, 1942.

KAGERO. U.S. Navy aircraft sank the *Kagero* on May 8, 1943.

SHIRANUI. Airplanes from Task Force 77 sank the *Shiranui* on October 27, 1944.

AKIGUMO. The USS *Redfin* torpedoed and sank the *Akigumo* on April 11, 1944.

Moffett, chief of the Bureau of Aeronautics, had argued that the only effective way to prevent an attack would be continuous offshore patrols to prevent enemy carriers from getting within range.

After overcoming the objections of the Naval General Staff to a strike by a fleet of carriers, using the force of his personality to the point of threatening to resign, Yamamoto implemented his plan. Beginning in February 1941, Commanders Minoru Genda, Mitsuo Fuchida, and Kosei Maeda trained air crews and completed strategy under a shroud of secrecy.

The task force assembled at Tankan, and departed for its mission on November 26, 1941, proceeding eastward in northern latitudes and observing radio silence. On December 2, 1941, due north of Midway Island, fleet commander Vice Admiral Chuichi Nagumo received a radio message from Yamamoto. The message said "Climb Mount Niitaka," which meant that the planned attack against Pearl Harbor should go forward. The carriers, battleships, and cruisers reached the launching point about 200 miles north of the Hawai'ian Islands at 6 A.M. on December 7, 1941.

Earlier a force of 16 fleet-style submarines had been deployed off Pearl Harbor, where five of them launched midget submarines. Two of the midgets succeeded in getting inside Pearl Harbor on December 7, but were sunk. One grounded on the north coast of Oahu, and its two-man crew was captured. The others did not return to the recovery area and this entire submarine effort accomplished very little.

By 9:45 A.M. on December 7, 1941, the last Japanese airplane, Commander Fuchida's, droned through the skies over Oahu on its way to the waiting Japanese fleet. Nagumo had moved the task force 40 miles closer, so that pilots would have an easier flight returning to their carriers. By 10 A.M. and for the next two hours, Vals, Kates, and Zekes (see JAPANESE AIRCRAFT) streamed back to their carriers. Two lost bomber pilots radioed, asking for a navigation fix, but Nagumo had ordered strict wireless silence. Cheering crewmen lined the carrier decks, counting the returning aircraft.

The Japanese had reason to celebrate and order another attack. Pearl Harbor was strewn with the wreckage of 19 ships, including most of the battleships of the U.S. Pacific Fleet (see PACIFIC FLEET, U.S.). The Japanese had destroyed at least 265 American planes with American casualties of 2,403 sailors, soldiers, and airmen dead and 1,178 wounded (see PEARL HARBOR: ACTION REPORT).

Measured against this the Japanese had lost only 29 planes, 55 airmen, and one submarine with a crew of 65 men. All the men on the midget submarines died except those captured from one that got stuck on the reef and all five of their midget submarines were lost.

The Japanese did not order another attack and they did not celebrate their victory for very long. Aboard the *Akagi*, Fuchida succinctly made his report, ending it with a recommendation for another attack. Nagumo had different ideas. He announced that the Pearl Harbor attack had achieved the anticipated results and ran up a signal flag on the *Akagi*'s masthead. The signal flag was the order for the task force to turn north and run for home. The Japanese task force slipped away as stealthily as it had arrived at Pearl Harbor.

Further Reading: Paul S. Dull, *A Battle History of the Imperial Japanese Navy: 1941–45* (Naval Institute Press, 1978); Donald M. Goldstein and Katherine V. Dillon, *The Pearl Harbor Papers: Inside the Japanese Plans* (Brassey's, 1999); Nathan Miller, *A Naval History of World War II: War at Sea* (Scribner, 1995).

—KATHY WARNES

Japanese American Internment Camps

War PANIC seized the UNITED STATES, particularly the west coast. Some officials worried that Japanese in America might spy for JAPAN. On February 19, 1942, President FRANKLIN D. ROOSEVELT authorized the relocation of 120,000 people of Japanese descent to internment camps. Two-thirds of the internees were American citizens. Canada interned 23,000 Japanese Canadians in British Columbia.

Ten major camps opened between March and October 1942. Nine closed in October and November 1945. Most camps housed fewer than 10,000 people, but two—Tule Lake, California, and Poston, Arizona—had populations nearing 20,000. Internees had only 48 hours to evacuate and were allowed to bring only a limited number of possessions. In camp, internees lived in barracks and used community washing, laundry, and eating facilities. Food and coal were sometimes rationed. Armed guards watched over the internees. Some died from inadequate medical care or from the stress of internment.

Tule Lake became the camp for those who disobeyed rules. In 1943 it was redesignated a segregation center, when it became home for those who refused to take a loyalty oath. Only 5,788 Japanese Americans renounced their citizenship rather than take the oath, and after the war only 357 declined to ask for their citizenship's return.

Public Proclamation 21 in December 1944 freed internees to return home in January 1945. After the war, some 5,000 Japanese and Japanese Americans either returned or went to Japan while others rebuilt their lives in the United States. Eighty-five percent of Japanese Americans lived on the west coast in 1940; only 42 percent did in 2000.

Although many accepted the internment as necessary, others regarded the detention as a violation of the detainees' right of habeas corpus. Habeas corpus challenges included *Hirabayashi v. United States* (1943) and *Korematsu v. United States* (1944), both ruled in favor of the United States.

The federal and some state governments began atoning for these camps in the 1970s. Internment camp time was covered under Social Security and federal civil service rules, and a 1984 law allowed some recovery of damages. Congress passed the Civil Liberties Act of 1988 recognizing the injustice of internment camps. It authorized payment of $20,000 to each of the 60,000 surviving internees and payments began in the early 1990s.

Further Reading: Karen Alonso, *Korematsu v. United States* (Enslow, 1998); Roger Daniels, *Prisoners without Trial* (Hill and Wang, 1993); Fusao Lawson Inada, *Only What We Could Carry* (Heyday Books, 2000); National Asian American Telecommunications, "Exploring the Japanese American Internment," www.jainternment.org/camps (cited November 2005).

—JOHN H. BARNHILL

ABOVE LEFT *Young evacuees arriving at the Turlock, California, center.* **ABOVE RIGHT** *A young girl waits with the family baggage before leaving by bus for a center.*

K

Kidd, Isaac (1884–1941)

By December 1941 Admiral Isaac Campbell Kidd was the commanding officer of Battleship Division One, with his flag on the battleship USS *Arizona* (see ARIZONA, USS). An Ohioan by birth, he had risen steadily through the ranks of the navy since his graduation from the naval academy at Annapolis, Maryland. By 1941, he was nearing normal peacetime retirement age, and command of Battleship Division One was intended to be his final posting. It is possible that he had chosen USS *Arizona* as his flagship based upon sentiment, since he had been its captain some years earlier. In a coincidence, the ship had been the division flagship at that time as well, and the admiral was none less than CHESTER NIMITZ.

Although no longer a young man, Kidd retained the erect bearing and energetic step of a much younger man, in large part because of his strong commitment to physical fitness. He had encouraged the organization of athletic teams among the ship's crew as a way of maintaining good levels of physical activity.

On the night before the attack, he had received the captain of the USS *Vestal*, a repair ship that was scheduled to do some work on USS *Arizona*. Although the actual direction of the work would be supervised by the ship's captain, Franklin Van Valkenburgh, naval protocol required a formal visit to the admiral before work began in the morning.

Those plans would not come to fruition, for everything would change at the moment the Japanese attacked shortly before 8:00 A.M. that

Sunday morning. Kidd was in his quarters in the section aft known as "flag country" when the attack began. He hurried to his duty station on the flag bridge, buttoning the jacket of his dress white uniform as he went. Several witnesses later recall having seen him uncharacteristically with one button undone, apparently having missed it in his haste to dress.

Jim Foster, a young Texan manning a gun that would normally be operated by 16 sailors, believes that he may well have been the last to have seen the admiral alive. He recalls the admiral slapped him on the shoulder and said, "Man your battle station, son." What happened afterward can only be conjectured from fragmentary and often conflicting accounts. There are arguments as to exactly where Kidd stood at the moment the explosion occurred. Some claim that he was standing on the flag bridge proper, while others suggest he took refuge in a small shelter nearby.

However, there is little question that he died instantly when engulfed by the blast in the forward powder magazine that broke USS *Arizona*'s back and killed most of the ship's complement. Foster is definite in recalling the complete destruction of the area, which he compares to pouring molten metal. Later, Kidd's academy class ring, partially melted but still identifiable, was found stuck to a mast. It has been hypothesized that his body was blown there before being consumed by the flames. The ring was subsequently returned to his widow. Kidd was one of several officers to receive a posthumous CONGRESSIONAL MEDAL OF HONOR as a result of the events of December 7, 1941.

Further Reading: Joy Waldron Jasper, James. P. Delgado, and Jim Adams, *The USS Arizona: The Ship, the Men, the Pearl Harbor Attack, and the Symbol that Aroused America* (St. Martin's Press, 2001); Michael Slackman, *Target: Pearl Harbor* (University of Hawai'i Press, 1990).

—LEIGH KIMMEL

Like Father, Like Son

ADMIRAL KIDD'S son, also named Isaac, was a midshipman at the time of the attack, and graduated shortly after his father's death. He had an illustrious career, and his last duty station was as commander in chief of the Atlantic Fleet. Throughout his career he remained adamant about the importance of never forgetting the lesson of PEARL HARBOR, and of always remaining vigilant against America's enemies. One of the coincidences of his life was having his career cross paths with that of Franklin Van Valkenburgh, Jr., son of the USS *Arizona*'s captain; the captain's son also found success in the Cold War navy.

AT LEFT *Machine-gunfire damage to the Hickam Base barracks remains unrepaired as a memorial.*
AT RIGHT *The post cemetery at Schofield Barracks.*

Kimmel, Husband E.
(1882–1968)

Admiral Husband Edward Kimmel was born in Henderson, Kentucky, a small town on the Ohio River. His father, Manning Marius Kimmel, was a West Point graduate who had the dubious honor of having fought on both sides in the American Civil War. As a young man, Kimmel hoped to attend West Point as well, but when he contacted his Congressman, he was informed that all appointments to West Point had been promised. However, the Congressman had available an appointment to the naval academy at Annapolis.

Determined to make the best of the situation, Kimmel tackled his studies with a verve, and graduated 13th in a class of 62. From there he launched a naval career of steadily developing success, building his reputation on hard work and attention to detail. He specialized in battleships and particularly in gunnery, and during World War I he helped the British Royal Navy improve their accuracy with a spotting technique he developed. Afterward, he was given his own independent command, and after alternating periods of staff and line work, attained flag rank.

Thus in the early months of 1941 he seemed a natural pick for replacing Admiral JAMES O. RICHARDSON, who had angered President FRANKLIN D. ROOSEVELT by repeatedly and bluntly stating that basing the Pacific Fleet (see PACIFIC FLEET, U.S.) in Hawai'i was foolish and dangerous. No sooner had Kimmel arrived, he tackled his new duties with an energy that left many of his staff struggling to keep up.

On the morning of December 7, 1941, Kimmel was at his home on Makalapa Hill, overlooking Pearl Harbor. He was preparing for an early game of golf with his opposite number in the army, Lieutenant General WALTER C. SHORT, when the telephone rang. It was the duty officer at fleet headquarters, relaying the message of Lieutenant William Outerbridge of the destroyer USS *Ward*, reporting the sighting of a Japanese mini-submarine. Even as Kimmel was trying to determine the significance of this report, he heard the first bombs falling outside. Immediately he knew this was war and told fleet headquarters to send a car to pick him up.

While he stood outside waiting for the car's arrival, he watched helplessly as one after another battleship took terrible damage. As an old battleship man, he could not help but recognize the extent of

A Private Sorrow

ALTHOUGH ADMIRAL Kimmel's disgrace and the subsequent personal attacks on him are well known, he also endured a deeply personal grief. All three of his sons served as naval officers in the war. The two elder sons followed in their father's footsteps to Annapolis, while the youngest had to gain his commission through a university Reserve Officer Training Corps (ROTC) program. His eldest son, Commander Manning Marius Kimmel, was the captain of the submarine USS *Robalo* when it was lost on July 2, 1944. According to the official reports, the sub went down with all hands when it struck a mine in the Balbac Strait, north of Borneo in the South Pacific. However, liberated American prisoners of war brought with them a story of a number of survivors of the USS *Robalo* who were captured by the Japanese and eventually killed.

the damage being done before his eyes, nor could he fail to understand the significance for his future. His next-door neighbor, the wife of Captain John B. Earle, saw him standing there and was immediately moved to sympathy by his expression of helpless horror.

ABOVE LEFT *Admiral Husband E. Kimmel, commander in chief of the Pacific Fleet.* **ABOVE RIGHT** *Secretary of the Navy Frank Knox at a press conference in Seattle, Washington, July 5, 1943.*

Moments later the official navy car arrived to take him to headquarters. As soon as he arrived, he gathered his staff in an effort to organize some kind of response. While they were standing by the great windows overlooking the harbor, there was a sudden noise. It was a bullet, piercing the glass and striking the admiral in the chest. However, the bullet's energy was already spent, and it did no more than bruise the admiral.

That bullet could have killed Kimmel, and he would probably have been acclaimed as a hero of the day, a brave but doomed defender. However, his rep-utation as a living man was to suffer grave injury. Within days he was relieved of command and sent back to the mainland to face one investigation after another. As the time passed, he became increasingly convinced that the navy was out to persecute him for December 7. He died an embittered man on May 14, 1968. One of his former staffers said that he died of a broken heart.

Further Reading: Edwin L. Beach, *Scapegoats: A Defense of Kimmel and Short at Pearl Harbor* (Naval Institute Press, 1995); Michael Gannon, *Pearl Harbor Betrayed: The True Story of a Man and a Nation under Attack* (Henry Holt, 2001); Gordon W. Prange, *At Dawn We Slept: The Untold Story of Pearl Harbor* (Viking, 1981).

—LEIGH KIMMEL

Knox, Frank A. (1874–1944)

As secretary of the navy, Frank A. Knox was the first government official outside Hawai'i to learn of the attack on Pearl Harbor. It was his responsibility to officially inform the president of the UNITED STATES. Knox's reaction, after the initial shock, was one of absolute amazement: "My God, this can't be true! This must mean the Philippines!" he exclaimed when Admiral HAROLD R. STARK broke the news to him. "No, sir," replied Stark. "This is Pearl!"

Just the day before, he had released his annual report to President FRANKLIN D. ROOSEVELT, boasting that the U.S. Navy was "the finest in the world" and that "we can defend ourselves in two oceans." Now, he had to tell Roosevelt that much of that navy had been sunk by Japanese bombers. And, as secretary of the navy, he would have to bear the brunt of criticism for the disaster.

To his credit, Knox moved swiftly. Within days, he flew to Pearl Harbor to personally inspect the attack site and report back to the president; on his recommendation, Roosevelt relieved Pearl Harbor's two top commanders, Admiral HUSBAND E. KIMMEL and General WALTER C. SHORT, of their commands.

Historians now generally agree that Kimmel was unfairly targeted as a scapegoat, though the navy has refused to posthumously exonerate him (see HISTORIANS' VIEWS; INVESTIGATIONS OF RESPONSIBILITY). To his death, Kimmel remained bitter at his treatment: in a 1954 book setting forth his defense, Kimmel charged that Roosevelt, Knox, and Stark were the true villains of Pearl Harbor and "must answer on the day of judgment like any other criminal."

Knox was a surprise choice to head the navy, the department for which Roosevelt had served as assistant secretary and for which he retained a special fondness. Though he had served in the Spanish-American War and World War I, Knox had no naval experience; a onetime general manager for the Hearst newspapers, he had most recently been publisher of the *Chicago Daily News*, which differed with Roosevelt on domestic matters, but supported his foreign policy.

Moreover, Knox was a Republican, and not just any Republican: in 1936, he had been the GOP candidate for vice president against Roosevelt, after barely losing the top spot on the ticket to Alf Landon. When Knox agreed to join his rival's cabinet, he was publicly and unceremoniously drummed out of the Republican Party. To that he replied: "I am an old soldier who fought in two wars, and if my Commander in Chief gave me a rifle and told me to start out again, I'd do it. I'm an American first and a Republican second."

His boasting about the navy's battle strength was unwise, given the administration's fear of general military unreadiness (see PREPAREDNESS) and became an embarrassment following the attack. But Knox oversaw a mammoth rebuilding effort and, before long, his words once again rang true.

Further Reading: Robert Barkdoll, "Kimmel Lays Pearl Harbor to Roosevelt," *Washington Post & Times-Herald* (December 7, 1954); Marquis Childs, "Secretary Knox," *Washington Post* (May 2, 1944); Otto Friedrich, "December Surprise," *New York Times* (September 1, 1991); "Knox Forecast of Jap Surprise Raid Disclosed," United Press (November 21, 1945); Walter Trohan, "Recalls Crisis Air on Pearl Harbor Eve," *Chicago Tribune* (December 7, 1965).

—ERIC FETTMANN

The soldier's chapel **ABOVE TOP** *and the base hospital* **ABOVE BOTTOM** *at Schofield Barracks.*

L

Lend-Lease

In a December 17, 1940, press conference, President FRANKLIN D. ROOSEVELT brought public attention to Britain's pressing financial need in the war against the Axis powers (see AXIS POWERS IN 1941): "If one's neighbor's house was on fire and one had a hose, one didn't say to him, 'Neighbor my garden hose cost me $15, you have to pay me $15 for it.' No, one connected the hose, helped put out the fire, and got the hose back afterward."

The idea of what was to be known later as Lend-Lease was the culmination of long study by the president and key members of the administration. The problem hinged on how best to assist the British, while remaining within the constraints imposed by the NEUTRALITY ACTS of the mid-1930s and, at the same time, taking into account isolationist feelings in the Congress and among the general public (see ISOLATIONISM).

The Neutrality Acts, which stated that once the president had declared a state of war existed between two countries, Americans could not sell or transport arms to them, were the first obstacle. A modification forbade loans to the belligerents (countries at war). In 1939 restrictions were eased to allow for "cash and carry" trading with warring nations. The administration decided that a solution must be found that left the acts in place, but still permitted needed aid.

Britain took full advantage of the legislative change, but soon found its requirements far outstripped its ability to pay cash from its gold

A WEATHER-WORN *old destroyer,* AT LEFT, *one of 50 being given by America to Britain as part of the U.S. Lend-Lease Act to aid England against Germany and the Axis, 1940.*

and dollar reserves. By 1940 this cash crunch had reached crisis proportions. Roosevelt, facing an election fight in November and never wanting to get out ahead of public opinion, moved cautiously in pointing out the importance of Britain's survival, without suggesting concrete steps for assistance that might give ammunition to his political opponents.

By the latter part of 1940, France had fallen and Britain was readying for a German invasion. In the UNITED STATES there was serious concern that war materials, provided to Britain in what could turn out to be a lost cause, might better be retained at home for American defense. At the same time the idea was emerging that aiding others contributed to American national security. This concept came to be the keystone of the Lend-Lease program.

After Roosevelt's reelection, Britain anticipated an early move by the United States to provide assistance, but the U.S. government was unresponsive. On November 23, the British ambassador, in a "calculated indiscretion," informed the press that "Britain was broke." Shortly thereafter, Roosevelt received a letter from Prime Minister WINSTON CHURCHILL setting forth Britain's perilous financial situation and the need for immediate assistance. According to presidential confidant Harry Hopkins, Roosevelt studied the Churchill letter at length, then expressed the outline of what was to become the Lend-Lease program.

On December 29, the president spoke directly to the American people in a "fireside chat." He said that for its own security America must go all out in support of nations like Britain, Greece, and China by becoming "the great arsenal of democracy." Encouraged by an enthusiastic response, the president immediately directed his administration to translate the broad outline of Lend-Lease into a legislative form.

The Treasury Department was tasked with the lead in preparing legislation that would give the president wide powers in providing Lend-Lease aid. Quietly, so as not to arouse anti-British sentiment in the Congress, the draft bill was coordinated with British experts, as well as with the State, War, and Navy departments. With speed unusual in Washington, D.C., the draft bill was completed and approved by Roosevelt on January 7, 1941.

The bill, carefully named "An Act to Promote the Defense of the United States" and happily, if not accidentally, given the number H.R. 1776, started through the Congress on January 10. From the beginning there seemed little doubt that the president had the power to force the bill through, but he preferred full and open debate on its provisions to marshal public opinion behind the Lend-Lease concept.

ABOVE LEFT *American-made revolvers shipped to England under Lend-Lease are unpacked at an English ordnance depot.* **ABOVE RIGHT** *An English girl, member of the Auxiliary Territorial Service, moves armfuls of American rifles just arrived from the U.S. under Lend-Lease. By war's end, 38 nations had benefited from Lend-Lease aid, valued at over $49 billion.*

Opposition centered on three main points: first, that it gave the president "unlimited, unprecedented, and unpredictable powers," second, that it increased the chance that the United States would be brought into the war, and third, that Communist Russia might be a beneficiary under the act. In addition to Treasury Secretary Henry Morgenthau Jr., administration leaders testifying in favor of the bill included Secretary of War HENRY L. STIMSON and Navy Secretary FRANK KNOX. Joining Republicans speaking in opposition were the former ambassador to Great Britain, Joseph P. Kennedy, and famed aviator Charles A. Lindbergh. The bill passed both houses of Congress without a serious fight and was signed into law on March 11.

Lend-Lease solved a critical British financial problem. Moreover, it organized the American defense production effort by assigning priorities to the various competing U.S. and foreign military agencies and speeded the conversion of American industry to a wartime footing. By war's end some 38 nations, principally the Soviet Union and those of the British Commonwealth, had benefited from Lend-Lease aid, valued at over $49 billion. This program was an early manifestation of the "special relationship" that Winston Churchill saw as existing between the United States and Great Britain. That relationship was to bind the two countries together during World War II and the Cold War to follow.

Further Reading: John Morton Blum, *V Was for Victory: Politics and American Culture During World War II* (Harcourt Brace Jovanovich, 1976); James MacGregor Burns, *Roosevelt: The Lion and the Fox* (Harcourt Brace Jovanovich, 1956); William L. Langer and S. Everett Gleason, *The Undeclared War, 1940–41* (Harper and Brothers, 1953); Robert E. Sherwood, *Roosevelt and Hopkins: An Intimate History* (Harper and Brothers, 1948).

—ALAN HARRIS BATH, PH.D.

Literature and Films

The American military disaster at Pearl Harbor has been depicted several times in novels and films. Although the same basic facts are presented in all of them, each incarnation puts these facts to startlingly different uses. The event has been employed as a government propaganda tool, a two-fisted paean to the enlisted man and an attack on the officer class, an indictment of American military leadership, and as a celebration of the "greatest generation." The various portrayals of December 7, 1941, tell us as much about America's changing popular understanding of history as about the historical date itself.

DECEMBER 7: CONSTRICTED DOCUMENTARY

The first American film about Pearl Harbor was made just weeks after the attack, in the early months of 1942. Secretary of the Navy FRANK A. KNOX authorized a project intended to provide "a complete motion picture factual presentation of the attack." Acclaimed director John Ford and cinematographer Gregg Toland were chosen by the Office of Strategic Services to collaborate on the film. Their documentary, *December 7,* was a debacle. Judged to be potentially harmful to national morale, the 83-minute working print of the film was confiscated by navy officials. The movie featured elaborate restagings of the day's military events. Some scenes were realistic enough to be presented as authentic footage in later documentaries. The movie also included a segment devoted to the navy's successful efforts to repair damaged ships and return them to duty. But the filmmakers risked censure when they attempted to explain why the attack on Pearl Harbor had succeeded.

Their analysis contained much inflammatory speculation, reflecting the American public mood in 1942. The film focused on two issues: American lack of PREPAREDNESS and Japanese American disloyalty. The movie features a fictional character, Uncle Sam, who is portrayed as being well-intentioned but also somewhat naïve and fatuous. He boasts on December 6 that Pearl Harbor is the "largest naval fortress in the world." Unconcerned about Japanese militarism because "3,400 miles separate Tokyo from Hawai'i," he proclaims that the PHILIPPINES and Singapore (see MALAYA AND SINGAPORE) might be in peril, but "it can't happen here." He is shown slumbering that night, his dreams filled with pretty island women whispering "aloha," intercut with disturbing visions of ADOLF HITLER and EMPEROR HIROHITO.

The bulk of the film's analysis dealt with the 135,000 Japanese Americans who lived in Hawai'i. Uncle Sam, proud of America's reputation as a "melting pot," insists that the Japanese Americans are "full-fledged American citizens" who "conduct themselves accordingly." The film includes an emotional real-life speech made by a Japanese American community leader at a patriotic rally. Japanese

ABOVE *The P40B, a plane used in the film* Tora! Tora! Tora!, *created jointly by American and Japanese filmmakers during the Vietnam era.*

Americans are also shown after the attack buying war bonds and donating blood. But another character, the folksy Mr. C, Uncle Sam's conscience, provides a very different viewpoint. The Japanese Americans, he tells Uncle Sam, are "hyphenated" citizens, with their own culture and morals. He warns: "When Tokyo speaks, they all listen." The film then provides a long sequence in which Japanese Americans going about their daily occupations—as gardeners, barbers, and dockworkers—are shown to be spying for JAPAN. In fact, the Japanese government relied for logistical information primarily on public sources such as the HONOLULU *Star-Bulletin* newspaper, which regularly provided details about the activities of the Pacific Fleet (see PACIFIC FLEET, U.S.). The film left the viewer to decide between the arguments for loyalty or disloyalty.

Significantly, navy officials reacted angrily to the accusations of unpreparedness but had only one objection to the portrayal of Japanese Americans. The sole sympathetic segment, the speech at the patriotic rally, was ordered cut. Ford was allowed to rework the movie, reducing the running length to 33 minutes. Most of the scenes that provided context and explanation were eliminated. The new version, which simply showed the drama of the attack and the scenes of navy salvage, won the Academy Award for best short documentary in 1943.

FROM HERE TO ETERNITY: PEARL HARBOR AS WATERSHED EVENT

During the 1950s, James Jones, a former army infantryman who had been stationed at Schofield Barracks in Oahu during the attack (see OAHU AIRFIELDS AND BASES), became an American literary sensation after he published his novel *From Here to Eternity* (1951). The book sold more than 2.5 million copies during the decade and won the National

Book Award. The success stemmed from the novel's reputation as a brutally honest account of the dysfunctional prewar American military. According to Jones, even with war looming, the daily life of the military in Hawaiʻi was consumed with non-military matters. Soldiers are portrayed as wasting their energies in stultifying routines, broken up by epic weekend bouts in HONOLULU's bars and whorehouses. Jones realistically depicted the military's profane, hypermasculine culture.

The novel presents the events of December 7 from the point of view of the enlisted men at Schofield Barracks. A typical Sunday morning finds many soldiers hungover or still inebriated. In the mess hall for breakfast, amid "their drunken laughter and horseplay and the clashing of cutlery," they hear what they guess to be dynamiting at Wheeler Field. Many of them crowd outside, where they see a red-haired soldier running down the middle of the street, shouting wildly. "Quite suddenly right behind him came a big roaring, getting bigger and bigger," and then an airplane emerges over the trees and shoots him down. The men gulp coffee and try to comprehend what is happening. Over the course of the attack, some of the soldiers behave bravely, a few cower in their bunks, and most of them mill around until belatedly given commands. The adrenaline and gunfire provide them with a sense of release after months of mundane activity. They do not realize the day's implications. Only when they see the devastation at Pearl Harbor later in the afternoon do they feel "a queasiness in the testicles."

Jones believed the attack represented a transformational event for America, not only militarily but also culturally and socially. He later wrote: "I remember thinking with a sense of the profoundest awe that…a watershed had been crossed which we could never go back over." *From Here to Eternity* emphatically portrays a prewar army of enlisted men bonding or scuffling over booze and poker, and officers grasping after their own careers. The novel's two protagonists, both quintessential "good soldiers," struggle with their own willfulness.

From Here to Eternity was adapted for film in 1953, at the height of Cold War McCarthyism—an era, director Fred Zinnemann later remarked, when "there was an *automatic* respect for Federal authority. To voice doubts about any of its symbols—the Army, Navy, or FBI—was to lay oneself open to deep suspicion." The Department of Defense refused to allow the filmmakers to shoot at Schofield Barracks or to use military equipment unless substantial changes to the story were made. The filmmakers reluctantly acceded to several of these demands: in particular, the condemnation of officers was toned down, so that a corrupt commander, given a promotion in the novel, is forced by his superiors to resign.

Nevertheless, *From Here to Eternity* became one of the finest—and bravest—mainstream Hollywood movies of the 1950s, a big-budget, glossy melodrama that still manages to retain much of the book's gritty critique. Zinnemann and screenwriter Daniel Taradash were particularly good at using film shorthand to imply what Jones had spelled out in graphic detail. Their ability to telescope gave clarity and intensity to issues explored in the 850-page, sometimes verbose novel.

For example, the book's depiction of a stockade, which fills more than 200 pages, is implied by one short but chillingly effective scene: a sadistic guard says, "Hello, tough monkey" to a newly arrived prisoner, grins, and grasps his truncheon. When the prisoner later dies after escaping, the viewer can imagine what must have happened to him. Like the novel, the film portrays the Pearl Harbor attack as a sudden, irreversible shock. Coming just a few minutes before the end of the picture, the attack renders insignificant the stories told during the previous two hours—personal histories that mean nothing when world history intrudes.

TORA! TORA! TORA! AND WORKS BY WOUK: A BROADER CONTEXT

Neither *December 7* nor *From Here to Eternity* attempts to offer substantive analysis of the military disaster. Rather, these works tell us how Americans during the 1940s and early 1950s responded emotionally to the event. *December 7* casts about for scapegoats, while *From Here to Eternity* offers an insider's exposé of military life. By the 1970s, filmmakers and novelists were able to appraise the attack with the benefit of cool hindsight, often drawing from historical scholarship. The film *Tora! Tora! Tora!* (1970) and Herman Wouk's novels *The Winds of War* (1971) and *War and Remembrance* (1978) pay attention to the context of world events in 1941 and to Japanese and American military logistics. These works offer a fair amount of factual and explanatory information. At the same time, the film and the novels sometimes have the feel of a textbook brought to life.

Tora! Tora! Tora! was created jointly by American and Japanese filmmakers. As a result, the picture has an admirable evenhandedness—a rarity in war movies. Taking a systematic approach, the film spends more than an hour laying the groundwork for the attack and then another hour depicting the military engagement, raising significant points along the way. American military leaders are shown to be complacent in their belief that Pearl Harbor is too shallow for a torpedo assault. Insisting that espionage is a more likely threat than aerial bombardment, they decide to guard planes at Hickam Field by lining them up together, unwittingly making them easy targets.

The movie also portrays successful efforts to intercept and decode Japanese diplomatic cables, which clearly indicate that an attack may be imminent. This sets off alarm bells among INTELLIGENCE experts; but official Washington is accurately depicted as a bureaucratic maze in which important information can be waylaid. When the military is finally placed on full alert, the response is slipshod and even lazy. For example, the movie shows an event from the morning of December 7: before the bombing commences, an American ship sinks a Japanese midget submarine operating just outside the harbor. When reported, this portent is ignored by a duty officer, who carps about the need for "confirmation." The "hero" of *Tora! Tora! Tora!* is the imaginative, disciplined Japanese navy. This raises the question of whether the film is too lenient in presenting the Japanese side of the story. Although the movie briefly notes that the country is allied with Nazi Germany, the Japanese navy at Pearl Harbor is shown to be honorable and admirable.

Produced during the Vietnam War, *Tora! Tora! Tora!* can be seen as reflecting an era in which American military authority was questioned. Although published only a year after the film, Wouk's *The Winds of War* and his subsequent companion novel, *War and Remembrance*, are more conservative works. They reflect the view of World War II that became enshrined in American public memory during the last decades of the 20th century: that of the "good war" fought by the "greatest generation." Wouk's protagonist is described as "something simple and almost obsolete ... a patriot." The 1,900-page epic dramatizes the historical record of World War II, beginning with the German invasion of Poland in 1939 and ending with Hiroshima in 1945. Unlike

James Jones's *The Pistol*

JAMES JONES was serving as an assistant company clerk at Schofield Barracks when the Japanese military attacked. He later recalled the day's absurdities. On Sunday mornings soldiers were allowed an extra half-pint of milk with breakfast; when the bombing began, the men ran outside to see what was happening, still gripping the milk cartons to make sure they would not be taken. With his milk in his hand, Jones suddenly realized that he was acting in a moment of history.

He crouched against a wall as a Japanese fighter swooped down: "As he came abreast of us, he gave a typically toothy grin and waved, and I shall never forget his face behind the goggles." Three of Jones's friends were killed while they slept in their bunks. A sailor told him about seeing a bomb land near a man who had begun climbing an exterior ladder on a ship. The force from the explosion blew the man through the ladder and into rectangular pieces that matched the size of the ladder openings.

Jones had been assigned guard duty on December 7. In this capacity he was given a pistol to carry. Soldiers typically were only allowed to carry rifles, and Jones remembered feeling protected and superior with the additional weaponry. This experience became the basis for his novella *The Pistol* (1958). The story involves a private who, because of clerical oversight, is able to keep a pistol for a few weeks following the attack. But soon he becomes obsessed with the pistol: he considers it to be his by right, his talisman of salvation, and he fears that it will be taken from him. Indeed, the men in his company try to take it, through scheming, thievery, and violence. Jones shows that in their common fear of the enemy, the soldiers quickly turn against each other. The private successfully defends his pistol from these antagonists, but in the end military bureaucracy triumphs. A clerk realizes his mistake, and the pistol is repossessed. All the effort and strife become instantly moot.

December 7 and *From Here to Eternity*, the novels—with their Olympian scope—do not provide any sense of the messier details of American wartime behavior.

The Pearl Harbor disaster is recounted efficiently but somewhat desultorily, in a few pages. Wouk places the attack within a larger historical context without delving into the day's military mistakes. He points out that the Japanese victory led to fundamental changes in naval strategy. Heavy-armored battleships, with their huge guns, had been regarded as the most important naval vessels, but at Pearl Harbor these ships had been sitting ducks. The attack anticipated the dominance of aircraft carriers in the Pacific war. Wouk suggests that the Japanese gambit was "such a foolish thing to do, such an outrageous gamble," that it succeeded brilliantly, precisely because American military leaders believed that the idea was foolish, outrageous, and therefore impossible. He also believes that over the long term, the attack became the "bullet" that destroyed Nazi Germany, because it brought the UNITED STATES into the war.

Further Reading: Philip D. Beidler, *The Good War's Greatest Hits: World War II and American Remembering* (University of Georgia Press, 1998); Akira Iriye, "*Tora! Tora! Tora!*," in Mark C. Carnes, ed., *Past Imperfect: History according to the Movies* (Henry Holt, 1995); Otohiko Kaga, *Riding the East Wind: A Novel of War and Peace* (Kodansha, 1999); Frank MacShane, *Into Eternity: The Life of James Jones, American Writer* (Houghton Mifflin, 1985); Fred Zinnemann, *A Life in the Movies* (Charles Scribner's Sons, 1992).

—TOM COLLINS

M

MacArthur, Douglas (1880–1964)

General Douglas MacArthur's role in the debacle of December 7, 1941, has been a subject of controversy and bitterness, particularly among those who believe the commanders in Hawai'i were dealt with in an unduly harsh manner. On that morning, MacArthur was in command of American forces based in the PHILIPPINES (see also PHILIPPINES, PREPARATION FOR ATTACK). It was 2:30 A.M. local time when news of the attack on PEARL HARBOR arrived in the headquarters of the U.S. Asiatic Fleet based in Manila, commanded by Admiral Thomas C. Hart. However, no one bothered to communicate the situation to MacArthur's army forces. It was only by luck that a signalman picked up a station from California. MacArthur was not informed until 3:40 A.M.

Even with this interservice communication failure, there should have been time to put the forces in the Philippines on full wartime alert. Yet, when the Japanese attackers arrived shortly after noon, most of the planes at Clark Army Air Base were on the ground, and were destroyed as readily as those at Hickam Air Base on Oahu. One bright spot was the relatively quick start of antiaircraft fire. However, the shells fell far short of their intended targets, and worse, much of the superannuated ammunition proved to be duds.

This failure, particularly in regard to the B-17 bombers, has been the target of the harshest criticism. By any rational consideration, MacArthur should have been doing *something* with bombers. Either

THE BOEING B17G, AT LEFT, *known as the "Flying Fortress," was one of the most famous airplanes ever produced. Best known for daylight bombings of strategic German industrial targets, the Flying Fortress served in every World War II combat zone. The B-17 prototype first flew on July 28, 1935, and the United States produced 12,726 B-17s through May 1945.*

ABOVE *General MacArthur surveys the beachhead on Leyte Island, soon after American forces swept ashore from a gigantic liberation armada aimed at the central Philippines, at the historic moment when the general made good his promise, "I shall return." 1944.*

was in fact the result of interpersonal conflict between MacArthur's chief of staff and his air commander.

One thing is certain: while the commanders in Hawai'i endured the destruction of their military careers and their reputations, MacArthur suffered no such indignity. Far from it, he continued in his command and became one of the first five-star generals in the American military. Only when he quarreled with President HARRY TRUMAN in the Korean War did his military career finally come to an end.

Further Reading: Richard Connaughton, *MacArthur and Defeat in the Philippines* (Overlook Press, 2001); John Costello, *Days of Infamy: MacArthur, Roosevelt, Churchill: The Shocking Truth Revealed* (Pocket Books, 1994).

—**LEIGH KIMMEL**

he should have been ordering them on the offensive, to fly north and bomb Japanese-held Formosa (Taiwan), or he should have put them into a defensive posture, flying south out of the range of attackers. But, until 11 A.M., he did nothing. By the time the orders came to start loading bombs, it was already too late. They were still in the process of readying the planes when the attackers arrived.

Accounts describe MacArthur as being in a state of shock that morning and assert that for nearly six hours he was not able to pull himself together to the point that he could give orders. Although Hart came to him in considerable distress, he did not then summon his air commander and require a complete report on the disposition of his forces, an inexplicable oversight. Some historians have suggested that the paralysis at headquarters

Malaya and Singapore

The British began construction of a major naval base in Singapore in 1923. Due to economic difficulties and some political opposition, work on the facilities proceeded slowly, with completion not until 1941. When completed, the Singapore base was huge and had virtually everything necessary to support significant naval forces throughout the region. The fortifications for the base were extensive, including 15-inch guns and bunkers. The defensive system was sufficiently impressive that the British press began calling Singapore the "Gibraltar of the East." This "Gibraltar" had two glaring weaknesses, however.

The first was that the major defensive line was oriented to protect against an attack from the sea.

Although Singapore is separated from Malaya to the northwest by only a narrow body of water, the Johore Strait, defenses in that area were minimal, primarily based on the assessment that the Malayan jungle would preclude an attack from the land side. The second weakness was that despite having a world-class naval base, the British actually stationed very few ships there permanently. The strategic assumption was that Atlantic-based ships could be sent to Singapore if a major threat erupted. By 1941, this assumption was clearly erroneous, with the British fleet having more than it could handle in the Atlantic and Mediterranean.

DEFEAT OF THE BRITISH

On December 8, 1941, the Japanese began landing troops in southern Thailand and northern Malaya, with some advance forces actually landing before the attack on Pearl Harbor. The Japanese forces, under command of General Tomoyuki Yamashita, numbered 27,000 for the initial offensive and another 83,000 follow-on forces. The assault troops consisted of some of the country's best-trained and most experienced soldiers. Defenders numbered slightly over 80,000 Indian, British, Australian, and Malay troops to protect all of Malaya and Singapore. The Commonwealth troops were scattered, defending British air bases dispersed throughout Malaya despite there being minimal Royal Air Force aircraft using these bases. The result was that the air bases were more valuable to the Japanese than they had been for the British defending them.

The Japanese made good use of their tanks, which the British did not have. Japanese troops also proved extremely effective at using infiltration tactics, frequently able to pass through defenders' lines to attack them from the rear. They also used some-18,000 bicycles to advance their forces rapidly. As a result,

by January 31, the defenders were driven off the Malayan mainland and on to Singapore.

Both sides had received reinforcements during the fighting in Malaya, so the defenders in Singapore still had about 70,000 troops despite their earlier losses and the Japanese had about 30,000. Commonwealth troops began to feverishly improve the defenses along the northern side of Singapore, but there simply were not enough troops to adequately man all of the defensive line. Meanwhile, the Japanese conducted almost daily air raids against Singapore in the latter half of January. As the assault became closer, artillery fire also increased significantly. British Prime Minister WINSTON CHURCHILL ordered that Singapore was to be defended to the death and that no surrender was to be allowed. He also ordered a "scorched earth" policy for all British military property.

During the night of February 8, the Japanese landed on the northwest side of the island. Although the Australian troops defending the sector fought hard, the Japanese soon had two divisions landed. By February 13, they had broken through the final defensive line around Singapore city. By this point, Japanese bombing and shelling were killing an estimated 2,000 civilians a day, with most of the bodies remaining unburied due to the dangers of recovering them. The same day, the British commander, Lieutenant General A. E. Percival, requested authority to surrender to avoid further bloodshed. Churchill agreed on February 14, and on the 15th, the Japanese accepted the unconditional surrender of the Commonwealth forces.

Further Reading: Ong Chit Chung, *Operation Matador: World War II: Britain's Attempt to Foil the Japanese Invasion of Malaya and Singapore* (Eastern University Press, 2003); Singapore Ministry of Defense, www.mindef.gov.sg/imindef/home.html (cited January 2006).

—LAWRENCE E. CLINE, PH.D.

Marshall Islands

The Marshall Islands, two parallel island chains located between Hawai'i and JAPAN, represented the easternmost edge of the Japanese Empire. Acquired from GERMANY after World War I, the Japanese Mandated Marshalls possessed strategic advantages because of their geographic location. Control of the Marshalls protected the right flank of General DOUGLAS MACARTHUR's forces as he worked his way up from the Solomon Islands. Additionally, the Marshalls provided vital naval bases and airstrips and were the proving ground where the UNITED STATES perfected its amphibious assault tactics.

Although the Marshall Islands are composed of 32 island groups, the American military was mostly concerned with only two: Kwajalein, located in the center of the Marshalls, and Eniwetok, further to the northwest. Kwajalein possessed two islands capable of supporting air bases. Eniwetok was ideal for a naval fleet base. After the battles of Midway (see MIDWAY, BATTLE OF) and Coral Sea, Japan had written off the Marshalls as expendable but were determined to defend them to slow the American advance.

Preparation for Operation Flintlock, the invasion of Kwajalein Atoll, began as early as November 1943, with air attacks aimed at destroying Japanese airpower in the region and establishing air superiority. Thanks to MAGIC (see CODES, JAPANESE), the Americans were able to break the Japanese codes and learn the exact locations of all Japanese planes in the area; by the day of the U.S. invasion only 15 of the Japanese aircraft still flew. Once air superiority was achieved, attacks focused on the atoll's bunkers and other defenses in the hope of making the landings as smooth as possible. A major naval bombardment preceded the landings in an effort to destroy all remaining defensive positions. The shelling was so intense that it is estimated that during the bombardment between 50 and 75 percent of Kwajalein's defenders were killed.

With Major General Holland M. Smith commanding the ground forces, nearly 54,000 strong, the landings began on February 1 at 9:30 A.M. Men of the 7th Infantry Division landed on Kwajalein Island at the southernmost tip of the atoll while the 4th Marine Division landed on Roi-Namur, at the northeast corner of the atoll, two hours later. The landing troops were supplied and equipped for every possible contingency to avoid the difficulties encountered at the landings in the Gilbert Islands. Because of the heavy preliminary bombardment, resistance was light except for a small pocket on Kwajalein Island. Roi-Namur fell on February 2 with Kwajalein falling two days later. Operation Flintlock cost the Americans 370 dead and 1,556 wounded. Only 100 of the 9,000 Japanese defenders were taken alive.

Shortly after launching Flintlock the Americans devised Operation Catchpole, the capture of Eniwetok Atoll. D-day was set for February 17 and preliminary bombing began on January 31. The landing force of 10,000 GIs and marines under the command of USMC Brigadier General T. E. Watson waded ashore at the first of the targeted islands midmorning on the 18th. As at Kwajalein, the resistance was light due in large part to the heavy bombarding provided by the navy. By February 24 all objectives had been taken at the cost of 200 Americans dead, compared with nearly 3,000 Japanese.

Further Reading: Philip A. Crowl and Edmund G. Love, *Seizure of the Gilberts and Marshalls* (Office of the Chief of Military History, Dept. of the Historical Branch, G-3 Division, Headquarters, U.S. Marine Corps, 1954); S. L. A. Marshall, *Island Victory* (University of Nebraska Press, 2001).

—CHRIS THOMAS

Marshall, George C. (1880–1959)

General George Catlett Marshall was the U.S. Army Chief of Staff when JAPAN bombed Pearl Harbor. He was appointed in 1939 by President FRANKLIN D. ROOSEVELT and was responsible for preparing the U.S. Army for war. He has been largely regarded as Roosevelt's most vital Joint Chief of Staff and the most important military mind during WORLD WAR II. However, he has received criticism for not acting fast enough in warning the fleet at Pearl Harbor of the potential threat for attack.

During the summer of 1941, U.S. relations with Japan had steadily deteriorated. In July Roosevelt had sanctioned an embargo on oil and steel to Japan (see SANCTIONS AGAINST JAPAN) that economically strangled the Japanese as they were heavily reliant on the UNITED STATES for oil. From July to December both nations failed in their attempts to negotiate a solution to their problems and war seemed imminent (see DIPLOMATIC RELATIONS). Marshall was aware that the Japanese were readying themselves for war. He was one of a select few allowed to read intercepted Japanese intelligence reports, known as MAGIC intercepts, that outlined Japanese preparations (see CODES, JAPANESE).

Debate still exists as to whether the United States should have been better prepared for the attack (see PREPAREDNESS). There were numerous warnings in the weeks and days leading up to the strike, yet American preparation remained minimal. The Army Signal Intelligence Service intercepted numerous Japanese messages, but the dispersal of this information was often poor and the intercepted messages often appeared to contradict one another. On December 6, the United States intercepted messages between Japan and a Japanese source in HONOLULU, but the exact details of the message could not be worked out. The following morning, at approximately 6:45 A.M. on the day of the attack, U.S. Army radars detected two Japanese aircraft 50 miles from Hawai'i. Inexplicably though, no action was taken.

The Japanese had intended to send American officials a message stating that they were ceasing negotiations with the United States and then follow with an immediate attack. The Japanese had planned to attack Pearl Harbor simultaneously with an attack on Malaya (see MALAYA AND SINGAPORE), but the attack on Malaya occurred almost two hours prior to Pearl Harbor. The United States had anticipated the attack on Malaya so this was hardly a surprise. Sadly, though, it took U.S. officials too long to realize that Pearl Harbor was also a target.

Marshall sent a warning to the fleet at Pearl Harbor to be on alert, but the message never reached the command headquarters; Pearl Harbor had already been attacked. When informed of the Japanese strike,

ABOVE *Gen. George C. Marshall with members of his General Staff in his office at the War Department Munitions Building, Washington, D.C., November 1941.*

Marshall was believed to have expressed great shock that Hawai'i had been struck. He had believed that the Japanese would strike targets closer to Japan, such as Singapore or the Dutch East Indies. Nevertheless, American officials including Marshall have been criticized for allowing evidence of an attack on Pearl Harbor to grow, while failing to act upon these warnings in a reasonable amount of time. Theories exist that the bombings were known and allowed to happen because it would ensure an American entry into the war (see HISTORIANS' VIEWS); however, a more valid reason is simply that negligence on the part of U.S. officials allowed the Japanese to strike Pearl Harbor with the fleet there left unprepared.

Further Reading: Peter Calvocoressi, Guy Wint, and John Pritchard, *Penguin History of the Second World War* (Penguin Books, 1999); Frederick D. Parker, *Pearl Harbor Revisited: United States Navy Communications Intelligence 1924–41* (National Security Agency, Center for Cryptologic History, 1994); Robert Stinnett, *Day of Deceit: The Truth about FDR and Pearl Harbor* (Touchstone Press, 2001); John Toland, *Infamy: Pearl Harbor and Its Aftermath* (Doubleday, 1986).

—DAVID W. MCBRIDE

ABOVE *The USS* Maryland *and the capsized USS* Oklahoma, *after the Japanese bombing attack on Pearl Harbor, December 7, 1941.*

Maryland, USS

The battleship USS *Maryland* was docked off Ford Island at Battleship Row throughout the attack on Pearl Harbor, trapped between Ford Island and other vessels. The USS *Maryland*'s position at mooring between Ford Island and the USS *Oklahoma* (see OKLAHOMA, USS) saved her from the extensive torpedo damage suffered by the USS *Oklahoma* and other vessels with broadsides facing open water.

Although the USS *Maryland* received two direct bomb hits in the Pearl Harbor attack, the crew was able to man all of the ship's antiaircraft batteries against Japanese aircraft. The USS *Maryland* was able to render assistance for fire control and rescue to sister ships immediately after the attack, and was left with several casualties and only slight damage to the vessel in comparison with other ships of the fleet.

The battleship was surrounded by smoke and flames from burning oil on the water's surface, and to her starboard side, the USS *Oklahoma* lay upside down on the harbor bottom. The USS *Maryland* was not sunk or irreparably damaged by the two direct bomb hits, as had been reported by the Japanese. The ship was quickly repaired and refitted by February 1942 for redeployment in August 1942.

The USS *Maryland* had a distinctive career in the war after Pearl Harbor. She was the flagship carrying Rear Admiral Harry W. Hill, as he commanded the southern force in the battle for the Gilbert Islands. Hill had trouble giving orders from the USS *Maryland* to the officers under him during the landing.

The USS *Maryland*'s communications center was situated in perfect position to be rendered temporarily inoperable by the concussive force of firing the ship's 16-inch guns. Firing those guns was necessary for "softening up" Japanese defenses before landing U.S. Marines. Because of the communications problem, and difficulty seeing the beach through the dust from shelling, Hill could not effectively coordinate the beginning and end of beach bombardment by ships, the air support for the invasion, and the landing of troops. As a result of this and other complications, the victory at Tarawa did not go as smoothly as planned.

It was two years later to the day after Pearl Harbor that the USS *Maryland* returned from this campaign and patrol duty in the area afterward. The battleship also took part in battering Japanese onshore defenses in the MARSHALL ISLANDS and then conducted similar actions off Saipan, where she was damaged by a nighttime Japanese torpedo raid. After speedy repairs, the USS *Maryland* saw action off the Palau Islands, and later the landings at Leyte, and intercepted the retreating Japanese naval forces at the battle of Surigao Straits. After contribution to actions off Okinawa, the USS *Maryland* missed the final battles in the Pacific; as the war ended, she was being refitted.

The ship's final mission of the World War II era was transporting thousands of ex-GIs back home from the Pacific theater. The USS *Maryland* was a Colorado-class battleship, commissioned on July 21, 1921, and decommissioned on April 3, 1947, then finally sold and scrapped in 1959. For her service in the war against the Japanese Empire, the USS *Maryland* was cited seven battle stars.

Further Reading: John Costello, *The Pacific War* (Rawson Wade, 1981); *The Dictionary of American Naval Fighting Ships* (Office of the Chief of Naval Operations, Naval History Division, 1959–1991); William L. O'Niell, *A Democracy at War: America's Fight at Home and Abroad in World War II* (Harvard University Press, 1993); Michael Slackman, *Target: Pearl Harbor* (University of Hawai'i Press, 1990).

—WILLIAM D. LAREMORE

Matsuoka, Yosuke (1880–1946)

Yosuke Matsuoka, a career diplomat, was instrumental in JAPAN's path to the Pearl Harbor attack, even if he was dismissed from office, a forgotten public servant, long before the attack happened. One of Matsuoka's most important contributions to Japan's entry into WORLD WAR II was his negotiation, while Japanese foreign minister, of the 1940 Tripartite Pact between GERMANY, Italy, and Japan.

Despite the foreign minister's faith in the Tripartite Pact, with communism as its stated enemy, Matsuoka had to rethink his policy when ADOLF HITLER and JOSEF STALIN signed a 10-year neutrality agreement in 1939.

Consequently, Matsuoka went to Moscow and negotiated a Soviet-Japanese neutrality pact in April 1941 (see RUSSIA–JAPAN RELATIONS). Despite years of viewing the Soviet Union as an ideological enemy, Matsuoka thought this pact would give Japan some time, avoiding a possible Soviet attack on Manchukuo or an air attack from the Soviet city of Vladivostok.

When Matsuoka returned from Moscow, he was upset to find that his government was in peace talks with the UNITED STATES. Alarmed by Matsuoka's seemingly antipeace position, Japanese Prime Minister Fumimaro Konoe forced Matsuoka out of his job in July 1941, when the majority of the Konoe government resigned en masse. Konoe, however, was quickly recalled by the emperor's officials to resume his position as prime minister, allowing him to form a new cabinet.

It appeared necessary to get rid of Matsuoka in this manner because Konoe felt unable to ask for his resignation. Matsuoka was immensely popular in Japan and the Axis allies (see AXIS POWERS IN 1941) were accustomed to working with him.

Despite Matsuoka's preeminent position in Japanese politics before he was forced out of office in 1941, he quickly drifted into obscurity. The forced retirement may have been a blessing to the former foreign minister, as he suffered from tuberculosis that was reportedly aggravated by his diplomatic European trip in April 1941.

History has not silenced Matsuoka's response to the Pearl Harbor attack. On the morning of the attack, one of his former aides visited him at home. The ailing former public servant lamented his role in negotiating the Tripartite Pact. Matsuoka called his role in that agreement the biggest mistake of his life.

He emphasized that his motivation was world peace with the ultimate aim of keeping the United States out of the war. However, he worried that people would think of him as the instigator of the Pearl Harbor attack and, because of this, lamented that he was to find no peace even after death.

Matsuoka's predictions the morning of the attack were partially correct. He did not escape notice by the International Military Tribunal for the Far East. Captured by Allied forces in 1945 (see ALLIES ON DECEMBER 7, 1941), he was returned to Tokyo and charged with aggression, probably due to his fervent support of Japan's expansionist policies. He escaped the gallows, however, dying in a Tokyo hospital on June 26, 1946.

Further Reading: Robert J. C. Butow, *Tojo and the Coming of War* (Princeton University Press, 1961); John Toland, *The Rising Sun: The Decline and Fall of the Japanese Empire, 1936–1945* (Random House, 2003); "Trial Watch: Yosuke Matsuoka," www.trial-ch.org/trialwatch/profiles/en/facts/p68.html (cited December 2005).

—MELISSA F. GAYAN

Memoirs, American

Americans created Pearl Harbor memoirs as narratives filled with a barrage of conflicting emotions: calm, surprise, disbelief, fear, anger, and reflection. Each begins with particularly ordinary Sunday routine. A Chinese photographer had a 7:00 A.M. appointment at the Pearl Harbor gates, and he waited patiently for his bus after grabbing a cup of coffee at the Swanky and Franky restaurant. Several sailors also recalled finishing their coffee. As sailor Theodore Mason depicted, "After a full breakfast of cereal, hot

> "BOMBS BEGAN to fall—metallic specks that reflected the sunlight fitfully as they wobbled down. The specks grew larger and more ominous. I felt totally helpless. These might well be the last few seconds of my life."
>
> —THEODORE MASON, a sailor stationed at Pearl Harbor on December 7, 1941

cakes, and syrup, skipping only the cold toast, I toyed with a final cup of coffee over a cigarette." John McGoran recalled his morning routine: "After finishing breakfast, I took my dirty dishes to the scullery below. Funny, but that's the way peace ended. Just then a sailor ran by, shouting crazily, 'The Japs are coming!'"

After the sudden realization of shattered calm in those few minutes before 8 A.M., the surprise shifted from disbelief to recognition upon sighting Japanese symbols on planes. The symbolic sun or "red meatball" brought sinking realizations that this was no drill. "Then I saw the rising-sun symbols on the near wing and the fuselage," one sailor recalled, "and remembered our aircraft identification drills. The plane was a Zero. The Japanese were attacking Pearl Harbor!"

Two sailors remembered remaining transfixed until torpedoes dropped from bomb bays. When Louis Peterson witnessed these "fish" slamming into the USS *Oglala*, the idea hit him: "It was no drill!" "The pilots' aim was very good," Mason noted. "Alongside the ships, the near misses sent up columns of water hundreds of feet high, accompanied by muffled explosions and spreading concentric shock rings."

As the fury intensified, needs and confusions escalated. "It was not courage that led me about the unprotected deck," Burdick Brittin began, "perhaps I was searching for something tangible to do." Or as Mason recalled, "Bombs began to fall—metallic specks that reflected the sunlight fitfully as they wobbled down. The specks grew larger and more ominous. I felt totally helpless. These might well be the last few seconds of my life."

The Chinese photographer caught in the midst of war hesitated to help because "I'm afraid some one will mistake me as a Jap and shoot me down," but he delivered equipment and sandwiches throughout the day. Other civilians near HONOLULU worked dil-igently at hospitals or shelters, saying "I want to do something."

MEN OF A SPECIAL KIND

Others experienced fleeting but dramatic moments of courageous patriotism. When the USS *California* unfurled her flag through the awful din, one sailor proudly recounted: "Some of us were crying unashamed tears. In that moment, which would live in history, I understood why men of a special kind were willing to die for abstractions named duty, honor, country." Another remembered the USS *Nevada*'s morning colors. "While machine-gun bullets sprayed around them, the band played the *Star-Spangled Banner* to the final note and the marines stood rigidly at 'present arms.' Then all broke for cover."

In the continental UNITED STATES, most seemed exceedingly calm that Sunday afternoon. Senator Tom Connally remembered taking "a relaxing drive" to Maryland but heard the news over the car radio. Admiral Arthur Radford recollected a peaceful Pensacola golf course until a navy car came racing up the fairway, honking, delivering the dispatch: "Japanese have attacked Pearl Harbor—this is no drill."

AT LEFT *U.S. sailors man their boats alongside the burning USS* West Virginia *on December 7.*

General GEORGE C. MARSHALL had galloped on his usual Sunday morning ride but then received an urgent telephone call from the War Department. Journalist Edward R. Murrow recalled Washington's crowds, comparing them to London's Battle of Britain: "The same look on their faces that they had in Downing Street." The news of Pearl Harbor came at 3:30 A.M., December 8, in the PHILIPPINES with the piercing sound of a battalion bugler's call to arms. Glen McDole would forever remember his lieutenant's announcement: "The Japanese have bombed Pearl Harbor and we are at war. From now on you are to stand by your guns at all times."

Anxious fears continued that Hawai'ian night. "By now the sun had set on the most evil day in the history of the U.S. Navy," Mason wrote. "No one knew what the casualties had been; no one knew what fresh disasters might be unleashed upon us in the hours ahead. The world, I began to learn that day, is not run by the best people but by the survivors." The governor declared martial law, but PANIC and rumors intensified on that "black out night." As Denver Gray described, "After dark, trigger-happy soldiers, sailors, and airmen fired tracer bullets into the darkened sky at the least provocation."

IN THE AFTERMATH

Other men received assignments to aid women and children. McGoran helped 200 women and children evacuate from Pearl Harbor's housing project to Honolulu's YMCA. "By 1700, the dormitory was filled to capacity," this reluctant sailor recalled, "and the distractions of settling in now gave way to an atmosphere of fear and tears." Hours dragged on as depicted in Mason's litany:

> None of us slept, although complete exhaustion was not far off, and our stomachs did not react to food. I remember my white uniform becoming filthy. I remember going around to the guns to cheer the men and I recall their grim looks of determination…I remember going through the wardroom where exhausted men had fallen in a dead stupor and where the dead air of the passageway was so repelling that I reeled drunkenly out on deck to vomit bile. I remember men in the crew looking searchingly into my eyes and, like a damned hypocrite, I remember smiling and joking.

When one exhausted sailor finally found "a glorious hot shower," emotions overwhelmed him. "I stayed there a long time," he began. "A feeling of elation possessed me. I was alive. The other men in the shower shouted and laughed and sang. I joined them. Suddenly, I felt ashamed of myself. How many of my shipmates were dead, wounded, hideously burned? We had suffered a shocking defeat at the hands of the Japanese Navy. Why was I singing? It took years, and additional combat experience, before I forgave myself for callously celebrating personal survival."

Pearl Harbor was no longer a paradise: "Oil was everywhere: spreading out from the sunken ships in pernicious rings, mottling the water, blackening the shore. Drifting on the slow currents were life rafts, life jackets, pieces of boats, and other flotsam. The air smelled of bunker oil, fire, smoke—and death."

Healing the wounded and finding the dead became immediate tasks; burials came later. One salvage diver described descents into absolute darkness because of the harbor's oil as these divers "developed a superior sense of touch, much as blind persons do…they could sense the presence of floating human bodies long before they felt them."

One sailor truly believed "the defeat at Pearl Harbor was basically attributable to the lack of effective anti-aircraft guns." This same sailor also thought

"FOR THE fourteen months preceding Pearl Harbor, I had been part of the battleship navy. I and my shipmates of the *California* had absorbed some of its pride and smartness and mystique. Those things had served us well on 7 December 1941. We had stood our ground, and we had done our duty. Some of us had done more. But only a very few had done less. We might have been defeated, but we were not broken by defeat. Ahead, there was a war to win—and we knew we would win it."

—FROM THE memoirs of
a Pearl Harbor survivor

ABOVE *The USS* Bowfin *was launched on the first anniversary of the attack on Pearl Harbor. She completed nine war patrols in two years of wartime duty, sinking 16 Japanese vessels. Decommissioned in 1971, the ship is now berthed in Pearl Harbor as the USS* Bowfin *Submarine Museum, next to the Arizona Memorial Visitor Center.*

Admiral HUSBAND E. KIMMEL and General WALTER C. SHORT had been "treated in a totally unfair and unethical manner." "Even today," this sailor recalled, "I can clearly visualize Admiral Kimmel running out to his lanai when the noise of battle alerted him to what was going on. What should he have done?"

INFUSED WITH DETERMINATION

Interestingly, Kimmel's own memoirs recount absolutely no description of his thoughts or actions on December 7—only defensive details of his actions before and after. "The fact that I then thought and now think my conclusions were sound," wrote Kimmel, "when based upon the information I received, has sustained me during the years that have passed since the first Japanese bomb fell on Pearl Harbor." Other enlisted men could not forgive: "When great men blunder, they count their losses in pride and reputation and glory. The underlings count their losses in blood."

Still, another sailor would not have chosen otherwise but to experience that December 7: "As for myself, given a second turn, I would choose to be in a vessel that was tied up along side the quays, exactly as we were." Another sailor lamented the lasting demise of the navy's power yet was infused with determination:

For the fourteen months preceding Pearl Harbor, I had been part of the battleship navy. I and my shipmates of the USS *California* had absorbed some of its pride and smartness and mystique. Those things had served us well on 7 December 1941. We had stood our ground, and we had done our duty. Some of us had done more. But only a very few had done less. We might have been defeated, but we were not broken by defeat. Ahead, there was a war to win—and we knew we would win it.

Further Reading: Sol Bloom, *The Autobiography of Sol Bloom* (G.P. Putnam's Sons, 1948); Blake Clark, *Remember Pearl Harbor!* (Modern Age Books, 1942); Tom Connally, *My Name Is Tom Connally* (Thomas Y. Crowell, 1954); Terry Dunnahoo, *Pearl Harbor: America Enters the War* (Franklin Watts, 1991); Stephen Jurika Jr., ed., *From Pearl Harbor to Vietnam: The Memoirs of Admiral Arthur W. Radford* (Hoover Institution Press, 1980); Tai Sing Loo, "How Happen I Were at Pearl Harbor on the Morning of Sunday, 7th of Dec. 1941," *United States Naval Institute Proceedings* (December 1962); Theodore C. Mason, *Battleship Sailor* (Naval Institute Press, 1982); John W. McGoran, "I Remember It Well," *Proceedings of the United States Naval Institute* (December 1979); Harry Mead, *20 Was Easy: Memoirs of a Pearl Harbor Survivor* (BookSurge, 2005); Edward C. Raymer, *Descent into Darkness* (Presidio Press, 1996); Joseph K. Taussig Jr., "A Tactical View of Pearl Harbor," in Paul Stillwell, ed., *Air Raid, Pearl Harbor!: Recollections of a Day of Infamy* (Naval Institute Press, 1981).

—**LISA L. OSSIAN, PH.D.**

ABOVE *The crash site of Japanese Lieutenant Fusata Iida, between the airfield hangars, Kaneohe Bay.*

"**I REALIZED** abruptly, however, that Lieutenant Iida was flying in a most unusual manner, quite different from his usual tactics. I watched his plane as it dove in its vertical, inverted position until it exploded on the ground between the Kaneohe airfield hangars."

—**LIEUTENANT IYOZO** Fujita, a Japanese pilot

Memoirs, Japanese

Masatake Okumiya and Jiro Horikoshi began their collective memoir titled *Zero!* with these words: "The attack on Pearl Harbor was a military feat so daring and so successful as to deserve a special place in history." The planning to successfully complete the mission took months of preparation, starting in May. "At the liaison conference of the 30th [November] the decision was made to go to war," recalled lead pilot Mitsuo Fuchida. Admiral ISOROKU YAMAMOTO's message explained the absolute importance of the collective plans: "The rise or fall of the Empire depends upon this battle; everyone will do his duty with utmost efforts."

After leaving Hitokappu Bay, carriers advanced toward Hawai'i in absolute radio secrecy. Minoru Genda recalled, "Day and night, or even when I awoke, whether in the Operations Room or in my room, I pictured to myself the situation in which we were, hearing the dashing of waves outside. Now we are advancing toward Pearl Harbor, not in a dream, but really, or 'May God help us.'"

"The ships pitched and rolled in the rough sea," Fuchida recalled, "kicking up white surf from the pre-dawn blackness of the water. At times wave spray came over the flight deck, and crews clung desperately to their planes to keep them from going into the sea." Fuchida began that day at 5:30 A.M.: "In my flying togs I entered the operation room and reported to the Commander in Chief, 'I am ready for the mission.' Nagumo grasped my hand firmly and said, 'I have confidence in you.'"

Fuchida also described the pilots' final briefing: "The room was not large enough for all of the men, some of whom had to stand out in the passageway. On a blackboard were written the positions of ships in Pearl Harbor as of 0600, 7 December. We were

230 miles due north of Oahu." One pilot remembered the day's absolutely unique emotions. "But when I woke up and came up to the bridge," Genda recalled, "to my wonder, I found myself quite unconcerned about anything, with all worldly thought and chimerical cares such as anticipation of troubles or the keenest desire for our success, absolutely cleared away. I have never experienced such a serene and quiescent mood in my life." Fuchida's memories captured the most detailed of moments:

On the flight deck a green lamp was waved in a circle to signal 'Take off!' The engine of the foremost fighter plane began to roar. With the ship still pitching and rolling, the plane started its run, slowly at first, but with steadily increasing speed. Men lining the flight deck held their breath as the first plane took off successfully just before the ship took a downward pitch…Fifteen minutes later 183 fighter bombers and torpedo planes had taken off from the flight deck of six aircraft carriers. This was the first wave of the total of 359 planes which I led into Pearl Harbor.

"This was the culmination of my every waking thought," Fuchida attempted to explain, "since that day, September 24, 1941, when Commander Genda had taken me aside at Kagoshima on the southern tip of Kyushu and said, 'Don't be alarmed, Fuchida, but we want you to lead our air force in the event that we attack Pearl Harbor!' And now December 7 was here, and our air armada was airborne. We flew through heavy clouds for 45 minutes… "At 7:53 A.M., when he was sure of surprise, Fuchida radioed the attack signal code words: *Tora! Tora! Tora!*"

After the attack began, Fuchida surveyed the rapid damage: "Black clouds of smoke rose from the airfields. A huge column of dark red smoke rose 1,000 feet into the air from the battleship *Arizona*.

Its powder magazine had exploded!" Juzo Mori flew his plane directly over the battleships along Ford Island. "I swung low and put my plane into satisfactory torpedoing position," he recalled. "It was imperative that my bombing approach be absolutely correct, as I had been warned that the harbor depth was no more than 34 feet." If he deviated at all in either speed or height, the torpedoes would falter and, as Mori explained, "all our effort would go for naught." "By this time I was hardly conscious of what I was doing," he remembered. "I was reacting from habit instilled by long training, moving like an automaton." Afterward, Mori felt compelled to reflect: "Is this really, I questioned, what is called war?"

Lead pilot Fuchida recounted a lasting thought. "My heart was ablaze with joy for my success," Fuchida recalled, "in getting the whole main forces of the American Pacific Fleet in hand. In the years that were to follow I would put my whole hate-flamed effort into conducting the war that ensued."

Fuchida recalled taking the time to assess the damage to the enemy. "After the second wave was headed back to the carriers," he began, "I circled Pearl Harbor once more to observe and photograph the results. I counted four battleships definitely sunk and three severely damaged. Still another battleship appeared to be slightly damaged and extensive damage had also been inflicted upon other types of ships. The seaplane base at Ford Island was all in flames, as were the airfields, especially Wheeler Field."

In addition to 359 planes, several MIDGET SUBMARINES engaged in the Pearl Harbor attack. One memoir, titled *I Attacked Pearl Harbor*, described a midget submarine's perspective. "My heart beat faster," Kazuo Sakamaki began as he described his preparations before the almost certain suicidal attack. "I packed my personal effects, wrote a letter of farewell to father, cleaned my body, changed into the uniform of the midget submarine, and sprayed perfume on it. This was the preparation for death. With my compass out of order it was more than a matter of ceremonial formality. I expected to die."

On December 7, this young man whose given name, Kazuo, means "peace boy," found himself at the narrow entryway of the harbor without functioning navigation, about to plunge into the *Pennsylvania*—nearly certainly meaning self-destruction. If not, Kazuo planned to climb aboard and "kill as many enemies as possible." "I made up my mind to do just that," he determined. "But the realization that I had failed tortured my mind and bitter tears rolled down my face incessantly. It was past noon, and if we should delay any more, the dark curtain of night would fall. With perspiration drenching my body, I started the ship toward the mouth of the harbor for the last time. I must have been half out of my mind. I did not care. I could not think. I just tried and tried. I was working blindly. I do not remember the rest of that afternoon." Later, he would become the first Japanese prisoner of war.

When Fuchida returned to his carrier after the two rounds, he recalled both his frustration and ultimate resignation as he tried, vehemently but respectfully, to argue for a third wave to decimate Pearl Harbor. "I had done all I could to urge another attack," Fuchida explained, "but the decision rested entirely with Admiral Nagumo, and he chose to retire without launching the next attack. Immediately flag signals were hoisted ordering the course change, and our ships headed northward at high speed."

Other pilots waited to attack the PHILIPPINES that same day, and Saburo Sakai expressed his confusion regarding Americans. "They squatted there like sitting ducks," Sakai observed. "The Americans had made no attempt to disperse the planes and increase their safety on the ground. We failed utterly to comprehend the enemy's attitude. Pearl Harbor had been hit more than five hours before; surely they had received word of that attack and expected one against these critical fields!"

The news of the Pearl Harbor attack reached Japanese ambassadors Saburo Kurusu and KICHISABURO NOMURA too late to provide any effective relief from their glaring error in delivering their war announcement from JAPAN an hour too late. A Japanese reporter in Washington, D.C., detailed the story for his memoir: "At about 2:30 P.M. they [Kurusu and Nomura] were ushered into [Cordell] Hull's presence and delivered the Japanese reply. Silently they listened to the gray-haired Secretary's stinging rebuke, in which he described the Japanese reply as 'crowded with infamous falsehoods and distortions.'" The ambassadors finally received the news after returning to the embassy. "I thought there was something very funny there," Nomura later related, "but I didn't get it." Looking back, Nomura believed that a dangerous incident in the Pacific might lead to war but had never imagined an attack on Pearl Harbor.

In the early nuclear age, Toshikazu Kase, a former member of the Japanese Foreign Office, wrote about what was learned from Pearl Harbor: "We have learned anew, victors and vanquished alike, that the sword and slaughter do not solve the woes and wants of mankind. For even as victory crowns the victor so shall it crucify him. Still more so in the atomic age."

Fuchida, lead pilot of Pearl Harbor, spent his last years praying for peace. "Eleven years after Pearl Harbor! Little did I dream that eventful morning," Fuchida concluded, "that my view of life would be so revolutionized. Today I am a Christian! I say it over and over again. This is the message I send to all mankind with a fervent prayer that there will be 'No More Pearl Harbor.'" (See also MEMOIRS, AMERICAN.)

Further Reading: Mitsuo Fuchida, *From Pearl Harbor to Golgotha* (Sky Pilots Press, 1957); Mitsuo Fuchida, "I Led the Air Attack on Pearl Harbor," *United States Naval Institute Proceedings* (September 1952); Shigeru Fukodome, "Hawai'i Operation," *United States Naval Institute Proceedings* (December 1955); Donald M. Goldstein and Katherine V. Dillon, eds., *The Pearl Harbor Papers: Inside the Japanese Plans* (Brassey's, 2000); Robert Guillain, *I Saw Tokyo Burning* (Doubleday, 1981); Toshikau Kase, *Journey to the Missouri* (Yale University Press, 1950); Masuo Kato, *The Lost War* (Alfred A. Knopf, 1946); Masatake Okumiya and Jiro Horikoshi with Martin Caidin, *Zero!* (E.P. Dutton, 1956); Gordon W. Prange, *God's Samurai: Lead Pilot at Pearl Harbor* (Brassey's, 1990); Kazuo Sakamaki, *I Attacked Pearl Harbor* (Association Press, 1949); Shigenori Togo, *The Cause of Japan* (Textbook Publishers, 2003).

—LISA L. OSSIAN, PH.D.

Midget Submarines

Admiral ISOROKU YAMAMOTO's initial plans for the attack on Pearl Harbor concentrated on executing a surprise aerial attack on U.S. forces. In later developments of the plan, the mission of the 27 I-class submarines evolved into one of reconnaissance and mop-up exercises. The Japanese were gravely concerned over which U.S. ships were at Pearl Harbor, particularly the location of the aircraft carriers, the primary focus of the attack. The I-class submarines were charged with performing pre-attack reconnaissance of the harbor and sinking any vessels that may report the position of the Japanese fleet. After the aerial attack, the submarines were directed to attack any U.S. ships that had managed to escape the harbor.

Initially the Japanese had developed their midget submarine to be used as a defensive weapon in the event of an American attack. The typical midget submarine weighed approximately 46 tons, was

The News in Tokyo

THE EYEWITNESS writer of *I Saw Tokyo Burning* recounted: "The Japanese people...were torn between the official slogans exhorting them to intransigence and a secret intuition that told them this was madness. Their strongest feeling on the morning of December 8 was one of consternation...Collectively, the nation had let itself be carried away by war hysteria, but individually, each Japanese, always so different when he is on his own, isolated from the group, feared the war. ...Tokyo was afraid. The Japanese were frightened by what they had dared to do."

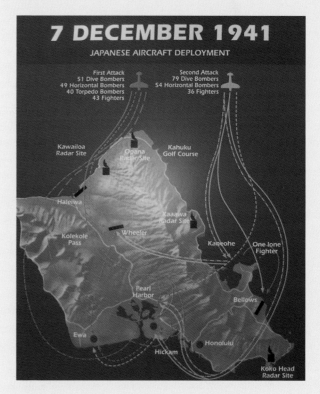

ABOVE *Japanese Aircraft Deployment on December 7, 1941. The first wave is shown on the left, in red, the second wave in orange on the right.*

78 feet long and 6 feet wide, with a crew of 2, and was capable of carrying 2 torpedoes. The mission of the midget submarine evolved into an offensive weapon system as JAPAN's policy became more aggressive militarily during the 1930s. Yamamoto had limited their involvement because a seaplane tender was required to deliver the midget submarine to within its 100-mile operating range. The odds of a tender being able to deliver the midget submarines within 50 miles of Pearl Harbor without detection were considered quite remote. In addition, Yamamoto considered Japanese suicide squads, or special attack forces, to be a waste of valuable resources in both men and material, and he included the midget submarines in that classification.

Yamamoto's final plan called for the midget submarines, carried by larger submarines, to be deployed several hours before the aerial assault, to use the cover of American ships to evade the submarine net and enter the harbor, and to finally launch their own attack once the aerial assault was complete and darkness had descended upon the harbor. The midget submarine commanders believed that waiting until dark not only increased the risk of detection, but also increased the likelihood of experiencing a shortage of oxygen. They convinced Vice Admiral Mitsumi Shimizu to alter the plan so that their attack would commence immediately after the aerial assault, thus taking full advantage of any chaotic conditions caused by the aerial assault.

At 6:30 A.M. on December 7 the USS *Antares* spotted a suspicious object in the water that turned out to be the conning tower of one of the midget submarines attempting to evade the submarine net by following another American ship into the harbor. Within minutes this submarine was sunk by the destroyer USS *Ward* and the activity was reported to the appropriate watch officer of the naval district.

Another midget submarine was sunk by one of the watch planes operating out of Ford Island. Unfortunately neither of these actions resulted in further patrols or defensive measures by either the U.S. Navy or Army. In the end Yamamoto was right to be so skeptical regarding the usefulness of the midget submarines: five of the submarines were sunk and another ran aground without inflicting any damage on the U.S. Fleet.

Further Reading: John Craddock, *First Shot: The Untold Story of the Japanese Minisubs that Attacked Pearl Harbor* (McGraw-Hill, 2006); Martin Gilbert, *The Second World War* (Henry Holt, 1989); Donald M. Goldstein and Katherine V. Dillon, *The Pearl Harbor Papers: Inside the Japanese Plans* (Brassey's, 1993).

—ABBE ALLEN DEBOLT

Midway, Battle of

The victory at Midway was a historic feat of arms by the U.S. Navy, and rightly called the battle that doomed JAPAN. The U.S. Pacific Fleet (see PACIFIC FLEET, U.S.) was outnumbered by 125 ships to 35. The Imperial Japanese Navy had been all-conquering and the Americans had yet to taste victory after the Pearl Harbor attack. Steaming toward Midway were four Japanese aircraft carriers of the Kido Butai, the carrier striking force, complete with surface escorts and an amphibious landing group. The UNITED STATES had only three carriers in the Pacific, and one of those was seriously crippled.

Admiral ISOROKU YAMAMOTO, who, against his better military judgment, had brilliantly planned and executed the attack on Pearl Harbor, had also advised the warlords that for six months he could sail unchallenged throughout the Pacific, but that thereafter he promised nothing. Six months to the day, the Battle of Midway ended in a decisive American victory. Japan lost four aircraft carriers and most of the pilots who had carried out the attack on December 7, 1941, and never again took the offensive in WORLD WAR II.

By the time of the Battle of Midway, June 4–6, 1942, Imperial Japan had conquered most of China, all of Southeast Asia and the East Indies, the PHILIPPINES, and Pacific islands from the Aleutians to New Guinea. The Japanese had bombed Darwin, Australia, and the British Fleet in India. It had rightly seemed as though the Rising Sun could rise at will wherever Japanese soldiers, sailors, and airmen went.

In the months after Pearl Harbor, the United States had lost WAKE ISLAND, GUAM, and the Philippines. Great Britain had lost all Asian colonies and the Raj of India was threatened. Similarly, France and the Netherlands had lost all Asian possessions to Japan. The United States began conducting carrier raids against Japanese forces as early as February 1942. In April 1942, the USS *Hornet* launched 16 B-25 bombers against the Japanese homeland. Results were modest but demonstrated to both America and Japan that there had been no final reckoning.

The very nature of naval warfare was changing. Though Japan outnumbered the United States in battleships, cruisers, and destroyers, the critical element to achieve command of the sea had become the aircraft carrier. In the Pacific, Japan had eight carriers and the United States four: the USS *Enterprise*, USS *Hornet*, USS *Yorktown*, and USS *Lexington*.

The most recent offensive Japanese naval endeavor prior to Midway had been in the South Pacific approaches to Australia. On May 7 and 8, 1942, carriers USS *Yorktown* and USS *Lexington* engaged

An Expected Attack

UNDER PRESSURE from Washington, D.C., to expect an attack elsewhere, Admiral Chester Nimitz based defensive plans on the work of his intelligence staff. Commander Edwin Layton, the fleet staff's intelligence officer, advised Nimitz nine days before the Battle of Midway that the Japanese would "attack on the morning of 04 June, from the Northwest on a bearing of 325 degrees. They would be sighted at about 175 miles from Midway around 0700 local time." Layton was off by only five degrees, five minutes, and five miles.

Forty-four years to the day after the Battle of Midway, President Ronald Reagan awarded the Distinguished Service Medal posthumously to Captain Joseph J. Rochefort, USN (Ret).

AT LEFT *A Navy fighter, June 4–6, 1942, during the attack on Midway. Six months to the day after Pearl Harbor, the Battle of Midway ended in a decisive American victory.*

two Japanese carriers, *Shokaku* and *Zuikaku*, in the Battle of the Coral Sea. The USS *Lexington* was sunk. The USS *Yorktown* and the Japanese carriers were damaged.

The U.S. victory at Midway was made possible by one of the greatest INTELLIGENCE coups in history. In Hawai'i, Fleet Radio Unit Pacific (FRUPAC), under Commander Joseph J. Rochefort, had worked tirelessly breaking Japanese naval codes and piecing together the Japanese offensive plans. Rochefort knew that the Kido Butai and a powerful amphibious force were bound toward Midway. He even knew the name of the Imperial Japanese Navy flag officer selected to oppose Pacific Fleet Commander Admiral CHESTER NIMITZ.

In order to confirm his suspicion that the Japanese had targeted Midway, Rochefort had a message sent to Midway in a low-level code that he assumed the Japanese had already cracked. The message indicated that there was a problem with the water distillation plant at Midway. When shortly thereafter the Japanese indicated in their coded messages that water equipment would be needed at the targeted attack point, it confirmed Rochefort's suspicion.

ABOVE *A Japanese Kaiten one-man suicide torpedo on display at Pearl Harbor. The Kaiten was not as successful as the Japanese military had hoped it would be.*

Nimitz mustered such forces as he could against the powerful fleet. The USS *Hornet* and USS *Enterprise* were at Pearl Harbor. On May 26, USS *Yorktown* returned from the Battle of the Coral Sea, trailing a ten-mile oil slick. Though the naval engineering estimate was that USS *Yorktown* needed three months in a shipyard, Nimitz stated, "We must have this ship back in three days." The USS *Hornet* and a new USS *Lexington*, under command of Admiral Raymond Spruance, headed to the aptly named "Point Luck," north of the Japanese force. USS *Yorktown* followed.

The initial attacks were a slaughter for the Americans, but the attacks had kept Japanese fighter cover low to the sea and in need of fuel, when fresh American squadrons arrived in 70-degree bombing dives. In a matter of moments, three Japanese carriers were fatally ablaze. The Japanese pilots still aloft attacked USS *Yorktown* mercilessly, with their own deaths imminent because of the lack of flight decks upon which to land. The USS *Yorktown* sank, and American bombers sank the fourth Japanese carrier. Yamamoto ceased battle and returned to Japan.

In New York City and Washington, D.C., Americans danced in the streets. The ships and planes that had attacked Pearl Harbor were now at the bottom of the Pacific, and most of their pilots were dead. However, as the USS *Enterprise* returned to Pearl Harbor, she was met with an eerie silence. Nobody could believe what an outgunned and outclassed American force had accomplished.

For his part, Nimitz signaled Washington, D.C., that his fleet would not rest until the Imperial Japanese Navy was reduced to impotence. And he wryly added that his command was "midway toward that objective."

Further Reading: Misuo Fuchida and Masatakee Okumiya, *Midway: The Battle that Doomed Japan* (U.S. Naval Institute Press, 1955); Edwin T. Layton with John Costello and Roger Pineau, *And I Was There*

(William Morrow, 1985); Walter Lord, *Incredible Victory* (Buford Books, 1998); Jonathan Parshall and Anthony Tully, *Shattered Sword: The Untold Story of the Battle of Midway* (Potomac Books, 2005); Gordon W. Prange, *Miracle at Midway* (Penguin Books, 1982); Ronald Spector, *Eagle against the Sun* (The Free Press, 1985).

—**RAY BROWN**

Mussolini, Benito (1883–1943)

As a young man, Benito Mussolini flirted with several political movements and even entertained the notion of leaving Italy to seek his fortune in the UNITED STATES. Like his future German ally, ADOLF HITLER, Mussolini served in the army during World War I, and was angered by the treatment of Italy at the postwar peace conference.

Mussolini was a primary participant in the formation of the Fascist Party that rose to power a decade prior to assumption of power by Hitler. Mussolini believed that as the first Fascist leader to achieve power, he was the senior partner in the German-Italian alliance. The 1915 Treaty of London had promised Italy sizable territory as a reward for entering the war on the Allied side. This, and other territorial arrangements, were ignored by President Woodrow Wilson at the postwar peace conference. As a result, Mussolini was driven to establish the empire he felt Italy was due and had been denied in 1919.

Mussolini's vision of an Italian empire extended from northeast Africa across the Mediterranean and into southeast Europe. His dream was seriously hampered by the reality of poor natural resources and a small and weak industrial base in Italy that could not support the armament program necessary for such an expansion. The lack of industrial and military preparedness forced Mussolini to request, and Hitler to agree to, a three-year timetable for the beginning of war at the signing of the Pact of Steel alliance in May 1939. When Hitler put aside the timetable and began the war with the invasion of Poland in September 1939, Mussolini initially kept Italy on the sidelines.

He assumed command of Italian forces and entered the war on June 10, 1940, certain that an easy victory and the attainment of an extensive empire were at hand. His dreams were destroyed when, due to poor planning and supplies, Italian forces met with disaster in France, the Mediterranean, and North Africa.

Desperate for a victory, Mussolini ordered, against the advice of GERMANY, an invasion of Greece that required German intervention to save Italy from yet another military disaster. Throughout the war, Italy's military catastrophes led to a growing reliance on German forces, tying the political and military fortunes of Mussolini and Italy to Germany and to a wider war.

Desperate to appear as a coequal in the alliance and to find a new enemy, Mussolini rather enthusiastically joined Germany in declaring war on the United States following the attack on Pearl Harbor. This action, as well as sending an Italian force to the Eastern Front to fight the Soviet Union, first cost Mussolini his political support and then his life in 1943.

Further Reading: R. J. B. Bosworth, *Mussolini's Italy: Life Under the Dictatorship, 1915–1945* (Penguin Group, 2006); Richard J. Samuels, *Machiavelli's Children: Leaders and Their Legacies in Italy and Japan* (Cornell University Press, 2003); Gerhard L. Weinberg, *Visions of Victory: The Hopes of Eight WWII Leaders* (Cambridge University Press, 2005).

—**ABBE ALLEN DEBOLT**

N

Neutrality Acts

In the aftermath of World War I, the realization grew that a war "to make the world safe for democracy" had done no such thing. As the world situation deteriorated in the mid-1930s, Congress enacted a series of Neutrality Acts to prevent the UNITED STATES from engaging in the risky behavior that had provided the justification for its entry into World War I. Unlike the neutrality legislation of 1916–17, which had tilted in favor of one belligerent (country at war), the 1930s neutrality laws were truly intended to keep the United States neutral. Like the legislation of 1916–17, however, they failed to keep the United States out of the war.

After Italy attacked Ethiopia in May 1935, Congress enacted a temporary neutrality act that gave the president the authority to embargo arms shipments to the belligerents should he determine that a state of war existed. He could also warn American citizens that they traveled on belligerent ships at their own risk. The act made no provision for embargoing war materiel, and was to expire on February 29, 1936. On October 5, President FRANKLIN D. ROOSEVELT declared that Italy and Ethiopia were at war, embargoed arms to both sides, and warned American citizens not to travel on Italian or Ethiopian ships. He called for a "moral embargo" of all trade with Italy, but American exports to Italy increased.

On February 12, Congress approved a 14-month extension of the 1935 Neutrality Act. The act continued the mandatory arms embargo and applied it to belligerents entering a war in progress. The Neutrality Act of 1936 prohibited loans or credits to belligerents, but it exempted short-term credits.

The United States declined to invoke the Neutrality Acts with the outbreak of the Spanish Civil War, because neither law applied to civil wars. In the absence of neutrality legislation applicable to civil wars, Glenn Martin Company sold the Spanish Nationalist government eight bombers on August 10, 1936, and Robert Cuse sought an export license to sell aviation parts to the rebels on December 28. Roosevelt could object but not prohibit.

When the 1936 act expired on May 1, the Neutrality Act of 1937 went into effect. This law covered civil wars as well as wars between nations. It gave the president authority to embargo strategic materiel and outlawed travel on belligerents' ships by Americans as well as loans to belligerents. It outlawed the arming of merchant ships trading with the belligerents and made cash-and-carry optional for two years. The cash-and-carry policy allowed materiel shipments to Allies for cash.

Because the neutrality acts were intended to render the United States neutral, it was disadvantageous when the Japanese occupation of China led to the outbreak of fighting on July 7, 1937. Had Roosevelt declared the fighting a state of war, he would have been prohibited from assisting the Chinese. Roosevelt chose not to refer to the war as war.

On August 17 he said he would wait and see. On August 19 the U.S. ship *Wichita* left Baltimore, Maryland, with 19 planes for China despite a Japanese blockade of the Chinese coast. On September 13, the U.S. Maritime Commission, under Joseph Kennedy, ordered the *Wichita*'s owners to unload the planes, which they did in San Pedro, California. The next day Roosevelt barred government-owned ships from carrying arms to either China or

JAPAN. U.S. exports continued, however, particularly through England. In 1938 U.S. aircraft companies sold $9 million worth of aircraft to Japan.

After the Munich Conference of September 12, 1938, Roosevelt wanted the option of exporting arms to France and England in the event of war. On January 4, 1939, in his State of the Union address, Roosevelt asked for all methods short of war to help Britain and France. Later that month it became known that Roosevelt planned to sell U.S. planes to France and England. In March, after GERMANY took Czechoslovakia, Roosevelt wanted a new neutrality law that would aid the allies. Cash-and-carry expired. The Vorys Amendment of June 29 allowed export of "implements" of war but continued to bar arms shipments. After England and France declared war on September 5, Roosevelt invoked the 1937 Neutrality Act.

The final neutrality act, designed by Bernard M. Baruch, was enacted on November 4, 1939. This act allowed belligerents to buy American arms and materiel as long as they paid in cash and shipped the materiel on their own vessels. The expectation was that the United States would not find itself drawn into war in order to safeguard a debt owed by belligerents. It also eliminated any chance that American vessels could be caught up in belligerent blockades. The act also gave the president the authority to designate combat zones and outlawed the passage of American vessels and citizens through those designated zones, including one around Britain. Two years later, after German submarines had repeatedly made travel by American ships difficult and after the destroyer *Reuben James* was torpedoed, Congress amended the 1939 act by authorizing the arming of merchant vessels.

When the Battle of Britain began in July 1940, Roosevelt allowed the training of British pilots and

European Neutrals in World War II

NEUTRALITY IS a difficult position to take in a climate of all-out war, especially for those in close proximity to a highly aggressive nation such as Nazi Germany. Some of Germany's small neighbors attempted to accommodate the aggressor, but they quickly became associates if not necessarily allies of the Axis. That fate befell Denmark and Norway in WORLD WAR II. Other countries sought to preserve themselves through Armed Neutrality, the approach taken by the small naval powers under the leadership of Catherine II of Russia in the 1780s when England and France were at war. Increasing defense capabilities seemed successful in Sweden and Switzerland, but the former managed to remain neutral mostly because it was far enough away to avoid the initial Nazi onrush. By the time Nazi conquests had brought the Germans close to Sweden, the German resources were depleted and the Allies were forcing Germany into a defensive stance. Switzerland survived by accommodating German demands for occasional troop movements through its territory. It also retained commercial links with Germany. Ireland said that it would take the British side if invaded by Germany and the German side if Britain stationed troops in Eire.

AT RIGHT *The Swedish flag. Sweden managed to remain neutral mostly because it was far enough away to avoid the initial Nazi onrush.*

the repair of British ships in the United States. By November Britain was short of cash, so Roosevelt proposed LEND-LEASE, enacted the next March. The initial appropriation was $7 billion. In March the U.S. Coast Guard seized 64 Axis ships for use in Lend-Lease convoys, and Roosevelt gave England 10 Coast Guard ships two days later. The American security zone established in the 1939 act was expanded to cover Greenland, where the United States established bases, and the list of war zones was modified to the advantage of Britain.

On April 11, when the USS *Niblack* fired depth charges at a German U-boat, the United States and Germany began an undeclared naval war. As the year progressed, the United States became increasingly involved on the side of the Allies, while expanding the authorized zones of travel for American vessels (see ALLIES ON DECEMBER 7, 1941; AXIS POWERS IN 1941).

When ADOLF HITLER invaded Russia in June, Roosevelt failed to invoke the Neutrality Act against Russia, and Congress provided $1 billion in Lend-Lease in October. American public opinion shifted as the United States extended its support to the Allies through the year.

In 1941 Congress approved a revision to authorize the arming of merchant ships, and U.S. ships continued to be attacked by German U-boats. The 1941 revisions authorized arming of merchant ships and their entry into belligerent ports and combat zones.

Further Reading: Wesley Marvin Bagby, *America's International Relations since World War I* (Oxford University Press, 1999); Michael E. Parrish, *Anxious Decades: America in Prosperity and Depression* (W. W. Norton, 1994); John N. Petrie, "American Isolationism in the 20th Century: The Impossible Dream," National Defense University Institute for National Strategic Studies, www.ndu.edu/inss/McNair/mcnair33/m33c4.html (cited December 2005).

—JOHN H. BARNHILL, PH.D.

Nevada, USS

On an otherwise horrifying morning, the USS *Nevada* stood as a beacon of hope as the Japanese attacked seven battleships in Pearl Harbor. Destroying these seven ships on Battleship Row was one of the prime Japanese objectives in its surprise attack. While 50 of the USS *Nevada*'s crew would perish on that morning, the actions of the crew in almost guiding the USS *Nevada* to safety were an incredible feat. The ship affectionately became known as "the ship that wouldn't die."

On the morning of December 7, 1941, the battleship's top officers had gone ashore. When the Japanese planes struck, the fate of the ship was left in the hands of junior officers and their crew. The first torpedo struck the ship at approximately 8:10 A.M. The torpedo caused massive flooding to the ship's port side, but the USS *Nevada* was one of the last ships to be struck and remained afloat. The blast also failed to dismantle the ship's antiaircraft guns. Almost 30 minutes after being struck, the USS *Nevada* began a gallant escape attempt out of the harbor in an effort to keep from being sunk.

Any escape attempt would be nearly impossible. The giant ship usually required hours to get her boilers ready to power the ship—but the USS *Nevada* crew had at least two of the boilers on at the time of the attack. The actions of the brave crew, under the leadership of solely junior officers, would be just as critical as the boilers to the ship's daring escape.

Edwin Joseph Hill had been in the navy since 1912 and had risen to the rank of chief boatswain. A native of Philadelphia, Pennsylvania, Hill was instrumental in ensuring that the USS *Nevada* could attempt her escape by releasing the ship from her mooring lines, even as Japanese gunfire rained down on them. He swam back to the ship and watched as the USS *Nevada* slowly struggled on her way to safety. When barely out of the harbor, the ship could go no farther and had begun to move out of control. Hill immediately worked to drop an anchor. Since the boat was in shallow waters, she would be unable to sink far below water. While trying to drop the anchor, Hill was killed by one of six Japanese bombs that fell on the USS *Nevada*. Hill, who was 48 years old, was posthumously awarded the Medal of Honor (see CONGRESSIONAL MEDAL OF HONOR); in addition, the escort ship USS *Hill* was named for him.

Donald Kirby Ross, of Beverly, Kansas, was the only other member of the ship's crew to receive a Medal of Honor. Ross was a machinists mate and had been in the navy since 1929. When the first torpedo struck the ship, Ross was below deck. He immediately made his way to the ship's dynamo rooms, which were responsible for keeping the ship running and providing the power to keep the ship's guns firing. If the dynamo room was unable to provide this power, the ship would be unable to move and defend herself.

A second wave of Japanese planes brought further damage to the battleship as she headed out of the harbor. The ship was already running on limited power, and now she was flooding. It was soon apparent that the USS *Nevada* could travel no farther. When the junior officers ordered the ship to drop anchor and prepare to defend herself, Ross's bravery ensured that she retained her power.

As the USS *Nevada* attempted to anchor, one of the Japanese bombs exploded into an air duct. The explosion carried into the dynamo room and Ross was temporarily blinded by the blast. With dangerous smoke filling the room, a blinded Ross ordered his men out of the room, as they would surely die from inhaling the gases. Ross remained, knowing that the ship was soon going to lose her power. He stayed for 15 minutes and made the necessary adjustments to transfer the control of the ship's power to a different room. Just before completing the transfer, Ross passed out. He was rescued by a crewmember, and upon regaining consciousness, returned to the smoke-filled room and successfully transferred the power.

The USS *Nevada* was able to hold off Japanese planes, in large part because Ross had ensured that the ship's power would remain on. When the Japanese finally ended their attack, the ship was badly hurt and the room to which Ross had transferred the power was filling up with smoke. Knowing that there were crew remaining below, Ross again went belowdecks, still blinded, and emerged with an unconscious sailor on his shoulder.

In the end, the USS *Nevada* would lay beached at Hospital Point. She had luckily sunk into shallow waters and thus only her lower half was submerged and flooded. This was a definite victory for its crew as the USS *Nevada*, over the course of two months, was salvaged and used later during the war (see SALVAGE OPERATIONS).

Further Reading: Walter Lord, *Day of Infamy: The Classic Account of the Bombing of Pearl Harbor* (Henry Holt, 2001); Naval Historical Center, "USS *Nevada* (BB-36), 1916–48," www.history.navy.mil/photos/sh-usn/usnsh-n/bb36.htm (cited January 2006).

—DAVID MCBRIDE

The Life of a Battleship

COMMISSIONED IN March 1916 and built at Quincy, Massachusetts, the USS *Nevada* was the first of a class of two 27,500-ton battleships. In mid-1918 she sailed to Britain for World War I service. Thereafter the *Nevada* was active in the Atlantic, Caribbean, and Pacific. The USS *Nevada* was modernized between 1927 and 1930 and returned to duty with the U.S. Battle Fleet, operating mostly in the Pacific.

After the damage inflicted December 7, 1941, the ship underwent vigorous salvage work and temporary repairs and was able to steam to the U.S. west coast in April 1942, where she spent the rest of the year receiving permanent repairs and improvements. She reentered combat work during the Attu landings in May 1943. Transferred to the Atlantic in mid-1943, she served during the Normandy invasion in June 1944 and the southern France operation in August and September. The USS *Nevada* then returned to the Pacific and assisted with the invasions of Iwo Jima and Okinawa in 1945, sustaining damage by a suicide plane on March 27 and an artillery shell on April 5. She spent the

ABOVE *The USS* Nevada *burns in Pearl Harbor, December 7.*

remaining months of WORLD WAR II in the eastern Pacific, awaiting the invasion of Japan.

At the end of the war, the USS *Nevada* headed back to Hawai'i. Too old to remain in the postwar fleet, she was used as a target during the July 1946 atomic bomb tests at Bikini Atoll in the MARSHALL ISLANDS. Damaged and contaminated by radiation after the testing, she was formally decommissioned in August 1946. Two years later, USS *Nevada* was towed out to sea off the Hawai'ian Islands and sunk by gunfire and torpedoes.

Nimitz, Chester (1885–1966)

Chester William Nimitz was a tall, white-haired Texan, born in Fredericksburg, a town settled primarily by Germans. Young Nimitz grew up working in the family's hotel. When he could not obtain an appointment to West Point, he instead accepted his Congressman's offer of an appointment to the naval academy in Annapolis.

Nimitz worked his way steadily up through the navy ranks. His ran his first destroyer command aground, but a sympathetic commanding officer transferred him to the submarine service. Nimitz soon became an expert, even drawing upon his childhood mastery of German to further research the submarines' diesel engines, traveling to GERMANY and speaking with the engineers who had developed the engines.

December 1941 found Nimitz in Washington, D.C., on a staff assignment with the Bureau of Navigation, preparing the fleet for a war that was clearly inevitable. On December 7, Nimitz was with his family. After a late midday meal, they gathered around the radio to listen to classical music, only to hear that the Japanese had attacked Pearl Harbor.

The admiral hurried to his office. For the next several days he worked to craft a response to the Japanese that could be executed by a badly crippled fleet. After a few days, President FRANKLIN D. ROOSEVELT determined that a change of command in Hawai'i was essential and that Nimitz was the man to do it. He headed to Pearl Harbor, where he spent the rest of the war.

Nimitz directed the early morale-boosting victories of James Doolittle's carrier-based raid on JAPAN and the battles of the Coral Sea and at Midway Island (see MIDWAY, BATTLE OF). He ended the war a fleet admiral, one of four authorized by Congress. He was present at the signing of the Japanese surrender instruments and subsequently held various staff posts ashore. Nimitz died on February 20, 1966, at his home on the grounds of Treasure Island Naval Station in San Francisco Bay.

Further Reading: Edwin T. Layton with John Costello and Roger Pineau, *And I Was There* (William Morrow, 1985); "Chester Nimitz," www.history.navy.mil/faqs/faq36-4.htm (cited January 2006); E.B. Potter, *Nimitz* (Naval Institute Press, 1975).

—LEIGH KIMMEL

ABOVE *President Roosevelt in conference with General MacArthur, Adm. Nimitz, and Adm. Leahy, while on tour in the Hawai'ian Islands, 1944.*

Nomura, Kichisaburo (1877–1964)

Many times in the years after Pearl Harbor, Kichisaburo Nomura said, "I must have been the worst-informed ambassador in history." On December 7, 1941, Nomura received an encoded message from his government in Tokyo. His instructions were to deliver the message to Secretary of State CORDELL HULL at 1 P.M. Washington time. The note was long and difficult to decipher. Nomura and special envoy Saburo Kurusu did not arrive at the State Department until 2 P.M.

At 2:20, they were ushered into Hull's office and handed him the memorandum, which concluded with the words: "The Japanese Government regrets to have to notify hereby the American Government that in view of the attitude of the American Government it cannot but consider that it is impossible to reach an agreement through further negotiations."

Hull looked at Nomura coldly. "I must say that in all my conversations with you during the last nine months, I have never uttered one word of untruth. This is borne out absolutely by the record. In all my 50 years of public service, I have never seen a document more crowded with infamous falsehoods and distortions—infamous falsehoods and distortions on a scale so huge that I never imagined until today that any Government on this planet was capable of uttering them." And with that, he waved them toward the door.

Hull had learned, just moments before the diplomats arrived, that Japanese bombers had begun their surprise attack at Pearl Harbor. Nomura would always insist that his government had never told him that the attack was coming.

Born into a family of Samurai warriors in Wakayama, JAPAN, on December 18, 1877, Nomura graduated from his nation's naval academy and embarked on a long military career. In 1932, he was attending a celebration in Shanghai when an assassin tossed a bomb into the crowd. The explosion robbed him of one eye and crippled one leg. His naval career over, he turned to diplomacy. He was appointed foreign minister in September 1939 and served in this post until December 1940, when he was named ambassador to the UNITED STATES. On his way to Washington, D.C., Nomura told reporters: "I am going to the United States for peace and not for war. There must be an understanding on both sides."

Nomura became a popular member of the diplomatic corps even as relations between Japan and America deteriorated (see DIPLOMATIC RELATIONS). Standing over six feet tall, he had a long, kindly face and a friendly manner. He later said that this affability was misinterpreted on both sides of the Pacific. "I was a patriotic Japanese," he once said, "but many people took me as pro-American."

Nomura had worked hard during his brief tenure to keep communications open between the two countries. He said in his memoirs that he had told his government that war was a mistake, but they were beyond listening. He returned to Japan in 1942. In 1953, he visited the United States again. He met with Hull and Eleanor Roosevelt, and the warmth of their greeting caused him to comment: "War is war, but in human conduct we can preserve the human touch." He died in May 1964 at the age of 86.

Further Reading: Donald M. Goldstein and Katherine V. Dillon, eds., *Pacific War Papers: Japanese Documents of World War II* (Potomac Books, 2006); Gordon W. Prange, *At Dawn We Slept: The Untold Story of Pearl Harbor* (Penguin Books, 1991).

—HEATHER K. MICHON

O

Oahu Airfields and Bases

The party had lasted all night and George Welch and Ken Taylor, young Army Air Corps lieutenants with the 15th Pursuit Group, stood outside an army barracks at Wheeler Field, the center for fighter operations in Hawai'i, watching the tropical sunrise. They decided to drive back to their own base at nearby Haleiwa Field. As Welch and Taylor walked to their car, they noticed 62 new Curtiss P-40 Tomahawks parked with wingtips touching to protect them against sabotage. Suddenly Japanese dive-bombers materialized out of the clouds. Parked planes disintegrated and buildings began to burn. Bullets spraying around him, Welch ran for a telephone and called Haleiwa.

"Get two P-40s ready! It's not a gag—the Japs are here!" he shouted.

Japanese Zeros (see JAPANESE AIRCRAFT) strafed Welch and Taylor three times as they drove to Haleiwa. Nine minutes later as they swung onto their field, the P-40s were armed and their propellers spinning. Welch and Taylor did not wait for orders. In two sorties, they managed to shoot down six enemy planes before they had to land, and later Welch was credited with four confirmed kills and Taylor with two. Both Welch and Taylor received the Distinguished Service Cross for extraordinary heroism.

All told, about 20 American fighter planes, including five obsolete Republic P-35s, managed to get airborne to counter the Japanese attack on the morning of December 7, 1941. Most of them were shot down, but they provided fierce and prophetic resistance.

CAUGHT BY SURPRISE, AT LEFT *Admiral Kichisaburo Nomura, Japanese umbassador to the United States, (left), and special envoy Saburo Kurusu (right), leave the U.S. State Department on December 7, 1941.*

Nomura had just delivered a message to U.S. Secretary of State Cordell Hull from the Japanese government which read, in part, "...it is impossible to reach an agreement through further negotiations."

Hull had learned, just moments before the diplomats arrived, that Japanese bombers had begun their surprise attack at Pearl Harbor. Nomura was unaware of the attack and would always insist that his government had never told him that the attack was coming.

The Imperial Japanese Navy had assembled the airborne attack force to strike Oahu's military installations to cripple the Pacific Fleet (see PACIFIC FLEET, U.S.) anchored at Pearl Harbor so that JAPAN would have a free rein in the South Pacific. They had to destroy air opposition so they attacked Hickam, Wheeler, and Bellows Fields with devastating firepower. The Japanese knew that if U.S. fighter planes could get into the air in significant numbers they would pose a serious threat to Japanese bombers and perhaps endanger the Japanese Striking Force's aircraft carriers.

The Japanese first attacked Wheeler Field, where flying pursuit groups of P-36s and P-40s were based, zooming straight down Oahu Island. The dive-bombers split and attacked from the east and west, beginning their runs at 10,000 feet and releasing their bombs at 500 feet. The fighters stayed above 15,000 feet but as soon as they encountered no air opposition, they assisted the dive-bombers in high-speed, low-level strafing runs.

The Japanese bombs heavily damaged Wheeler Field, destroying almost half of the P-40s on the ground, but smoke from one of the first hangars hit partially covered the P-36s so just a few of them were destroyed. The badly damaged hangars included one where much of Wheeler's aircraft and machine-gun ammunition had been stored. Thirty-three men were killed and 73 wounded. Although Schofield Barracks, adjacent to Wheeler Field, was not a primary target, at least two Zeros hit several structures at Schofield on the way to Wheeler Field. Of approximately 140 planes on the ground at Wheeler, mainly P-40 and P-36 pursuits, nearly two-thirds were destroyed or put out of action.

Shortly after the Japanese hit Wheeler Field, a squadron of about 50 dive-bombers and fighters attacked Hickam Army Airfield adjacent to the Pearl Harbor Navy Yard. They first bombed the Hawai'ian Air Depot's engineering building and hangar area where bombers were parked wingtip to wingtip. Fearing sabotage from the large local Japanese population, the U.S. Navy had bunched the planes together in one place where they could be carefully guarded. They made easy targets for Japanese aviators, who broadened their attack to include the huge new consolidated barracks, mess hall, base theater, the post exchange, and other buildings. Many men were killed as they slept in the 3,200-man barracks, the largest in the Army Air Forces at the time. The mess hall in the center of the building took a direct hit that killed 35 men eating breakfast. Several cooks seeking shelter in a walk-in cooler died from the concussion of later blasts.

Japanese maps showed the area just behind the consolidated barracks as an underground fuel storage dump, but the Army Air Forces had located the fuel storage dump elsewhere and the baseball field built on that location received many direct bomb hits.

Many men at Hickam Field responded heroically. One man lugged a machine-gun to the roof of a

ABOVE *Wheeler Field. A P-40 destroyed in the Japanese attack. The Japanese dive-bombers began their runs at 10,000 feet and released their bombs at 500 feet.*

hangar. Another climbed into a parked B-18, mounted a .30 caliber machine-gun in the nose, and kept firing at the Japanese until incendiary bombs hit the plane and burned it. Altogether, 189 men died at Hickam Field and 303 were wounded. About two-thirds of the B-17, B-18, and A-20 bombers at Hickam were also wrecked or damaged enough to keep them grounded.

The Japanese waited until about 8:30 A.M. to attack Bellows Field in Waimanalo, when a single Japanese fighter flew in over the ocean and fired its machine-guns at the tent area. Soon nine more fighters arrived and thoroughly strafed the field, destroying several P-40s. Members of Wheeler Field's 44th Pursuit Squadron who were at Bellows for gunnery training rushed out to arm their P-40 Warhawks. The Japanese fire killed one pilot as he climbed into his airplane and shot down another pilot at the end of the runway. The third pilot got airborne but Japanese fire quickly gunned down his plane, which crashed into the ocean. He managed to swim ashore despite his wounds.

The Japanese planes also attacked the U.S. Navy and U.S. Marine Corps air stations on Pearl Harbor's Ford Island, at Ewa to the west of Pearl Harbor, and Kaneohe Bay near Bellows Field. The attack reduced Ewa's airplanes, which were mainly carrier-type bombers and fighters, from nearly 50 operational planes to less than 20. Japanese planes attacked Ford Island and Kaneohe, where several squadrons of long-range PBY patrol seaplanes were based, in successive waves. Ford Island, in the middle of Pearl Harbor, was headquarters of Patrol Wing Two and some sources say that the first bomb of the Pearl Harbor attack struck there, prompting the message, "Air Raid, Pearl Harbor—this is no drill." In all, the Japanese destroyed 33 PBY patrol seaplanes and other aircraft on Ford Island and gutted one big hangar.

A major navy patrol seaplane base was located at Kaneohe Bay, on the east coast of Oahu. Some of the buildings at Kaneohe were still being constructed, while it already housed three patrol squadrons and 33 PBYs on the ground or floating just offshore when the Japanese raiders arrived. The Japanese destroyed all but six of the PBYs and the survivors were damaged. Only the three Kaneohe Bay PBYs that were out on patrol were fit for service at the end of the Japanese raid. Altogether the Japanese destroyed 92 navy aircraft and damaged 31; the Army Air Corps sustained 96 planes lost and 128 damaged.

Admiral ISOROKU YAMAMOTO, the mastermind of the Pearl Harbor attack and commander of the Imperial Japanese Navy, had particularly wanted to catch the three U.S. aircraft carriers at Pearl Harbor. He almost did include the USS *Enterprise* in the tally. She was returning to Pearl Harbor from Wake Island, but heavy seas kept her from arriving at Pearl Harbor on time, which would have meant her demise. Many of her scouts and bombers that flew in ahead of the ship, however, were caught in the initial Japanese attack, and five planes were lost.

Around 7:30 P.M. on December 7, 1941, as it was getting dark, Navy Lieutenant Fritz Hebel was leading his Wildcat fighters from the USS *Enterprise* toward Ford Island after completing a search mission. The men on the ground were still nervous from the morning attacks and no one knew for sure whether or not the Japanese would return. As Hebel's fighters came in for a landing the whole sky was crisscrossed with tracer bullets from ship antiaircraft guns. Hebel and three other navy pilots were killed by friendly fire.

The sequel to the Japanese attack played at Bellows Field on December 8, 1941. The Japanese had launched five two-man MIDGET SUBMARINES against Pearl Harbor, and the American forces sank all of them except one, which drifted out to Bellows Field and grounded on the reef. One Japanese crewmember drowned after escaping from the submarine. The other, Ensign Kazuo Sakamaki, washed ashore and was captured. Air Force personnel dragged the midget submarine off the reef and onto the beach. Bellows Field captured the first American prisoner of war and the first war prize one day after the Japanese attack on Pearl Harbor. (See also OAHU FORTS.)

Further Reading: "George Welch, Ken Taylor, Fritz Hebel," Aviation History On-Line Museum, www.aviation-history.com (cited March 2006); Naval Historical Center, "Pearl Harbor Raid," www.history.navy.mil (cited March 2006); U.S. Army Corps of Engineers, Office of History, "Did You Know?" www.usace.army.mil/history (cited March 2006).

—KATHY WARNES

Oahu Forts

The U.S. military presence increased sharply in Hawai'i during its territorial years, beginning in 1898. Fort Shafter was built in 1905 and construction of Pearl Harbor Naval Base was begun in 1908. Several small forts were built on Oahu's south shore. Schofield Barracks was built in 1909 on a base covering over 14,000 acres.

After World War I, Hawai'i became the home of the U.S. Pacific Fleet (see PACIFIC FLEET, U.S.). Hickam Field, Kaneohe Naval Air Station, and the U.S. Marine Corps Air Station, later known as Barbers Point, had joined the growing list of properties taken over by the military.

In 1905, the U.S. War Department began construction at Fort Shafter as part of an ambitious building program that included the army's Fort DeRussy, Fort

Ruger, and Schofield Barracks. The fort was named for Major General William R. Shafter, commander of the expeditionary force that liberated Cuba in 1898. In June 1907, the 2nd Battalion, 20th Infantry Regiment became the first unit stationed in the barracks facing Palm Circle. Over the decades, the post's key location between Pearl Harbor and HONOLULU led to its gradual expansion, including a hospital, ordnance depot, antiaircraft regiment, and signal depot.

From 1921 through World War II, Fort Shafter served as an antiaircraft artillery post and on December 7, 1941, the Coast Artillery batteries established gun positions on the parade field and sustained the only known casualties on the post. Fort Shafter was strafed during the attacks. Some of the fixed antiaircraft units at Fort Shafter defended the fort against the Japanese planes.

Fort DeRussy was an army reservation built in 1915 in order to protect Honolulu and Pearl Harbor as part of the U.S. territory. Initially large cannons were located in two battery locations within the fort, and later on, the cannons were replaced with antiaircraft guns. The Hawai'ian Coast Guard Artillery Command located its headquarters at Fort Ruger and four Coast Artillery regiments were stationed at Fort Armstrong, Fort Barrette, Fort DeRussy, Diamond Head, Fort Kamehameha, Kuwaaohe Military Reservation (Fort Hase), and Fort Weaver. None of them played a major role in the December 7, 1941, attack.

During the late 1930s and early 1940s the U.S. military instituted selective service, numerous training exercises, the mobilization of the National Guard, and the doubling of the Army Department's strength to 43,000 soldiers, including the Air Corps. The Hawai'ian Department's two main tasks were to protect the Pacific Fleet from sabotage and defeat any invasion. In April 1941, the army chief of staff reported to President FRANKLIN D. ROOSEVELT that

"Don't Worry about It"

AS 21-YEAR-OLD army private Joseph McDonald neared the final minutes of his 14-hour overnight shift at the switchboard at Fort Shafter, the switchboard lit up with a call. A few minutes after 7:00, Private Joseph Lockard, along with his partner, Private George Elliot, of the army's fledgling SCR-270 radar system at Opana radar station near Kahuku Point, called McDonald to report a large flight of incoming planes 136 miles north of Oahu. McDonald was stationed at Fort Shafter's information center as a member of the 580th Signal Aircraft Warning Company the day of the attack. He wanted the officer in charge, Lieutenant Kermit Tylor, to recall army plotters, who had just left the night shift, to the information center at Fort Shafter. The plotters worked on a large table map of the islands and plotted all radar sightings.

Tyler said, "Don't worry about it," in regard to the Lockard and McDonald reports, because he believed that the radar operators were seeing a dozen U.S. B-17 bombers flying in from the U.S. west coast. McDonald also argued that the radar sightings should have been reported to Wheeler Field, but none of his superiors passed on the message. About an hour later Japanese bombs struck Hickam Field.

History and Pearl Harbor conspiracy advocates have been harsh in their judgment of Tyler. Throughout the years since the Pearl Harbor attack, books and Hollywood films have ridiculed him and at the least, cast him as incompetent. Daniel Martinez, a National Park Service historian based in Hawai'i, thinks the historical verdict on Tyler has been somewhat unfair. Martinez points out that in 1941, Tyler was a fighter pilot. Born in Iowa and raised in Long Beach, California, Tyler was assigned to the Army Air Corps' 78th Pursuit Squadron at Wheeler Field in central Oahu. On December 7, 1941, Tyler was working as the pursuit officer at the Fort Shafter Information Center on the 4 A.M. to 8 A.M. shift, only the second time he had done so.

ABOVE *A navy patrol plane and gun crew with an improvised mount, in front of a hangar. Ford Island Naval Air Station.*

Tyler's task as pursuit officer was to help the more experienced officers assign planes to intercept enemy aircraft, but those officers did not have to work on Sunday morning, December 7. The crew of enlisted men plotting aircraft positions on a large map finished their shift at 7 A.M. When the telephone rang about six minutes later, Tyler and McDonald were alone. Lockard and Elliot, the Opana radar station operators, reported that they had spotted something big on their radar scope that was moving very quickly.

"Even had Kermit Tyler seized upon the idea that this was a threat, he had no ability to contact the airfields to warn them to scramble the planes. There was no telephone system yet to call and issue a warning," Martinez said.

In 1970 Tyler and his family were invited to the premiere of *Tora! Tora! Tora!* Film representatives told him that he played a role in the picture, so he proudly brought his family to see the film. His scene featured a drunken soldier at a bar complaining that he had just been called up to Fort Shafter. The drunken soldier was supposed to be Tyler.

"The island of Oahu, due to its fortification, its garrison, and its physical characteristics, is believed to be the strongest fortress in the world."

Between 1911 and 1914 the Army Corps of Engineers built four batteries: Selfridge, Hasbrouck, Hawkins, and Jackson, adding a fifth, Battery Closson, in 1920. These batteries were key sections of Oahu's "ring of steel," which included Forts Armstrong, DeRussy, and Ruger, along with Ford Island Military Reservation. Other forts and military reservations supporting artillery were developed in the 1940s, particularly after the attack of December 7.

After General WALTER C. SHORT assumed command of the Hawai'ian Department of the Army in February 1941, he moved into Quarters 5, the commanding general's residence on Palm Circle. On Sunday morning, December 7, 1941, as he was dressing for his regular Sunday morning golf match with his navy counterpart Admiral HUSBAND E. KIMMEL, he heard machine-gun fire from the direction of Pearl Harbor. He placed his command on the highest alert. On December 17, 1941, he was relieved of his command and retired shortly after. (See also OAHU AIRFIELDS AND BASES.)

Further Reading: Mike Gorden, "Don't Worry about It," *Honolulu Advertiser* (December 7, 1999); "The Hawai'ian Department 7 December 1941," www.usarpac.army.mil/history/dec7_hawndept.asp (cited February 2006).

—KATHY WARNES

Oklahoma, USS

The USS *Oklahoma* was completely destroyed when the Japanese attacked Pearl Harbor, suffering the second-highest number of casualties. The ship was authorized by Congress on March 4, 1911, and was built by the New York Shipbuilding Corporation in Camden, New Jersey, in the fall of 1912. Two years later, on March 23, the USS *Oklahoma* was launched by Lorena J. Cruz, the young daughter of the governor of Oklahoma. The USS *Oklahoma* was commissioned in Philadelphia on May 2, 1916, and first set sail under the command of Captain Roger Welles. Classified as a *Nevada*-class battleship, the USS *Oklahoma* had a displacement of 27,500 tons and a top speed of 20.4 knots. The ship was built with VTE reciprocating machinery and experienced problems with vibration throughout her 30-year lifespan.

In her early days of service in World War I, the USS *Oklahoma*'s most harrowing experience was an encounter with Sinn Fein, a group of Irish rebels, in which several crewmen were drowned. The USS *Oklahoma* served an as escort for President Woodrow Wilson when he sailed to France in December 1918 and accompanied the president home from Europe in the summer of 1919 after he had signed the Treaty of Versailles.

After World War I, the USS *Oklahoma* traveled the world, taking part in training exercises and rescue missions, which included rescuing Americans stranded by the outbreak of the Spanish Civil War. The crew loved to brag about a baby being born on board during the latter rescue attempt. After a chance encounter with a tugboat carrying railroad cars in 1940, the USS *Oklahoma* crew joked about being the only battleship that had ever sunk a freight train. On September 16, 1927, reconstruction began on the USS *Oklahoma* and continued until July 15, 1929.

When the Pacific Fleet (see PACIFIC FLEET, U.S.) was ordered to Pearl Harbor in May 1940, the USS *Oklahoma* took up residence in Hawai'i. Far from being a deterrent as had been predicted, the fleet proved to be a prime target for attack. At 7:55 A.M., on December 7, 1941, the first wave of Japanese bombers and fighters arrived over Pearl Harbor, just as the morning clouds were breaking up. The Japanese had been ordered to take out all battleships and aircraft carriers but were stymied in the latter attempt, because the carriers had been moved out to sea. However, the vessels along Battleship Row, particularly the older ships that had been positioned outboard, took the brunt of the attacks.

Unlike the USS *Arizona*, USS *California* (see CALIFORNIA, USS), and USS *West Virginia* (see WEST VIRGINIA, USS), which sank outright, the USS *Oklahoma* capsized. All told, 415 were killed, including 20 officers and 395 enlisted men. One of the officers was Father Schmitt, the ship's chaplain, who as the senior officer aboard, refused to leave the sinking ship. The crew had been allowed to sleep in that Sunday morning, and many men were still belowdecks.

Thus, the true horror of the attack on the "Okey," as she was known to her crew, was that most of the 415 casualties died not from bombs or torpedoes but from being trapped inside the ship's wreckage. Due to the efforts of Julio De Castro, a civilian dockworker, and a number of sailors who launched a rescue campaign, 32 men were cut out of the ship's hull. Until December 10, noises could be heard from inside the ship, where men were trapped below the water line, beyond the help of would-be rescuers. Despite the horrendous losses, 986 men survived the attack on the USS *Oklahoma*, including 62 officers and 924 enlisted men.

The ship had been pelted with at least five Japanese Type-91 aerial torpedoes and one bomb, in addition to being strafed with machine-gun blasts. Two events increased the loss of life and hastened the sinking of the USS *Oklahoma*. A panicked novice neglected to push a button on the bridge that would have given the men below five precious minutes of warning before the USS *Oklahoma* was hit. Second, the hatches on the "blisters," the airtight compartments that were supposed to keep the ship upright if struck by a torpedo, were normally closed. On December 7, they had been opened because of an admiral's inspection scheduled for the following day. In 1943, the USS *Oklahoma* was salvaged in a massive rescue operation (see SALVAGE OPERATIONS). After being turned upright, she was patched and refloated. While under tow en route from Hawai'i to California in May 1947, the USS *Oklahoma* sank.

Further Reading: *Dictionary of American Naval Fighting Ships* (Naval History Division, 1959); Robert O. Dulin Jr. and Stephen Bower Young, *Trapped at Pearl Harbor: Escape from Battleship* Oklahoma (North River Press, 1991); William H. Garzke and Robert O. Dulin Jr., *Battleships: Allied Battleships in World War II* (Naval Institute Press, 1980); Benjamin W. Labaree et al., *A Maritime History* (Mystic Seaport, 1998); John Lehman, *On Seas of Glory: Epic Battles of the American Navy* (The Free Press, 2001).

—ELIZABETH PURDY, PH.D.

ABOVE *Rescue crews line the hull of the 29,000-ton* USS Oklahoma *which capsized after being blasted by Japanese warplanes.*

P

Pacific Fleet, U.S.

On December 7, 1941, the U.S. Pacific Fleet (USPACFLT) consisted of three aircraft carriers, eight battleships, eight cruisers, 29 destroyers, 500 other ships, and 390 planes. The Pacific Fleet was not destroyed at Pearl Harbor, yet the surprise attack was a resounding and humiliating defeat. In two hours, 18 warships had been sunk, others damaged, 188 aircraft destroyed, 155 planes damaged, and 2,403 servicemen lost. The carriers USS *Lexington* and USS *Enterprise* were at sea on December 7. The USS *Saratoga* was in port in San Diego, California.

In the aftermath of the attack the commander of the Pacific Fleet, Admiral HUSBAND E. KIMMEL, was aware that he still had a formidable force available, and the Japanese attack had not touched the invaluable fuel stocks or critical repair facilities. Still, the Pacific Fleet would undergo profound changes after the attack.

By the summer of 1944 the Pacific Fleet had little resemblance to the old order of battle in 1941. The Pacific Fleet became the largest and most lethal seagoing force in world history. The old battleships were relegated to patrol of the west coast of the UNITED STATES. New fast carriers, new amphibious forces, and new submarines were the means of offensive victory.

APPROACH TO WAR

In the years following World War I, U.S. military forces, particularly the army, fell on hard times. Money and equipment were scarce and

SAILING TO THE SOUTH PACIFIC AT LEFT *Photographed from the deck of a Coast Guard combat transport, this parade of ships was symbolic of America's farflung supply lines in the Pacific. The convoy was carrying men and materials to the South Pacific battle lines. November 6, 1943.*

promotions quite slow. The navy did not fare nearly so badly as the army, but it was by no means ready for war when it came.

In December 1941 the United States had three fleets—the Atlantic, the Pacific, and the Asiatic. Both the Atlantic and Pacific Fleets were under the overall command of Commander in Chief, U.S. Fleet, which had the unfortunate acronym CIN-CUS (pronounced "sink us,"), which was changed to Chief of Naval Operations (CNO) after the sinking of so many U.S. ships on December 7.

The navy was still built around the battleship and the concept of "the decisive battle," which was a gunnery action. Eighty percent of all Annapolis naval academy graduates went to battleships after graduation. To make the best of certain disarmament agreements, the navy had converted some ships to aircraft carriers and had even built some new carriers. Still, the prophets of airpower at sea were only a growing minority, and the concept of amphibious landing was not highly regarded at the time. Though the marines were restructured during the inter-war years to undertake that mission, the navy was little more than an interested observer. Commander Richmond Kelly Turner advised the Naval War College class of 1937 that the purpose of the fleet was to create situations for decisive battles like Jutland or Trafalgar. Yet Turner later became famous for commanding the amphibious forces in the Pacific during WORLD WAR II. He never entered into a surface battleship engagement.

During the inter-war years, the U.S. Navy had a series of contingency plans for war, all given a color designation for who the enemy might be—red for Great Britain, green for Mexico, black for GERMANY, and so on. Conflict with JAPAN was designated Plan Orange and was "played" 127 times by U.S. Navy officers at the Naval War College prior to World War II.

Though the plan had an assumption that the PHILIPPINES would be held, many officers thought the islands would fall to Japan. Though the level of reality of Plan Orange is a matter of debate—to some minds the war games were a forerunner of victory, to others an exercise in futility—it can be said that a generation of officers became familiar with the peculiar geography and hydrography of the vast Pacific region, where the largest naval war in history would be fought.

AFTERMATH OF DEFEAT AT PEARL HARBOR

Kimmel, who after the attack on Pearl Harbor mused that a stray Japanese bullet in his office might have done well to have hit him, was relieved by Admiral CHESTER NIMITZ as commander in chief of the U.S. Pacific Fleet. Nimitz, a submariner, had until then been in Washington, D.C., in charge of navy personnel. The subsequent investigations into the attack found Kimmel guilty of errors of judgment and not coordinating army-navy efforts to defend Hawai'i (see INVESTIGATIONS OF RESPONSIBILITY). In May 1942, Kimmel decided to take early retirement.

During the war, Kimmel was employed by Frederick R. Harris Incorporated, which did secret work for the navy. He died in 1968 in Groton, Connecticut, a bitter man. The level of his culpability had long been officially decided, but remains to this day a matter of historic controversy (see HISTORIANS' VIEWS).

Nimitz assumed command of the Pacific Fleet in a modest ceremony on the deck of a submarine 10 days after the Pearl Harbor attack. To the surprise of many, not least of whom were the officers themselves, he retained almost all of Kimmel's staff. This decision would serve him well in the coming months and years, in terms of ease of transition, competence, and loyalty.

Addressing the Sailors

ON SEPTEMBER 15, 1942, with the fighting in Guadalcanal raging on land and in the water, Admiral Chester Nimitz spoke the following at an awards ceremony for men of the Pacific Fleet:

"Much has been accomplished since those critical opening days of the war, but much remains to be done. At this very moment our forces, in which all of the four armed services—the Navy, Marine Corps, Coast Guard and Army—are represented, are stubbornly and successfully resisting the powerful efforts of the Japanese to eject us from our hard-won positions in the southeastern Solomons. Slowly but surely we are tightening our grip—not without losses—but with losses disproportionately small compared with those of our enemy.

"Do not for one minute assume that we have the Japanese on the run. While we may not like many of their characteristics, we cannot deny that they are brave, skillful, and resourceful fighters, who frequently prefer death to surrender. They are dangerous antagonists, but they have learned by now that we also are dangerous antagonists who are willing and know how to fight.

"We have had losses and we must expect more losses before this war is won, but must not be dismayed by such prospects. Successful war against a powerful enemy cannot be waged without losses. Nor can we expect to be fully trained and ready before fighting. We will never reach that stage in our training where we will be ready to the last gaiter button. We must fight to the best of our ability with what we have when we meet the enemy. Time and not state of training is the determining factor. He who gets there 'fastest with the mostest' is still a good guide to success.

"We will win this war only by fighting. All the nation's productive output will be of no avail unless we are willing to come to grips with the enemy. Suitable targets present themselves only rarely to our guns, bombs, and torpedoes. On those rare occasions our tactics must be such that our objectives are gunned, bombed, or torpedoed to destruction. This our enemy will understand and respect. Such resolution will be rewarded. When things look bad for our side remember that the prospect may be, and probably is, even tougher and blacker to the other fellow."

ABOVE *Inspection aboard a U.S. submarine at the New London submarine base in Connecticut.*

THE U.S. ASIATIC FLEET

The Pacific Fleet based at Pearl Harbor was not the only U.S. naval force in the Pacific. Admiral Thomas C. Hart commanded the Asiatic Fleet responsible for the protection of the Philippines and American interests in Southeast Asia and China. The Asiatic Fleet consisted of fleet headquarters in the Philippines, which amounted to one heavy cruiser, one light cruiser, 13 old destroyers, 29 submarines, five gunboats, one yacht, six minesweepers, two tankers, six motor torpedo boats, and a number of minor auxiliaries. The fleet also included the USS *Langley* (CV-1), a converted collier, which was the navy's first aircraft carrier, and the Fourth Marine Regiment (the China Marines) in Shanghai, China—though shortly before commencement of hostilities with Japan, these China Marines were deployed to Corregidor and Bataan (and ultimately the Bataan Death March and harsh imprisonment).

The U.S. Asiatic Fleet did not exist past February 1942. The Japanese onslaught was relentless. American, British, Dutch, and Australian (ABDA) forces were cobbled together in an effort to defend the East Indies and Southeast Asia from the Japanese forces. There were a number of engagements, but the issue was never in doubt. ABDA and the U.S. Asiatic Fleet ceased to exist by March 1942.

Hart, already past retirement age, and with both his flagship and sole aircraft carrier at the bottom of the ocean, returned to Washington, D.C., for work on the navy's General Board. Hart led one of several investigations of the defeat at Pearl Harbor, conducting interviews in the Pacific theater so that important lessons would not be lost.

ORGANIZING FOR VICTORY

The vast oceanic area indicated that the Pacific would be predominantly a naval theater. However, personalities and politics demanded other considerations. Though General DOUGLAS MACARTHUR's ordered escape from the Philippines had been onboard a PT boat commanded by Medal of Honor awardee John Bulkeley and thence by plane over vast ocean waters, neither MacArthur, nor the army, nor his political supporters would stand for his leading a command subordinate to a U.S. Navy Flag officer. Similarly, the navy was not about to stand for an army officer unfamiliar with the mysteries of sea-holding power to command naval forces. The Pacific theater became a divided command, contrary to war-fighting doctrine and basic principles of command.

The central Pacific was commanded by Nimitz, who retained command of the Pacific Fleet, but it also had land and air components commanded by general officers of other services. The southwest Pacific theater—the approaches to Australia, most of the Solomon Islands, New Guinea, most of the East Indies, and the Philippines—was commanded by MacArthur. He would have a modest subordinate naval component, but most strike forces were sent in by Nimitz. The arrangement was not the best, but the vast reaches of the Pacific did not leave either Nimitz or MacArthur looking for additional work.

The Pacific Fleet was organized into the 3rd and 5th Fleets. The 3rd Fleet proceeded with operations under Admiral William F. Halsey and his staff. While the 3rd Fleet was deployed, Admiral Raymond Spruance and his staff planned the next operation. Upon return of the 3rd Fleet, they would simply trade places with Halsey and his team became the 5th Fleet. The arrangement worked remarkably well. Halsey was known as a "sailor's admiral." "Bull" Halsey, the Patton of the Pacific, was a bit coarse, extremely aggressive, beloved of his sailors, and enormously outspoken. Spruance was known as an "admiral's admiral." Quiet and gentlemanly, his standing orders, policies, and procedures were more organized than those of the 3rd Fleet. Spruance was a bit more cautious than Halsey, but neither was ever defeated in battle. Eventually, by the time of the great central Pacific offensive of 1944, there were enough ships and sailors for two fleets, so the 3rd and the 5th could be at sea at the same time.

There was also the somewhat lighter and more amphibian 7th Fleet under Admiral Thomas C. Kincaid, which became the naval component of MacArthur's southwest Pacific area. The 7th Fleet worked with the 3rd in the victory in the Philippines.

GROWING THE FLEET AFTER PEARL HARBOR

Before the attack on Pearl Harbor, the Pacific Fleet consisted of nine battleships, three aircraft carriers, 12 heavy cruisers, eight light cruisers, 50 destroyers, and 33 submarines. There were also a number of auxiliaries. When the landings at Okinawa began on April 1, 1945, the invasion force of the 5th Fleet possessed 1,300 ships. At the surrender of Japan on September 2, 1945, there were 234 Allied ships in Tokyo Bay alone, the vast majority of these American, and all under command of Nimitz. A Japanese diplomat who was part of the formal surrender party later spoke of the sight and stated that he had then wondered to himself, "How did we ever think we could defeat these people?"

Between July 1940 and September 1945, U.S. Navy personnel strength grew from 203,127 to 4,064,455. These figures include the U.S. Marine Corps and the U.S. Coast Guard. The majority of these people served in the Pacific theater.

AT LEFT *War production–drive poster, drawn by well-known cartoonist Garrett Price. September 1942. Poster drives were common, promoting enlistment for both men and women, recycling of items such as paper, rubber, scrap metal, and nylon hosiery, and keeping the public's mind focused on the war effort.*

Early in the war, the United States lost four aircraft carriers to enemy action—the USS *Lexington* at Coral Sea, the USS *Yorktown* at Midway, the USS *Wasp* at Guadalcanal, and the USS *Hornet* at Santa Cruz. Indeed, after the Battle of Midway, Nimitz for a time had only two operational carriers in his command. However, during World War II the United States built and commissioned 17 fleet carriers and almost 100 smaller aircraft carriers. Additionally, logistics support ships as well as amphibious ships developed to a level new in world history. The Pacific Fleet needed to be self-sustaining for months at a time across thousands of miles. The scale was quite an adjustment for the British Pacific Fleet, which arrived in 1945. Similarly, the amphibious force, under Turner, had to embark, transport, land, and support not only division-strength marines and soldiers, but eventually whole armies, as at Okinawa.

SUBMARINES

A crucial element of the Pacific Fleet was the submarine force. U.S. submarines in the Pacific operated out of Pearl Harbor and Brisbane, Australia (the latter a part of MacArthur's area of responsibility). Commander, Submarine Forces Pacific (COMSUBPAC) for most of the war was Vice Admiral Charles A. Lockwood.

Though plagued early in the war by defective torpedoes and commanding officers not up to wartime responsibilities—almost 30 percent were relieved of command in 1942—the submarine force eventually provided a critical blow to Japanese sea power. U.S. submarines sank 1,300 Japanese ships, including a battleship, eight aircraft carriers, and 11 cruisers. Constituting less than 2 percent of the navy's personnel strength, U.S. submariners were responsible for 55 percent of Japan's maritime losses. Twenty-two percent of the submariners were killed in ac-

tion. Submariners were also the most highly decorated branch of the armed forces: seven captains were awarded the Medal of Honor. Commander Sam Dealy of the famous USS ("Hit 'em Again") *Harder* was awarded five Navy Crosses and the Medal of Honor. Many submarine commanding officers were incredibly brave and resourceful.

The Pacific Fleet was the largest and arguably most successful armada in the history of the world. The accomplishments in technological advance and decisive victory may well be without equal. The victory in the Pacific rendered the United States the dominant and unchallenged sea power in the Pacific and the world for the remainder of the 20th century and into the 21st century.

Further Reading: Clay Blair, *Silent Victory* (Naval Institute Press, 2001); John Costello, *The Pacific War* (William Morrow, 1982); Walter Lord, *Incredible Victory* (Burford Books, 1988); Samuel Eliot Morison, *History of U.S. Naval Operations in World War II* (University of Illinois Press, 2002); E. B. Potter, *Nimitz* (Naval Institute Press, 1976); Gordon Prange, *At Dawn We Slept* (Penguin Group, 2001); Ronald Spector, *Eagle against the Sun* (Random House, 1985); John Toland, *Infamy: Pearl Harbor and Its Aftermath* (Penguin Group, 1982).

—RAY BROWN

Panay Incident

The *Panay* incident involved an attack by Japanese aircraft on the USS *Panay* in China on December 12, 1937. The attack left three killed and 43 sailors and five civilian passengers wounded.

The USS *Panay*, launched in Shanghai in 1927, was one of a series of U.S. Navy gunboats assigned to the Yangtze Patrol of the Asiatic Fleet. Her mission was to protect American lives and property against Chinese warlords and bandits and to guard U.S. in-

The Yangtze Patrol

THE U.S. Navy maintained warships along the Yangtze River in China from 1854 to 1942. Many of the missions were simply to show the flag, but the ships' crews also were involved in repeated operations against pirates, bandits, and warlords. Virtually all the major European countries and Japan also kept warships and gunboats along the Yangtze.

Following the Boxer Rebellion in 1900, the U.S. Navy formally organized the Yangtze Patrol, initially based in Shanghai and later Hankow, and the South China Patrol, headquartered in Hong Kong. The first gunboats were a mix of U.S.-built vessels, Spanish gunboats captured in the Spanish-American War, and later, some built locally. In late November 1941, three of the five U.S. gunboats in China sailed to Manila. The USS *Wake* was seized in port on December 8, and the USS *Tutuila* was handed over to the Chinese government after her crew was flown to India in January 1942.

terests after the Japanese invasion of China. In December 1937, the USS *Panay*, under the command of Captain James Hughes, was assigned the mission of evacuating the remaining Americans from the city of Nanking as Japanese forces advanced toward the city. Three Standard Oil tankers, the *Mei Ping, Mei An*, and *Mei Hsia*, sailed with the *Panay*.

The Japanese naval commander in Shanghai was notified of the USS *Panay*'s movements. Despite this, the Japanese army commander ordered Japanese aircraft to attack "any and all ships" in the Yangtze River north of Nanking. After the Japanese navy verified this order, its aircraft launched a bombing attack that continued for about two-and-a-half hours, until the USS *Panay* sank. Surviving crew members of the ship were taken on board one U.S. vessel and two British ships and evacuated.

The Japanese claimed that the attack was unintentional and that they did not realize that the *Panay* was a U.S. vessel due to "poor visibility." A U.S. Navy board determined, however, that the ship was flying a clearly visible U.S. flag, and this was verified by newsreel footage taken at the time of the attack. President FRANKLIN D. ROOSEVELT reportedly was furious and initially called for "a forceful response." Despite the president's anger, however, the general reaction among most Americans and politicians seemed to be muted.

Part of the relatively calm response was probably due to the rather quick Japanese diplomatic response to the attack. On December 24, the Japanese government formally apologized, promised to punish those responsible, and offered reparations. On April 22, 1938, Tokyo paid reparations of $2,214,007.36 to officially settle the incident. One interesting aspect of the Japanese response to the attack on the *Panay* was the reaction of the Japanese public. Within days of the incident, members of the public were offering their condolences, including sympathy cards and letters from schoolchildren and private visits to the wife of the U.S. ambassador to Tokyo by wives of Japanese officials, reportedly without their husbands' knowledge. Private contributions from Japanese also flowed in. Many of these donations also were from schoolchildren and pensioners, and some were as little as two yen.

The USS *Panay* incident did not lead to any direct military response, but it was one more milestone in the steadily growing tensions between the UNITED

STATES and JAPAN. It also indicated the growing belligerency of the pro-war faction among the commanders of the Japanese army.

Further Reading: Manny T. Koginos, *The Panay Incident: Prelude to War* (Purdue University Studies, 1967); Hamilton Darby Perry, *The Panay Incident: Prelude to Pearl Harbor* (Macmillan, 1969).

—LAWRENCE E. CLINE, PH.D.

Panic

In the days following the Japanese attack on Pearl Harbor, cities along the west coast of the UNITED STATES and others throughout the country fell into panic as rumors of further attacks flourished. The next day, the *San Francisco Chronicle* reported planes being spotted over the city. The following night, military officials ordered blackouts of coastal cities.

Seattle, the city closest to what would become the Alaskan front, practiced air-raid drills throughout 1942, and in the Los Angeles area, local officials granted police officers the authority to enforce city-wide blackouts by breaking light bulbs if necessary. On the east coast, fears of possible German incursions spread as well. This initial panic touched off a series of measures designed to protect the United States from direct attack or internal subversion, principally sabotage. While many of the rumors proved erroneous, continental defenses remained as a few failed Axis operations sustained American anxieties on both the Atlantic and Pacific coasts.

Following the attack on Pearl Harbor, west coast residents saw soldiers move in to guard against invasion, sabotage, and insurrection. Soldiers and police officers stood guard around harbors, airfields, railways, bridges, and reservoirs. In the days to come,

Los Angeles Blacks Out

THE INITIAL attack on Pearl Harbor led to a series of blackouts intended to prevent a similar attack in the Los Angeles area. The Long Beach City Council passed an ordinance on December 9, 1941, authorizing the police department broad powers to force compliance. If no other means were available to turn out the lights, policemen were to pull circuit-breaker switches or break lights. Captain Richard B. Coffman, the commander of the 11th Naval District, which includes Los Angeles and the surrounding communities, ordered retail establishments along the coast closed by 4:30 P.M. All lights within 15 miles of the harbor were ordered out. Coffman advised residents to refrain from unnecessary travel or telephone use to keep transportation and communication lines free for military use. Those businesses near the harbor that needed to remain open received a fresh coat of black paint over their windows.

Headlines of the **Chicago Daily News** ABOVE LEFT *and the* **Honolulu Star-Bulletin** ABOVE RIGHT *on December 8, 1941, reflect the shock of the nation over the bombing of Pearl Harbor.*

stories of panic filled the newspapers. The U.S. Navy and Air Force searched unsuccessfully for Japanese carriers off the coast of northern California, as San Francisco Bay area residents received reports that enemy planes had circled the city the night before. Only a few days later, Eleanor Roosevelt, who was traveling to the west coast with civil defense director and mayor of New York City Fiorello La Guardia to shore up civil defense organization and morale, received false reports that San Francisco was under Japanese attack.

Officials in Los Angeles reported "imminent" attacks from Japanese aircraft. Naval forces in Southern California braced for a large air and sea invasion from a reported 34 enemy ships waiting to attack off the coast of Los Angeles. One report suggested a Japanese ship lay silent only a few miles from Catalina Island. These kinds of rumors only fueled panic further. In the end, it seems floating logs and migrating whales served as target practice for aircrews on edge.

Investors in the stock exchange reacted somewhat predictably to the panic that ensued from Pearl Harbor. The sound of air-raid sirens in New York City created anxiety among small investors, but using the term *panic* to describe market activity would be hyperbole. Traders reacted with nervousness, dumping Pacific Coast securities with sharp losses for companies that were believed to be overly exposed to air raids; however, total market activity was up and net losses were not large.

In the end, the initial reaction of panic subsided, replaced by a more consistent alertness. By the end of the next year, Axis powers (see AXIS POWERS IN 1941) were on the defensive and authorities focused less attention on building civil defenses. However, the panic that the attack on Pearl Harbor produced led to heightened alertness with varied consequences. On the one hand, U.S. Coast Guard Beach Patrols successfully thwarted covert sabotage by GERMANY. On the other hand, rumors of enemy aircraft over American cities and of ships lurking offshore demonstrated the degree to which the attack on Pearl Harbor and other bases in Hawai'i had unnerved the general public. (See also HONOLULU.)

Further Reading: Roy Hoopes, *Americans Remember the Homefront: An Oral Narrative of the World War II Years in America* (Penguin Group, 2002); Robert C. Mikesh, *Japan's World War II Balloon Bomb Attacks on North America* (Smithsonian Books, 1990); Bert Webber, *Silent Siege III: Japanese Attacks on North America in World War II* (Webb Research Group, 1992).

—CHAD PARKER

Pearl Harbor: Action Report

At 7:49 A.M. on December 7, 1941, Mitsuo Fuchida, a Japanese Imperial Navy pilot, led his fleet of 183 Japanese fighter planes down the eastern side of Oahu, then banked west and flew along the southern coast past the city of HONOLULU. As he swept toward Honolulu, Fuchida radioed to the *Akagi*, the 1st Japanese Air Fleet flagship. History and Hollywood have recorded his radio message as "*Tora! Tora! Tora!*," the Japanese word for "tiger." The literal translation of his message is the Japanese word *totsugeki*, which means "charge," and *ra* which is the first syllable of *raigeki*, meaning "torpedo attack." His three-word message actually broadcast the news of the successful torpedo attack on Pearl Harbor to his superiors, Admirals Chuichi Nagumo and ISOROKU YAMAMOTO.

Fuchida believed that the torpedo attack on Pearl Harbor had been a complete surprise, but he had miscalculated. The Japanese had inadvertently warned both the U.S. Navy and the U.S. Army of their impending attack. Patrolling in the pre-dawn darkness of December 7, 1941, the USS *Ward* had reached a restricted zone off the entrance of Pearl Harbor when the minesweeper *Condor* reported that she had spotted a submarine periscope at 3:42 A.M. Almost three hours later, a patrol plane also spotted the periscope and used a smoke pot to mark its location. The USS *Ward* fired her guns and dropped depth charges and radioed the news of the incident to Pearl Harbor and in turn Pacific Fleet Commander Admiral HUSBAND E. KIMMEL was informed of the incident. Kimmel did not act on this warning. This submarine was one of the five Japanese MIDGET SUBMARINES that attempted to enter Pearl Harbor as part of Yamamoto's plan of attack. The USS *Ward*'s crew later was cited for firing the first shot in the Pearl Harbor attack.

Army Signal Corps Privates Joseph Lockard and George Elliot experienced this same inaction by their superiors. They were operating the Opana Radar Site near Kahuku Point on the northern tip of Oahu using equipment designed to be an early warning system. At 7:02 A.M. they spotted the approach of the Japanese planes that would shortly attack Pearl Harbor. Elliot called the Information Center and told them about the unusual incoming flight. Lockard talked to Air Corps Lieutenant Kermit A. Tyler, stressing the direction and size of the flight. Tyler told Lockard, "don't worry about it." This was the first time that U.S. military forces used radar in warfare.

The American forces at Pearl Harbor had much to worry about in the next two hours. At dawn on December 7, 1941, Nagumo's task force of six heavy aircraft carriers and 24 supporting vessels arrived undetected about 200 miles north of Oahu. At 6 A.M., 183 planes took off from six Japanese carriers and winged south toward Oahu. The airborne armada consisted of torpedo bombers, dive-bombers, horizontal bombers, and fighters (see JAPANESE AIRCRAFT); they arrived at Oahu shortly before 8:00 A.M. The Japanese planes bombed and strafed the navy air bases at Ford Island and Kaneohe Bay, the Marine airfield at Ewa, and the Army Air Corps fields at Bellows, Wheeler, and Hickam (see OAHU AIRFIELDS AND BASES). Other planes assaulted the ships moored in Pearl Harbor, the crews aiming their guns, bombs, and torpedoes at the seven battleships anchored along Battleship Row and the USS *Pennsylvania* (see PENNSYLVANIA, USS) in dry dock across the channel. Yamamoto had planned the simultaneous attacks to destroy the American planes before they could get into the air to intercept the Japanese. The Japanese attacked in two waves using a total of 359 planes.

ABOVE *The Japanese American owner of this store, a graduate of the University of California, was forced to close as a result of evacuation orders. He placed the "I am an American" sign in the window on December 8, 1941.*

Within minutes after the Japanese planes swooped out of the clouds firing their guns and dropping their bomb and torpedo payloads, they had hit all of their battleship targets. The USS *West Virginia* (see WEST VIRGINIA, USS) sank almost immediately and the USS *Oklahoma* (see OKLAHOMA, USS) turned turtle and sank. An armor-piercing bomb ignited the forward ammunition magazine of the USS *Arizona* (see ARIZONA, USS) and the explosion and fire killed 1,171 crewmen. The USS *Arizona* suffered the most casualties of any of the battleships and made up about half the total number of Americans killed at Pearl Harbor. The Japanese also damaged the USS *California* (see CALIFORNIA, USS), USS *Maryland* (see MARYLAND, USS), USS *Tennessee* (see TENNESSEE, USS), and USS *Nevada* (see NEVADA, USS) in varying degrees during the first half hour of the raid.

About 8:30 A.M., the Japanese planes lessened the fury of their attack and the USS *Nevada* took advantage of the lull. Chief Boatswain E. J. Hill cast off the lines under fire and swam back to the ship. Later while on the forecastle attempting to let go the anchors, several bombs exploded, blew him overboard, and killed him. Despite the damage that the Japanese had inflicted upon the USS *Nevada*, Lieutenant Commander Francis J. Thomas managed to get her moving within 40 minutes of the attack and headed down the channel. Before she could clear the harbor, the second wave of Japanese planes, which had been launched a half hour after the initial force, appeared overhead. They focused their attacks on the USS *Nevada*, attempting to sink her in the channel so that she would block the narrow entrance to Pearl Harbor. The harbor control tower ordered the USS *Nevada* to beach herself at Hospital Point. Thomas obeyed the order and the channel remained unblocked.

The Japanese attack on Pearl Harbor ended shortly before 10 A.M., two hours short of when it began. The damage assessment amounted to at least a year's depletion of U.S. fighting power in the Pacific. Twenty-one ships from the U.S. Pacific Fleet (see PACIFIC FLEET, U.S.) were sunk or damaged. The majority of American airplanes were hit before they could take off, with 188 totally destroyed and 159 damaged. The American death toll numbered 2,403, including 68 civilians, most of whom were killed by antiaircraft shells landing in Honolulu. There were 1,178 military and civilian personnel wounded.

By comparison, Japanese losses were negligible. Less than 10 percent of the attacking force, 29 planes out of 353, failed to return to their carriers. However, the Japanese had failed to damage any of the three American aircraft carriers. On November 28, Kimmel sent the USS *Enterprise* to deliver U.S. Marine Corps fighter planes to Wake Island. The USS *Enterprise* made the delivery on December 4 and on December 7 steamed 200 miles outside Pearl Harbor. On December 5, Kimmel sent the USS *Lexington* to deliver 25 scout bombers to Midway Island, and the last Pacific carrier, USS *Saratoga*, had left Pearl Harbor for upkeep and repairs on the west coast. The Japanese force failed to damage the shoreside facilities at the Pearl Harbor Naval Base that later helped America to win the war. Fortunately for the Americans, the tanker *Neosho*, berthed at the southern end of Battleship Row, had finished transferring aviation fuel to the adjacent oil tanks on Ford Island five minutes before the first attack. If the tanker or the tank farm had been hit, the fire storm would have engulfed the nearby USS *Maryland*, USS *West Virginia*, and USS *Tennessee*. However, the *Neosho*'s antiaircraft guns were in action by 8:10 A.M. and, at 8.42 A.M., she started to move away to a safer part of the harbor. The USS *Arizona* was considered too badly damaged to be salvaged, the USS *Oklahoma*, although raised from the harbor, was considered too old to be worth repairing, and the *USS Utah* also was not considered worth repairing (see SALVAGE OPERATIONS).

Further Reading: Department of Defense, 50th Anniversary of World War II Commemorative Committee, *Pearl Harbor: 50th Anniversary Commemorative Chronicle*, "A Grateful Nation Remembers" (The Committee, 1991); Joseph Lockard, "Pearl Harbor Revisited: Reflections," Historical Electronics Museum Newsletter, November 1991, www.history@ieee.org (cited March 2006); Gordon W. Prange, *God's Samurai: Lead Pilot at Pearl Harbor* (Potomac Books, 2003); World War II action reports, the Modern Military Branch, National Archives and Records Administration, www.history.navy.mil/docs/wwii/pearl/ph59.htm (cited March 2006).

—KATHY WARNES

Pennsylvania, USS

In the early 1940s, as WORLD WAR II continued in Europe and as hostilities with JAPAN mounted, the USS *Pennsylvania* (BB-38, 1916–48) was one of the ships assigned to Pearl Harbor, Hawai'i, with the idea that the Pacific Fleet (see PACIFIC FLEET, U.S.) would serve to deter foreign attackers. As the third navy ship named for the second state, the *Pennsylvania* had been authorized by Congress on August 22, 1912, and commissioned in June 1916 at a total cost of $12,993,579.23. Classified as a "super-dreadnought" battleship, along with her sister ship, the USS *Arizona* (see ARIZONA, USS), the USS *Pennsylvania* was designed with a displacement of 31,400 tons and a top speed of 21 knots. She was armed with twelve 14-inch guns, fourteen five-inch guns, four three-pounders, and two 21-inch torpedo tubes. Captain H. B. Wilson was the first commander of the USS *Pennsylvania* when she sailed from Newport News at 10:11 A.M. on March 16, 1915, after being christened by Elizabeth Kolb of Germantown. When she set sail, the USS *Pennsylvania* was considered the world's biggest battleship.

After serving as a flagship in the Atlantic Fleet, the USS *Pennsylvania* was sent to France in 1918. Because the USS *Pennsylvania* and the USS *Nevada* were the only oil-burners in the U.S. Navy, they were considered "too modern" for active fighting in the military theater where other ships were fueled by coal, which was more readily available.

After the end of World War I, the USS *Pennsylvania* reverted to the role of navy flagship and was assigned to the Battle Fleet where she traversed the Atlantic and the Pacific, as well as the Mediterranean. Following a cruise to Australia and New Zealand in the mid-1920s, the USS *Pennsylvania* was returned to the Philadelphia Navy Yard to be modernized to better equip her for participating in naval drills.

The crew of the USS *Pennsylvania* generally referred to the ship as "The Pennsy," "The Mighty Penn," or "The Old Falling Apart." The latter nickname was derived from the USS *Pennsylvania's* ten-

ABOVE *The USS* Pennsylvania, *flagship of the Pacific Fleet, suffered only slight damage. The wrecked USS* Downes *is shown at left, and the USS* Cassin *at right.*

dency to sound as if she were coming apart during attacks as she discharged a heavy volume of fire. On the morning of December 7, 1941, when the Japanese attacked Pearl Harbor, the USS *Pennsylvania* was in dry dock. Plans to return her to Battleship Row had fortuitously been delayed. Because she was not initially in the line of attack, the USS *Pennsylvania* was able to return fire at Pearl Harbor and was afterward able to continue to wage war against Japan, motivated by the rallying cry, "Remember Pearl Harbor."

On the morning of December 7, most of the crew of the USS *Pennsylvania* was belowdecks, and the chaplain was making preparations for the 8 A.M. mass. All men were on board because overnight leaves had been canceled in response to the volatile political situation. By the time the call to General Quarters summoned the crew to their assigned positions, some of the crew had already begun firing the 50-caliber Browning machine-guns. At 7:57 A.M., explosions were heard, and the air defense siren was sounded. After observing an attack force of a large number of Japanese aircraft, crewmembers knocked locks off ammunition boxes and began loading other weapons in order to return fire. Some time between 8 A.M. and 8:30 A.M., the crew of the USS *Pennsylvania* noted that the USS *Nevada* (see NEVADA, USS) had managed to get under way but was halted by a number of Japanese bombs.

According to an official navy report of February 15, 1942, the USS *Pennsylvania* lost 26 enlisted men and two officers on December 7. Most of those deaths occurred when a five-inch gun mount was felled by a 500-pound bomb, which had been dropped from a Japanese plane at a height of 10,000 to 12,000 feet and had penetrated casemate nine on the starboard side of the ship. The bomb caused the boat deck to open both upward and downward; and guns were put out of commission. The galley was also hit, and

fuel from the service tanks ran onto the lower decks. Among the 29 men wounded, injuries ranged from severe burns to multiple wounds. Most of the damage to the USS *Pennsylvania* was derived from machine-gun bullets, but a large part of the destruction occurred when a portion of a torpedo tube from the USS *Downes* hit the forecastle of the ship. Fire was a major problem on board the ship, and the loss of ammunition destroyed in the attack made it difficult to return fire.

Some two weeks after the attack, the USS *Pennsylvania* sailed to San Francisco for repairs (see SALVAGE OPERATIONS). She was structurally updated and equipped with new antiaircraft machine-guns to fit her for participation in various operations in Alaska and Asia and in patrolling the coasts of Hawai'i. Chiefly, the USS *Pennsylvania* was used to attack Japanese strongholds while invasions were carried out. In her final attack against Japan, the USS *Pennsylvania* received heavy damage when she was hit by a Japanese torpedo in August 1945 in Okinawa, making her the last ship to be damaged by enemy fire in World War II.

The USS *Pennsylvania* was subsequently deemed too old for service and was relegated to target duty. Her final duty was to serve as a target during the July 1946 Bikini Atoll atomic bomb test, thus providing evidence for studies on the effects of residual radioactivity. Because of the radioactivity, the USS *Pennsylvania* was scuttled at Kwajalein on February 10, 1948.

Further Reading: *Dictionary of American Naval Fighting Ships* (Naval History Division, 1959); William H. Garzke and Robert O. Dulin Jr., *Battleships: Allied Battleships in World War II* (Naval Institute Press, 1980); Benjamin W. Labaree et al., *A Maritime History* (Mystic Seaport, 1998); John Lehman, *On Seas of Glory: Epic Battles of the American Navy* (The Free Press, 2001); "USS Pennsylvania," www.usspennsylvania.com (cited March 2006).

—ELIZABETH PURDY, PH.D.

Philippines, Preparation for Attack

While the attack on Pearl Harbor was under way, the Philippine Islands were already on alert for possible attack, and even a potential invasion. The possibility of Japanese aggression could not be underestimated as was shown in China in the 1930s, and the general belief among American military planners was that an attack against the UNITED STATES would most likely occur at the PHILIPPINES.

American forces based in the Philippines would pose a considerable hindrance to Japanese expansion in the Pacific region, as well as a threat to the Japanese home island of Kyushu, which could be reached by bombers based in the Philippines. Military strategists and planners in Washington, D.C., were aware of this, and therefore measures were taken to deter Japanese aggression and defend the Philippines against a Japanese attack.

Abandoning an earlier plan to withdraw completely from the area, President FRANKLIN D. ROOSEVELT instead ordered a buildup of forces in the Philippines beginning in 1940, most notably the movement of additional bombers to Philippine base airfields. General DOUGLAS MACARTHUR was called out of retirement to oversee military forces in the Philippines. Unfortunately, the presence of bombers was a nullified advantage following the surprise bombing conducted by the Japanese air force within hours after the assault on Pearl Harbor.

In the event that war broke out with JAPAN, the official strategy to protect the Philippines was detailed in the plan for war against Japan, known as War Plan Orange. The plan detailed a Philippine-American force holding the Bataan Peninsula and the island of Corregidor to prevent an invading force from securing a beachhead in Manila Bay, until the expected arrival of help came from the forward U.S. naval base at Pearl Harbor.

As time went on, American war planners saw the Philippines as a certain loss in the event of an attack. This was primarily because the distance from the Philippines to the nearest U.S. naval assistance was immense, making the territory nearly indefensible. There was also an assumed likelihood of GERMANY being a greater threat, which would require more military resources in the Atlantic and European theater.

Due to the Japanese surprise strike at Pearl Harbor, there was no way to send any part of the devastated American fleet in time to assist Philippine-American defenders. The Philippines were temporarily lost to the Empire of Japan.

Writers and scholars assign MacArthur differing degrees of blame because of his unrealistic attempt at defending the whole of Luzon's coastline with undertrained and poorly equipped soldiers, his lack of preparedness for defending the key airfields, and his delay in properly supplying and preparing the forces that eventually took defensive positions at Bataan and Corregidor. The defenders of Bataan and Corregidor in 1941 bravely held their positions as long as possible despite being poorly supplied and having almost no hope for the arrival of help.

Further Reading: Peter Calvocoressi, Guy Wint, and John Pritchard, *Total War: The Causes and Courses of the Second World War* (Penguin Books, 1975); John Costello, *The Pacific War* (Rawson, Wade, 1981); David Reynolds, *From Munich to Pearl Harbor: Roosevelt's America and the Origins of the Second World War* (Ivan R. Dee, 2001); John Toland, *The Rising Sun: The Decline and Fall of the Japanese Empire, 1936–45* (Cassell and Company, 1970).

—WILLIAM D. LAREMORE

Philippines

The Philippines represented a key defensive position for the UNITED STATES at the start of WORLD WAR II. Geography was the main reason: Manila is 5,000 miles from Pearl Harbor, but only 1,800 miles from Tokyo. Although this increased the strategic importance of the islands, it also meant that supporting them in case of war would be extremely difficult. Politics and diplomacy also played a role: the United States had agreed to grant the Philippines gradual independence and was turning over many defense responsibilities to the emerging commonwealth; also, as a result of the Washington Naval Treaty of 1922, the United States agreed to limit its fortifications in the Pacific.

On December 7, the forces defending the Philippines consisted of slightly over 31,000 U.S troops and Philippine Scouts, and some 100,000 Philippine troops (see PHILIPPINES, PREPARATION FOR ATTACK). About nine hours after the attack on Pearl Harbor, the Japanese began air attacks against Philippine military installations—which knocked out about half the U.S. aircraft and caused the withdrawal of most of the navy's surface vessels—and then began landing troops on islands north of Luzon. JAPAN's ground forces consisted of about 57,000 troops, a significantly lower figure than the troop strength of the defenders. The Japanese, however, had the advantage of having a wide choice of landing sites, and most of the troops of the Philippine army were poorly trained and badly equipped. Japanese forces made a series of landings on December 8, 10, 12, 22, and 24, continually moving toward Manila. During these operations, the Japanese suffered only about 2,000 casualties.

AT LEFT *Gen. Douglas MacArthur, center, wades ashore during initial landing operations at Leyte, Philippines, on October 20, 1944.*

The Japanese commander, General Homma, was instructed that he must complete the operations in Luzon Island in 50 days; half his forces would then be detached for operations elsewhere.

General DOUGLAS MACARTHUR concluded that his forces could not hold the main island of Luzon, so on December 26, Manila was declared an open city, and the remaining U.S. and Philippine forces withdrew to the more defensible Bataan Peninsula, which was about 25 miles long and 20 miles wide. The defense was aided by the Japanese decision to remove one of their best divisions to operations in the Dutch East Indies and replace it with lesser-quality troops. This gave the U.S and Philippine troops a welcome respite in early January. Allied troops established strong defensive positions and—after having their initial defense line broken— repulsed a series of Japanese attacks and attempts at amphibious landings. By early February, the Japanese had suffered about 7,000 combat casualties and another 10,000 to 12,000 dead of disease.

The defenders, however, suffered from shortages of food, medical supplies, and ammunition, and malaria spread widely. Daily rations were reduced to 1,000 calories, mostly rice with protein provided by mule, monkey, water buffalo, or lizard meat. Many medical supplies, particularly quinine to combat malaria, had been lost or abandoned during the retreat. By the end of March, U.S. commanders reported that about 75 percent of their troops were unfit for duty. Morale also reportedly plummeted as it became clear that the U.S. troops could expect no relief forces, and especially after MacArthur and his primary staff were evacuated to Australia on March 12.

The Japanese began their final offensive against Bataan on April 3. The exhausted defenders could not hold the attackers and the corps commander surrendered his forces on April 9. Since individual units were cut off, their commanders had to surrender on a piecemeal basis. The movement of the prisoners to prisoner-of-war camps became known as the Bataan Death March due to the some 600 Americans and 5,000 to 10,000 Filipinos who died on the trek. In part, the high numbers of deaths were the result of the soldiers' weakened physical condition and poor planning by the Japanese, but the mortality rate was exacerbated by the brutality of many of the Japanese guards.

The heavily fortified island of Corregidor off the coast of Bataan continued to hold out. After several weeks of heavy shelling, the Japanese landed forces on Corregidor the night of May 5. By the end of May 6, General Jonathan Wainwright began surrender negotiations. On May 8, Wainwright ordered all U.S. and Philippine forces to surrender, but it took until June 9 for all forces to do so. A few small units and individuals continued to fight on as guerrillas.

Further Reading: William H. Bartsch, *December 8, 1941: MacArthur's Pearl Harbor* (Texas A&M University Press, 2003); Donald Knox, *Death March: The Survivors of Bataan* (Harvest, 2002); William Manchester, *American Caesar: Douglas MacArthur, 1880–1964* (Little, Brown, 1978); Eric Morris, *Corregidor* (Cooper Square Press, 2000).

—LAWRENCE E. CLINE, PH.D.

Preparedness

Admiral ISOROKU YAMAMOTO, the Japanese architect of the surprise attack on Pearl Harbor, remarked to several different cabinet members in Japan in 1940, "In the first six to 12 months of a war with the United States and Great Britain I will run wild and win victory upon victory. But then, if the war continues after that, I have no expectation of success."

Even though he believed that the attack on Pearl Harbor was a blunder and that JAPAN could not win a protracted war with the UNITED STATES, Yamamoto carefully planned and executed the attack so successfully that, as he anticipated, it temporarily halted and then threw the U.S. military machine into overdrive to overcome its devastating effects. The focal points of Yamamoto's plan were meticulous preparation, surprise, and using aircraft carriers and naval aviation in new and creative ways (see JAPANESE AIRCRAFT; JAPANESE FLEET). At the center of Yamamoto's plan were six aircraft carriers surrounded by 24 supporting vessels. A separate group of Japanese submarines would sink any American battleships that escaped the Japanese carrier force.

In many respects Japan's longstanding isolationist and militaristic policies predestined Pearl Harbor. Ironically, these same policies in the United States produced very different results. The United States was partially prepared for war, but could not unite its citizens to officially declare war until Pearl Harbor. Americans from President FRANKLIN D. ROOSEVELT down to the man on the street who considered Japanese people "the yellow peril" and vastly inferior fighters and human beings significantly underestimated the ferocity, tenacity, and resilience of the Japanese people.

In a reverse historical irony to American isolationism, on March 31, 1854, Commodore Matthew Perry, with a powerful fleet at his command, persuaded the Japanese to agree to open the country to foreign trade after 200 years of isolation from the rest of the world. Japanese statesmen realized that the old policy of isolation was definitively ended,

and because Japan was compelled to associate with other nations, some Japanese rulers resolved to make Japan strong enough to dominate them. By the mid-1920s Japan had politicized its distrust of the United States, partially because of long-standing American policies toward Japan, including the 1924 Exclusion Act prohibiting further immigration from Japan. Japan also viewed the United States as an empire-building rival after a struggle over domination of Hawai'i. Winning the 1904 Russo-Japanese War inflamed Japanese nationalism and convinced some factions in the country that Japan was well on its road to world domination.

Documents like the "Tanaka Memorial" drew the attention of the world to Japanese expansionist dreams. Premier Baron Giichi Tanaka, who had become Japanese premier as the leader of the aggressive military party, sent his memorial advocating Japanese world domination to the emperor on July 25, 1927. The document foreshadowed Japan's September 18, 1931, invasion of Manchuria, the northernmost province of China, an event that many historians consider the real beginning of WORLD WAR

ABOVE LEFT *A poster promoting more production and military preparedness.* **ABOVE RIGHT** *Submarine construction in Groton, Connecticut, August 1943.*

11. Manchuria was 6,000 miles from San Francisco, but over the next 10 years Japanese policy aggressively worked toward expanding to encompass all of the South Pacific, and eventually the western coast of the United States.

In the next decade, the militarists also prevailed over those desiring more conciliatory policies toward the United States. The United States increased military and financial aid to China, began to strengthen its military power in the Pacific, and stopped shipping oil and other raw materials to Japan (see SANCTIONS AGAINST JAPAN). In response, Japan's leaders decided on a program of seizing the resources of Southeast Asia. This put the United States and Japan on a collision course toward war.

Despite its own episodes of empire-building, the United States practiced isolationist policies from colonial times, and during the 1920s and 1930s, most Americans opposed becoming involved in Europe's alliances and wars. The beginning of World War II in September 1939, the 1940 German military successes in Europe, and the Battle of Britain jolted many Americans wide-awake and made them wonder if the western hemisphere would be next. Others still backed the noninterventionist America First Committee in 1940 and 1941, but the isolationists did not have enough political clout to derail the LEND-LEASE Act, aid to Britain, and other interventionist measures. The Roosevelt administration tried to persuade a reluctant nation to face the Axis powers, for by now imperial Japan had acquired allies (see AXIS POWERS IN 1941). Representatives of Nazi GERMANY, Fascist Italy, and imperial Japan signed the Tripartite Pact in Berlin on September 27, 1940, formalizing the partnership of the Axis powers. The Tripartite Pact was a warning to the United States to remain neutral or fight a war on two fronts.

Although the United States had sporadic imperialistic episodes before and after Perry's invasion of Japan in 1854, it reluctantly joined the last year of World War I. After World War I, the major nations undertook large new capital expenditures to build battleships and battle cruisers. By 1920, the United States had already laid down the keels for five battleships and four battle cruisers. Japan began a program that called for eight battleships and eight battle cruisers and in 1921 Britain ordered four large battle cruisers with plans for four matching battleships. The United States initiated a treaty to limit the largest ships and on February 6, 1922, five nations signed the Washington Naval Treaty, which limited the naval armaments of each major world power. Representatives of the United States, the British Empire, the Empire of Japan, the French Third Republic, and Italy signed the treaty and the U.S. Senate ratified it on March 29, 1922.

The treaty limited the capital ship tonnage and total tonnage for aircraft carriers. In Europe the treaty affected planned building programs for most of the countries that signed it. Almost all of the countries built fewer battleships, but also converted existing battleships and battle cruisers. This produced World War II fleets consisting primarily of ships laid down before World War I. The United States built no new battleships until the keel of the USS *North Carolina* was laid in October 1937, a period of almost 20 years. Japan terminated the treaty in 1934, and the later attack on Pearl Harbor caused the U.S. Navy to convert from a battleship fleet to a carrier-based force. Overall, some historians say the Washington Naval Treaty enabled Japan to arm at a gallop, while hobbling the United States and European nations.

International disarmament agreements like the Washington treaty, decreasing military budgets, and rivalries between the service branches of the military for scarce dollars drastically affected U.S. preparedness at Pearl Harbor. Defense budgets had focused on building battleships instead of on aviation. When Billy Mitchell demonstrated that airplanes could sink battleships off the coast of Virginia in 1921 (see AIRPLANES VERSUS SHIPS), the navy declared the test void since Mitchell had violated its guidelines. The Bureau of Aeronautics increased its development of the aircraft carriers that would help win the Pacific in World War II, and the Air Corps began to push its agenda toward aerial combat. Still, on December 3, 1941, Japan had 10 aircraft carriers compared to the three then available to the U.S. Navy in the Pacific Ocean.

For the first half of 1941, U.S. military strategy and preparations were aimed at actively fighting the Atlantic war and maintaining a defensive posture in the Pacific. For some time the United States had been decoding Japanese messages (see CODES, JAPANESE) and U.S. officials knew early in the month of July 1941 that Japan had decided on further aggression to the south. Even though it had broken the Japanese code, the U.S. government did not cohesively evaluate Japanese intentions, and continually overestimated U.S. preparedness.

President Roosevelt theorized that the American navy could block Japan from the Aleutian Islands to Hawai'i, from Howland to WAKE ISLAND to GUAM. Great Britain would take over from the American line to Singapore (see MALAYA AND SINGAPORE). The president thought that Japan could be brought to its knees within a year.

As well as the American generals, the HONOLULU press seriously underestimated Japanese strength. The *Honolulu Advertiser* said in a lead editorial on December 3, 1941: "Unless there is an immediate and complete reversal of Tokyo policy, the die is cast. Japan and America will travel down the road to war. Such a course should be sad for Japan to contemplate. She is the most vulnerable nation in the world to attack and blockade. She is without natural resources. Four years of war have already left deep scars. She has a navy, but no air arm to support it."

At this point the Japanese attack force was more than halfway to Pearl Harbor. Yamamoto would get his six months to run wild and more, successfully attacking the United States at Pearl Harbor and leading the Japanese navy to its early victories in the Pacific. In a final irony, when the United States decoded a Japanese message in 1943 that included Yamamoto's itinerary, 18 American P-38s ambushed and shot down his plane near Bougainville. In the end the admiral had motivated his enemy to become prepared.

Further Reading: *Honolulu Advertiser* (December 3, 1941); Harold L. Ickes, *The Secret Diary of Harold L. Ickes* (Simon and Schuster, 1954); Taro Sakamoto, *The Six National Histories of Japan* (UBC Press, 1991); James C. Schneider, *Should America Go to War: The Debate over Foreign Policy in Chicago, 1939–41* (University of North Carolina Press, 1992).

—KATHY WARNES

ABOVE LEFT *A war production–drive poster.* **ABOVE RIGHT** *A boarding house in Hawai'i displays a sign discouraging the passage of rumors.*

R

Rankin, Jeannette (1880–1973)

As the first woman elected to the U.S. Congress, social reformer and political activist Jeannette Pickering Rankin holds a distinct place in American history. Rankin is remembered as the only member in either house of Congress to cast a dissenting vote against declaring war on JAPAN after the attack on Pearl Harbor that took place on December 7, 1941. The only female in Congress in 1917, Rankin was one of 50 members of Congress who voted against American entry into World War I. In 1940, Rankin won her bid to return to the House of Representatives on an isolationist platform, and she remained devoted to this cause even after public opinion swung to a pro-war position in the wake of Pearl Harbor.

As an avid pacifist, Rankin had been strongly influenced in her opposition to American involvement in WORLD WAR II by the findings of the Nye Committee, which advanced the belief that the Allies, chiefly through the influence of British Prime Minister WINSTON CHURCHILL, along with munitions makers, were lobbying for American involvement in the war. When President FRANKLIN D. ROOSEVELT tried to help the Allied cause by proposing the LEND-LEASE deal that allowed the UNITED STATES to provide the Allies with military equipment in exchange for American military bases, Rankin joined other isolationists in voting against the measure. Eleanor Roosevelt reportedly attempted to win Rankin's support for the war by inviting her to a secret meeting at the White House, along with other influential female politicians. Rankin did not move from her antiwar position.

Even before 1941, historians believe Roosevelt had become firmly convinced that American entry into World War II was inevitable. Isolationists, however, remained determined to prevent such action (see ISOLATIONIST PRESS). Everything changed at 7:55 A.M. on December 7, 1941, when the Japanese attacked the U.S. Pacific Fleet (see PACIFIC FLEET, U.S.) as it was docked at Pearl Harbor, Hawai'i, crippling America's naval strength and striking a severe blow to its defensive position. Roosevelt reacted to Pearl Harbor by asking Congress to declare war on Japan. Rankin learned of the impending vote from a radio announcement while aboard a train en route to Detroit. Unable to sleep, Rankin spent the night of De-

cember 7 in an upper berth, dreading the coming day. On December 8, Rankin left the train at Pittsburgh and returned to Washington, D.C. Upon arriving in the capital, she spent the day driving around in her car, thus ensuring that she remained inaccessible to anyone who would seek to influence her vote.

Members of Congress were so unified in their reaction to Pearl Harbor that debate on the declaration of war lasted a scant 40 minutes (see CONGRESSIONAL REACTION). The vote to declare war on Japan was 388–1. When casting her vote against American entry into World War I, Rankin had opted to let her vote speak for itself. In 1941, however, Rankin was determined to make her voice heard. She wanted to get the declaration referred to committee and tem-

Women in Congress

IN 1916, women were not allowed to vote in national elections or in most state elections. Nevertheless, three women ran for congressional seats on major party tickets. Only Jeannette Rankin, a pacifist Republican from Montana, was successful in winning a seat in the House of Representatives. Rankin's victory placed her in an all-male setting in which females were generally considered incapable of making rational political decisions. Even though Rankin was an avid activist on many issues, she found it almost impossible to make her voice heard in Congress and chose not to run for reelection in 1918.

By the time that Rankin returned to the House of Representatives in 1941, women had won the right to vote through the Nineteenth Amendment (1920) to the U.S. Constitution. Rankin was joined in the House of Representatives by four other women: Democrat Mary T.

Norton (New Jersey) and Republicans Frances P. Bolton (Ohio), Edith Nourse Rogers (Massachusetts), and Margaret Chase Smith (Maine). In 1948, Smith became the first woman to be elected to the U.S. Senate.

AT LEFT *Jeannette Rankin, America's first female member of the House of Representatives, ca. 1917.*

porarily off the House floor. Rankin repeatedly tried to gain recognition, but Speaker Sam Rayburn (D–Texas) was just as determined to head her off and refused to allow her to speak. Her colleagues repeatedly told her to sit down. They tried both booing and cajoling to pressure her to make the declaration of war unanimous. Nevertheless, she stood firm. When her name was called, Rankin replied that she could not go to war and, therefore, would not send anyone else.

Amid the boos, hisses, and catcalls that followed her vote, Rankin fled to a telephone booth in the cloakroom. Afterward, a hostile crowd met her, as the district police escorted her to her office in the Cannon House Building. When verbally attacked by a group of army officers in the crowd, Rankin chided them for drinking and continued on her journey. She remained behind her locked office door for the rest of her day. Around the country, reaction was almost unanimous in castigating Rankin for her antiwar stand. She did, however, receive unexpected support from William Allen White of the *Emporia Gazette*, who praised Rankin for her bravery even as he disagreed with her position. Future president John F. Kennedy later remarked that Rankin was one of the most fearless women in American history.

Keeping a relatively low profile for the rest of her congressional career, Rankin frequently voted "present," even on declarations of war against Germany and Italy. She chose not to run for reelection. When she left Congress, Rankin had a statement printed in the *Congressional Record*, without reading it on the House floor. Her statement of December 8, 1942, a year after the vote on the declaration of war against Japan, reiterated her position that military INTELLIGENCE was available that could have prevented the Japanese attack on Pearl Harbor. She continued to blame the British for manipulating the United States into joining the war. Rankin closed her statement by announcing her continued support for free speech and free inquiry. Thereafter, Rankin alternated her time between her home state of Montana and her adopted state of Georgia. She was devastated when the United States dropped the atomic bomb upon the Japanese cities of Hiroshima and Nagasaki in 1945, even though it brought about the end of World War II.

Further Reading: Marcy Kaptur, *Women of Congress: A Twentieth-Century Odyssey* (Congressional Quarterly, 1996); Christine A. Lunardini, *From Equal Suffrage to Equal Rights: Alice Paul and the National Woman's Party, 1910–28* (New York University Press, 1986); Jeanette Rankin and Sue Davidson, *Heart in Politics: Jeanette Rankin and Patsy T. Mink* (Avalon Publishing Group, 1994).

—ELIZABETH PURDY, PH.D.

Richardson, James O. (1878–1974)

On January 6, 1940, Admiral James O. Richardson succeeded Admiral C.C. BLOCH as CINCUS, the Commander in Chief, U.S. Fleet, with responsibility for the Atlantic and eastern Pacific Ocean area and for all naval patrol planes assigned to the U.S. Fleet and the U.S. Asiatic Fleet. When Richardson subsequently met with President FRANKLIN D. ROOSEVELT at the White House, he bluntly told the president that the American fleet should not have been transferred from California to Pearl Harbor in May 1940. The base at Pearl Harbor was strategically significant to the UNITED STATES because it was located midway between the

Memoirs of Admiral James O. Richardson

IN HIS account of events leading to the Pearl Harbor attack, Richardson was adamant that President Roosevelt had intentionally created a situation that would force Congress to declare war on Japan. Roosevelt had been doing everything he could to aid the Allies since World War II had begun on September 1, 1939, with the German invasion of Poland. Many of his opponents believe that Roosevelt froze all Japanese assets in the United States, halted American trade with Japan, and prevented the Japanese from receiving necessary supplies from other sources in order to force Japan to act. Roosevelt had already essentially ordered American ships at sea to prepare for battle before war was officially declared on December 8, 1941, the day after the Pearl Harbor attack.

west coast of the United States and a Japanese military base on the MARSHALL ISLANDS. However, Richardson believed that at least two-thirds of the American fleet should remain on constant alert at sea.

After a period of leave at Pearl Harbor, Admiral HAROLD R. STARK, the chief of Naval Operations, extended the Pacific Fleet's stay in Hawai'i because he believed that its presence at Pearl Harbor was essential to protect the U.S. mainland from enemy attack (see PACIFIC FLEET, U.S.). Richardson had re-

peatedly insisted that the facilities at Pearl Harbor were inadequate for the protection of the U.S. ships and their crews.

Despite his misgivings, Richardson established a plan for joint army and navy protection of Pearl Harbor. When Stark brought up the possibility of using antitorpedo nets at Pearl Harbor, Richardson replied that antitorpedo nets were neither necessary nor practical.

On February 1, 1941, after only 13 months, Richardson was replaced as CINCUS by Admiral HUSBAND E. KIMMEL. Richardson was subsequently assigned to a series of minor jobs until his retirement in 1947. Well aware of what had happened to Richardson, Kimmel kept his concerns about the inadequate defense of Pearl Harbor to himself. His instructions were to divert Japanese attention from Southeast Asia by capturing the CAROLINE ISLANDS and Marshall Islands, playing havoc with JAPAN's trading routes, and defending GUAM, Hawai'i, and the U.S. mainland from enemy attack. It was understood that naval forces at Pearl Harbor were preparing for a possible war with Japan.

On November 19, 1945, Richardson testified before a Congressional joint committee, laying the blame for the inadequate defense of Pearl Harbor on Roosevelt, who had died seven months earlier and was, thus, unable to defend his strategy. Richardson told Congress that Roosevelt had suggested an American blockade of Japan as early as 1940. Richardson's testimony gave new life to the theory that Roosevelt had coldheartedly left Pearl Harbor unprotected in order to propel the United States into WORLD WAR II.

Although Richardson had completed a personal account of the events leading up to the attack on Pearl Harbor, he chose, out of respect for Stark, a close friend, not to publish the account until after

Stark's death. In the memoir, Richardson stated that Stark had been grossly negligent in his responsibilities. Richardson maintained that the War Department had issued orders that only General GEORGE C. MARSHALL was authorized to place Pearl Harbor on full alert. According to Richardson, Marshall was unavailable when Stark learned of a possible enemy attack. As a result, Stark made no preparations to protect Pearl Harbor. When Richardson was asked to head the navy's investigation into the attack on Pearl Harbor, he declined, stating that he had already drawn his own conclusions and was, therefore, unable to be objective during an investigation.

Further Reading: Charles R. Anderson, *Day of Lightning, Years of Scorn: Walter C. Short and the Attack on Pearl Harbor* (Naval Institute Press, 2004); Edward L. Beach, *Scapegoats: A Defense of Kimmel and Short at Pearl Harbor* (Naval Institute Press, 1995); James O. Richardson, *On the Treadmill to Pearl Harbor: The Memoirs of Admiral James O. Richardson* (Department of the Navy, Naval History Division, 1973).

—**ELIZABETH PURDY, PH.D.**

Roosevelt, Franklin D. (1882–1945)

Franklin D. Roosevelt was president of the UNITED STATES on December 7, 1941. The attack on Hawai'i started at 7:53 A.M. local time, and Roosevelt was informed of the attack while eating lunch. The Japanese delivered their declaration of war to Secretary of State CORDELL HULL in Washington, D.C., at 2:30 P.M. Roosevelt learned later in the day from British Prime Minister WINSTON CHURCHILL that the Japanese had also made attacks, on a much smaller scale, on British territories in the Pacific.

For his speech to the nation the next day, Roosevelt was presented a text declaring December 7 "a date which will live in world history..." Roosevelt edited these words to proclaim "a date that will live in infamy." He gave his speech via radio at 9:30 A.M. Within the hour, the U.S. Senate voted unanimously and the U.S. House of Representatives voted 388–1 to declare war on JAPAN, the lone dissenting vote coming from Republican JEANNETTE RANKIN of Montana, a pacifist who had also voted against the declaration of World War I. Roosevelt signed the declaration at 4:10 P.M. The European Axis powers, honoring their treaties with Japan, declared war on the U.S. within days (see AXIS POWERS IN 1941).

Roosevelt is the only president to have had a third term, and he also won a fourth, serving longer than any other president. His first two terms were marked by the Great Depression and his efforts to revolutionize the way the U.S. government dealt with social problems. The 1940 presidential campaign was marked by Roosevelt's emphasis on having kept the United States out of the war, as the leading nations of Europe, and even neighboring Canada, were already at war with GERMANY.

Franklin Delano Roosevelt was born in Hyde Park, New York, on January 30, 1882, the only child of James Roosevelt and Sara (Delano) Roosevelt; Roosevelt's only sibling was a son more than 27 years older from his father's first marriage. James Roosevelt was a railroad executive. The family was distantly related to President Theodore Roosevelt. One peculiarity is that Franklin's branch of the family pronounces their surname ROSE-e-velt, while Theodore's branch pronounces it ROOZ-e-velt. Roosevelt attended Groton School and matriculated at Harvard, graduating in 1904. He next received a law degree from Columbia and went into private practice in New York City.

On March 17, 1905, Roosevelt married his fifth cousin, Eleanor Roosevelt, in New York City. They had six children: one daughter and five sons, including two named Franklin D. Roosevelt Jr. (the elder FDR Jr. died in infancy). The five who lived to adulthood had among them 16 marriages. All four of Roosevelt's sons served in the military during the war and earned decorations.

Roosevelt's political career began in 1910 when he was elected to the state senate from Dutchess County, in the Hudson River Valley north of New York City. He was reelected to the senate in 1912 but instead went to Washington, D.C., to serve as assistant secretary of the navy in the administration of President Woodrow Wilson. He ran in the Democratic primary in 1914 for the U.S. Senate but lost. (This was the first time the country elected senators, the constitutional amendment providing for their direct election having only recently passed.) In 1920, he was the Democratic nominee for vice president on a ticket with James Cox of Ohio. The Democrats lost to Republicans Warren G. Harding and Calvin Coolidge.

ABOVE LEFT *A formal portrait of President Franklin Delano Roosevelt, ca. 1933.* **ABOVE RIGHT** *Roosevelt signing the declaration of war against Japan, December 8, 1941.*

Following this defeat, Roosevelt practiced law in New York and was an executive in banking. In August 1921, he was stricken with polio while vacationing at his summer home on Campobello Island, New Brunswick, Canada. Roosevelt adapted reasonably quickly to his paralysis. An avid driver, he traveled throughout the country in a customized car containing controls he had pioneered for use by the disabled. In 1928, he returned to the political sphere and was elected governor of New York. His administration was marked by efforts to uproot corruption from the state government, but he was ineffectual at reforming New York City government. He had more success in the sphere of public works, including the development of parks and hydroelectric generation on the St. Lawrence River. This emphasis on public works would also mark his early years as president. He was reelected as governor in 1930.

The Democratic Party nominated Roosevelt for president in 1932. Voters were preoccupied with the poor performance of the economy since the stock market crash of 1929. President Herbert Hoover and his administration had made at best a modest effort to overcome the Depression but Roosevelt won the election in a landslide.

Roosevelt was the victim of an assassination attempt on February 15, 1933, several weeks before taking office. An anarchist, Giuseppe Zangara, shot at the president-elect and missed, but he killed the mayor of Chicago, Anton Cermak, and wounded four others. Zangara was executed for the murder of Cermak only two weeks after the mayor's death.

Roosevelt's first term started with a busy time known as the First 100 Days. The president's economic recovery plan was called the New Deal. Some of the New Deal agencies and acts created in the 100 Days were the Tennessee Valley Authority, the National Recovery Administration, the Public Works Administration, the Federal Deposit Insurance Corporation, the Civilian Conservation Corps, the Agricultural Adjustment Act, and the Federal Emergency Relief Act. It is perhaps fitting that the president who was the fountainhead of these agencies mostly referred to by their initials was himself the first of a series of presidents known by his initials, FDR. Another set of agencies, including Social Security, was established later in the first term and have become a more permanent part of American life than the early New Deal agencies, which served mostly to alleviate the Depression.

The public apparently approved of the New Deal. Roosevelt was reelected in 1936 by the biggest electoral college landslide to that time, losing only Maine and Vermont to Republican Alf Landon, governor of Kansas. Roosevelt spent much of his second term battling the Supreme Court, which was busy at work dismantling the New Deal on Constitutional grounds. Roosevelt proposed an unpopular scheme that would let him appoint extra justices. It was defeated, but Roosevelt soon made the first of his nine appointments to the Court.

When Germany invaded Poland in 1939, Roosevelt sided with those who supported the United States's traditional isolationist stance. In the 1940 election, Roosevelt defeated Wendell Willkie, the only major party presidential nominee of the 20th century who never held office. Roosevelt's margin was less than that by which he had defeated Hoover and Landon, but it was solid nevertheless. Roosevelt gave his famous "Four Freedoms" speech in January 1941, two weeks before his third term started. He enumerated the great freedoms for which democracies aspire as freedom of speech, freedom of worship, freedom from want, and freedom from fear.

ABOVE *Mrs. Eleanor Roosevelt arriving at the Naval Air Station in Trinidad, British West Indies, March 12, 1944.*

Early in his third term, Roosevelt was working at alternatives to war. The LEND-LEASE Act was passed in March, to appease those who did not want the United States giving arms to warring allies but were able to allow "leasing" arms to them. The Atlantic Charter for peace was proclaimed in August. But at the same time, there were rumblings pointing to war. The United States occupied Iceland starting in July and DOUGLAS MACARTHUR was readied for command in the Pacific.

Roosevelt's cabinet met on December 5 and reviewed military INTELLIGENCE that indicated the Japanese were preparing for war. They had no idea that Japan would be attacking Hawai'i within a few hours. Their informed speculation was that the Japanese were preparing to engage the British in Southeast Asia. It was later learned that there had existed at this point intelligence, in the form of Japanese communications that were being decoded within the military, that indicated an imminent attack on

Pearl Harbor (see G-2 AND ARMY INTELLIGENCE). This failure of communication within the military intelligence apparatus led to a centralization of intelligence gathering under Roosevelt within the executive office of the president for the remainder of the war. After the war, the Central Intelligence Agency was created, and the military hierarchy was reorganized under the jurisdiction of a single cabinet member, the secretary of defense. (Previously, there had been both a secretary of war and a secretary of the navy.)

On December 6, intelligence decoded 13 of 14 parts of a Japanese message that indicated an imminent attack somewhere in the Pacific (see CODES, JAPANESE). Roosevelt tried to appeal to the emperor of Japan for peace at this point, but no reply was received.

During the 1944 presidential election, the United States was completely occupied with the war. Roosevelt argued, "Don't change horses in the midstream." He was reelected to an unprecedented fourth term over New York Governor Thomas E. Dewey. Also on the Democratic ticket was Roosevelt's third vice president, Senator HARRY TRUMAN of Missouri.

The most significant event of Roosevelt's uncompleted fourth term (he died on April 12, 1945) was the "Big Three" conference at Yalta with Winston Churchill and JOSEF STALIN in February 1945. After the war, many in the West faulted this assemblage for ceding eastern Europe to Soviet domination. Others argued that some accommodation of the Soviets was necessary to achieve the military defeat of Germany. Historians have long speculated whether the declining health of Roosevelt and his obvious physical exhaustion at the time of Yalta were factors in the Americans and British giving so much ground to the Soviet Union at the conference.

Further Reading: James MacGregor Burns, *Roosevelt: The Lion and the Fox* (Harcourt Brace, 1956); Kenneth S. Davis, ed., *FDR* (Random House, 1972–2000); Frank Freidel, *Franklin D. Roosevelt: A Rendezvous with Destiny* (Little, Brown, 1990); George T. McJimsey, *The Presidency of Franklin Delano Roosevelt* (University Press of Kansas, 2000).

—**TONY L. HILL**

The Death of a President

FRANKLIN D. Roosevelt died at his winter home in Warm Springs, Georgia, on April 12, 1945.

Roosevelt's death shocked most Americans. Despite his obviously failing health, the younger generation had no recollection of anyone else being president. Roosevelt was buried at Springwood, his family home in Hyde Park. His wish for a monument was that a desk-sized block of granite be installed on Pennsylvania Avenue. To many in Washington, this was not enough of a monument, and planning began for a permanent monument. Forty years later, the commission had reached an impasse on the monument and its design, and proposed the rather weak solution that the Washington Monument be renamed the Washington-Roosevelt Monument. (Signs to this effect were placed there in the 1980s.) It was not until the 1990s that a plan for a permanent memorial was agreed upon, and the Roosevelt Memorial opened in 1997 on eight acres between the Potomac River and the Tidal Basin in Washington, D.C.

Russia-Japan Relations

The most significant fact concerning the Soviet Union on December 7, 1941, is that it was not the target of the Japanese attack, although that option had been given consideration. Russia and JAPAN had long viewed each other as threats, and they had fought each other on several occasions. For Japan to go to war with either the United States or the Soviet Union in 1941 required it to find a way to secure its rear against the other. During World War II, the press and government officials referred to the Union of Soviet Socialist Republics as "Russia."

Russia had become an Asian power by occupying Siberia in stages from the 16th to the 19th century. It earned Japan's ire when, along with GERMANY and France, it intervened diplomatically to compel Japan to return some occupied territories after the First Sino-Japanese War (1894–95). The Russo-Japanese War (1904–05), fought to determine which country would have predominant influence in Manchuria (northeastern China) and Korea, was the first time in the modern era that an Asian power defeated a European power. Japan, along with several other countries, intervened in the Russian Civil War (1918–20), but Japan's military contingent was the largest and remained for the longest period of time. It occupied eastern Siberia and sponsored an anti-Bolshevik regime, the Far Eastern Republic, which collapsed when Japanese forces withdrew in 1922.

Under civilian governments, Japan then took a more conciliatory turn, withdrawing from northern Sakhalin Island and recognizing the Soviet government in 1925. After the onset of the Great Depression, however, Japan set out to create an economically self-sufficient empire in East Asia, which put it on a collision course with other powers. Domestically, it also suppressed the Japanese Communist Party and denounced the Communist International (or Comintern, the worldwide association of Communist parties, based in Moscow) as subversive, although it avoided the disruption of diplomatic relations at the time by publicly accepting the fiction that the Comintern had no connection to the Soviet government.

The occupation of Manchuria by Japan's Kwantung Army in 1931–32, and the establishment of the puppet state Manchukuo, brought the Japanese Empire to the border of the Soviet Union, causing unease in Moscow. The Soviet Union was not in a position to respond forcefully at the time, although it began building up its forces in the Far East from an estimated eight infantry divisions and 200 aircraft in 1932 to 30 divisions and 2,500 aircraft in 1939. In an apparent effort to turn "imperialist" states against each other, however, Karl Radek (an official of both the Soviet foreign ministry and the Comintern) wrote in the U.S. journal *Foreign Affairs* that this was an occasion for the United States to defend its interests in East Asia by taking action to stop Japanese aggression. Japan joined Germany and Italy in the Anti-Comintern Pact in 1936. Moscow provided military equipment to the Nationalist government of China when Japan attacked it in 1937.

In the late 1930s the mounting tensions came to a head over the ill-defined borders of Manchukuo. There were several brief border incidents in 1936 and 1937. In 1938 a Japanese division seized a disputed high ground called Changkufeng, near Lake Khasan, but withdrew after the Soviets counterattacked with two divisions. The following year the Kwantung Army penetrated into Mongolia, a Russian client state since the late Tzarist era, but it was devastated by a Soviet counterattack using aircraft, heavy armor, and artillery.

The time had come for Japan to reevaluate its stance toward Moscow. The Soviet army had performed far beyond expectations despite an extensive and bloody purge of its officer corps earlier in the decade. Then, in August, in disregard of the Anti-Comintern Pact, Germany signed a nonaggression treaty with the Soviet Union, seemingly nullifying its usefulness as an ally. At the same time, Japan's war with China was lasting far longer and tying down far more troops than expected. Thus, Tokyo determined in 1939 that war with the Soviet Union would not be possible, at least not until the China situation was resolved and the position of Germany clarified.

By mid-1940 Tokyo and Moscow had signed a treaty regarding the Manchukuo-Mongolia border and Japan was actively exploring the possibility of expansion to the south, rather than the north, in the hope that the natural resources of Southeast Asia could be used to sustain the war effort in China. Japan was also considering the possibility that war with the United States, Britain, and the Netherlands could result; all of them had colonial territories in the region of Southeast Asia (the PHILIPPINES; MALAYA AND SINGAPORE; and Indonesia).

In September Japan, Germany, and Italy renewed their alliance through the Tripartite Pact, which sought to deter intervention by outside powers—presumably the United States, conceivably the Soviet Union—with the prospect of a two-front war. Any attempt to interfere with the ambitions of either Germany or Japan would result in war with both. The treaty also permitted Japan to seize the Asian colonies of countries conquered by Germany. Foreign Minister YOSUKE MATSUOKA, however, was soon discussing with JOSEF STALIN the possibility of expanding the treaty to include the Soviet Union, in the name of preventing Anglo-American world he-gemony. Although that did not occur, Japan and the Soviet Union signed a neutrality pact in April 1941. To the extent that the neutrality pact held, Japan had secured its rear for a move to the south.

Two months later, however, in June 1941, the situation changed again. Without consulting Japan, and in violation of the nonaggression pact of 1939, the Germans invaded the Soviet Union. Hitler immediately called on Japan to invade Siberia while his forces were tying down much of the Soviet army in Europe. A Japanese attack, of course, would also prevent the 30 divisions and 16 tank brigades stationed in Siberia from reinforcing the European front.

The Japanese now faced the need to choose between advancing northward and advancing southward, but in July they decided to keep their options open by preparing for both. Troops were transported into Manchukuo, for a possible move into Siberia, and also into French Indochina—France having already fallen to Germany—for a possible move farther south. The preference was still to go south, although some argued that they could quickly take the Soviet Far East and then move south. For his part, Prime Minister Fumimaro Konoe believed that the Germans had violated their treaty provisions by attacking first, and by not consulting Japan, they had put Japan in a predicament and did not deserve help. Japan would repeatedly advise the two to reconcile. Nevertheless, Japan was prepared to move northward if the Soviet Union collapsed. Aside from the strategic and economic advantages of controlling eastern Siberia, Japanese leaders did not relish seeing the Germans in East Asia.

Vyacheslav M. Molotov, the Soviet foreign minister, requested from the United States a "warning" to help deter Japan, by which he was presumed to mean an offer of help if Japan attacked. Unprepared to commit the country to war for the Soviet Union,

President FRANKLIN D. ROOSEVELT responded by allowing the British to forward U.S. equipment to the Soviets for use against the Germans, and by taking certain measures intended to deter Japanese aggression against anyone (see SANCTIONS AGAINST JAPAN). These measures included an oil embargo, which would make military operations difficult, and the dispatch of long-range bombers to the Philippines, which would remind Japan of its vulnerability if it should provoke war with the United States.

These actions may have helped save the Soviet Union, although they proved counterproductive for the United States. Deprived of oil for its ongoing war in China, Japan decided to honor its neutrality pact with the Soviets and to seize the oilfields of the Dutch East Indies (Indonesia). For its part, Moscow also respected the neutrality pact, refusing, for example, to allow U.S. bombers to attack Japan from Siberia, at least until the collapse of Germany in 1945 removed the threat of a two-front war.

Assuming the United States and Britain would stand with the Netherlands, Japanese forces were to seize the British and American colonies and attack key military installations, including those at Pearl Harbor, before the Allies had time to mobilize resistance. In October 1941, General HIDEKI TOJO replaced Konoe as prime minister and the Japanese army and navy received orders to prepare for war in the south. Richard Sorge, a Soviet spy with connections at the German embassy in Tokyo, reported on Japanese policy debates and military preparations until his arrest in October. He was not privy to Japanese plans, but he believed the Soviet Union to be safe at least until spring. With the pressure easing on the Soviet Union's Asian frontier, Stalin ordered half of the forces in Siberia redeployed westward, where they helped halt the German offensive outside Moscow in December.

Further Reading: Alvin D. Coox, *Nomonhan: Japan against Russia, 1939* (Stanford University Press, 1985); Waldo Heinrichs, "The Russian Factor in Japanese-American Relations, 1941," in Hilary Conroy and Harry Wray, eds., *Pearl Harbor Reexamined: Prologue to the Pacific War* (University of Hawai'i Press, 1990); James William Morley, ed., *The Final Confrontation: Japan's Negotiations with the United States, 1941* (Columbia University Press, 1994); Boris Slavinsky, *The Japanese-Soviet Neutrality Pact: A Diplomatic History, 1941–45* (RoutledgeCurzon, 2004).

—SCOTT C. MONJE, PH.D.

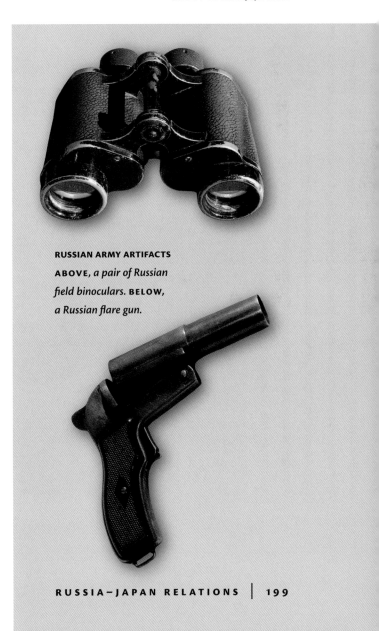

RUSSIAN ARMY ARTIFACTS
ABOVE, *a pair of Russian field binoculars.* **BELOW,** *a Russian flare gun.*

DEPOSIT OLD SIL
& NYLON HOSE

S

Salvage Operations

Probably the funniest salvage story from Pearl Harbor involved an old soldier and a husky sergeant in the lull after the first attack. The old soldier suddenly realized that he had left his false teeth in his locker, and started back to get them.

"Where do you think you're going?" the sergeant demanded.

"I've got to get my teeth," the old soldier told him.

The husky sergeant grasped the old soldier firmly by the arm and pulled him back. "Hell man, they ain't dropping sandwiches," he said.

When the last Japanese Zero (see JAPANESE AIRCRAFT) disappeared over the Pearl Harbor horizon after two hours of bombing, torpedoing, and strafing, the anchorage was dotted with the wreckage of 19 ships, including most of the battle line of the Pacific Fleet (see PACIFIC FLEET, U.S.) and clouds of smoke hung over the water like a huge black shroud. Luckily the carriers had been out to sea. The Japanese had destroyed approximately 265 American planes and American casualties totaled 2,403 sailors, soldiers, and airmen dead and 1,178 wounded. Tallied against this the Japanese lost 29 planes and 55 airmen, one submarine with a crew of 65 men, and all five of their MIDGET SUBMARINES.

On December 7, 1941, Rear Admiral William R. Furlong commanded the minelayer USS *Oglala*, flagship of the Pacific Fleet mine force. The USS *Oglala* was docked near Battleship Row and as he stood on the USS *Oglala*'s deck, Furlong saw three aerial torpedoes strike the water and head for the USS *Oglala*. One of the torpedoes hit and sank the USS *Oglala*, which rolled over on her side and capsized at a 90-degree angle.

A few hours after the attack, Furlong inspected one of the Japanese charts taken from a captured midget submarine. The chart was covered with tissue paper, and a Japanese officer had sketched the latest information received from Japanese agents at Pearl Harbor. An error in the chart caused the sinking of Furlong's ship, the USS *Oglala*. The Japanese believed that the battleship USS *Pennsylvania* (see PENNSYLVANIA, USS), flagship of the fleet, was at the pier where the USS *Oglala* lay, but the USS *Pennsylvania* had been moved to a dry dock. The cruiser USS *Helena* was inboard of the USS *Oglala* at the same dock. The USS *Oglala* had a flag up and this may have fooled the Japanese pilot who torpedoed the minelayer.

Francis W. Scanland, captain of the USS *Nevada* (see NEVADA, USS), beached his destroyer on a mud point where she remained upright and did not block the channel. The USS *California* (see CALIFORNIA, USS) settled in the mud at her moorings, listing five to seven degrees, with only her high turrets above the water. Also hit at her moorings, the USS *West Virginia* (see WEST VIRGINIA, USS) leaned to port. The fact that her starboard bilge hooked against the USS *Tennessee* (see TENNESSEE, USS) beside her kept the USS *West Virginia* afloat. Broken in half by the explosion of her forward magazine, the USS *Arizona* (see ARIZONA, USS) rested on the bottom. In eight minutes the USS *Oklahoma* (see OKLAHOMA, USS) rolled over 150 degrees, and on the other side of Ford Island, the USS *Utah* also lay with her bottom in the air. A heavy bomb hit the floating dry

ABOVE *Sunken Japanese ships in Manila Bay were refloated by Navy salvage crews, towed to deeper water and resunk. Battered ships were left afloat. August 1945.*

dock containing the destroyer USS *Shaw*, which was blown in two by the explosion of her forward magazine. The explosion on board the USS *Downes* beside her ignited the USS *Cassin* and she fell off her blocks in dry dock. The battleships USS *Maryland* (see MARYLAND, USS) and USS *Tennessee* and the cruisers USS *Raleigh* and USS *Honolulu* were damaged by bombs.

Later Furlong remarked that "if the Navy Department had immediately named all of the vessels damaged on December 7, the Japs might have been back the next week. Any one can see that if such a statement had been given out on Dec. 7, it would have been the greatest service one could have rendered the enemy."

Five days later Furlong was made commandant of the Pearl Harbor Navy Yard in charge of all salvage operations. Furlong's salvage superintendents included Captain J. M. Steele, who commanded the USS *Utah*. Next came Captain Homer N. Wallin, who received the Distinguished Service Medal for his work on the USS *California* and USS *West Virginia*. Commander F. H. Whitaker of Beaumont, Texas, was most concerned with raising and patching the USS *Oklahoma* so she could go into dry dock. Whitaker also prepared for the turning over of the capsized USS *Utah*, and did considerable salvage in the sunken USS *Arizona*.

Furlong's first major task was organizing men and materials. He had to acquire divers, burners, mechanics who could work in diving suits under water, pumpers, electricians, and laborers. Once the ships were floated, he had to have all types of artisans who could rebuild the vessels. "We needed boats, barges, pumps and a great variety of special kinds of materials. We had some difficulty, particularly in getting the special kinds of pumps and hoses," Furlong said.

The Pearl Harbor salvage job was constantly delayed because the ships that could be most quickly repaired and sent into battle had first priority at the dry docks. Furlong also had to contend with the long arm of the military deploying men working on the Pearl Harbor damaged ships to more urgent jobs, slowing down the work on the battleships. He noted that a positive factor was that the oil that flooded the interiors of all the ships as a result of the explosions preserved the metal under water, making it possible to save most of the sunken ships.

Navy and civilian divers spent about 20,000 hours underwater in about 5,000 dives. They worked long, exhausting hours to recover human remains, documents, ammunition, and other items from the oil-fouled interiors of ships that had been under water for months. Workers spent endless hours cleaning the ships and getting them ready for shipyard repair. They had to do most of their work wearing gas masks to protect themselves against toxic gases.

By 1943, Furlong could look back at a successful Pearl Harbor operation. The battleship USS *Oklahoma* had been capsized at her moorings but had been righted. The battleships USS *Nevada*, USS *California*, and USS *West Virginia*, inoperable when the Japanese planes left, were refloated, patched, and sent to sea again in 1942. The battleships USS *Pennsylvania*, USS *Maryland*, and USS *Tennessee* were repaired and returned to service. The USS *Shaw* was repaired and sent back to the fleet. The USS *Oglala* had been patched and refloated in 1942. The cruisers USS *Raleigh* and USS *Honolulu* were speedily repaired; the seaplane tender USS *Curtiss*, repair ship USS *Vestal*, and the floating dry dock *YFD-2* were put back into service, or at least were readied to steam to the mainland for final repairs. The most seriously damaged of these ships, USS *Raleigh* and USS *Shaw*, were returned to active duty by mid-1942.

Midget Submarine

A FINAL salvage irony occurred 60 years later on August 28, 2002, when the research teams in Hawai'i's Undersea Research laboratory submersibles *PISCES IV* and *PISCES V* discovered a 78-foot Japanese submarine lying upright at a depth of 1,200 feet. The submarine was one of five Japanese midget submarines that participated in the Pearl Harbor attack and was believed to be the one sunk by the destroyer USS *Ward* over an hour before the attack. Divers examining the submarine discovered a bullet hole in the conning tower and both of its torpedoes still intact. It is believed to contain the remains of two Japanese crewmen. The bullet hole in the conning tower and the unfired torpedoes provided physical evidence to support the U.S. contention that it had fired first against JAPAN in WORLD WAR II. The U.S. State Department and the Japanese government debated the ownership and disposition of the submarine.

The two destroyers USS *Cassin* and USS *Downes* had been damaged beyond economical repair, but 50 percent of their main and auxiliary machinery and practically all of their guns had been reclaimed for use on other ships. Starting in December 1941 and continuing into February 1942, the Navy Yard stripped the USS *Cassin* and USS *Downes* of serviceable weapons, machinery, and equipment. This materiel was sent to California, where it was installed in new hulls. These two ships came back into the fleet in late 1943 and early 1944. The USS *Arizona* permanently rested on the bottom of Pearl Harbor (see ARIZONA, USS MEMORIAL), but its main and secondary gun batteries had been recovered. Ammunition from the damaged ships was usable after reprocessing. The target ship USS *Utah* also remained on the bottom of Pearl Harbor.

Furlong estimated that the Pearl Harbor salvage had restored a small fortune to the navy. He figured that each battleship represented a total investment of $70 million to $90 million, a cruiser $50 million, and a destroyer $20 million. "When we finish with a damaged ship the repairs are permanent. We put in all new wiring, install the latest guns, streamline and modernize them throughout. They go out better than when they were hit," he said.

Further Reading: C.A. Bartholomew, *Mud, Muscle, and Miracles: Marine Salvage in the United States Navy* (Naval Historical Center, 1990); Nathan Miller, *A Naval History of World War II: War at Sea* (Scribner, 1995); "Pearl Harbor Attack," www.history.navy.mil (cited March 2006); "Pearl Harbor Salvage Operations," *New York Times* (May 23, 1943); "Submarine Expedition," *Honolulu Advertiser* (August 29, 2002).

—KATHY WARNES

Sanctions against Japan

When JAPAN occupied Manchuria and invaded China in the 1930s, the UNITED STATES and other governments were reluctant to go to war, so they imposed diplomatic sanctions on Japan. After Japan ignored sanctions by the League of Nations and withdrew from the league, the United States attempted to coerce Japan by prohibiting the sale to Japan of oil, petroleum, and steel. The sanctions failed, leading the United States into war with Japan, as well as GERMANY and Italy.

Relations between the United States and Japan worsened after 1931, the year in which Japan occupied Manchuria, making that northern Chinese territory into the puppet state of Manchukuo. The U.S. secretary of state, HENRY L. STIMSON, wanted to impose sanctions against Japan, but President Herbert Hoover disapproved. When the League of Nations attempted sanctions in 1933, Japan left the league effective in 1935. U.S. trade with Japan continued.

Japan had long bought steel from the United States. In December 1934, the same month that Japan renounced the treaty controlling the size of its navy, Japan bought shells from Fort Stevens in Washington state. The exporter said the shells were not going to be converted to war materiel. The American attitude was that trade with either side in a conflict was acceptable. Liberal groups such as the Washington Commonwealth Federation agitated for an embargo, but that was not the popular view. During the Depression many Americans earned money salvaging scrap metal.

On October 6, 1937, President FRANKLIN D. ROOSEVELT declined to call for collective action against Japan, although he had just the day before called for a quarantine of world lawlessness. Rather, a meeting occurred at Brussels of the 18 nations that had signed the 1922 Nine-Power Treaty guaranteeing Chinese territorial sovereignty. On November 24 the attendees issued a statement asking Japan to cease its aggressive actions.

The 1937 invasion of China by Japan caused a marked deterioration of Japanese-American relations. The USS *Panay* was an American gunboat patrolling the Yangtze River in Nanking, China. During the Japanese bombing of Nanking, the USS *Panay* served as a shelter for foreign embassy staff. Japanese warplanes bombed the USS *Panay* and a British gunboat without warning or provocation on December 12, 1937, sinking the USS *Panay* and causing major damage to the British vessel. The attacks caused three deaths and 48 injuries and outraged American public opinion. Japan initially claimed that the pilots had not seen the painted American flags on the gunboat's sides and decks. Japan apologized and paid an indemnity (see *PANAY* INCIDENT).

After the *Panay* incident, in 1938 the U.S. government asked private businesses to cease shipments to Japan and asked banks to discontinue credits to Japan. Many businesspeople backed the move because they wanted to keep Japanese goods from the American market. Others preferred to continue trade.

On February 24, 1939, Chinese American children of cannery workers began picketing a Japanese ship in Astoria, Washington. After the school board ordered the children back to school, the movement spread to the mothers, then the longshoremen's union, which refused to load scrap metal. The movement spread over opposition by ship owners and adverse arbitration rulings. Reluctantly, longshoremen resumed loading scrap as Europe neared war.

Legislation to embargo the sale of steel scrap to Japan died in Congress as Roosevelt opposed it and Japan threatened to boycott American cotton. Between January and August 1940, Washington state's ports loaded 70,898 tons of steel for Japan. Finally, on September 26, 1940, Roosevelt embargoed scrap effective October 15. As late as October 11, scrap was loaded in Seattle. The embargo overlooked melted scrap, so the shipment of ingots continued until shortly before December 1940.

The Japanese began fortifying the MARSHALL ISLANDS in early 1940. The Marshalls lie between Hawai'i and the PHILIPPINES, and the Japanese presence threatened American communications. In response, in June 1940, Roosevelt moved the Pacific Fleet (see PACIFIC FLEET, U.S.) from California to Pearl Harbor. The intent was to provide a show of force and deter potential attacks on American, British, and Dutch colonies in East Asia. Hawai'i was within striking distance for Japanese forces, so Roosevelt was running a risk.

While Britain was struggling to hang on against Germany and Italy, Japan demanded in July 1940 that Britain stop shipping materiel through Burma to the Chinese Nationalists in China's west. The British acceded, but the United States increased its assistance to the Chinese. It also introduced restrictions on the sale of war-related materiel, including oil and scrap metal. The 1940 Japanese occupation of northern Indochina as the first step toward taking the oil of the Dutch East Indies led the United States to impose an embargo on the export of oil, aviation fuel, and scrap metal, arms, munitions, and other potential war materiel to Japan. Additionally, Roosevelt froze Japanese assets in American banks.

Japan's aggressiveness in the 1930s led to the ABCD encirclement, with Japan hemmed in by the Americans, British, Chinese, and Dutch. American sanctions hardened the hostility of Japanese militarists. From the Japanese perspective, the United States was interfering in the natural Japanese sphere of influence. The Japanese declared that they would expand their influence by creating the GREATER EAST ASIA CO-PROSPERITY SPHERE.

Deteriorating relations with the United States led Japan to look for allies. The result was the Tripartite Pact of September 27, 1940, made between Germany, Italy, and Japan, in which Japan's sphere was acknowledged and agreed to in a mutual defense treaty. Neither Germany nor Italy expected Japan to start another war. On April 3, 1941, to protect Manchukuo, Japan and the Soviet Union signed a nonaggression pact (see RUSSIA–JAPAN RELATIONS).

Stimson Doctrine

THE JAPANESE conquest of Manchuria did not sit well with the Western powers. The consensus in Washington, D.C., and the other capitals was that the best course was to do nothing that might aggravate the situation. Although he initially agreed that pacification of Japan was necessary, U.S. Secretary of State Henry L. Stimson came around to the view that threats and collective sanctions were necessary. President Herbert Hoover was a pacifist who refused to allow Stimson to pursue sanctions. Stimson did send the Japanese a note on January 7, 1932, informing them that the United States would never recognize Japanese sovereignty over territory taken by force. This was the Stimson or Hoover Doctrine.

Even as a member of the Axis, although angered by Allied opposition to its war with China and its inability to get oil, Japan continued to negotiate with the United States until the beginning of the war (see ALLIES ON DECEMBER 7, 1941; AXIS POWERS IN 1941). Prime Minister Fumimaro Konoe sent Admiral KICHISABURO NOMURA to the United States in April 1941 to negotiate a settlement under which the United States recognized Japanese hegemony in east Asia.

In July 1941 Japan seized FRENCH INDOCHINA. The Japanese poured troops into the Indochinese staging area for the attack on the European colonies in Southeast Asia. Roosevelt, on July 25, 1941, froze all Japanese assets in the United States. At the time, the United States provided 80 percent of Japan's oil, so Japan was without imported oil critical to its economy. Japan began negotiations with the United States to ease or lift these damaging restrictions, negotiations that continued through the fall of 1941. The British and Dutch government in exile also imposed sanctions, so by August Japan was unable to get virtually any rubber or oil for the war against China and the expansion into Southeast Asia.

American demands that Japan leave Indochina and China would have made Japanese military and economic hegemony in Asia impossible. Japan promised to end its southward march, to not attack the Soviet Union, and to not declare war on America if the United States and Germany went to war. Japan wanted China in return. Roosevelt refused. The Japanese government fell in October 1941, and the militant General HIDEKI TOJO became Japan's ruler.

Japan had built a strategic reserve, and it could have lasted two years before it ran dry. And the Americans were willing to grant Manchukuo, if only Japan would leave China and abandon the Greater East Asia Co-Prosperity Sphere. Japanese militarists were adamantly opposed to abandoning either China or the sphere. Sanctions failed again, hardening the militarists, who replaced Konoe in October 1941 with the hard-line Tojo. Sanctions had failed. Negotiations had failed. The freeze was the final blow to Japanese hopes of avoiding confrontation with the United States. War was imminent, and the remaining question was where the Japanese would attack.

Further Reading: Robert Dallek, *Franklin D. Roosevelt and American Foreign Policy, 1932–45* (Oxford University Press, 1995); Jonathan G. Utley, *Going to War with Japan, 1937–41* (Fordham University Press, 2005).

—JOHN H. BARNHILL, PH.D.

Short, Walter C. (1880–1949)

Lieutenant General Walter C. Short was the commander of Hawai'ian Department, the army's largest overseas department, at the time of the Japanese attack on December 7, 1941. He began his military career during World War I as assistant chief of staff to the Third Army.

In February 1941, Short was asked to take military command of Hawai'i, with department headquarters at Fort Shafter. When he sailed on the SS *Graceful Matsonia*, steaming west through the Pacific to take the command of the base at Pearl Harbor, he did not know that it would be his last army assignment. Short would be remembered by some as the commander who had parked fighter planes wingtip to wingtip on the Hawai'ian airfields around Pearl Harbor.

To others, he was made a scapegoat for the miscalculations of top military and civilian officials. A careful study of events preceding the fateful day of December 7 revealed that it was a combination of many factors and circumstances that culminated in the Japanese attack (see INVESTIGATIONS OF RESPONSIBILITY; HISTORIANS' VIEWS). When the warning came, it was too late for Short to do anything about it.

Situated about five miles west of HONOLULU on the southern coast of Oahu, Pearl Harbor is one of the largest natural harbors in the eastern Pacific Ocean. After the outbreak of WORLD WAR II, there was expansion of the facilities at Pearl Harbor, with equipment updating and the addition of the U.S. Signal Corps. The army chief of staff, General GEORGE C. MARSHALL, had visited Pearl Harbor and because of his concern, security was placed on high alert starting in July 1941. But by November there was slackness, and a series of events occurred that was beyond the control of Short or even his navy counterpart, Admiral HUSBAND E. KIMMEL.

The Americans believed a Japanese attack was imminent, most likely somewhere in Southeast Asia. The decoding of Japanese messages (see CODES, JAPANESE) on December 6 made clear the Japanese intent. The next day another message said that diplomatic relations with the UNITED STATES would be broken, and that this message would be delivered to officials in Washington, D.C., at 1 P.M. local time, which would be early morning in Pearl Harbor. An alert message was sent by telegraph to Pearl Harbor, but a radio link with Hawai'i failed. The message was received at Oahu headquarters at noon, but all hell had broken loose four hours before.

Short was having his usual golf match with Kimmel at the time of the Japanese attack. He could hear the sound of heavy firing from the direction of Pearl Harbor and ordered his command on alert. He went straight into his command post in Aliamanu Crater to direct the units under his command, including the Hawai'ian Coast Artillery Command, Hawai'ian Air Force and Aircraft Warning, and Antiaircraft Artillery. But it was a belated move and untold damage had been done by the Japanese. Without guidance from the State Department, both Short and Kimmel had different theories dating from late October.

Short thought that his units would be made targets of a sabotage attack, and Kimmel planned his moves in a traditional way in case of war. It was not that Short was sitting idle, as he had achieved some safety measures by mid-November. But the Japanese sneak attack, which was well executed and conceived much earlier, left the American people, the War Department, the Department of State, and the Hawai'ian command flabbergasted. Now there was a search for scapegoats upon whom to lay the blame,

and it was Short and Kimmel who bore the brunt. Secretary of the Navy FRANK A. KNOX conducted an inquiry, which put the blame on both for dereliction of duty. Both had allegedly ignored repeated warnings and believed in a submarine attack, not attack from planes. Short and Kimmel were relieved of their duties on December 17.

Short had failed in his primary duty of protecting Pearl Harbor against air and sea attack. The reports of subsequent inquiries conducted by the special commission of the president (1942) and congressional investigation (1946) blamed Short and Kimmel for not taking adequate measures to protect Pearl Harbor. The latter report put the blame on the War Department also, as it did not direct Short to take adequate measures and inform him about negotiations between the United States and JAPAN. The inquiries did not find valid reasons for courts-martial. Perhaps Short's main faults lay in limited use of radar surveillance and in his strong belief that adequate defense should be against sabotage, and not against air attack. The chain of command, beginning with the army chief of staff, also was to be blamed, but as commanders on the spot, the record claimed Short and Kimmel failed in their duty, whatever might be the circumstances.

There were attempts to clear the names of both officers, and the Pearl Harbor Survivors Association honored Short and Kimmel in 1999, in the presence of their sons, who were also military officers. The U.S. Senate in 2000 resolved that the Japanese attack was not due to dereliction of duty by Short and Kimmel and that they had performed their duties well. However, the White House in June 2002 did not restore their war ranks. After being stripped of his command, Short retired from the army and worked for the Ford automobile company until his death in 1949.

Further Reading: Charles R. Anderson, *Day of Lightning, Years of Scorn: Walter C. Short and the Attack on Pearl Harbor* (Naval Institute Press, 2005); Henry C. Clausen and Bruce Lee, *Pearl Harbor: Final Judgement* (Da Capo Press, 2001); Husband E. Kimmel, *Admiral Kimmel's Story* (Regency, 1955); U.S. Congress, *Report Before the Joint Committee on the Investigation of the Pearl Harbor Attack* (Government Printing Office, 1946).

—PATIT PABAN MISHRA

Stalin, Josef (1879–1953)

Josef Stalin was born Iosif Vissarionovich Dzhugashvili in Gori in the Russian imperial province of Tbilisi, now the Republic of Georgia. After dropping out of a Russian Orthodox seminary, he became active in the Marxist revolutionary movement. He was repeatedly arrested and exiled to Siberia but regularly escaped and returned to St. Petersburg. Although he was in exile in eastern Siberia when the February 1917 Revolution deposed Tzar Nicholas II, he soon returned to the capital.

To what extent he participated in the October Revolution has been the subject of some debate. While he was in power, Stalin magnified his own role as the great hero, as part of his cult of personality. However, it has since been suggested that Nikita Khrushchev and his successors actually went to the other extreme, minimizing Stalin's contribution to the revolution as a way of distancing themselves from its excesses and asserting that Stalin despoiled a movement that was originally pure and noble.

Once the Bolsheviks were in power, Stalin took the position of general secretary of the Communist Party and proceeded to make himself indispensable to Bolshevik leader Vladimir Ilich Lenin. By the time Lenin's health began failing in the early 1920s, Stalin controlled enough key bureaucratic functions that he was able to outmaneuver his foremost rival, Leon Trotsky, and take complete power after Lenin's death.

After he assumed total control of the Soviet Union, Stalin initiated his ambitious Five Year Plan, which was to totally transform the nation from a backward agricultural nation to a modern industrial

AT LEFT *Teheran, Iran. December 1943. Standing outside the Russian Embassy, left to right: General George C. Marshall, chief of staff, shaking hands with Sir Archibald Clark Kerr, British ambassador to the Soviet Union; Harry Hopkins; Marshal Stalin's interpreter; Marshal Josef Stalin; Foreign Minister Molotov; and General Voroshilov.*

one. The entire nation was mobilized along the lines of an army in the field, and whole industrial cities were constructed from the ground up. In addition, the countryside was to be transformed into an agricultural proletariat working on state-owned farms and on collective farms. However, the plan that looked so splendid on paper soon proved to be anything but in actuality. Because it was completely unacceptable to suggest that the headlong rush to industrialization could have caused the failures, such as industrial accidents and completely inappropriate sequences of construction, the problems had to be blamed upon outside wreckers. Combined with the assassination of Leningrad Party Secretary Sergei Kirov, the state of affairs soon spun into a Great Terror, which Stalin used to destroy all rivals actual and potential. Anyone who might potentially pose a threat was killed or imprisoned.

However well Stalin might be able to eliminate enemies within the Soviet Union, he could not eliminate all those from without. In particular, there was the problem of Nazi leader ADOLF HITLER, whom Stalin simultaneously admired and hated. In the late 1930s, Stalin negotiated a nonaggression pact with Hitler, dividing Poland between them. Some historians have said that Hitler was the only man whom Stalin ever trusted, and this mistake led to his being caught completely by surprise when the Nazis came pouring across the Soviet border on June 6, 1941.

As a result, Stalin was neck-deep in a desperate fight for survival on December 7, 1941. Because his purges of the Red Army had destroyed almost all his competent commanders and he had replaced them with his incompetent acolytes, such as Klimenty Voroshilov and Semyon Budyonny, the Nazis had been able to make enormous advances onto Soviet territory in a matter of days. Whole Soviet divisions were encircled and taken prisoner due to catastrophically bad leadership. Leningrad was encircled and settling in for a desperate siege that lasted almost three years. Nazi forces were on the outskirts of Moscow.

Even in the chaos of the panicky withdrawal of government offices from Moscow, there have been questions of whether Stalin may have known about the planned Japanese attack on Pearl Harbor, or at least the intention of JAPAN to initiate hostilities with the UNITED STATES. However, one thing is certain—the resulting entrance of the United States into the war on the side of the Allies was enormously beneficial to Stalin (see ALLIES ON DECEMBER 7, 1941).

Although the United States had been quietly aiding Britain through the LEND-LEASE program, because the two nations shared a common history and culture, Americans had been largely aloof from the Soviet dictatorship, which represented a political and economic system diametrically opposed to democracy and free-market capitalism. Some members of Congress had even publicly expressed hope that Hitler and Stalin would end up in a mutual death grip and both dictatorships would be destroyed. Now that the United States and the Soviet Union had a common cause, materiel aid began pouring into the beleaguered Soviet Union via the Bering Strait and Siberia, enabling Stalin's forces to hold out.

Not only did the Soviets hold out, but they won, and as a result of the agreement at the Yalta Conference of February 1945, they were allowed to take Berlin. Stalin remained in complete control of the Soviet Union until his death on March 5, 1953.

Further Reading: Robert Conquest, *The Great Terror: A Reassessment* (Oxford University Press, 1990); Simon Sebag Montefiore, *Stalin: The Court of the Red Tzar* (Alfred A. Knopf, 2004); Donald Rayfield, *Stalin and His Hangmen: The Tyrant and Those Who Killed for Him* (Random House, 2004).

—LEIGH KIMMEL

Stark, Harold R. (1880–1972)

At the time of the Pearl Harbor attack, Harold Raynsford Stark was the chief of Naval Operations, the U.S. Navy's most senior operational officer. A tall, white-haired man with the air of a professor, he seemed easily bullied by the more forceful personality of Richmond Kelly Turner. Stark's quickness to give way was at least partially responsible for the so-called "mutiny on the second deck," in which Turner usurped significant responsibilities for the analysis and distribution of INTELLIGENCE materials. It has often been speculated that this act of organizational empire building played a critical role in the intelligence failure that made the surprise at Pearl Harbor possible.

Stark's location on the night of December 6, 1941, has been the subject of intense controversy, particularly by those who would exonerate the commanders in Hawai'i. It has often been alleged that he was attending a play. However, Stark subsequently testified that, while he clearly recalled having seen *The Student Prince* while it was playing at the National Theater, he could not connect the play with his activities that particular night.

It can be said with certainty that on the morning of December 7, Stark was indeed taking care of naval business. At 9 A.M. Washington, D.C., time, the 14th and final part of the Japanese diplomatic message was decoded, and the chief of the Office of Naval Intelligence, Vice Admiral Theodore Wilkinson, delivered it to him (see CODES, JAPANESE). While they were discussing how to respond, a final message came through, instructing the Japanese ambassador to submit the entire message to U.S. Secretary of State CORDELL HULL at 1 P.M. local time.

Wilkinson then suggested Stark should notify Admiral HUSBAND E. KIMMEL, commander of U.S.

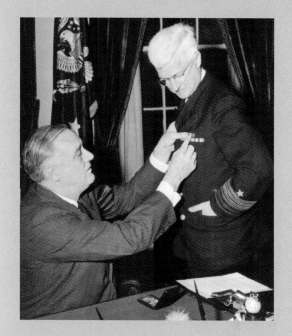

ABOVE *President Roosevelt pins a Gold Star in lieu of a second Distinguished Service Cross to Admiral Harold R. Stark, chief of Naval Operations. The citation was for his work building a large peacetime, two-ocean navy. The White House, April 9, 1942.*

naval forces at Pearl Harbor. Stark picked up the phone, but hesitated at the time difference. Deciding that it would be an ungodly time to call solely on the basis of a diplomatic ultimatum rather than signs of troop movements, he did nothing.

Historians have long debated what, if any, difference Stark could have made had he followed through his initial gesture. On one hand, the warning might have prevented total tactical surprise. The base would have been warned, and there would have been just enough time to put it on a war footing. Perhaps many of the gunners would not have been in the position of having nothing with which to fight, their ships being under peacetime conditions with all ammunition locked away in lockers.

On the other hand, there was no way to avert the strategic surprise. For too many years the American public and Congress had ignored the news coming from Europe and Asia of two aggressive powers fighting their way into empire. Both Congress and the people trusted the oceans to preserve America's isolation. As a result, military and naval appropriations were far too small to create the sort of military the nation really needed, and much of what the UNITED STATES had in the Pacific was being diverted to help Britain fight the Nazis.

In fact, some historians have even suggested that such a last-minute warning could have had catastrophic results, especially had Kimmel tried to meet the JAPANESE FLEET at sea. Fleet Admiral CHESTER NIMITZ often said it was God's own providence that the fleet was at anchor that morning, where the sunken battleships could be salvaged and men could escape to safety.

Further Reading. Edward L. Beach, *Scapegoats: A Defense of Kimmel and Short at Pearl Harbor* (Naval Institute Press, 1995); Henry C. Clausen and Bruce Lee, *Pearl Harbor: Final Judgement* (Crown Publishers, 1992); Gordon Prange, *At Dawn We Slept: The Untold Story of Pearl Harbor* (Penguin, 1981); John Toland, *Infamy: Pearl Harbor and Its Aftermath* (Doubleday, 1982).

—LEIGH KIMMEL

Stimson, Henry L. (1867–1950)

Henry L. Stimson was the secretary of war on December 7, 1941. He was born in the city of New York on September 21, 1867, and studied at Yale University and Harvard Law School. He came into the limelight as secretary of war between 1911 and 1913. Under President Herbert Hoover's administration (1929–33), he was the secretary of state. He strongly believed that the UNITED STATES should not recognize any territory seized by force, and although Hoover did not implement the Stimson Doctrine after the Japanese invasion of Manchuria in 1931, Stimson remained committed to it.

A debate continued in the United States about entering WORLD WAR II. Ultimately the interventionists won against the isolationists. President FRANKLIN D. ROOSEVELT began to initiate full-scale mobilization and in this he found Stimson helpful. A pro-Allied Republican favoring the policy of compulsory military training and repeal of the NEUTRALITY ACTS, the 72-year-old Stimson was named secretary of war by the Democratic administration in 1940.

Throughout the latter part of 1940 and early part of 1941, U.S. assistance to the Allies was increasing, and Stimson worked toward this effort. In the wake of Japanese advances in Southeast Asia, Stimson urged the president to limit oil and scrap material to JAPAN. He reiterated strong action against Japan with an oil embargo (see SANCTIONS AGAINST JAPAN). In the face of German submarine attacks, Britain was finding it difficult to convoy supplies from the United States under the LEND-LEASE program of January 1941, and Stimson advocated a policy of America convoying the vessels itself. A quarter of the Pacific Fleet (see PACIFIC FLEET, U.S.) was diverted to the Atlantic in May. The secretary was convinced that the United States eventually would join the war. From May to December 1941, a series of actions by Japan and GERMANY took the United States closer to entering the war as a belligerent. The Nazi invasion of the Soviet Union in June resulted in the extension of the Lend-Lease program to Moscow, and the U.S.

Navy was playing an active role after the actions of Nazi submarines in September.

The Tripartite Pact of September 1940 between Japan, Germany, and Italy extended the Axis into Asia (see AXIS POWERS IN 1941), and by July 1941 Japanese forces were in Indochina. Japanese assets were frozen in the United States. The American air force was strengthened in the PHILIPPINES due to Stimson's urging in September. In November, the Japanese government continued negotiations with the United States (see DIPLOMATIC RELATIONS). But neither country would yield over the question of Japanese control of China.

Stimson advised the president on November 6 against any move toward cessation of armament movement for six months. On November 25 Roosevelt had told him and other American officials that there might be a surprise Japanese attack. A Japanese naval task force was sailing on the same day from the Kuriles toward Hawai'i, and a warning was sent to the American naval base in Pearl Harbor. Another Japanese convoy was moving south of Taiwan as reported by Stimson on November 26, and the War Cabinet that met two days afterward viewed with alarm the Japanese moves.

Roosevelt's final appeal of December 6 to the Japanese emperor produced no result. The next day the Japanese planes struck the American naval base at Pearl Harbor. On December 8, Roosevelt declared war on Japan—but not on Germany and Italy despite insistence from Stimson. On December 11, both declared war on the United States.

Stimson had mobilized American resources before and after December 7 to the best of his ability. He was an author of American wartime strategy and played an important role in converting the isolationist foreign policy into an active involvement in world affairs. Some scholars say he has been unfairly

ABOVE *Col. C. R. Morris adjusts the blindfold on Secretary of War Henry Stimson, preparing to draw the first numbers in the Selective Service National Lottery, while President Roosevelt looks on. October 29, 1940.*

criticized for treatment of Japanese Americans. After the Allied victories in 1944, Stimson spoke out on moral grounds against the terror bombings of Germany and Japan. He continued to remain as secretary of war until 1945. Some of his important publications were *American Policy in Nicaragua* (1927), *Democracy and Nationalism in Europe* (1934), *The Far Eastern Crisis* (1936), and *On Active Service in Peace and War* (1948). Stimson died on Long Island, New York, on October 20, 1950.

Further Reading: Godfrey Hodgson, *Colonel: The Life and Wars of Henry Stimson, 1867–1950* (Knopf, 1990); Paul A. C. Koistinen, *Arsenal of World War II: The Political Economy of American Warfare, 1940–45* (University Press of Kansas, 2004); Elting L. Morison, *Turmoil and Tradition: A Study of the Life and Times of Henry L. Stimson* (Houghton Mifflin, 1960); Henry L Stimson and McGeorge Bundy, *On Active Service in Peace and War* (Harper, 1948).

—PATIT PABAN MISHRA

THE SOLEMN PRIDE
THAT MUST BE YOURS
★★ TO HAVE LAID ★★
SO COSTLY A SACRIFICE
UPON THE ALTAR
OF FREEDOM

T

Tennessee, USS

When commissioned on June 3, 1920, with Captain Richard H. Leigh in command, the USS *Tennessee* (BB-43) was the most advanced warship in the U.S. fleet. The USS *Tennessee* and her sister ship, USS *California* (BB-44; see *CALIFORNIA,* USS), were the first American battleships built to a "post-Jutland" design with greater underwater hull protection and fire-control systems for both the main and secondary batteries. Her 14-inch guns could be elevated to 30 degrees rather than the 15 degrees of earlier battleships, increasing the gun range by 40 percent to 35,000 yards. Construction had begun on the U.S. Navy's fifth vessel named USS *Tennessee* on May 14, 1917, at the New York Navy Yard. She was christened by Helen Lenore Roberts, daughter of the governor of Tennessee, on April 30, 1919.

After trials on the east coast, the USS *Tennessee* sailed via the Panama Canal to her home port of San Pedro, California, arriving in June 1921. For the next 19 years the USS *Tennessee* performed exercises and took part in annual fleet operations designed to keep her at the peak of efficiency. As a deterrent to Japanese aggression in the Far East, the battle force centered at San Pedro was ordered by President FRANK-LIN D. ROOSEVELT to change its base of operations to Pearl Harbor, Hawai'i, in the spring of 1940.

On the morning of December 7, 1941, the USS *Tennessee* was on Battleship Row in Pearl Harbor. She was moored on the starboard side to a pair of massive concrete quays located on Ford Island.

THE 30-FOOT STATUE OF LADY COLUMBIA, AT LEFT, *in the National Memorial Cemetery of the Pacific, known as the "Punchbowl," represents all grieving mothers. In ancient times, the extinct volcanic Punchbowl Crater was known as the Hill of Sacrifice, and was the site of royal burials and sacrifices. Today, more than 32,000 servicemen and women from four wars are buried here.*

The USS *West Virginia* (see WEST VIRGINIA, USS) was berthed next to her on the port side. Just ahead of the USS *Tennessee* was the USS *Maryland* (see MARYLAND, USS), with the USS *Oklahoma* outboard (see OKLAHOMA, USS). The USS *Arizona* (see ARIZONA, USS) was about 75 yards behind the USS *Tennessee* with the repair ship USS *Vestal* berthed outboard. When the Japanese attack began, the USS *Tennessee* was able to man her guns and get her steam up, but was unable to move. The USS *West Virginia* took sustained damage and began to list heavily, trapping the USS *Tennessee* against the quays to which she was moored. The USS *Oklahoma* capsized and sank bottom up.

When the USS *Arizona* and the USS *West Virginia* exploded, fuel oil ignited, and flames and dense smoke surrounded the USS *Tennessee*. At about 8:30 A.M. two bombs hit the USS *Tennessee*. The first struck gun turret III, but the bomb burned rather than exploded. The second bomb exploded upon striking the center gun of the forward "high" turret. Bomb fragments sprayed forward and fatally wounded commanding officer Captain Mervyn S. Bennion.

When the USS *Arizona's* magazines erupted, the USS *Tennessee* was covered with burning oil and debris that started a number of fires on the main deck and in the officers' quarters on the deck below. Shipboard burning was brought under control by 10:30 A.M., but oil was still burning around the USS *Arizona* and the USS *West Virginia* and continued to threaten the USS *Tennessee* as she was trapped against the quays for two more days. Compared to the other battleships around her, however, the USS *Tennessee* was relatively undamaged. Only five members of her crew died as a result of the attack, and less than 20 were seriously injured. While the effectiveness of the ship's antiaircraft fire may have been

Remember Pearl Harbor

IN OCTOBER 1944 the USS *Tennessee* played a major role in the invasion of the PHILIPPINES, providing air defense rather than shore bombardment until the Japanese navy made one final attempt to destroy the American landing fleet in Leyte Gulf. Pearl Harbor's surviving battleships avenged that attack on the night of October 24–25, 1944, in the Battle of Surigao Strait between Leyte and Dinagat Islands. The USS *Tennessee* joined the USS *West Virginia*, USS *Maryland*, USS *California*, and USS *Pennsylvania* as part of the battle line that destroyed a Japanese force that included the battleship *Yamashiro*. The battle was the last in naval history to take place solely between all-gun warships. It was also the last battle in which one force was able to "cross the T" of their opponents. This maneuver had been a staple of ships of the line since the 17th century and enabled the USS *Tennessee* and her sister ships to bring all their firepower to bear on the Japanese.

ABOVE *Foreground: the USS* West Virginia. *Background: the USS* Tennessee. *December 7, 1941.*

a factor, the USS *Tennessee* was lucky. Being moored inboard sheltered her from torpedo attack, and of the two bombs that hit her, one did not explode and the other spent itself on a gun barrel.

The USS *Tennessee* remained trapped until December 16, when she moved under her own power to the Pearl Harbor Navy Yard for four days of temporary repairs. The intense heat had warped every piece of hull plating above the waterline and ruined most of the electrical wiring. On December 20, the USS *Tennessee*, USS *Pennsylvania* (see PENNSYLVANIA, USS), and USS *Maryland* left Pearl Harbor for the Puget Sound Navy Yard with a screen of four destroyers. Working around the clock, shipyard craftsmen repaired the USS *Tennessee's* damage, and she went back to war on February 26, 1942.

The ship's role was not to be the one for which she had trained for two decades. Naval warfare had changed, and the USS *Tennessee* was too slow to keep up with aircraft carriers and other fast ships. Her heavy turret guns still served well for shore bombardment and gunfire support for troops ashore. On April 12, 1945, the USS *Tennessee* survived a kamikaze attack during the battle for Okinawa. The USS *Tennessee* earned ten battle stars for WORLD WAR II service and was one of only two battleships to receive a Navy Unit Commendation.

The USS *Tennessee* was placed in the inactive fleet until March 1959, when her name was struck from the Naval Vessel Register. In July, she was sold to the Bethlehem Steel Company and scrapped.

Further Reading: Myron J. Smith, *Volunteer State Battlewagon: USS Tennessee (BB-43)* (Pictorial Histories, 1992);"USS Tennessee (BB-43)," in James L. Mooney, ed., *Dictionary of American Naval Fighting Ships* (Naval Historical Center, 1991); Jonathan G. Utley, *An American Battleship at Peace and War: The U.S.S. Tennessee* (University Press of Kansas, 1991).

—ROBERT D. BOHANAN

Tojo, Hideki (1884–1948)

Hideki Tojo found himself in a position of responsibility for the Japanese civilian population after Prime Minister Fumimaro Konoe's resignation in October 1941. The resignation was a result of Konoe's inability to reconcile civilian and military goals during negotiations with the UNITED STATES, especially how to deal with the United States freezing U.S.-based Japanese assets and imposing an oil embargo on JAPAN (see SANCTIONS AGAINST JAPAN). The U.S. stance was in response to Japan's southward expansion according to its GREATER EAST ASIA CO-PROSPERITY SPHERE policy.

Tojo quickly acclimated himself to protecting both civilian and army interests. He kept his post as minister of war after becoming prime minister. Tojo came to support using military force in the Pacific after he perceived continued negotiations with Allied governments as a failure. He realized that military action was a necessity when he received an unacceptable 10-point proposal from U.S. Secretary of State CORDELL HULL on November 26, 1941 (see DIPLOMATIC RELATIONS). As the former army minister, he knew if Japan removed its military forces from China, as the Hull proposal demanded, it would only result in a military revolt.

Tojo was clearly kept out of the Japanese navy's plans to bomb Pearl Harbor in a surprise attack. Witnesses report Tojo flew into a rage at hearing the navy advocate what he considered a dishonorable action. After recovering from his outburst, Tojo agreed to support the plan only if Japan offered prior notification of the attack. Despite viewing the navy's attack plans as shameful, Tojo knew that Pearl Harbor was a necessary target because the United States had moved its naval forces there from California in 1940.

ABOVE LEFT AND RIGHT *Japan's Prime Minister General Hideki Tojo planned the subterfuge of sending Saburo Kurusu to negotiate in Washington while the Japanese launched a surprise navy air attack on Pearl Harbor.*

Toyoda, Teijiro (1885–1961)

As foreign minister in Fumimaro Konoe's third government, Admiral Teijiro Toyoda played a key role in Japanese-U.S. relations from July to October 1941. Toyoda served in the Japanese navy from 1905 to 1941 and retired from active duty a vice admiral. In April 1941 he became a naval reserve admiral and entered the Konoe cabinet as minister of commerce and industry. With the formation of his third government in July 1941, Konoe named Toyoda foreign minister.

During his brief tenure Toyoda faced an insoluble national crisis when the UNITED STATES, Britain, and the Dutch Empire froze Japanese assets in response to Tokyo's occupation of southern FRENCH INDOCHINA. Convinced that only through a summit could JAPAN have sanctions lifted and avoid war, the foreign minister devoted the bulk of his energies to bringing about a meeting between Konoe and President FRANKLIN D. ROOSEVELT. With the collapse of Konoe's final cabinet in October 1941, Toyoda temporarily left government service, though he would return to serve several prime ministers in various capacities, as well as a short term in the postwar Japanese legislature, the Diet.

Toyoda's long association with the navy, desire to avoid war with America, and close relationship with Tokyo's ambassador to the United States, Admiral KICHISABURO NOMURA, all influenced Konoe's selection of Toyoda to replace the pro-Axis and anti-American YOSUKE MATSUOKA in July 1941. While an early supporter of the Axis pact (see AXIS POWERS IN 1941), Toyoda saw the alliance as a means to deter the United States and conclude the war in China, rather than as an instrument to facilitate even greater Japanese expansion.

The Japanese committed the first act of war without war being declared against the United States. The Japanese government officially declared war on December 8. That day found Tojo speaking to the nation via radio, defending Japan's decision to attack in the face of western countries determined to dominate the world. Later that day, despite his radio message, Tojo appeared to forget that his country was at war when he appeared outside his home in his riding clothes. He was promptly stopped by his secretary, who questioned his destination, asking what would happen to the country if he were injured riding. Despite the fact that the reproof came from a subordinate, Tojo reportedly went back inside without a word.

Further Reading: Robert J. C. Butow, *Tojo and the Coming of War* (Princeton University Press, 1961); John Toland, *The Rising Sun: The Decline and Fall of the Japanese Empire, 1936–45* (Random House, 2003).

—**MELISSA F. GAYAN**

Within days of accepting the post of foreign minister, Toyoda faced as great a crisis in Japanese-American relations as any Japanese diplomat ever had. Japan's advance into southern French Indochina led Roosevelt on July 25 to freeze all Japanese assets in the United States, thus bringing American trade with Japan to a virtual halt. Britain and the Dutch Empire soon followed suit. Faced with economic ruin at home and military collapse abroad, Konoe approached War Minister HIDEKI TOJO and Navy Minister Oikawa Koshiro on August 4 in order to secure their support for his plan to meet with Roosevelt and break the diplomatic logjam. Early Japanese efforts to secure Roosevelt's agreement to meet with Konoe foundered. Convinced that only a leaders' conference could avert war, Toyoda met U.S. Ambassador JOSEPH GREW in an attempt to persuade him to urge his superiors to agree to the summit.

Despite Toyoda's best efforts and Grew's decision to endorse the meeting, Secretary of State CORDELL HULL and others convinced Roosevelt to delay acceptance until negotiators concluded preliminary discussions concerning an end to the current undeclared Sino-Japanese War, the postwar evacuation of Japanese forces from China, the restoration of the Open Door, and Japan's relation to the Axis. Toyoda thus spent the bulk of his tenure trying to meet American conditions for a summit. He met frequently with Grew, who supported a Konoe-Roosevelt summit, and took extraordinary pains to ensure that negotiations for a leaders' conference remain secret, so as not to arouse the fury of military extremists and pro-Axis sympathizers.

Toyoda managed to mollify American concerns over Japan's relation to the Axis by remaining largely silent even as Berlin and Washington, D.C., waged war on the high seas. As early as August 5 he informed the United States that Japan would accept American mediation to end the conflict with China. He could not, however, overcome American objections over the stationing of Japanese troops in postwar China, as War Minister Tojo and Sugiyama Gen, chief of the Army General Staff, clung to their position that Japanese forces would remain indefinitely in Inner Mongolia, north China, and Hainan Island. Unable to convince the army to soften its position and Roosevelt to hold the summit, Konoe and his entire cabinet resigned on October 14.

Further Reading: Chihiro Hosoya, "The Role of Japan's Foreign Ministry and Its Embassy in Washington, 1940–41," in Dorothy Borg and Shumpei Okamoto, eds., *Pearl Harbor as History* (Columbia University Press, 1973); Nobutaka Ike, ed., *Japan's Decision for War: Records of the 1941 Policy Conferences* (Stanford University Press, 1967); William Morley, ed., *Japan's Road to the Pacific War: The Final Confrontation* (Columbia University Press, 1994).

—SIDNEY PASH

Truman, Harry (1884–1972)

U.S. Senator Harry Truman was asleep in Columbia, Missouri, when Pearl Harbor was attacked. On December 8, he voted in favor of going to war against the Japanese, and volunteered his services to help the military. Speaking to the man he considered his political idol, Truman told Army Chief of Staff General GEORGE C. MARSHALL that he was capable of training young artillerymen for battle.

During World War I Truman had served as commander of Battery D, 129th Field Artillery Regiment, 35th Division, and thus he believed was capable of passing on his knowledge. Truman was 56 years old at the time. Marshall smiled at the suggestion but told Truman he was not needed.

Truman was born on May 8, 1884, in Lamar, Missouri, and grew up in Independence, Missouri. He first entered politics in 1922 when he was elected as a Jackson County Judge. He served two terms as the county judge and then won a seat in the U.S. Senate in 1935.

When the Japanese attacked Pearl Harbor, Truman was still a senator, a position he would hold until 1944 when he accepted President FRANKLIN D. ROOSEVELT's offer to run as his vice president. Truman would only serve 82 days as vice president before becoming president of the UNITED STATES on April 12, 1945, immediately after Roosevelt died.

Truman won reelection in 1948 and then left politics in 1952, choosing not to run against Dwight Eisenhower. During his time in office he would see the end of World War II, the dropping of the atomic bombs, the beginning of the Cold War and the Korean War, and would recognize the state of Israel. His Truman Doctrine and passage of the Marshall Plan were crucial to rebuilding Europe after the war. Domestically, he desegregated the armed forces in 1948.

Truman left office as one of the nation's most unpopular presidents; his hard work and honesty has gained appreciation after some of the more corruptive presidencies of the 1960s and 1970s. Truman died on December 26, 1972.

Further Reading: Robert H. Ferrell, ed., *Off the Record: The Private Papers of Harry S Truman* (Harper and Row, 1980); Alonzo L. Hamby, *Man of the People: A Life of Harry S Truman* (Oxford University Press, 1995); David McCullough, *Truman* (Simon and Schuster, 1992).

—DAVID W. MCBRIDE

ABOVE TOP *President Harry S Truman in a formal presidential portrait from 1945. Truman became president on April 12, 1945, upon the death of Franklin D. Roosevelt.* **ABOVE BOTTOM** *President Truman announces Japan's surrender, at the White House in Washington, D.C., August 14, 1945.*

Pearl Harbor and the Atomic Bomb

WHEN TRUMAN became president in 1945, one of his earliest decisions would be how to bring an end to the war in the Pacific. He faced various scenarios that included using the atomic bombs that had recently been made available. He also had the option of waiting for the Soviet Union to enter the war in the Pacific, which was set for early August 1945. Finally, he had the option of launching an invasion on mainland Japan in November; however, such an order would surely result in tremendous American casualties.

Debate continues over whether Truman should have dropped the atomic bombs on JAPAN. While he may have had alternatives, he was genuinely concerned with keeping American casualties to a minimum, and the memories of Pearl Harbor were still fresh in the collective American consciousness. In a meeting with British Prime Minister WINSTON CHURCHILL in July 1945, Truman stated that he felt that the Japanese lacked military honor following their attack of Pearl Harbor.

In his private papers it is also possible to see how the attack on Pearl Harbor affected his decision-making process. On August 6 Truman issued a public statement following the dropping of the first atomic bomb, stating that "The Japanese began the war from the air at Pearl Harbor. They have been repaid many fold." Three days later he gave another statement following the second bomb. Again Truman would bring up Pearl Harbor: "Having found the bomb we have used it. We have used it against those who attacked us without warning at Pearl Harbor, against those who have starved and beaten and executed American prisoners of war, against those who have abandoned all pretence of obeying international laws of warfare."

While the attack on Pearl Harbor was not the primary reason for the president's decision to use the bombs, the image of the Japanese as a treacherous enemy that had struck Pearl Harbor in a cowardly fashion helped to sustain a negative image of the Japanese that was only further aided by the vicious fighting that took place in the Pacific during the war. As a result, there was very little sympathy for the Japanese when the bombs were dropped.

ABOVE *A dense column of smoke rises more than 60,000 feet above the Japanese port of Nagasaki, the result of an atomic bomb dropped on the industrial center on August 9, 1945. Over 30 percent of the city was destroyed, and nearly 150,000 people were killed or wounded. Three days earlier, on August 6, 1945, the* Enola Gay *dropped the first atomic bomb on the Japanese city of Hiroshima. The device contained the equivalent of 12,500 tons of TNT, destroyed an area of five square miles, and took the lives of approximately 140,000 of Hiroshima's 350,000 residents.*

U

United States

The attack on Pearl Harbor broke forever the belief that America could remain aloof from the struggles of international affairs. For decades, the nation had attempted to insulate itself from the growing world conflict through policies of neutrality and isolation. The policy of neutrality was abandoned on December 7, 1941. It was not that the United States had been oblivious to the events that were happening around the world, but rather, it had sought to follow a policy that would prevent engagement in world conflict.

Throughout the 19th century, the United States had followed a policy of westward expansion that tended to engage the military on its frontier and to prevent much in the way of engagement overseas. Economic factors gradually earned the United States a place on the world stage. In spite of the Monroe Doctrine of 1823, which declared that the United States would not get itself involved in the affairs of Europe, the United States had created commercial concerns throughout the world. After the occupation of the PHILIPPINES during the Spanish-American War, American interests had reached the western Pacific Ocean and extended into the Caribbean. It had gained control over Puerto Rico, Hawai'i, and GUAM.

THE UNITED STATES IN WORLD WAR I

By the advent of World War I, there were conflicting opinions as to the American neutrality policy, in spite of President Woodrow Wilson's

THE TIME OF YOUR LIFE *First staged in 1939, William Saroyan's drama was touted as a microcosm of America, wearied by World War I and following a policy of neutrality as World War II developed in Europe. The photo* **AT LEFT** *is from a 1939–40 production by the American Theatre Guild, starring Eddie Dowling, Julie Haydon, Gene Kelly, and Charles de Sheim. William Saroyan refused to accept the 1940 Pulitzer Prize for Drama for* The Time Of Your Life, *stating that art could not be patronized by wealth.*

declaration in August 1914 that Americans should be impartial in thought and action. However, Allied war propaganda was intense and successful in garnering some American public support. Yet progressives, socialists, and feminist groups clamored for neutrality, and the U.S. administration continued to proclaim neutrality, as American interest was not directly at stake. Gradually, there emerged a pro-Allied policy, although the country did not join the war.

Compared to the loan amount of $27 million to GERMANY, the Allies received some $2.3 billion over the period 1914–16. The United States had closer business ties with the Allies, and that was one reason for the increased volume of trade. The British fleet effectively blockaded the Central powers, preventing American goods from reaching Germany or Austria-Hungary. Economic prosperity of the United States became closely interwoven with Allied success, and American industry prospered with munitions and food orders.

A German victory would have spelled disaster for the American economy. The situation began to change when Germany acted against the shipping interests of the United States after the February 1915 announcement that Germany would not spare merchant shipping around the British Isles. On May 7, 1915, the sinking of the British liner *Lusitania* resulted in the loss of 128 American lives, arousing public opinion against Germany. The torpedoing of the French vessel *Sussex* in March 1916 resulted in the president warning of a break in diplomatic relations.

On January 31, 1917, Germany resorted to unrestricted submarine warfare against neutral as well as belligerent shipping. The American administration could no longer hang onto neutrality. The United States declared war on April 6, 1917. The war ended with the surrender of Germany on November 11, 1918. The United States became a creditor nation with $11.7 billion in credits, and the dollar became the most important currency in

AT RIGHT *A United States Navy recruiting poster from World War I, created by Howard Chandler Christy, 1917. The poster reads, "Gee!! I wish I were a man/I'd join the Navy/Be a Man and Do it/United States Navy Recruiting Station."*
AT FAR RIGHT *American soldiers return home after serving overseas in World War I. The parade in honor of returned fighters is passing the Public Library in New York City. 1919.*

international money markets. Nonintervention and isolationism again became the predominant political mood. In March 1920, the U.S. Senate rejected both the Versailles Treaty and participation in the League of Nations.

THE INTERWAR PERIOD

At the 1922 Washington Naval Conference, the Great Powers made an effort to limit the major fleets through a strategic arms agreement. The United States was successful in abolishing the Anglo-Japanese alliance of 1902 and making Japan agree to a 5:5:3 tonnage ratio, in favor of the United States and Britain. The agreement also precluded fortification of the formerly German islands in the Pacific that had been awarded to Japan as League of Nations mandates.

In January 1923, French and Belgian troops marched into the German Ruhr area, and the United States used its financial clout to avert a crisis by arranging a loan of $200 million to Germany. The administration of President Calvin Coolidge had made it clear that American loans would come only if peace and security were maintained in Europe. The administration of Herbert Hoover took an active part in the Kellogg-Briand Pact (1928), which "outlawed" war and renounced the use of force as an instrument of foreign policy. All the major powers that were later involved in World War II signed the pact.

The decade of the 1930s saw mounting financial, diplomatic, and military crises. The crash of the New York Stock Exchange in October 1929 led to an international economic depression. The rise of totalitarian dictatorships in Germany and Italy, coupled with the militarism of Japan, was soon going to change the world order based on the Treaty of Versailles. A series of events occurred, beginning with the Japanese invasion of China's Manchuria in 1931, which led the world toward another world war. The American response was to keep intact its political and economic influence at a time of global depression and aggressive foreign policy on the part of Germany, Italy, and Japan. Isolationism was to be maintained unless the security and defense of the nation were directly threatened.

From the beginning of the 20th century, U.S.-Japanese relations had worsened in several stages. By the Root-Takahira Agreement of 1908, both the United States and Japan had agreed to maintain the territorial integrity of China and the status quo in the Pacific. The Washington Conference of 1921–22 had temporarily created a lull in the naval arms race in the Pacific. It also reaffirmed the "Open Door" policy, and relations between the United States and Japan relaxed for the time being.

The Japanese occupation of Manchuria in flagrant violation of the League of Nations Covenant met with verbal condemnation. U.S. Secretary of State HENRY L. STIMSON had said the United States should not recognize territory acquired in violation of the Open Door policy or Chinese integrity. Japan withdrew from the League of Nations in March 1933. The Anti-Comintern Pact was signed between Japan and Germany on November 25, 1936, and Italy joined it after one year. In the summer of 1937, Japan invaded five northern provinces of China, which was met with strong disapproval by President FRANKLIN D. ROOSEVELT, who said in October that the aggressor must be "quarantined."

The United States condemned the Japanese action, but opposed sanctions (see SANCTIONS AGAINST JAPAN). The inaction of other nations made Japan more confident, and it set up a puppet government in China in 1938. It was committed fully to establishing a new order in East Asia (see GREATER

EAST ASIA CO-PROSPERITY SPHERE), and it was poised for expansion into Southeast Asia.

THE U.S. DECISION TO ENTER WORLD WAR II

Peace in Europe was shattered on September 1, 1939, when Germany attacked Poland and World War II broke out after a fragile peace of two decades. After the spectacular success of the Axis powers in 1939 and 1940, the United States gave up military neutrality. Roosevelt said that the country would remain neutral, but he could not ask Americans to remain neutral in thought. The president called a special session of the Congress in September 1939 and Congress revised the neutrality laws, permitting belligerents to purchase arms on a "cash and carry" basis. The United States increased its assistance to the Allies through sales of arms, petroleum, and machinery, sold on a cash basis and shipped aboard Allied or other foreign-registered ships.

In September 1940, the United States agreed to supply Britain 50 naval destroyers in exchange for a lease on Caribbean naval bases. The LEND-LEASE program of January 1941 allowed the president to sell, lease, and lend armaments to any country important for defense of the United States. Britain, and afterward the Soviet Union, benefited immensely from the program. When shipment of supplies became difficult due to German submarine attacks, a policy of convoying the vessels by the United States began. One-fourth of the Pacific Fleet (see PACIFIC FLEET, U.S.) was diverted toward the Atlantic in May 1941.

The signing of the Atlantic Charter in August 1941 between Britain and the United States emphasized American commitment to self-determination and freedom, along with the "destruction of Nazi tyranny." By the fall of 1941, the United States had moved from the status of a benevolent neutral to a belligerency short of war.

The United States also was getting ready on the home front, enhancing its military potential and unleashing a massive mobilization plan. The country was preparing to produce sufficient munitions. The industrial mobilization plan began in 1939 with the immediate task of having more weapons, planes, ships, tanks, and ammunition.

Prior to the mobilization effort, the U.S. Army was ranked 17th in size among the major countries. The army budget submitted in January 1940, with selective service implemented, set a target of 1,000,000 soldiers. The U.S. Congress approved in September 1940 the Burke-Wadsworth Act, providing the first peacetime conscription.

The army possessed 27 infantry, five armored, and two cavalry divisions; 35 air groups; and a host of supporting units by the autumn of 1941. The strength of the army was 1,643,477 personnel in 1941. The national defense budget amounted to $1.12 billion in 1939 and $10.5 billion in 1940. New plants for the manufacture of some 50,000 airplanes were planned.

The United States was thus far more prepared for war in 1941 than it had been in 1917. The motivation to become a belligerent was provided on that fateful day, December 7, 1941, in Pearl Harbor.

Further Reading: James L. Abrahamson, *America Arms for a New Century: The Making of a Great Military Power* (The Free Press, 1981); Robert A. Divine, *The Reluctant Belligerent: American Entry into World War II* (John Wiley & Sons, 1979); Justus D. Doenecke, *From Isolation to War, 1931-1941* (H. Davidson, 1991); Donald M Goldstein and Harry J. Maihafer, eds., *America in World War I* (Brassey's, 2004); Alan L. Gropman, *Mobilizing U.S. Industry in World War II* (National Defense University, 1996); Akira Iriye, *The Globalizing of America, 1913-1945* (Cambridge University Press, 1993); David Titus, ed., *Japan's Road to the Pacific War: The Final Confrontation Japan's Negotiations with the United States, 1941* (Columbia University Press, 1994); Allan M. Winkler, *Home Front USA: America during World War II* (H. Davidson, 1986).

—PATIT PABAN MISHRA

Roosevelt's Address to Congress, December 8, 1941

YESTERDAY, DECEMBER 7, 1941—a date which will live in infamy—the United States of America was suddenly and deliberately attacked by naval and air forces of the Empire of Japan. The United States was at peace with that Nation and, at the solicitation of Japan, was still in conversation with its Government and its Emperor looking toward the maintenance of peace in the Pacific. Indeed, one hour after Japanese air squadrons had commenced bombing in Oahu, the Japanese Ambassador to the United States and his colleague delivered to the Secretary of State a formal reply to a recent American message. While this reply stated that it seemed useless to continue the existing diplomatic negotiations, it contained no threat or hint of war or armed attack. It will be recorded that the distance of Hawai'i from Japan makes it obvious that the attack was deliberately planned many days or even weeks ago. During the intervening time the Japanese Government has deliberately sought to deceive the United States by false statements and expressions of hope for continued peace. The attack yesterday on the Hawai'ian Islands has caused severe damage to American naval and military forces. Very many American lives have been lost. In addition American ships have been reported torpedoed on the high seas between San Francisco and Honolulu. Yesterday the Japanese Government also launched an attack against Malaya. Last night Japanese forces attacked Hong Kong. Last night Japanese forces attacked Guam. Last night Japanese forces attacked the Philippine Islands. Last night the Japanese attacked Wake Island. This morning the Japanese attacked Midway Island. Japan has, therefore, undertaken a surprise offensive extending throughout the Pacific area. The facts of yesterday speak for themselves. The people of the United States have already formed their opinions and well understand the implications to the very life and safety of our Nation. As Commander in Chief of the Army and Navy I have directed that all measures be taken for our defense. Always will we remember the character of the onslaught against us. No matter how long it may take us to overcome this premeditated invasion, the American people in their righteous might will win through to absolute victory. I believe I interpret the will of the Congress and of the people when I assert that we will not only defend ourselves to the uttermost but will make very certain that this form of treachery shall never endanger us again. Hostilities exist. There is no blinking at the fact that our people, our territory, and our interests are in grave danger. With confidence in our armed forces—with the unbounded determination of our people—we will gain the inevitable triumph—so help us God. I ask that the Congress declare that since the unprovoked and dastardly attack by Japan on Sunday, December 7, a state of war has existed between the United States and the Japanese Empire.

W

WACs

The Women's Army Corps (WAC) began on July 3, 1943, after having been originally structured as the Women's Army Auxiliary Corps (WAAC), an organization established to work alongside the army, primarily in support services. Massachusetts Congresswoman Edith Nourse Rogers introduced the bill to create the separate Army Corps in May 1941; however, she failed to receive sufficient support prior to the Japanese bombing of Pearl Harbor. But, with General GEORGE C. MARSHALL's support, Congress approved the bill and recruitment began.

The WAAC, it was argued, would allow men to be relieved from noncombatant work and reassigned to combat duty. The army began enrollment of women in earnest and established training facilities and living quarters and began appointment of women at home and abroad. Similar to men, rank determined one's pay grade. WAAC grades were analogous to those of enlisted men and included auxiliary, junior leader, leader, staff leader, technical leader, first leader, and chief leader. While pay was less at the start, by the end of 1942, the army compensated them equally to men of equivalent grade.

The first WAAC trainees were sent to units of the Aircraft Warning Service (AWS) to replace volunteer civilian workers. Others would go on to work for the Army Air, Ground, and Supply Forces as mechanics, drivers, typists, file clerks, and other administrative and support positions. The Army Air Forces received nearly 40 percent of WAACs and

AT LEFT *A Women's Army Corps (WAC) enlistment poster calls attention to the widespread need for support services in the war effort. The poster also encapsulates a somewhat romanticized image of feminine beauty in World War II America. Created by Bradshaw Crandall, the poster was published by the Recruiting Publicity Bureau, United States Army, in 1943.*

assigned them duties for everything from weather forecasters and radio operators to sheet metal workers and air traffic controllers. The Army Service Forces employed WAACs in mixing and analyzing ordnance and as mechanics and electricians. A much smaller number worked for the Army Ground Forces, although with great reluctance from many male officers. The majority performed office work in the states, but some served overseas as well. The first overseas WAACs served in Algiers for General Dwight D. Eisenhower performing mainly clerical work.

While the work of the WAAC was essential to the war effort, in the summer of 1943 Rogers pushed through a bill that transformed the WAAC into the WAC, making it part of the army, rather than an auxiliary. WAC activities were now governed by military regulations and WAC servicewomen followed the army chain of command. The new organization allowed women to receive the same rank as men, up to lieutenant colonel, with the director being granted the rank of colonel with no possibility of promotion. There was a general understanding within the army that all generals and colonels, except the director of the WAC, have combat training and experience. This requirement effectively excluded women from attaining these ranks. The change in status was one that related more to how the WAC was administered within the army's existing organizational structures. The jobs women performed were much the same.

By the end of the war, more than 150,000 women had served in the WAC. While the number is substantial, the proposed recruitment goal set by Con-

African American WACs

WHILE WOMEN trying to serve in the army faced certain discrimination from male officers, African American women faced a second obstacle: race. Like African American men, women found themselves serving in all-black units and were commanded by black officers. Black and white women shared training facilities, but shopping and entertainment remained strictly segregated. As African American WAC Charity Adams Early remembered, African Americans "were kept in the dirty and most unmilitary position as the unsung support personnel."

ABOVE LEFT *The first member of the U.S. Army WAC Detachment FWD COMZ to step ashore in France is Sgt. Nancy E. Carter of Charlottesville, Virginia, July 15, 1944.* ABOVE RIGHT *WAC Pvt. Joy Caldaronello and Pvt. Jane Lee Wolford brew a cup of hot coffee while on bivouac in France, November 1, 1944.*

gress from the beginning was 150,000. There was also competition from domestic industry. While there was some public support for the drafting of women into the WAC in late 1943 to fill army positions, Congress never seriously considered this option and recruitment failed to meet expectations.

With the end of the war in Europe on May 8, 1945, demobilization of the WAC began. While many women, like many of their male counterparts, looked forward to returning home, others desired to remain in the army; however, no plans were made for women in postwar programs. By the end of 1946, the WAC was a mere shell of the wartime organization. But within two years, Congress granted army requests to make the WAC a permanent fixture of the U.S. Army. In 1978 the army eliminated the WAC and folded women into a single army corps with men. (See also WAVES.)

Further Reading: Charity Adams Early, *One Woman's Army: A Black Officer Remembers the WAC* (Texas A&M Press, 1989); Bettie J. Morden, *The Women's Army Corps, 1945–78* (Center of Military History, U.S. Army, 1992).

—CHAD PARKER

Wake Island

Wake Island lies roughly halfway between JAPAN and Hawai'i and was attacked by Japanese forces on December 8, 1941, as part of Japan's massive Pacific offensive that began with the surprise attack on Pearl Harbor. Despite the manpower shortage, the soldiers and civilians stationed on Wake and its sister islands, Wilkes and Peale, defended the atoll for over two weeks and inflicted major losses on the Japanese. On De-

ABOVE *Marine Brigadier General Lawson H. M. Sanderson affixes his signature to the Wake Island surrender document. Japanese Rear Admiral Shigematsu Sakaibaara, at left, sits with pen in hand ready to sign. Between them is the Japanese interpreter, and at right, in the baseball cap, is Larry Watanabe, Honolulu-born Japanese, with the U.S. Army as an interpreter.*

cember 23, the garrison surrendered in the face of overwhelming odds.

The strategic position of the island played a key role in air travel between the continental UNITED STATES and U.S. possessions in the PHILIPPINES. When tensions heightened between America and Japan in the 1930s, the military urged that Wake's defenses be strengthened. Despite the efforts of over 1,000 civilian and military workers, Wake's defenses were not completed before Japan attacked.

Although the ranking officer on Wake was Commander Winfield Scott Cunningham of the U.S. Navy, elements of the 1st Marine Defense Battalion under Major James Devereux made up the bulk of military men on the island. Devereux's marines were supplemented by small detachments of army and navy personnel. In total, there were 519 military personnel on the island when the Japanese attacked.

Due to the lack of radar equipment, inadequate observation posts, and the roar of the surf, the defenders on Wake could not see or hear enemy planes until they were overhead. The island had sufficient antiaircraft guns, but only enough men to man a third of them. The initial attacks destroyed all but four of the F4F Wildcat fighters available for aerial defense.

The Japanese attempted a landing on December 11, but their fleet fell into an ambush set by Wake's coastal defenses and suffered heavy damage without landing a single soldier. The JAPANESE FLEET, commanded by Rear Admiral Kajioka, sustained damage to three cruisers, lost two destroyers, and suffered 700 dead compared to only four wounded Americans. Although the defenders suffered fewer casualties than they inflicted, each casualty sustained or piece of equipment lost was irreplaceable. After the failed first invasion, Japan returned to daily bombing and shelling in order to soften up the island for a second attempt.

Japan launched the second landing on December 23 with a larger force, including carrier support, and withheld preliminary bombardments to avoid giving the island advance warning of the attack. Additionally, Japan took advantage of their numerical superiority by making several landings all over the island to further stretch the already thin defenses.

The invasion began before dawn and consisted of 1,000 men with an additional 500 in reserve. Wake's defenders, grouped in small pockets throughout the island, fought heroically, sometimes even hand-to-hand, before giving ground. Despite the stoic effort, by mid-afternoon it was clear that the island could not be held and the order was given to surrender. Although Japan won the battle, they did so at the cost of 820 killed and 333 wounded. The Americans suffered 120 killed, 49 wounded, and two missing. Those who survived were taken to prisoner-of-war camps in China, Korea, and Japan's Hokkaido Island and held until the end of the war in 1945.

Further Reading: Chet Cunningham, *Hell Wouldn't Stop: An Oral History of the Battle of Wake Island* (Carroll and Graf, 2002); Bill Sloan, *Given Up For Dead: America's Heroic Stand at Wake Island* (Bantam Books, 2004); John F. Wukovitz, *Pacific Alamo: The Battle for Wake Island* (Penguin Group, 2003).

—CHRIS THOMAS

Wallace, Henry A. (1888–1965)

On the morning of December 7, Vice President Henry Agard Wallace was in New York City, together with his former cabinet colleague, Secretary of Labor Frances Perkins, to meet with Latin American officials for a discussion of Pan-American unity. Less than 10 months had passed since Wallace had taken office as President FRANKLIN D. ROOSEVELT's surprise choice, over strong opposition within the Democratic Party because of his left-liberal views and reputation as a "mystic," to succeed John Nance Garner as vice president.

In that time, the former secretary of agriculture had made short shrift of the vice presidency's sole constitutional mandate—presiding over the Senate—to pursue a more activist role. In July 1941, Roosevelt had created the Economic Defense Board, a policy and advisory group concerned with international economic issues and defense mobilization, and made Wallace its chairman, the first time a vice president had ever been given an administrative position. Two months later, Wallace was named to head another new agency, the Supply Priorities and

Allocations Board (SPAB), designed to speed the production and delivery of war materiel to the Allies (see ALLIES ON DECEMBER 7, 1941).

His most important role, however, was not made public: two months before Pearl Harbor, Wallace had met with Roosevelt and Vannevar Bush, a former dean and now head of the National Defense Research Committee, to discuss whether or not to proceed with development of an atomic bomb; during his term as vice president, Wallace served on a five-member committee that oversaw the Manhattan Project, making him one of the few people in government privy to the atomic secret.

Wallace first learned of the Pearl Harbor attack from a passerby who had heard a news flash; minutes later, the White House operator tracked him down and told him that an airplane was waiting to take him to Washington, D.C. By 8:30 P.M., he was back at the White House, where, with the rest of the cabinet, he heard a grim Roosevelt disclose the details of U.S. losses during the attack (see PEARL HARBOR: ACTION REPORT).

That night, Wallace remained at the White House for urgent conversations with Roosevelt. "We were all drawn very close together by the emergency," he wrote later. "Americans are really good when they really get up against it." Though personally inclined toward pacifism, he had long urged the president to "go to the absolute limit in your firmness in dealing with Japan," saying that "the entire Axis will be impressed and the psychology of the American people will be strengthened."

The next morning, Wallace was in the office of the Senate Foreign Relations Committee, working with Majority Leader Alben Barkley on the precise script and procedures for that afternoon's historic joint session to hear Roosevelt's call for a declaration of war. He entered the House chamber together with the elderly and infirm Senator Carter Glass, a conservative Virginia isolationist, in what was meant as a visible show of solidarity and unity (see CONGRESSIONAL REACTION). Later that evening, Wallace convened a meeting of SPAB, at which the agency released a public statement: the time for national defense had ended, it said. From now on, the sole objective was victory.

Further Reading: John C. Culver and John Hyde, *American Dreamer: A Life of Henry A. Wallace* (W. W. Norton, 2000); Edward L. Schapsmeier and Frederick H. Schapsmeier, *Prophet in Politics: Henry A. Wallace in the War Years* (Iowa State University Press, 1970).

—ERIC FETTMANN

WAVES

The WAVES (Women Accepted for Voluntary Emergency Service) was established as an organization for women in the U.S. Navy during WORLD WAR II. A bill authorizing the WAVES was

ABOVE *Lovel Lees (left) Sp(Y)3/c and Catherine S. Pinzhoffer (right) Sp(Y)3/c give radio directions to incoming planes at NAS Anacostia, D.C. Control Towers.*

signed on July 30, 1942, with Mildred A. McAfee as the organization's director. Members were part of the navy reserve and had full military status and eligibility for veterans' benefits.

Thousands of women were recruited for the WAVES. Never before had American women been offered such a large role in the service of their country, nor had there ever been such an urgent need for their service. Men who worked at shore stations were needed for sea duty, and the WAVES took their places. They received the same ratings and pay. The call went out for all women to volunteer, even if they had no special skills. If a woman passed physical and educational requirements, she was accepted.

The WAVES were responsible for a variety of tasks. Many of the vital aspects of running the navy's day-to-day operations were held by men who were needed for sea duty. The WAVES took over many clerical, administrative, technical, and communications positions. They were involved in radio work, office duties, and the like, but also included jobs traditionally held by men, including aviation gunner instruction, aeronautical engineering, mechanics, aviation ground crew, navigation instruction, aviation ordnance, finance, and chemical warfare. WAVES also took over the "Link Trainer," which taught pilots the principles of flying on the ground. Women also had the opportunity to become officers, and many did.

Basic training lasted four weeks, taking place at the Naval Training School in the Bronx, New York. From there, some WAVES received additional training in specialist work before being transferred to naval air stations, naval shore stations, naval hospitals, agricultural and mechanical colleges, and teachers' colleges.

During World War II, approximately 100,000 women served with the WAVES. By the end of the war, there were around 86,000 women still actively serving. The organization became part of the regular navy and naval reserve in 1948. Joy Bright Hancock, who served in both world wars, became the first director of women in the regular navy. (See also WACS.)

Further Reading: James E. Seelye Jr. and Casey M. Stark, eds., *Ideals, Courage, and Hope: Selections from the University of Toledo Veterans History Project Interviews* (University of Toledo Libraries, 2004); Emily Yellen, *Our Mothers' War: American Women at Home and at the Front During World War II* (Free Press, 2004).

—JAMES E. SEELYE JR.

West Virginia, USS

The hull of the second USS *West Virginia* (Battleship No. 48 to the Navy) was laid down on April 12, 1920, by the Newport News Shipbuilding and Drydock Company of Newport News, Virginia. The ship, known as "Wee Vee," was sponsored by Miss Alice Wright Mann of Mercer County, daughter of millionaire coal mine operator Isaac T. Mann, a prominent West Virginian. The ship was launched on November 19, 1921, commissioned under the command of Captain Thomas J. Senn, on December 1, 1923. Her specifications included a displacement of 33,590 tons; length of 624 feet; draft of 30 feet and 6 inches; speed of 21 knots; complement of 1,407 crewmen; armament of eight 16-inch guns, twelve 6-inch guns, and two 21-inch twin-turret guns. The USS *West Virginia* became the flagship for the commander, Battleship Divisions, Battle Fleet, on October 30, 1924.

During the remainder of the 1920s, the ship took part in various army-navy maneuvers to test the defenses of the Hawai'ian Islands, cruised with the fleet from Hawaiʻi to the Caribbean Sea and the Atlantic Ocean, and from Alaskan waters to Panama. In the 1930s, the ship carried out routine training missions with the fleet. In order to keep pace with technological developments in ordnance, gunnery, and fire control, as well as engineering and aviation, the ship underwent modifications designed to increase her battle capacity.

In the closing years of the 1930s, it became evident that the UNITED STATES would become involved in another war on a grand scale with the most probable enemy being JAPAN. This reasoning produced the dispatch of the fleet to Hawaiʻian waters in the spring of 1939, and the retention of the fleet at Pearl Harbor in 1940. As 1941 progressed, the USS *West Virginia* carried out a schedule of intensive training maneuvers, based on the Pearl Harbor force operating in various task forces and groups in the Hawaiʻian area. This routine continued even through the unusually tense period that began in November and extended into the next month. Such at-sea periods were usually followed by in-port upkeep, with the battleship mooring to masonry quays along the southeast shores off Ford Island in the center of Pearl Harbor. On Sunday, December 7, 1941, the USS *West Virginia* lay moored outboard of the USS *Tennessee* (see TENNESSEE, USS) at berth F-6 with 40 feet of water beneath her keel. Shortly before 8 A.M., Japanese planes, flying from a six-carrier task force, started their well-planned attack on the fleet at Pearl Harbor.

The USS *West Virginia* officially took five 18-inch aircraft torpedoes in her port side and two bomb hits; those bombs were 15-inch armor-piercing shells fitted with fins. The first bomb penetrated the superstructure deck, wrecking the port casemates and causing that deck to collapse to the level of the galley below. Four casemates and the galley caught fire

Casualties

ONE OF the first casualties of the attack was the ship's commanding officer, Captain Mervyn S. Bennion. Bennion arrived on the bridge of the USS *West Virginia* early in the heat of the battle only to be struck down by a bomb fragment hurled from an explosion on the battleship USS *Tennessee*. Bennion, hit in the abdomen, fell to the deck, mortally wounded. He clung tenaciously to life long enough to be involved in the conduct of the ship's defense up to his last moment. For his courage and devotion to duty, Bennion was awarded the Congressional Medal of Honor posthumously (see CONGRESSIONAL MEDAL OF HONOR).

In all, 107 crewmembers of the *West Virginia* were killed in action as a result of the Japanese attack on December 7. Untold numbers of others were injured; some by enemy bombs, torpedoes and strafing; some by flying debris; and many received burns either from the raging fires onboard the ship or from the oil and gasoline fires that engulfed the waters as sailors abandoned ship. Perhaps the most cruel of all deaths were those that were not discovered until well after the ship was pumped out and refloated many months later. During ensuing repairs, workers located 70 bodies of USS *West Virginia* sailors who had been trapped below when the ship sank.

immediately, with the subsequent detonation of the ready-service projectiles stowed in the casemates.

The second bomb hit further aft, wrecking one Vought OS2U Kingfisher floatplane atop the "high" catapult on Turret III, and pitching the second floatplane to the main deck below. The projectile penetrated the 4-inch turret roof, wrecking one gun in the turret itself. Although the bomb proved a dud, burning gasoline from the damaged aircraft caused some damage. Later examination revealed that USS *West Virginia* had taken not five but seven torpedo hits. The ship was abandoned, settling to the bottom of the harbor on an even keel.

In the after-action report from the senior surviving officer of the USS *West Virginia*, Lieutenant Commander William White, to the commander in chief, Pacific Fleet, White stated that he had been in his cabin dressing when at 7:55 A.M., he felt two heavy shocks on the hull of the ship (see PACIFIC FLEET, U.S.; PEARL HARBOR: ACTION REPORT). By the time he had reached the quarterdeck, the ship was beginning to list rapidly to port. As he proceeded along the starboard side of the ship, he felt a third heavy shock to port side. Another heavy explosion threw him to the deck. The ship continued to list up to, by his estimation, as much as 25 degrees. In order to keep the ship from capsizing, he ordered the ship to be counterflooded. As the result of this action, the ship settled to the bottom in an upright position.

In July 1944, emerging from extensive modernization, the USS *West Virginia* rose, phoenix-like, from the destruction at Pearl Harbor to take her rightful place as the flagship of the fleet.

Further Reading: "Battle Report" and "Crew Lost at Pearl Harbor on December 7, 1941," www.usswestvirginia.org (cited January 2006); *Dictionary of American Naval Fighting Ships* (Department of the Navy, National Historical Center Publishers).

—**FRANK R. DURR**

World War II, Causes of

George Kennan, diplomat and historian, called World War I the great seminal tragedy of the 20th century. By this he meant that the seeds had been planted either in the war or the peace settlement for many of the later tragic events of the 20th century, including WORLD WAR II.

The effects of World War I on GERMANY cannot be overestimated. During the war the German people had been fed a constant diet of propaganda that said Germany was on the verge of winning the war. Then, suddenly, in November 1918 they found out that not only had they lost the spring and summer campaigns of 1918, but the entire war. In 1919 the German delegation was summoned to Versailles, France, not to take part in the discussion of the terms of the peace, but to sign the already prepared treaty. This was the only part that Germany played at Versailles.

In the Treaty of Versailles, Germany had to accept full responsibility for causing the war under Article 231. There were further humiliations including the loss of German territory, the payment of a huge indemnity, and the reduction of the German military to 100,000 troops with no tanks, airplanes, submarines, or capital ships.

The roots of World War II in Asia also lay in the diplomatic settlement of World War I. JAPAN emerged from World War I as the leading power in the Far East. Japan obtained League mandates over the MARSHALL ISLANDS, the Mariana Islands, and the CAROLINE ISLANDS, all of which were former German possessions.

In addition, at Versailles Japan was awarded the former German leaseholds of Kiaochow and Shantung in China, despite protests from the UNITED STATES and China. Despite these territorial gains, the Japanese felt cheated by the Versailles Treaty. They had expected more.

The Italians walked out of the treaty negotiations at Versailles after they had been informed that they would not receive the Austrian territory they had been promised for joining the Allied side. So they, along with Germany and Japan, were severely disappointed by the Treaty of Versailles. Since Japan and Italy believed that they had not received their fair share of the spoils of war they were not inclined to support the treaty.

In Russia revolutionaries were focused on winning their own civil war after pulling out of the war in 1917. Moreover, they had not been invited to participate in the discussions at Versailles.

HITLER'S PATH TO DOMINATION

Thus the ingredients for the failure of the peace were present. When the armistice was signed on November 11, 1918, the German army was still in France, giving rise to the "stab-in-the-back" theory that Germany had been stabbed in the back by Jews, communists, and socialists. All parties in Germany, on the left and on the right, were opposed to the Versailles Treaty.

In 1922 BENITO MUSSOLINI led a march on Rome and seized control of the government. In Germany, ADOLF HITLER started his long rise to power after being discharged from the German army in 1919; he would not achieve power in Germany until January 30, 1933. Later Hitler and Mussolini would sign a "Pact of Steel" in which they joined forces. From the moment Hitler came to power, he planned to go to war. Germany was going to have to wage a ruthless war of annihilation and subjugation in the east to acquire what Hitler claimed was much-needed living space.

Starting in 1933 steps were taken that ultimately would lead to the outbreak of the war with Poland on September 1, 1939, and thus the start of World War II. In 1933 Hitler withdrew from the League of Nations. In 1934 he signed a nonaggression pact with Poland for the purpose of removing them as an ally to France. In June 1934 Hitler purged the SA (the *Sturmabteilung*, or Storm Troops), killing its leader, Ernst Roehm, as well as several hundred members of the paramilitary organization in the Night of the Long Knives to gain the confidence of the German army. Hitler needed the German army

AT LEFT *Adolf Hitler (shown to the left of center) accepts the ovation of the Reichstag after announcing the peaceful acquisition of Austria. Berlin, March 1938.*

on his side for the war he was planning, but he had no further use for the SA, who had been important as "bully boys" aiding his rise to power. In August 1934, Marshal von Hindenburg, the aged hero of the Battle of Tannenberg and the president of Germany, passed away. Hitler occupied the two offices of chancellor and president. He then had the German army swear a personal oath of allegiance to Hitler, not to the government of Germany, as had previously been the case.

In 1935 Mussolini invaded Abyssinia. In March 1936 Hitler remilitarized the Rhineland, a direct violation of the Treaty of Versailles. France and Britain did nothing, which only encouraged Hitler. Then, in 1936, the Spanish Civil War broke out. Hitler and Mussolini backed Francisco Franco, leader of the fascist forces, while JOSEF STALIN backed the loyalist forces. The Germans tested their new military hardware in Spain, but refused to send three divisions of German troops as Franco had requested. As Hitler expected, the Spanish Civil War dragged on, distracting France and Britain from what was going on in Germany. In effect, by 1936, there already was a preview of World War II going on in Spain.

Hitler continued his military buildup with large-scale army maneuvers in the fall of 1937. Also in that year, despite several economic shortages because of lack of foreign exchange, Hitler indicated in his talks with his generals and diplomats that Germany would soon embark on a more aggressive foreign policy. Hitler was opposed in this policy by the commander in chief of the army General Werner von Fritsch, the war minister General Werner von Bloomberg, and the German foreign minister Konstantin von Neurath. They all told Hitler that Germany was not prepared for war. This, of course, was not Hitler's opinion and he used a se-

ries of charges to dismiss all three of them. Hitler replaced von Neurath with Joachim von Ribbentrop, whose loyalty to the *Führer* was unquestioned. At the same time Hitler also retired or transferred a number of other high army officers in the military and appointed himself as war minister. He also appointed General Wilhelm Keitel as his chief military advisor. This marked a turning point in Hitler's policy, as he now controlled both the military and the diplomatic corps.

In February 1938, Hitler, in discussions with the Austrian Chancellor Kurt Schuschnigg, demanded concessions that would have ended Austrian independence. Schuschnigg called for a plebiscite to determine if Austria wanted to remain an independent nation. This action put Hitler in a rage. Enormous pressure was placed on Austria to capitulate to the German demands, which Schuschnigg finally did. Arthur Seyss-Inquart was appointed chancellor and the Germans marched into Austria to cheering crowds.

The next move by Hitler was the annexation of the Sudetenland of Czechoslovakia. The Sudetenland was an area of Czechoslovakia populated by ethnic Germans. British Prime Minister Neville Chamberlain and French Premier Edouard Daladier acceded to Hitler's demands to avoid another war that most officials thought would be similar to World War I. Both Chamberlain and Daladier believed it was better to appease Hitler's demands, rather than risk another war. Hitler had said that this would be his last demand. At Munich, Germany, on September 29, 1938, Hitler, Mussolini, and Hermann Goering, chief of the *Luftwaffe* (German air force), were able to get Chamberlain and Daladier to agree to their demands. Chamberlain returned to London to cheering crowds, a hero, because he had been able to maintain the peace.

Shortly after Munich, Hitler ordered the high command of the army to prepare to occupy the remainder of Czechoslovakia, which took place in March 1939. Hitler's opinion of Chamberlain and Daladier was that he had met them at Munich and they were worms.

Britain knew that Hitler could not be trusted. Britain and France gave guarantees to Polish independence. Hitler never believed that Britain would go this far and he was outraged. He ordered the high command of the army to prepare "Case White": a September 1, 1939, invasion of Poland. The chief of the German General Staff, General Franz Halder, enthusiastically backed Hitler in this undertaking. While plans were being formulated for the invasion of Poland, Hitler's foreign minister, von Ribbentrop, negotiated a Nazi-Soviet nonaggression pact with the Soviet Union. In this pact, Hitler promised to Stalin the Baltic states of Lithuania, Latvia, and Estonia and the eastern part of Poland and Romania. In return the Soviet Union would provide Germany with vital shipments of raw materials and food. Hitler assured Stalin of peace between the two countries.

Britain thought that the pact was of little significance, since the Soviet Union and Germany were ideological enemies. Germany was fascist and the Nazis' avowed enemies were the Judeo-Bolsheviks of the Soviet Union, who were communists. Hitler always lumped the two together and spoke of them as Judeo-Bolsheviks. On September 1, 1939, Hitler launched an attack on Poland in the belief that Britain and France would not honor their obligations to Poland. Much to his consternation they did, and World War II was started.

Italy remained neutral until the German campaign in France in May–June 1940. When Mussolini saw that the British and French were unable to mount an offensive against the Germans, he joined forces with the Nazis. Germany's nonaggression pact with the Soviet Union remained in effect until the morning of June 22, 1941, when Germany invaded the Soviet Union as the last trainload of raw materials was crossing the border into German-occupied Poland.

Mein Kampf

ADOLF HITLER set out his policy in *Mein Kampf* (*My Struggle*), which he wrote in Landsberg Prison in 1924, while serving nine months of a five-year sentence for his attempt to overthrow the government in his Beer Hall Putsch on November 9, 1923. In this book, Hitler related that Germany had to acquire *Lebensraum* (living space) in the east of Europe to grow and to acquire natural resources that Germany needed, such as oil, iron ore, copper, and food. The only natural resource that Germany had in abundance was coal. If Germany did not acquire living space, according to Hitler, it was destined to become a third-rate power. According to Hitler, eastern Europe and the Soviet Union were populated by subhuman Slavs, whom the Germans would subjugate, while eliminating the educated elite in these lands.

ABOVE *Title page from a 1939 edition of Hitler's Mein Kampf.*

JAPAN'S PATH TO WORLD WAR II

In Japan during in the 1930s, the Cherry Society was a group of dissident military officers who wanted to change the country through a military revolution. They encouraged military violence, which led to the assassination of Prime Minister Hamaguchi Yuko in 1930, and Prime Minister Inuka Ki in 1932. The Cherry Society believed that it was the duty of the military to weed out corrupt ideas in Japanese society such as democracy and materialism.

Japan moved quickly to industrialization but lacked natural resources. The country had to import oil, iron, rubber, cotton, wood, wool, and minerals. Foodstuffs, especially meat, also had to be brought into the island nation. By 1937, out of a population of 70 million, 37 million were living in cities. Only in coal was Japan self-sufficient thanks to the mines in Korea, which had become a protectorate of Japan in 1910, and in Manchuria, China, invaded starting in 1931. The 1930s world depression hit hard in Japan and curtailed trade with other countries for the natural resources that Japan needed to maintain its industrial development. The Japanese military leaders thought that the only solution to Japan's economic problems was to exploit the natural resources in China. There were risks in undertaking such a course, but the leaders in Japan were willing to take them and it appeared that the remainder of the world was occupied with its own problems. In Europe, Britain and France were focused on the rise of Hitler, while in the Soviet Union, Stalin was involved with the purges of the military. The United States appeared relatively secure in its policy of isolation and noninvolvement in world affairs. In the 1930s the colonial powers Japan faced in Asia were Indochina, Burma, Malaya, the PHIL-IPPINES, the Dutch East Indies, Britain, France, the United States, and the Soviet Union; however, none of these seemed to be beyond the ability of Japan to overcome.

Chiang Kai-shek, the leader of China, was determined not to let Japan take any more Chinese territory. In Japan, at this time, the spirit of Bushido, or the warriors' code, dominated society. This code entailed the philosophy of achieving either victory or death. Moreover, there was to be no mercy for the enemy. The Japanese then undertook a brutal assault of the city of Nanking, an event often referred to as the Rape of Nanking. During this attack on Nanking, 250,000 Chinese were killed, tortured, or raped. Crimes of unspeakable horror were committed by the Japanese army, almost all of which have been fully documented by reporters.

In August 1938 and May 1939 the Japanese Kwantung Army was defeated in battles on the Manchurian-Siberian-Mongolian border by the Soviet army led by General Georgi Zhukov and his Siberian troops. He almost completely annihilated the

ABOVE Aftermath of the Japanese bombing of Shanghai's South Station. China, August 28, 1937.

Japanese 10th Army. The Japanese discontinued their policy of moving north into Siberia and decided to move south into Java, Sumatra, and Borneo to secure much-needed raw materials and foodstuffs.

On the other hand, the Japanese were successful in China but were unable to bring the war to a satisfactory conclusion. The vast space of China and the lack of clear objectives contributed to the slow Japanese advance. The prime minister of Japan, Prince Konoe, argued that it was high time to move south as soon as possible. By September 1941 it was decided that war with the United States was inevitable—especially since U.S.-imposed trade sanctions against Japan were further crippling the military expansion. Japanese leaders agreed that they could achieve a victory if they struck first, as they had at Port Arthur against the Russians in the 1904–05 war.

In October 1941 Prince Konoe resigned under pressure and General HIDEKI TOJO became prime minister. On November 5, 1941, Tojo and other Japanese ministers discussed their options and agreed to review plans for the movement south, including the plan developed by Admiral ISOROKU YAMAMOTO to strike the U.S. naval base at Pearl Harbor. They had to strike Pearl Harbor if they planned to move south.

While the Japanese were pursuing a policy of negotiating with the United States, they were planning for war. The United States knew that the negotiations were just a sham because it had broken the Japanese diplomatic code (see CODES, JAPANESE). On November 1, 1941, Japan made its final proposal to U.S. Secretary of State CORDELL HULL. The Japanese proposal promised: (1) to get out of China in 25 years; and (2) to get out of Indochina and southern China if the United States would sell Japan one million tons of aviation fuel. The United States rejected both of these terms and offered instead these demands: (1) withdraw from China and Indochina immediately; (2) accept the Chiang Kai-shek government as the legitimate one in China; and (3) resign from the pact with Germany and Italy. Japan refused. Meanwhile, back in Japan, Tojo ruled that unless the United States met Japanese demands for hegemony in Asia by November 25, 1941, then war plans would be put into effect and Japanese forces would attack Pearl Harbor. With the U.S. rejection of the Japanese proposals, the strike force sailed from Japan in the center of a storm, along the northern route to Pearl Harbor.

Japan had already decided in 1940 that they had enough oil for three years of peacetime, one and one-half years of defensive war, or six months of offensive war. They chose the third option. Their strategy was to move south and seize the natural resources, including oil, in Java, Sumatra, and Borneo. In order to do this they had to take the Philippines or neutralize them, defeat the British fleet at Singapore, and neutralize the U.S. Pacific Fleet (see PACIFIC FLEET, U.S.) at Pearl Harbor. Then they would set up a defensive perimeter and hold it in the belief that the United States would not have the willpower to retake those territories; the United States would tire and negotiate a settlement favorable to Japan. History proved them quite wrong (See also WORLD WAR II, RESULTS OF.)

Further Reading: Iris Chang, *The Rape of Nanking: The Forgotten Holocaust of World War II* (Penguin Group, 1998); James William Morley and Kamikawa Hikomatsu, eds., *Japan's Road to the Pacific War* (Columbia University Press, 1994); Williamson Murray and Allan R. Millett, eds., *Calculations: Net Assessment and the Coming of World War II* (The Free Press, 1992); Cameron Watt, *How War Came: The Immediate Origins of the Second World War* (Knopf, 1990); Gerhard L. Weinberg, *A World at Arms: A Global History of World War II* (Cambridge University Press, 2005).

—ANDREW R. CARLSON, PH.D.

World War II, Results of

WORLD WAR II turned the world upside down and inside out. It altered social, political, economic, and cultural life forever. Colonial empires that had been in existence for several hundred years fell apart. In their place there were ethnic minorities engaging in civil war and insurgency movements that continue to the present day. Migrations of people, forced and voluntary, would see millions of people homeless. Countries that had been in depression prior to the war emerged as economic superpowers. The world became bipolar, as the various countries aligned themselves with either the UNITED STATES or the Soviet Union. Countries that had always prided themselves on being first-rate powers now retreated to a second-rate status.

Education became available to people of talent. In the United States the G.I. Bill enabled millions to attend higher education, while in other countries opportunities that had been open only to the elite were now open to many. The war also gave stimulus to the civil rights movement in the United States.

Countries that had been steeped in a class system now had to reward those who had borne the battle for their country. This was true in both the Allied countries as well as those of the Axis. Totalitarian countries became democratic. Entire countries had been laid waste in the war. Even in countries not damaged by the war, such as the United States, vast migrations of people took place. People who would have not ventured very far away from their birthplace prior to the war had now seen the world and moved about freely. Over 60 million people lost their lives in the conflict. Entire families were consumed by the Holocaust.

"A RUBBLE HEAP, A CHARNEL HOUSE": POSTWAR EUROPE

Following World War II, Europe was described by WINSTON CHURCHILL as "A rubble heap, a charnel house, a breeding ground of pestilence and hate." Fifty million people were in places different than they had been at the start of the war. Another 16 million were classified as displaced persons, which included many people brought to Germany for labor and those who fled before the advancing Soviet army. The Americans and British forced six million people to return to their homeland. Of this number 10 percent were executed, 20 percent were cleared of any charges, and 70 percent were reeducated in labor camps, in which many died before completing their reeducation.

After 1945 GERMANY was divided into zones of occupation by the British, French, American, and Soviet forces. The British zone was in the north of Germany, while the American zone was in the south, and the French zone in the Rhineland. The Soviet zone consisted of the eastern part of Germany. The city of Berlin was also divided between the four countries into zones of occupation with the

ABOVE *What remains of the city of Darmstadt, Germany, a city of 110,000 people, after a daylight saturation air raid on September 12, 1944.*

British, French, and American sector in the west and the Soviet sector in the eastern part of the former German capital.

In 1949 two Germanys were formed, the Federal Republic of Germany, which consisted of the Allied occupation zones, and the German Democratic Republic, which was the Soviet zone. The capital of the Federal Republic of Germany was at Bonn. The division of Germany would continue until October 2, 1990, when the two countries were reunited into one Germany.

After the war Germany became a haven of black marketing and bartering, where anything of value could be exchanged for food or cigarettes. One of the biggest problems faced by the Allies was how to feed the German populace and stem the spread of disease. Fuel was also in short supply. The mission of the U.S. Army after the war, in addition to occupation duties, was a relief mission to stave off starvation and disease. The main provider of food and medicine was the United States, because Britain and France had been ravaged by the war. The United Nations Relief and Rehabilitation Organization, founded in 1944, provided millions of tons of food, clothing, and industrial equipment.

The Marshall Plan, named after former General GEORGE C. MARSHALL, was passed by Congress in 1947. The plan was instituted to stimulate economic growth in Europe, including Germany, and to assist countries that were in danger of being taken over by communism.

In Germany the Nuremberg trials were showcased after the war. Many of the leading Nazis committed suicide or escaped the country. ADOLF HITLER, Joseph Goebbels, and Heinrich Himmler committed suicide, while Martin Bormann disappeared, only to be found dead years later in the ruins of Berlin. The International Military Tribunal was convened in 1945 in the ruins of the city of Nuremberg. This trial of major war criminals lasted for a year. Martin Bormann was tried in absentia. The four judges—each represented one of the Allied victors: Britain, France, the United States, and the Soviet Union— found 19 of the defendants guilty of crimes. Eleven were hanged, but Goering escaped this fate by committing suicide. Rudolf Hess was sentenced to life in prison, where he died in 1997 at the age of 93. Albert Speer, who was responsible for munitions, was given 20 years in prison; Karl Dönitz, head of the German navy and the last chancellor of Germany, received 10 years in prison; while Konstantin von Neurath, the former foreign minister, received 15 years in prison.

THE SOVIET UNION AFTER THE WAR

The war was a great consolidating experience in the Soviet Union. It was called the Great Patriotic War. It gave the Soviet people a sense of pride and cohesion that was not eroded until 1989. Of course Soviet propaganda played a large role in this consolidation.

Two superpowers emerged from World War II, the United States and the Soviet Union. The United States was in a dominant position until 1949 as the only country to have an atom bomb, but the Soviets test-fired one in 1949 and continued research on more powerful bombs. The United States also continued to work on developing more powerful bombs and produced a hydrogen bomb, the destructive potential of which made the bombs dropped on Hiroshima and Nagasaki pale in significance. The United States and the Soviet Union engaged in an arms race during the Cold War that lasted until 1989, when the Soviets lost their dominance over their eastern European satellite nations. The arms race and the talk of "Star Wars" missile systems and "trillion dollar" defense budgets was something the Soviets were unable to keep up with.

The development by Germany of the V2 and V4 rocket programs led to the development of the intercontinental ballistic missiles with nuclear warheads. The space race between the United States and the Soviet Union owed much to the German scientists who had worked on the rockets in Germany. Many German scientists were taken to the Soviet Union, while Dr. Werner von Braun and his associates came to the United States. The U.S. space program owes a great debt to the German rocket program. In the development of flight technology, the jet plane of the postwar era also owes much to the German jet program developed during the war.

GREAT BRITAIN, FRANCE, AND THE NEW STATE OF ISRAEL

Great Britain and France were relegated to the status of second-rate powers. Both of them emerged from the war exhausted, both in terms of manpower and in economic potential. Britain's colonial possessions were lost one after another and the policy was to let them go without a struggle. The age of colonialism died after World War II. France, on the other hand, fought unsuccessful wars in Indochina and Algeria to hold on to its colonial possessions, one reason being that CHARLES DE GAULLE said that France needed them for greatness. However, France lost those colonies after protracted and costly wars. Asia and Africa underwent many changes as former colonial powers lost their hold on their colonial empires. The fighting in former Dutch Indonesia ended in November 1945, and it was obvious to the British and the Dutch that they could not revert to the colonial status that existed before the war. In India, Egypt, the Middle East, and Africa there were movements for independence. What started as a trickle after World War I now turned to a flood, as World War II broke the dam. The colonial empires of Italy, Great Britain, France, the Netherlands, Spain, and Portugal all succumbed to this movement. Some of them resisted the rising tide for independence and fought long wars, all of which failed. Many former colonies gained independence only to disintegrate into civil war, which in many cases turned into wars of genocide. Some of these genocidal wars continue to the present day.

The state of Israel was created in the Middle East for Holocaust survivors. The creation was opposed by Palestine and this struggle continues unabated. Much of the violence in the world today is a result of the unwillingness of people to accept the post–World War II political settlements.

CHINA AND KOREA

After World War II China again fell into civil war with Chiang Kai-shek fighting the Communists under Mao Zedong. Mao won and took China down a bloody road through the Cultural Revolution.

On August 15, 1945, Korea was liberated. JAPAN had held suzerainty over Korea from 1905 to 1910 and treated it as a protectorate from 1910 on. Before plans for Korean independence could be implemented, the military occupied the country and it was divided into two separate zones. The Soviet zone in the north was established on August 10, 1945, and the U.S. occupation began on September 8, 1945, in the south. The military leaders of the Soviet Union and the United States agreed that the Soviets would accept the surrender of Japan north of the 38th Parallel, while the United States would accept the surrender south of it.

As time went on the 38th Parallel became the dividing line as relations between the United States and the Soviet Union deteriorated. The division

AT RIGHT *The Punchbowl, location of the National Memorial Cemetery of the Pacific, where servicemen and women from four wars are buried. In ancient times, the extinct volcanic Punchbowl Crater was known as Puowaina (Hill of Sacrifice). It was the site of secret royal burials and the sacrifice of those who offended certain taboos.*

along the line of the 38th Parallel made no political, topographical, geographical, economic, or military sense. Korea, which had been under the Japanese yoke for so long, was now divided into two parts. In December 1945 the United States and the Soviet Union announced the Moscow Agreement for the establishment of a trusteeship over Korea. This was opposed by the Korean people, but was backed by the Communists. A joint United States–Soviet Union Commission in 1946 and 1947 failed to reach an agreement on economic and administrative coordination between the north and south zones of occupation.

The issue went before the General Assembly of the United Nations on November 14, 1947. The United Nations Commission, which arrived in Seoul in January 1948, was blocked in its efforts to work in the north. As a result the Temporary Commission on Korea decided it would only observe elections in the south. On May 10, 1948, democratic elections were held in the south and on May 31, 1948, the elected National Assembly was convened and Dr. Syngman

Rhee, who had spent 40 years in the United States, was elected as its chairman. The National Assembly adopted a democratic constitution on July 12, 1948. However, on July 25, 1950, North Korea invaded the south and the peninsula was ravaged for several years. When the north was driven back, the Chinese intervened. When the war ended, the division between the north and south was again set at the 38th Parallel. The south has prospered since then, while the north has continued under Communist domination and become a nuclear threat.

JAPAN: RECONSTRUCTION AND REFORMATION

When Japan surrendered on August 15, 1945, a great deal of work had to be done. The country was occupied by U.S. troops and the Japanese military machine dismantled and destroyed. A democratic government had to be instituted. General DOUGLAS MACARTHUR became the military governor and political parties reemerged. Political, religious, and civil liberties were established. The country that had been destroyed by bombing had to be rebuilt.

Formation of the United Nations

THE UNITED Nations was established on October 24, 1945, to maintain world peace and foster international cooperation. The charter of the United Nations was drafted during the war by the United States, Britain, and the Soviet Union and remains the same today. The General Assembly controls much of the work of the United Nations. The United Nations has a 15-member Security Council that is dominated by the five permanent members: China, France, Russia, Britain, and the United States, who have veto power over resolutions. The primary function of the Security Council is to maintain international security and peace. Its decisions are binding on the member states. The United Nations is headed by the Secretary General, who is usually an important person in the area of international diplomacy and is able to take independent initiatives.

The emperor was allowed to remain on the throne and on January 1946, he repudiated his divinity and stated that Japanese people were not superior to other races, nor destined to rule a great empire. An election was held on January 12, 1946. Women were enfranchised and the voting age was lowered from 25 to 20, and from 30 to 25 to hold office. Land reforms were undertaken.

Chinese and Soviet reparation demands on Japan were a serious obstacle to the reconstruction of Japan. The land of the rising sun was forced to give up its colonial empire that had been acquired over the past 50 years. Seven million Japanese, both military and civilians, who were scattered around the empire were returned to Japan by March 1947. Allied forces had to act quickly to get the Japanese military and civilians out of areas they had conquered before a bloodbath of revenge could take place. Most of them were repatriated within 10 months of the surrender and helped to maintain the peace in Japan.

One advantage that Japan had was that it was the only country in the Far East that was not torn apart by civil unrest. Furthermore, Japan was not divided into zones of occupation. It was mainly an American operation, although some British were involved. Moreover, the Japanese were willing to submit to American occupation. The rebuilding of Japan was started with aid from America.

The last session of the Diet, under the old constitution, ended on March 31, 1947, and the old parliamentary system dissolved. A new Democratic Party (Minshuto) came into being at the same time, and a new constitution on May 3, 1947. The new constitution was American-inspired and war as an instrument of Japanese policy was renounced. Sovereignty resided in the people, and the emperor became a symbol of Japan and of the unity of the people. The emperor could no longer act without the advice and approval of the cabinet. The cabinet was responsible to the Diet. The majority of the members of the cabinet, including the premier, had to be members of the House of Representatives. The military was left out completely because the cabinet members had to be civilians. There was a Bill of Rights that gave equal rights to women. There was a provision for judicial review by a new Supreme Court that could rule on the constitutionality of legislation.

The educational system was also reformed and made more democratic. The divine rights of Japan were abandoned. The martial and ultranationalistic Shinto ideology was done away with. Peaceful concepts were stressed. The textbooks were changed from a rendering of the military exploits of Japan to the achievements of science and literature. Free thought and inquiry were introduced into higher education, which was made available to women and people of talent, instead of the economically fortunate few.

Japanese war criminals were brought before the International Military Tribunal Far East, which was a court of 11 judges selected from the Allied countries. They tried and convicted 25 of 28 who were indicted as Class A war criminals. These were policy makers responsible for the decision to go to war. Seven were hanged, 16 sentenced to life in prison, and two received lesser sentences. HIDEKI TOJO, unrepentant to the end, was hanged. On December 7, 1945, in a show-trial in Manila, Generals Tomoyuki Yamashita and Massaharu Homma were tried and executed. There were also Class B and Class C suspects, who had committed crimes against prisoners of war, such as Allied airmen. In the six years following the war, 5,700 were tried and half were convicted, with about 1,000 executed. However, many who had committed unspeakable crimes escaped punishment, often because of Allied desires to protect them, such as General Ishili Shiro, a medical doctor, who had commanded Unit 731, where prisoners of war and civilians in occupied countries were used as guinea pigs in medical experiments such as vivisection.

Japan continues to the present day to struggle with World War II. The educational system is reluctant to portray in textbooks Japanese activities committed during the war, such as using Korean middle-school girls for "comfort women" for Japanese troops in Korea, the killing of prisoners of war, and other war crimes.

The war has been over for more than 60 years, but it continues to shape the world in which we live, as well as the future. (See also WORLD WAR II, CAUSES OF.)

Further Reading: Michael Hogan, *The Marshall Plan: America, Britain and the Reconstruction of Europe, 1947–52* (Cambridge University Press, 1987); Philip R. Piccigallo, *The Japanese on Trial: Allied War Crimes Operations in the East* (University of Texas Press, 1979); Howard Schonberger, *Aftermath of War: Americans and the Remaking of Japan, 1945–52* (Kent State University Press, 1989); Ann Tusa and John Tusa, *The Nuremberg Trial* (Simon and Schuster, 1984).

—ANDREW R. CARLSON, PH.D.

World War II

The UNITED STATES was not officially at war with JAPAN until December 8, 1941, the day after the Japanese bombing of Pearl Harbor. In the case of GERMANY, ADOLF HITLER, who was in a pact with Japan and Italy, declared war on the United States on December 11, 1941, much to the consternation of his generals. His generals were adamantly opposed to declaring war on the United States because they were already having problems on the eastern front outside Moscow. When the United States entered the war, Germany and Japan had been at war for a number of years (see also WORLD WAR II, CAUSES OF).

EUROPEAN THEATER

The war in Europe started with the German attack on Poland on September 1, 1939. The "Phony War" followed, because although Great Britain and France had pledged to come to the aid of Poland, nothing happened over the winter of 1939–40. During the "Phony War," the French did not train for the coming war, as did the German *Wehrmacht*, but concentrated on building fortifications. The French army was inflexible and lacked the capacity to respond quickly. The next German operation was *Weserübung* (Operation Weser) in the early spring of 1940, in which Germany moved into Denmark and Norway. The operation was a tremendous gamble by

Germany, for it hoped to capture Norwegian ports and air bases before Great Britain could mount an effective response. Once they had captured the airfields, the *Luftwaffe* (German Air Force) would control the seas off Norway. The Germans were successful; the British were unable to counter the combined German naval force, paratroopers, and infantry as they captured the key cities of Narvik, Trondheim, Bergen, and Oslo.

The next German attack in the west, *Fall Gelb* (Operation Yellow), took place on May 10, 1940, when Nazi forces unleashed an offensive on the Netherlands, Belgium, and France. The Dutch surrendered on May 15, 1940, and King Leopold of Belgium capitulated on May 28, 1940. By the end of May, the British expeditionary forces found themselves driven back to the beaches of Dunkirk in France, from which they were able to evacuate 350,000 troops by June 3; however, they were forced to leave all of their equipment behind. The troops that were taken off the beaches would become the cadre of the British army in World War II. The evacuation was the high-water mark of the British army, but WINSTON CHURCHILL warned the House of Commons on June 4, 1940, that "Wars are not won by evacuations." After Dunkirk, for all practical purposes, France stood alone. Hostilities were ended on June 22, 1940. Germany had achieved a treaty with France, in which the northern part of the country would be under German control, while the south, Vichy France, would be under the control of the aged hero of World War I, General Philippe Pétain, who negotiated the treaty with Germany.

PACIFIC THEATER

In the Far East, Japan had been involved in China and Manchuria since 1931, although the war there

ABOVE LEFT *Headlines of the* Toledo Blade, *December 9, 1941, show the fear that the Japanese were about to bomb U.S. cities.* **ABOVE RIGHT** *A Combat Mobile Pigeon Coop. Pigeon communications were important in World War II, as radios did not always work.*

did not start in earnest until 1937, with a vicious Japanese attack on the city of Nanking. Japan had fought a border war with the Soviet Union on the Mongolian-Soviet border in 1939–40 and was soundly defeated. At that point, Japanese strategists decided instead of moving north into Siberia they would move south into Java, Borneo, and Sumatra to obtain much-needed raw materials. In 1940 Japan moved into northern Indochina and in July 1941 into southern Indochina and Thailand.

The Japanese knew if they were going to move south they had to conquer or neutralize the PHILIP- PINES Islands and neutralize the American fleet at Pearl Harbor and the British fleet at Singapore. Ad- miral ISOROKU YAMAMOTO planned the attack on Pearl Harbor for December 7, 1941, and the attack on the Malaya peninsula, taking the British port at Singapore and the Philippine Islands. Japan had conquered a large empire in the Far East with lit- tle more than 15,000 casualties, dead and wounded. They were able to do this because of the ferocious fighting spirit of the Japanese soldiers who were well led, highly trained, and well disciplined in the tenets of Bushido (warrior philosophy).

GERMAN VICTORY

While the Soviets were not at war with anyone they moved into Poland to take their share of the coun- try after the German invasion, which was a se- cret attachment to the Nazi-Soviet nonaggression pact signed in late August 1939. In 1940 the Soviets moved into Lithuania, Latvia, and Estonia under the pretext of protecting these countries from unnamed enemies. When JOSEF STALIN made the same de- mands on Finland, he had a war on his hands. On March 13, 1940, Marshal Carl Mannerheim, com- mander in chief of the Finnish army, persuaded his government to turn over the Karelian Isthmus to the Soviets. The Soviets suffered horrendous casu- alties in the war with Finland and it was in effect a humiliating defeat. The difficulty the Soviets had with smaller Finland convinced Hitler that the So- viet army was rotten to the core and all he had to do was "kick in the door and the whole rotten struc- ture would come tumbling down." The Japanese had gained a different impression of the Soviet army in 1939 when General Georgi Zhukov smashed the Jap- anese 10th Army.

To this point the German victories had been be- yond their own expectations. Cheering crowds greeted the troops returning from France. Germany was convinced that, at last, Britain would come to its senses and make peace. However, the govern- ment had changed from Neville Chamberlain, who had appeased Germany, to Winston Churchill, who was ready to take on the Nazis. Churchill had opposi- tion, particularly from Lord Halifax, who attempted to convince his colleagues that Britain could avoid a disastrous war by coming to terms with Hitler. How- ever, Hitler never presented a firm offer. Churchill worried whether he could obtain assistance from the United States, but by the end of June, Churchill had financial and economic assistance.

The Germans believed, after their great victories on the continent, that the war was over. General Al- fred Jodl believed it was only a matter of time until Britain capitulated. Germany spent June and July 1940 waiting for peace feelers from Britain, while Hitler was on vacation. However, no overtures were forthcoming from Britain. Hitler and his General Staff had misjudged the British resolve.

At this time the British had broken the German secret Enigma code and were deciphering messages; the Germans were confident that they had devel- oped a code that could not be broken. Ultra, as the code-breaking came to be known, would play a large

ABOVE LEFT *The Italian Civilian Rehabilitation. An American AMG officer pours a helmetful of beans into the hat of an Italian citizen in Monghidoro, Italy, November 2, 1944.* **ABOVE RIGHT** *Cleaning up Naples. American salvage equipment being used to clear away debris in the port area of Naples, Italy.*

part in World War II. It was a great security coup for the Allies (see ALLIES ON DECEMBER 7, 1941) and a great security failure for Germany.

If the Germans were going to invade the British Isles they would have to achieve either naval or air superiority. Achieving naval superiority was out of the question because of the size of the British fleet, so it would have to be air superiority. The Germans started to bomb Britain, but by August 1940 it was already apparent that they were not up to the task of achieving air superiority. The planned invasion of Britain, code-named Operation Sea Lion, finally had to be postponed. Finally in May 1941 the air campaign was called off because Hitler was now planning his attack on the Soviet Union.

Germany's prospects of victory in France prompted BENITO MUSSOLINI to declare war on France and Britain on June 10, 1940. This cemented the Rome-Berlin Axis (see AXIS POWERS IN 1941), which came about after Mussolini's Abyssinian War in 1936. Mussolini was determined to turn the Mediterranean Sea into an Italian Sea, by re-creating the Roman Empire. But Mussolini was a thorn in Hitler's side rather than adding to the Axis war strength. He undertook campaigns in Albania and Greece. Once he got bogged down there he had to call upon Germany for assistance. Some historians point to the German rescue of Mussolini in the Balkans as the reason why Germany failed to reach Moscow before the Russian winter set in. Originally, the assault on the Soviet Union was to take place on May 15, 1941. It was postponed until June 22, 1941. The weather in the spring of 1941 was extremely wet and not suitable for German tank operations. The ground was saturated with water from heavy rainfall. By June 22, though, the weather and soil were excellent for *Blitzkrieg* (lightning war). Thus, little credence can be placed in this theory.

In July 1940 the British undertook their first attack in North Africa against the Italians, who collapsed, forcing the Germans to get involved there by February 12, 1941, under General Erwin Rommel. Germany subjugated Yugoslavia and Greece and attacked the British-held island of Crete in an airborne assault code-named Operation Merkur. The Germans severely underestimated the number of British forces on Crete, as well as the Allied loyalty of the local population. Moreover, the use of Ultra enabled the British to know that the German attack would be on the airfields. Yet, despite this intelligence the British commander on Crete expected a seaborne attack. The bulk of the Commonwealth troops were prepared for the assault to come from the sea and most antiaircraft guns were focused on the Suda-Bay-Canea sector. Only a single infantry battalion held the Maleme airfield. Despite horrendous casualties, the Germans were victorious. Crete would have been an ideal base to cut off Romanian oil shipments to the Germans through the Aegean Sea. It could also have been used as a launching site for bombing raids on the Ploesti oil fields in Romania.

Despite having signed the Nazi-Soviet nonaggression pact in August 1939, the Germans attacked the Soviet Union on June 22, 1941, with 3,000,000 men, 3,000 tanks, and many planes. It was probably the best-trained, best-equipped army in history to that point and their initial victories were very impressive. However, they had not been able to agree on a single objective, so they went for all of them: Leningrad in the north, Moscow in the center, and the Caucasus in the south. The destruction of Soviet tanks, artillery pieces, airplanes, and troops was very impressive as well as the number of prisoners taken. By July 3, 1941, the German commander, Franz Halder, noted in his diary, "The campaign against Russia has been won in 14 days." By August the Germans halted their troops, assuming they had destroyed the Red Army, but the Soviets were busy calling up millions of reserves, creating new divisions and separate brigades during the summer of 1941. The Germans had been overly optimistic and had underestimated the Soviet Union's perseverance.

Finally on September 6, 1941, Hitler agreed with Halder that the main drive should be directed against Moscow. The attack would be launched in October—another German mistake, as the rough Russian winter approached. Moreover, the German army was having serious difficulties with equipment breaking down and logistical problems. By December 1941 the Germans were in the suburbs of Moscow. The German troops were exhausted, supplies were not being received, the troops had summer uniforms, and the vehicles had no antifreeze. Then there was a heavy snowfall and the temperature plummeted. Some German generals wanted to set up a defense line, but none of them dared to propose this to Hitler. General Gerd von Rundstedt had captured Rostov on November 24, 1941, and then ordered a retreat to the Mius River to set up a defense line—and Hitler fired him.

THE TIDE TURNS

In December, in subzero temperatures, Soviet General Zhukov and his crack Siberian troops unleashed a counterattack on the north and south flanks of the German army. By December 10, the Soviets came close to overwhelming Army Group Center and cut Panzer Group Three's escape route. The German army was faced with a nightmare—below zero temperatures, vehicles that would not run, inadequate clothing, no rations, blinded by the snow, and weapons that would not function because of the extreme cold. Nevertheless, Hitler decided that they had to stand and fight where they were.

By the end of January 1942 the Soviet drive had petered out and the Germans had established some stability outside Moscow. Many historians today are of the opinion that Germany had lost the war by December 1941—and not at Stalingrad in 1942 as is often presented. By December 1941 the Soviets had torn the heart out of the German army. Germany suffered 750,000 casualties and of the 3,000 tanks that started the campaign only 146 were fully operational.

In the Pacific, the Japanese seized the natural resources in the South Pacific and set up a defensive perimeter. Japan had carriers as far as the Indian Ocean, raiding ports in India and Ceylon. During the week of April 6–9, 1942, they sank two British cruisers and a carrier. However, the United States was aware of Yamamoto's strategic aim because of intercepted radio traffic. Japan felt safe behind this defensive perimeter. Then on April 18, 1942, Lieutenant Colonel JAMES DOOLITTLE bombed Tokyo with bombers, which had taken off from the carriers USS *Enterprise* and USS *Hornet*. Three other bombers followed with bombing raids on other Japanese cities. While the bombers did not do a great amount of damage, it was a great psychological blow to the Japanese because the bombs were almost dropped on the Imperial Palace. It was also a great psychological boost to the United States because it had struck back at Japan.

Now Japan realized it had to expand its defensive perimeter, and it seized territory in northern China and other Pacific islands. In May 1942 the Americans and the Japanese met in the Battle of the Coral Sea. It was not a victory for either side; however, American aviators were able to stand up to the superior JAPANESE FLEET, despite losing the

The Decision to Use the Atom Bomb

PRESIDENT HARRY Truman's decision to use the atomic bomb has, in recent years, become a matter of controversy. In 1945, however, Truman's decision to deploy the atomic bomb was based upon casualty estimates of a land invasion offered by national intelligence services and the unfathomable militaristic attitude of Japanese leaders who failed to accept surrender, even in the face of the destruction of a majority of their major cities by American airpower, vowing that the Japanese nation would fight to the death if necessary. The United States is the only country in the world to have used nuclear weapons in wartime against an enemy nation, but many have since tested nuclear weapons in preparation for war. Although the nature of radiation was not clearly understood, the hope was that the fighting could be stopped by employing the nuclear weapon in an effort to save American lives. In the end, the responsibility for the use of these weapons rested on Truman's shoulders, a fact that he freely admitted and after he made the decision to use them.

carrier USS *Lexington* and having the carrier USS *Yorktown* heavily damaged, while seven Japanese ships were sunk.

THE UNITED STATES ON THE OFFENSIVE

Then in June 1942 a battle took place between the Japanese and American fleets in the Battle of Midway. In this encounter four Japanese carriers were sunk, while the United States lost only the USS *Yorktown.* The United States also lost a destroyer and 147 planes and 362 men, but the Japanese suffered 3,057 dead and 322 planes lost along with their pilots. These were Japan's most experienced pilots. It had taken five years of training to get them to this point of expertise. Now they were lost. The Japanese naval air force would never be the same. Midway was the turning point in the Pacific war: after Midway the United States was on the offensive.

Following the Battle of Midway the Allies undertook operations against New Guinea and when Japan started to build an airfield on the island of Guadalcanal, to cut the supply lines of the United States to send men and materials to Australia, an attack was planned against the island in August 1942. After months of bitter fighting the Japanese on Guadalcanal were defeated and the airfield they had started was completed by the Americans and named Henderson Field.

While the war was being fought in the Pacific and in the Atlantic, operations were launched in North Africa when the Americans came to the assistance of the British. German General Rommel had arrived in February 1941 and attacked the British to assist the failing Italian efforts. Up to this point American leaders had pushed for a direct assault on the continent of Europe; however, the ill-fated attack at Dieppe, France, revealed that this would require more preparation. In November a combined force of British and American troops landed in Algeria and Morocco, code-named Operation Torch. They pushed the German troops to Tunisia. From Tunisia the Allies crossed the Mediterranean Sea to the island of Sicily.

GERMANY RETREATS

The Germans were locked in a life-or-death struggle at Stalingrad in September–November 1942. Surrounded, lacking supplies, Marshal Friedrich von Paulus surrendered the German 6th Army in February 1943. It was a catastrophic defeat for Germany, although the Soviets had suffered even worse casualties. Of the 91,000 Germans who surrendered only 5,000 would live to see Germany again. Starting in February 1943 it would be a constant battle between retreating German troops and advancing Soviet armies. By the summer of 1943 the Soviets had a superior number of troops and weapons, despite the fact that Germany was killing them by the thousands and destroying vast amounts of Russian equipment. While there would be victories for Germany, it was be a retreat that continued until the final battle in Berlin in the spring of 1945.

Being overly cautious, the Allies waited until July 10, 1943, to launch Operation Husky on the island of Sicily. The Germans were deceived into believing that the Allied attack would come in the Balkans and Greece. A combined British-American effort drove the Germans to Messina, from which they were able to escape over the straits of Messina to the mainland of Italy with their equipment. While the Germans continued to fight in Italy until the end of the war, Operation Husky opened the Mediterranean to Allied merchant shipping. The attack on Sicily also resulted in the overthrow of Mussolini. The fighting up the Italian peninsula was bitter and protracted. The landings at Salerno in September

1943 and later at Anzio were some of the most difficult and hard-fought of the war. As the Allies moved up the Italian peninsula, the German General Albert Kesserling, who was a defensive genius, continued to set up new defensive lines after the Allies had breached one after another. Some of the most difficult fighting involved Allied Polish troops around Monte Cassino.

THE END OF THE WAR IN EUROPE

As the war was progressing in the Mediterranean, combined British-American airpower continued to pound Germany. However, Stalin still wanted the Allies to launch a second front in the west to take the pressure off the Soviet troops. At one point he threatened to make a separate peace with Germany, which would have placed the Allies in an untenable position.

The second front in the west was finally opened in France on June 6, 1944, with the D-Day landing. Once the beachhead had been established the Allies moved across France, with French forces liberating Paris. In December 1944, the Germans made a final attempt to drive the Allies back in the Battle of the Bulge. But by January 1945 the Allies were on the offensive again. The Supreme Allied commander, General Dwight D. Eisenhower, decided to let the Russians take Berlin, because at the Yalta Conference it had been decided to divide Germany into zones of occupation and Berlin would be in the Russian zone. Moreover, he knew that taking Berlin would result in enormous casualties. This proved to be true as 361,367 Soviet troops were killed in the final battle for the German capital. In April and May 1945, Allied forces freed German concentration camps revealing the horrors that had occurred during the war. The American-Soviet forces met on the Elbe River and on May 8, 1945, the war in Europe was over.

THE END OF THE WAR IN THE PACIFIC

While war in Europe had ended, the war in the Pacific was still being fought. The U.S. strategy was divided between General DOUGLAS MACARTHUR's drive up the southwest Pacific, and Admiral CHESTER NIMITZ's drive across the central Pacific. Theoretically, the United States should have taken only one route, but in the end it worked out well because the Japanese never knew where the next attack would come from.

While the U.S. Navy was destroying the Japanese navy, the U.S. Marines and Army were conducting operations on the islands of Tarawa, Kwajalein, Eniwetok, Saipan, GUAM, and Tinian after capturing the MARSHALL ISLANDS and the Marianas Islands. The United States started to bomb Japan from bases in the Marianas with B-29 bombers. The casualties the Americans took were high, but the worst was still to come on Iwo Jima and Okinawa in February and April 1945.

With the war already over in Europe, America was becoming war weary. The casualty figures had been running at about 35 percent in the Pacific war. The main Japanese home islands still remained to be taken, despite Japanese losses from bomber raids on Tokyo and other cities from May to August 1945. The Tokyo raid alone killed 100,000 and destroyed large sections of the city.

The first phase of the invasion of Japan was set for November 1, 1945, at Kyushu, while the second phase would start on March 1, 1946. In the initial assault it was estimated that there would be 268,000 Allied casualties out of an invasion force of 760,000. In the second phase 1,000,000 casualties were estimated. Japan had 2,500,000 troops in the home islands, with another 2,000,000 in reserve. Japan could also count on another 20,000,000 citizens who would help the army by attacking the in-

vaders with sharpened sticks. These were Japanese boys and girls and the elderly. Japan also had 10,000 planes, of which 5,000 were kamikaze, and 3,000 suicide torpedo boats. The casualties on the Japanese side would have been even more terrible than on the American side; they would have been in the millions. The Japanese military was still in control in Japan and was going to stage an all-out defense of the home islands.

On August 6, 1945, Colonel Paul Tibbets took off from Tinian in a B-29 named *Enola Gay*, after his mother. The first of two atomic bombs, Little Boy, was dropped on Hiroshima, killing more than 100,000 people. (On August 8 the Soviet Union declared war on Japan and moved 1.6 million troops into Manchuria, killing 350,000 Japanese soldiers.) On August 9 the second bomb, Fat Man, was dropped on Nagasaki. On August 15 the emperor, for the first time, made a radio broadcast and spoke to the Japanese people, saying it was time to end the war. As the emperor was speaking, there was a plot by the Japanese military to stop him from delivering his speech, but it did not succeed. On September 2, 1945, on the battleship USS *Missouri*, MacArthur accepted the Japanese surrender.

Further Reading: Steven Ambrose, *D-Day, June 6, 1944: The Climactic Battle of World War II* (Simon and Schuster, 1994); Winston S. Churchill, *The Second World War* (Houghton Mifflin, 1986); I. C. B. Dear, ed., *The Oxford Companion to World War II* (Oxford University Press, 1995); Richard B. Frank, *Downfall: The End of the Imperial Japanese Empire* (Random House, 1999); Christopher Moore, *Fighting for America: Black Soldiers, the Unsung Heroes of World War II* (Random House, 2005); Herman J. Obermayer, *Soldiering for Freedom: A GI's Account of World War II* (Texas A&M University Press, 2005); Sir Charles Webster and Nobel Frankland, *The Strategic Air Offensive against Germany* (Battery Press, 1961); Gerhard L. Weinberg, *A World at Arms: A Global History of World War II* (Cambridge University Press, 2005); Thomas W. Zeiler, *Unconditional Defeat: Japan and the End of World War II* (Scholarly Resources, 2004).

—ANDREW R. CARLSON, PH.D.

Y

Yamamoto, Isoroku (1884–1943)

Admiral Isoroku Yamamoto, born Isoroku Takano on April 4, 1884, in Tokyo, was the youngest child of a former samurai. He changed his name to Yamamoto at the age of 32 at the request of the Yamamoto family, which was in need of male heirs. Yamamoto was a brilliant naval student who rose quickly through the ranks. Perhaps one of the great ironies of Yamamoto's plan to attack Pearl Harbor was the fact that the man who championed the attack was both knowledgeable and fond of the UNITED STATES. He made several trips to the United States between 1916 and 1928 as a tourist, student, and staff member of the Japanese embassy.

In an era of large battleships, Yamamoto argued against the building of large ships in favor of a navy built around airpower. To this end he trained as a pilot, commanded an aircraft carrier, and as the head of the Japanese military aerodynamics division, he placed the order for the famous Zero fighter plane. Prior to Yamamoto's plan, the Japanese naval strategy envisioned a defensive war that called for the Japanese navy to take on the American navy in Japanese home waters. However, this plan did not support Japanese plans for military operations south of their home islands. At the conclusion of World War I, JAPAN viewed the United States as its primary enemy and as the major hindrance to Japanese control of Southeast Asia. Throughout 1940 Yamamoto advised against war with the United States and in a January 1941 letter stated his doubts whether

AT LEFT *Photo of official portrait of Isoroku Yamamoto by Shugaku Homma, 1943.*

Japanese politicians fully realized the effort and sacrifices required to defeat the United States.

As early as January 1941, Yamamoto was beginning to outline a plan that called for a decisive strike primarily aimed at American aircraft carriers. It was Yamamoto's hope that such a strike would cripple the U.S. Fleet and buy enough time for Japan to complete its Asian conquests. In the end, the American aircraft carriers survived to form the nucleus of a new fleet. Yamamoto was killed on April 18, 1943, when his plane was shot down en route to Bougainville Island.

Further Reading: Hiroyuki Agawa, *The Reluctant Admiral: Yamamoto and the Imperial Navy* (Harper and Row, 1974); John Craddock, *First Shot: The Untold Story of the Japanese Minisubs That Attacked Pearl Harbor* (McGraw-Hill, 2006); Martin Gilbert, *The Second World War* (Henry Holt and Company, 1989).

—ABBE ALLEN DEBOLT

ABOVE *Fleet Admiral Isoroku Yamamoto, commander in chief of the Japanese Navy Combined Fleet.*

Commander Minoru Genda

IF ADMIRAL Yamamoto was the visionary who conceived of the attack on Pearl Harbor, Minoru Genda was the architect who brought the vision to life. Genda was the archetype of a fighter pilot: aggressive and daring. The first in his flight class in November 1929, Genda became well known in the Imperial Navy in the 1930s for rejecting the defensive role of the fighter plane in favor of using carriers and their fighters in an offensive, aggressive role. Genda's reputation as a bold planner with a good eye for detail led to his transfer in February 1941 to the 11th Air Fleet to assist the study group in planning for Pearl Harbor.

In late February 1941, Genda provided a draft that outlined an early morning attack on Pearl Harbor and Oahu using a variety of aircraft; his plan was adopted in nearly its entirety. Genda's suggestion to land 10,000 to 15,000 troops to occupy Oahu was rejected. While at sea, Genda proposed to task force commander Admiral Nagumo four different plans to put into operation after the completion of the second wave of attacks on Pearl Harbor. In essence, these plans called for keeping the fleet in the area for several days to seek and destroy any remaining American warships. In the end, Nagumo ignored Genda's plans to press the attack and decided to return to home waters.

ABOVE CELEBRATING SURRENDER *In one of the most famous images from World War II, a sailor kisses an American woman in Times Square, New York City, in celebration of the Japanese surrender on August 14, 1945.*

INDEX

A

Abe, Zenji, 112, 113
Abukuma, 114, 115
advertising (1941), 49
African Americans
    daily life (1941), 47
    as WACs, 230
Agee, James, 44
Agricultural Adjustment Act, 195
aircraft carriers, 1–3
    built during World War II, 174
    Japanese, for Pearl attack, VII, 3, 5, 114. *See also specific carrier names*
    origin and evolution, 1–3
    U.S., lost in war, 174
    U.S., on December 7, VII, 149, 170, 173, 179
airplanes
    A-20 bombers, 163
    B-17 bombers, VII, XIV, XV, 33, 163, 165
    B-18 bombers, 163
    Billy Mitchell and, 4, 5, 187
    bombing from, 4–5. *See also* dive-bombers
    destructive power proven, 5
    fighting against Pearl attack, XV, 161, 163
    growing reliance on, 170
    Japanese. *See* Japanese aircraft
    post-World War II, 244
    ships vs., 3–6
    U.S., damage/destruction summary, VII
    from USS *Enterprise*, coming to help, XV, 163
    World War I service, 4
    See also dive-bombers; Japanese aircraft; torpedo planes
Akagi, VII, XIV, 5, 111, 114, 115, 116, 177
Akigumo, 115
Allies, 6–9. *See also specific country names*
Ambassador Nomura. *See* Nomura, Kichisaburo
America First, XI, 8, 35
America First Committee, 103, 104
Anteres, USS, 85, 148
Anti-Comintern Pact, 66, 99, 197, 198, 225
anti-Semitism, 9
antitorpedo nets, 4, 192
appeasement, 17, 238
Arare, 115
Arcadia conference, 9–10
Argus, HMS, 2, 3
Arizona, USS, 10–13
    annual commemoration wreath, 14
    attack/destruction of, IX, XIV, 12, 13, 120, 144, 179, 202, 216
    Battleship Row position, 11
    casualties, 13
    construction of, 10
    heroism aboard, XIV, 13, 39
    memorialized before formal Memorial, 14, 50
    natural protective casing around, 16
    Nimitz commanding, 11
    pre-attack exercises, 11
    recognizing bravery aboard, 39
    salvage operation, 13–14, 203, 204
    service record, 10–11
    survivor story, 12

"tears" of oil, 10, 50
top officers. *See* Kidd, Isaac (Admiral); Van Valkenburgh, Franklin
World War I service, 10
Arizona, USS Memorial, 13–16
    dedication, 13
    design, 15
    development process, 14–15
    Elvis benefit concert for, 15
    funding, 15
    names of killed, 13
    oil bubbling from, 10, 50
    opposition to, 14
    as preparedness symbol, 15
    shrine room, 15
    structural/fuel leakage concerns, 15–16
    survivor list, 13
    U.S. flag on sunken mainmast, 13
articles, reader's guide to, XII
Asiatic Fleet, 170, 172
    Admiral Thomas Hart and, XIII, 133, 172
    Commander in Chief of, 170, 191
    end of, 172
    Pacific Fleet ships diverted to, 226
    Panay incident, 174–176
    receiving message of attack, XIII, 133
    USS *Pennsylvania* and, 180
    vessels, on December 7, 1941, 172
Atlantic Charter, 83, 103, 195, 226
Atlantic Fleet
    Commander in Chief of, 170
    Isaac Kidd (son) and, 120
    receiving message of attack, XIII
    USS *Nevada* transferred to, 157
atomic bombs
    Bock's Car and, 81–82
    debate over using, 221
    decision to use, 81, 221, 252
    destruction caused by, 221
    dropping of, 81–82, 220, 221, 252, 255
    Enola Gay and, 81, 221, 255
    inducing surrender, 80, 82, 255
    Manhattan Project, 233
    Pearl Harbor attack influencing use of, 221
    Soviet Union developing, 243
    tests, 157, 181
    USS *Nevada* as target for, 157
A-20 bombers, 163
Australia, 29
    attacked, 29, 149
    Caroline Islands and, 33
    MacArthur to, 184
    troops in Malaya, 135
    war response, 29
Axis powers, 16–20
    birth of, 17
    disorganization of, 19–20
    European associates of, 155
    leading up to, 16–17
    See also Germany; Hitler, Adolf; Japan; Mussolini, Benito; Tripartite Pact

B

Battleship Row
    attack of, VII
    ship positions, 11, 215–216
    See also specific battleship names
battleships
    as core of navy, 170
    damage/destruction summary, VII
    as of December 7, 1941, 169, 173
    Japanese, 114, 115
    See also specific battleship names
B-18 bombers, 163
Bellows Field, 51, 114, 162, 163–164, 178
Bennion, Mervyn S., 40, 216, 235
Benny, Jack, 45, 48
"Big Three" conference, 196
Birmingham, USS, 1
blame, for Pearl Harbor attack, 97–101
    Admiral Kimmel and, 86, 97, 98, 99, 100, 208
    army investigation, 99–100
    "back door to war" theory, 85, 86
    C.C. Bloch and, 22, 84, 86
    Clark investigation, 99
    Clausen investigation, 100
    communication/intelligence failures, 83, 84–86, 95–97, 195–196, 208
    Douglas MacArthur and, 100
    George C. Marshall and, 24, 98–99, 100, 137–138
    government officials, 82–83, 84, 86
    Harold R. Stark and, 22, 62, 123, 193, 211–212
    Hart investigation, 98
    historian views, 82–87
    Husband Kimmel and, 86, 96, 97, 98, 99, 100, 208
    initial investigations, 98
    Joint Congressional Committee and, 100–101
    Knox investigations, 97–98, 100, 122–123, 208
    navy investigation, 99
    obvious scapegoats, 97
    President Roosevelt and, 82, 85, 86, 95–96, 101, 192
    radar operating procedures, 84–85
    Walter C. Short and, 22, 96, 97, 98–99, 207, 208
    Winston Churchill and, 95–96
    See also preparedness
Blitzkrieg, 88, 250
Bloch, C.C., XII, 21–22, 84, 86
Bloom, Sol, 9
Bock's Car, 81–82
Bolton, Frances P., 190
Bormann, Martin, 243
Bowfin, USS, 143
Brandstetter, Frank, IX, X
British Chiefs of Staff, 10, 68
British Commonwealth, 22–29
    African front, 7, 18, 22, 253
    Arcadia conference and, 9–10
    declaring war on Japan, 25–26
    in Far East, 22–24
    Japanese attacks on, 22–24
    reactions to Pearl attack, 24–26, 68–69
    solidarity with America, 35
    standing alone against Axis, 17–18
    See also Churchill, Winston; Hong Kong; Malaya
Brooke, Alan, 23, 25
Brooke-Popham, Robert, 23, 24
Brown, William, 90
B-17 bombers, VII, XIV, XV, 33, 163, 165
Bulkeley, John, 172

C

California, USS, 31–32
    avenging Pearl attack, 216
    Battleship Row position, 11, 31
    evacuation of, 31, 32
    heroism aboard, 31–32, 40
    post-attack position, 202
    survivor memoirs, 141, 143
Caroline Islands, 33–34, 108, 192, 236
Cassin, USS
    attack of, XIV, 203
    damaged, 203
    parts salvaged, 204
casualties, from December 7
    American, 116, 169, 201
    Japanese, 116
Central Intelligence Agency, creation, 196
Chamberlain, Neville
    appeasement of Hitler, 238
    Hitler opinion of, 238
    Winston Churchill taking over for, 249
Cherry Society, 240
Chiang Kai-shek, 9, 35, 109, 110, 111, 240, 241, 245
Chickuma, 114, 115
China
    document foreshadowing invasion of, 185–186
    Greater East Asia Co-Prosperity Sphere, 69–71
    history with Japan, 108–109
    Japan invading, 16–17, 70, 109, 225, 240, 241
    Nanking atrocities, 16, 70, 109
    Neutrality Acts and, 154
    reparation demands to Japan, 246
    triggering Japanese embargos, 70, 109, 110, 204
    U.S. aid to, inflaming Japanese, 206
    Yangtze Patrol, 174, 175
Churchill, Winston, 23, 34–36
    to America, 35
    Arcadia conference and, 9–10
    "Big Three" conference attendance, 196
    blame for Pearl Harbor and, 95–96
    hearing of Pearl attack, 26
    journal entry, 28
    response to Pearl attack, VIII, 26, 28, 34–35
    Roosevelt and, 9–10, 35
    speech immediately after Pearl attack, 34
    See also British Commonwealth
Civilian Conservation Corps, 195
Clark, Carter W., 99
Clausen, Henry C., 100
codes, German, 96, 249
codes, Japanese, 36–39
    "east wind rain," 50, 83, 84, 99
    encryption method, 36–37
    JN-25, 38–39
    PURPLE, 37–38, 95, 96
    signaling attack on U.S., 36, 50, 83, 84
    See also Intelligence
coding devices
    German, 96
    Japanese, 36, 38
Cold War, 14–15, 127, 220, 243–244
Commander in Chief, U.S. Fleet (CINCUS), 21, 85, 170, 190, 191
Congress
    approving Marshall Plan, 243
    approving WAC bills, 229, 231
    declaring war on Japan, 20, 41

Hawai'i statehood and, 76–77, 79
isolationism and. *See* isolationism
joint committee investigating attack, 100–101, 192, 208
Neutrality Acts, 103, 153–155, 226
opposing entry into war, 17, 103
reactions to Pearl attack, 40–41
women in, 189, 190
Congressional Medal of Honor, 39–40
Japan raid recipient (Doolittle), 56
Pearl Harbor recipients, 13, 32, 39–40, 156, 235
PT-boat recipient, 172
submariner recipients, 174
Connally, Tom, 141
Coral Sea, Battle of, 150, 158, 174, 252–253
Craigie, Robert, 26
cruisers
Japanese, 114, 115
U.S., on December 7, 169, 173
culture (1941), 42–45
entertainers, 45, 48
literature, 44–45
movies, 42–43, 48
music, 45, 48
radio, 45, 47
Cunningham, Winfield Scott, 231
Curtiss, USS, XIII, 203
Cuse, Robert, 154

D

daily life
in 1941, 47–50. *See also* culture (1941)
panic after attack, 176–177
damage, as memorial, 50–51
damaged ships. *See* salvage operations; *specific ship names*
dc Gaulle, Charles, 52–53
opposing Japan in Indochina, 58
political career, 53
reactions to Pearl attack, 52
Dealy, Sam, 174
Death toll, of attack, IX
December 7 documentary, 127–128
declarations of war
by Hitler, on United States, 20, 63–64, 247–248
by Italy, 151, 250
by Japan, 53–54, 218
by Soviet Union, 255
by United States, 20, 41, 193
Denmark, X, 155, 248
Depression
fostering isolationism, 17
fostering Nazism, 67
fueling Japanese expansionism, 109, 197, 240
impacting 1941 culture, 42, 45, 47, 49
Roosevelt responding to, 193, 194–195
World War II overshadowing, 242
destroyers
Japanese, 114, 115
U.S., on December 7, 173
Devereux, James, 231
diplomatic relations, 54–55
chronology of Japanese activities, 81
failing plans, 54–55
interwar period summary, 225–226
preparing for war during, 54, 241
dive-bombers
armor-piercing bombs, 5

attack of, 4–5, 111, 112, 161, 162
firing at, 12
number on mission, 113–114
specifications, 113
documentary film, 127–128
Dole, James Drummond, 78, 79
Dole, Sanford B., 77–78
Dole Pineapple, 78–79
Dönitz, Karl, 243
Doolittle, James, 55–56
Doolittle's raid, 55, 56, 158
Downes, USS
explosion on, 203
torpedo tube hitting *Pennsylvania*, 181
USS *Cassin* sagging onto, XIV
Duke of York, HMS, 9–10

E

"east wind rain," 50, 83, 84, 99
Eisenhower, Dwight D., 8, 220, 230, 254
Enigma code, 96, 249
Enola Gay, 81, 221, 255
Enterprise, USS, 149
avoiding Pearl destruction, 163, 169, 179
Doolittle's raid from, 56, 252
eerie Pearl Harbor return, 150
fighter planes, into Ford Island firefight, XV, 163
Japanese ships sunk by, 115
Midway success, 150
pilots, killed by friendly fire, XV, 163
entertainers (1941), 45, 48
European theater, of World War II, 248, 254. *See also specific countries*

F

fashion trends (1941), 49
Fat Man, 255
Federal Emergency Relief Act, 195
films. *See* movies
Finn, John William, 40
Flaherty, Francis, 40
fleet. *See* Japanese fleet; Pacific Fleet (U.S.)
Fleet Radio Unit Pacific (FRUPAC)
breaking codes, 150
enabling Midway success, 39, 97, 150
top officer, 97
See also codes, Japanese; intelligence
Force Z, 22–23, 27–28
Ford Island
attack/damage summary, 163
battleships alongside. *See* Battleship Row
damage marks at, 50–51
Fort Armstrong, 164
Fort Barrette, 164
Fort DeRussy, 164, 166
Fort Hase, 164
Fort Kamehameha, 164
Fort McKinley, 90
Fort Ruger, 164, 166
Fort Shafter, 207
as antiaircraft artillery post, 164
Fuchikami telegram to, XIV, XV
radar report of Japanese planes to, 165
Fort Weaver, 164
"Four Freedoms" speech, 48, 195
France
appeasement of Hitler, 238

D-Day, 254
declaring war on Germany, 17, 65
falling to Germany, 17, 57, 110, 248
German prospects of victory, 250
isolationism and, 102
Italy declaring war on, 250
supporting Poland, 238–239, 248
United Nations and, 246
U.S. response to war (early), 65–66, 154
See also de Gaulle, Charles; French Indochina
freedoms, four, 48, 195
French Indochina, 57–59
  countries comprising, 57
  French government removed, 58
  French resistance in, 58
  full Japanese occupation, 58
  Japanese bases in, 57–58
  Japanese takeover of, X, 57–59, 70, 110, 206–207, 249
  Japanese withdrawal negotiations, 55, 57, 111, 207, 241
  triggering Japanese sanctions, 206–207
  Vietnam resistance (Viet Minh), 58–59
Friedman, Elizebeth, 38, 96
Friedman, William F., 37, 95, 96
From Here to Eternity, 51, 128–130, 131
FRUPAC. *See* Fleet Radio Unit Pacific (FRUPAC)
Fuchida, Mitsuo
  leading Pearl attack, 111–114, 116, 177–178
  memoirs on, 144–147
  pre-attack speech to crew, 144
  reactions to attack success, 145
  surveying damage, XIV, 144–145
  "*Tora! Tora! Tora!*" message, 13, 144, 177
  urging third attack to decimate Pearl, 146
Fuchikami, Tadao, XIV, XV
fuel stocks unharmed, 114, 169, 179
Fuqua, Samuel G.
  Arizona heroism, XIV, 13, 39
  Medal of Honor, 13, 39
Furlong, William R., 201–202, 203, 204

G
G-2, 61–63. *See also* intelligence
Geiger, Roy, 72
Genda, Minoru, 258
  envisioning carriers delivering attack planes, 3
  memoirs, 144
  planning attack, 112, 116, 258
  pressing for third strike, 114, 258
Germany, 64–68
  attacking Soviet Union, X, 6–7, 210, 251
  Blitzkrieg, 88, 250
  declaring war on United States, VIII, 20, 63–64, 247–248
  invading Poland, 65
  Japan alliance, VIII, 19–20, 109–110. *See also* Tripartite Pact
  nonaggression pact with Soviet Union, 17, 18–19, 66, 198, 210, 239, 249, 251
  Reichstag, 63, 64, 67, 88
  retreat of, 253–254
  rise of Nazis, 67
  Soviet Union repelling, 251–252, 253
  tide turning against, 251–252
  U.S. response to war (early), 65–66
  war criminals from, 243
  withdrawing from League of Nations, 237
  World War I and, 224–225, 236
  World War II causes and, 236–239

World War II victories, 249–251
  See also Hitler, Adolf
Germany, Federal Republic of, 243
Goebbels, Joseph, 88, 243
Goering, Hermann, 238, 243
Gratz, Tucker, 14
Gray, Denver, 142
Great Britain. *See* British Commonwealth
Great Depression. *See* Depression
Greater East Asia Co-Prosperity Sphere, 69–71
Greater East Asia doctrine, X
Grew, Joseph, 71
  critical of Roosevelt negotiations, 71
  diplomacy with Japan, 55, 71, 219
  on Pearl attack, X
  receiving declaration of war, XIV, 53
  warning of impending attack, 71
Grotjan, Genevieve, 38
Guam, 71–72
  America taking control, 223
  battle to retake, 72
  casualties, 72
  expected attack on, 86, 192
  under Japanese control, 71–72
  soldier hiding 28 years on, 72
  taken by Japan, 71, 149
Guggenheim, Alicia, 105
Guggenheim, Harry, 105

H
Halsey, William F., XIII, 84, 172, 173
Hamakaze, 115
Hart, Thomas
  commanding Asiatic Fleet, 172
  end of Asiatic Fleet and, 172
  heading navy investigation, 98
  Philippines loss and, 134
Hawai'i, 76–79
  to 1898, 73–76
  1898 to 1942, 76–79
  America and, 76–79, 90–92
  blackouts/curfews after attack, 92
  Japan/U.S. struggle over, 185
  Kamehameha I, II, III, and IV, 74–75, 76
  Kamehameha the Great, 74
  kapu laws, 75
  Oahu airfields and bases, 161–164. *See also* Bellows Field; Hickam Field; Wheeler Field
  Oahu forts, 164–166
  pineapple production, 78–79, 92
  sugar plantations, 78
  as U.S. Territory, 76–79
  war effort contributions, 92
  See also Honolulu
Hearst, William Randolph, 104–105
Hebel, Fritz, 163
Helena, USS, XIII, 202
Hess, Rudolf, 243
Hewitt, Henry K., 100
Hickam Field
  attack of, VII, XIII, 112, 162, 165
  casualties, 163
  clustered plane targets at, 130, 162
  damage summary, 114, 163
  heroism at, 162–163

Hiei, 114, 115
Hill, Edwin Joseph, 39–40, 156, 179
Hill, Harry W., 138–139
Hill, USS, 156
Hill of Sacrifice. *See* Punchbowl Cemetery
Himmler, Heinrich, 243
Hirohito, Emperor, 80–82
    decision to attack United States, 111
    final pre-attack message from Roosevelt, 71, 96
    involvement in attack plans, 80
    negotiations with, 71
    surrendering to U.S., 80, 82
    as symbolic leader, 80, 246–247
Hiryu, VII, 5, 111, 114, 115
historian views, 82–87
    Charles Tansill, 82–83, 85
    Gordon Prange, 86–87
    Roberta Wohlstetter, 83–86, 96
Hitler, Adolf, 87–88
    Axis partners and, 16–20
    death of, 243
    declaring war on United States, VIII, 20, 63–64, 247–248
    dismissing dissenters, 238
    on keeping U.S. out of war, 66
    Mein Kampf (My Struggle), 239
    Mussolini and, 19, 151, 237–238, 239, 250
    night and fog decree, 87
    Pact of Steel, 237, 251
    path to domination, 237–239
    response to Pearl attack, 88
    rise of Nazism and, 67
    speech declaring war, 64
    violating Versailles Treaty, 16, 237–238
    See also Germany
Hong Kong, 88–89
    expected attack on, 88
    Japanese attacks on, 6, 24, 88–89, 227
    Japanese takeover of, 25
Honolulu, 89–92
    American military to, 90
    beaches during wartime, 92
    as capital of Hawai'i, 89–90
    December 7, 1941, 91–92
    wartime entertainment, 92
Honolulu, USS, 203
Hoover, Herbert
    aboard USS *Arizona*, 11
    opposing sanctions against Japan, 205, 206
    as pacifist, 206
    Roosevelt defeating, 194
Hoover Doctrine, 206
Horikoshi, Jiro, 144
Hornet, USS
    Doolittle's raid from, 56, 252
    launching bombers against Japanese homeland, 149
    loss of, 174
    Midway success, 150
    sinking *Hamakaze*, 115
Hughes, James, 175
Hull, Cordell, 92–93
    death of, 93
    learning of attack, 159, 161
    negotiating with Japan, 53–54, 55, 57, 83, 111, 217, 219
    Nobel Peace Prize recipient, 93
    political career, 92–93
    receiving declaration of war, 193
    receiving message of severed diplomatic ties, VII–VIII, IX, 81, 96, 146, 159
    response to Nomura, IX, 159
    10-point proposal to Tojo, 217, 241
    testifying at investigation, 101
    warned of attack, 71
    warning military of possible attack, 93

I

Iida, Fusata, 51
Indochina. *See* French Indochina
intelligence
    centralization of, after attack, 195–196
    communication failures regarding attack, 83, 84–86, 95–97, 195–196, 208
    coordination, 63
    "east wind rain" foretelling attack, 50, 83, 84, 99
    Enigma code (German), 96, 249
    failing to break JN-25 code, 38–39
    G-2 and, 61–63
    impacting Midway victory, 39, 97, 149, 150
    MAGIC intercept system, 38, 62, 91, 99, 136, 137
    MID (Military Intelligence Division), 61–63
    one-pointed focus of, 38–39
    Pacific Theater, 95–97
    personnel types, 61
    predicting U.S. attack, 36, 50, 83, 84, 196, 208
    PURPLE code (Japanese), 37–38
    Signal Intelligence Service (SIS), 36, 37, 38, 39, 61, 62, 95, 137
    Ultra code (German), 249–250
    warning of Pearl attack, 62
    women cryptanalysts, 38
    See also codes, Japanese; Fleet Radio Unit Pacific (FRUPAC)
internment camps
    in Britain, 35
    reparation payments for, 117
    in United States, 35
interwar period summary, 225–226
investigations of responsibility. *See* blame, for Pearl Harbor attack
isolationism, 101–104
    affecting Pearl Harbor attack, 185, 186
    America First and, XI, 8, 35, 103, 104
    building threats against, 103–104
    early 20th-century proponents, 102
    in Japan, 185
    melting to support war, 40–41, 233
    negative connotations of, 101, 102
    in 19th century, 102
    political party perspectives, 103
    President Roosevelt and, 103
    press promoting, 104–105
    pressure against entering World War II, 18
    rise of, 17
    U.S. history of, 186
isolationist press, 104–105
Israel, 220, 245
Italy. *See* Mussolini, Benito

J

Japan, 107–110
    assets frozen, 54, 213, 219
    Cherry Society, 240
    China and, background history, 108–109
    China invaded by, 16–17, 70, 109, 225, 240, 241
    chronology of activities, 81
    December 7 casualties, 201

decision to attack United States, 110–111, 241
declaration of war against, 20, 41, 193
declaration of war by, 53–54
embargos. *See* sanctions against Japan
expansionist policy, 80, 185–186, 206
German alliance, VIII, 19–20, 109–110. *See also* Tripartite Pact
Greater East Asia Co-Prosperity Sphere, 69–71
industrialization of, 240
isolationism, giving rise to Pearl Harbor, 185
military atrocities, 16, 70, 89, 109
nonaggression pact with Soviet Union, 110, 111, 206
path to World War II, 240–241
rapid rise of, 107–108, 109
reconstruction and reformation, 245–247
rise of militarism, 109
Soviet Union and, 109, 110, 111, 206
Soviet Union declaring war on, 255
surrendering to U.S., 80, 82, 255
tide turning against, 252–253
United States rebuilding, 246–247
U.S. Congress declares war on, 20
war criminals from, 247
Japanese aircraft, 111–114
    attack of, VII, 4–5, 111–114
    carriers originated from, VII
    codenamed Kate, 111, 113
    codenamed Val, 111, 113, 114
    pilot leading attack. *See* Fuchida, Mitsuo
    planes used for attack, 113–114
    Zeroes, 27, 111, 113, 114, 140, 257
    See also dive-bombers; torpedo planes
Japanese fleet, VII, 114–116
    aircraft carriers, VII, 3, 5, 114. *See also specific carrier names*
    battleships, 115
    cruisers, 114, 115
    destroyers, 114, 115
    fate of, 115
    surprise attack history, 114
    targets destroyed, 116
    See also Nagumo, Chuichi
Japanese Americans
    as Americans (in 1942 documentary), 128
    internment camps, 35, 117
JN-25 code, 38–39
Jones, Herbert, 31–32, 40
Jones, James, 128–129, 131
    From Here to Eternity (book and film), 51, 129–130, 131
    The Pistol, 131

K

Kaga, VII, 5, 111, 114
Kagero, 115
Kaneohe Bay
    damage marks at, 51
    heroism at, 40
Kase, Toshikazu, 26, 146
Kasumi, 115
Kate (Japanese aircraft), 111, 113
Kennedy, John F., 8, 191
Kennedy, Joseph P., 127, 154
Kidd, Isaac (Admiral), 119–120
    Medal of Honor to, 13, 39, 120
    military career, 119
    night before attack, 11, 119
    taking *Arizona* command, 11
Kidd, Isaac (son of Admiral), 120

Kido Butai, 114, 115
Kimmel, Husband, 121–122
    aftermath of attack and, 169, 170
    on December 7, 121–122
    defense concerns of, 192
    denied legal counsel, 98
    deploying aircraft carriers pre-attack, 179
    exoneration of, 99, 100
    honored by Pearl Harbor Survivors Association, 208
    indications of war and, XI, 22, 84, 85–86, 96
    memoirs, 142–143
    military career, 121–122
    near-death during attack, 122
    relieved of command, 122, 123
    response to submarine sighting, 178
    responsibility for attack and, 86, 96, 97, 98, 99, 100, 208
    sailor perspectives on, 142, 143
    as scapegoat, 122, 123, 208
    sons as naval officers, 121
Kimmel, Manning Marius, 121
Kincaid, Thomas, 173
Kirishima, 114, 115
Knox, Frank A., 122–123
    authorizing documentary of attack, 127
    investigations of responsibility, 97–98, 100, 122–123, 208
    political career, 123
    receiving message of attack, XIII, 122
    supporting Lend-Lease Act, 127
    surprise choice for navy head, 123
Konoe, Fumimaro
    Axis relations, 66, 198
    forcing Matsuoka out, 139
    opposed to war, 54
    pressing to meet Roosevelt, 54, 219
    pushing for Asian hegemony recognition, 206
    resignation of, 54, 110, 217, 219, 241
    Toyoda and, 218, 219
    urging China withdrawal, 110
Korea
    Japan annexing, 70, 108
    North, 245
    Russo-Japanese War and, 197
    South, 245
    supplying coal to Japan, 240
Kurusu, Saburo
    deceptive negotiations, X, 53, 55, 218
    delivering message to Hull, IX, 159

L

La Guardia, Fiorello, X, 8, 177
labor unions, 48
Langley, USS, 3, 172
League of Nations
    Germany withdrawing from, 237
    Japan violating terms of, 35, 225
    Japan withdrawing from, 204, 205, 225
    sanctions against Japan, 204, 205
    United States rejecting, 102, 225
Leigh, Richard H., 215
Lend-Lease Act, 125–127
    as "An Act to Promote the Defense of the United States," 126
    benefits of, 127
    described, 18, 47, 195
    helping Britain/Allies, 18, 66, 68, 154–155, 186, 226
    isolationists opposing, 189
    Neutrality Acts giving rise to, 125, 154

neutrality risked with, 66
opposition to, 189
passage of, 18, 126–127, 195
Roosevelt announcing plans for, 47
for Soviet Union, 155, 210, 212
Let Us Now Praise Famous Men, 44
Lexington, USS, 149
avoiding Pearl destruction, 169, 179
Battle of Coral Sea and, 150, 252
sinking of, 150, 174, 252
sinking *Zuikaku*, 115
literature
in 1941, 44–45
From Here to Eternity (book and film), 51, 129–130, 131
The Pistol, 131
War and Remembrance, 130–131
The Winds of War, 130–131
Lockard, Joseph L., 84, 165, 178
Lockwood, Charles A., 174

M

MacArthur, Douglas, 133–134
accepting Japanese surrender, 255
escape from Philippines, 172
as Japan military governor, 245
losing Philippines, 133–134, 182, 184
"Operation Olympic" opposition, 80–81
perspective on Hirohito, 80
to Philippines, 184
power struggle, 172
responsibility for attack and, 100
MAGIC intercept system, 38, 62, 91, 99, 136, 137
Malaya, 135
invasion imminent, 22–23
Japanese attacks on, VIII, 24–25, 26–27, 137, 227
Japanese takeover of, 26–28, 35, 135
Manchuria. *See* China
Manhattan Project, 233
Marshall, George C., 137–138
declining Truman training offer, 219–220
designing chain of command, 10
guilty of preparedness neglect, 24
Pearl preparedness and, 24, 137–138, 207
receiving message of attack, XIII
responsibility for attack and, 98–99, 100, 137–138
warning of Pearl attack and, 62, 137–138, 193
Marshall Islands, 136
atomic bomb test in, 157
Japanese expansion and, 71, 108, 205–206, 236–237
location of, 136
U.S. capturing, 136, 139, 192, 254
Marshall Plan, 220, 243
Maryland, USS, 138–139
attack of, 112
avenging Pearl attack, 216
Battleship Row position, 11, 138, 216
commissioning of, 139
damage to, 179, 203
decommissioning of, 139
fighting against Pearl attack, 138
as flagship, 138–139
Gilbert Islands battle, 138–139
Marshall Islands service, 139
repaired/reactivated, 138, 203, 217
service after Pearl attack, 138–139
Mason, Theodore, 140, 144

Matsuoka, Yosuke, 139–140
death of, 140
force out of office, 139–140, 218
Hitler support pledge, 66
International Military Tribunal charges, 140
lamenting Tripartite Pact, 140
negotiating Tripartite Pact, 139
nonaggression pact with Soviet Union, 19, 110, 139, 198
reactions to Pearl attack, 140
war perspective, 17, 110, 139, 140
McAfee, Mildred A., 234
McCormick, Robert, 104–105
McDole, Glen, 142
McGoran, John, 140, 142
Mein Kampf (My Struggle), 239
memoirs, American, 140–143
memoirs, Japanese, 144–147
midget submarines, 114, 116, 147–148, 202, 204. *See also* submarines, at Pearl Harbor
Midway, Battle of, 148–151
American fleet loses, 253
cryptanalysts (intelligence) affecting, 39, 97, 149, 150
expected attack on, 149
Japanese attacks, 114, 227
Japanese carriers lost, 150
as turning point, 148–149, 253
USS *Yorktown* lost, 150, 174, 253
Missouri, USS, 255
Mitchell, William (Billy), 4, 5, 187
Molotov, Vyacheslav M., 66, 198
movies
in 1941, 42–43, 48
attack documentary, 127–128
From Here to Eternity, 51, 128–130, 131
Tora! Tora! Tora!, 130–131, 165
Murrow, Edward R., 47, 142
music (1941), 45, 48
Mussolini, Benito, 151
climb to power, 151, 237–238
declaring war on France and Britain, 250
declaring war on United States, 151
Hitler and, 151, 237–238, 239
overthrow of, 253
Pact of Steel, 237, 251
reaction to attack, XV
recognizing appeasement weakness, 17

N

Nagumo, Chuichi, 258
aircraft carrier captain, 5
hearing *"Tora! Tora! Tora!"*, 177
launching attack, 1, 16
post-attack plan alternatives, 258
receiving go-ahead message, 111, 116
task force arriving for attack, 178
third-wave consideration, XIV, 16, 114, 146, 258
Nanking, 16, 70, 109
National Recovery Administration, 195
navy. *See* aircraft carriers; battleships; cruisers; Pacific Fleet (U.S.); ships; submarines
Neutrality Acts, 65, 103, 125, 153–155, 226
Nevada, USS, 156–158
as atomic bomb test target, 157
attempted escape, 156, 179
Battleship Row position, 11
as beacon of hope, 156–157

decommissioning of, 157
destruction of, 157
grounded at Hospital Point, XIII, 157, 179, 202
heroism aboard, 39–40, 156–157, 179
holding off Japanese planes, 157
oil-burner "handicap," 180
repaired/reactivated, 157–158, 203
New Deal, 44, 103, 194–195
news focus (1941), 47–48
Niblack, USS, 155
night and fog decree, 87
Nimitz, Chester, 158
    fleet size under, in 1945, 189
    given Pacific Fleet command, 158, 170
    Guadalcanal address to sailors, 171
    MacArthur and, 172
    military career, 158
    reactions to Pearl attack, 158, 212
    regretting Pearl as memorial, 14
    as submarine expert, 158
    USS *Arizona* and, 11, 119
    See also Midway, Battle of
Nomura, Kichisaburo, 159
    deceptive negotiations, X, 55, 206
    delivering message to Hull, VII–VIII, IX, 146, 159
    Teijira Toyoda and, 218
Norton, Mary T., 190
Norway, X, 155, 248
Nuremberg trials, 243
Nye, Gerald, 8
Nye Committee, 189

O

Oahu
    airfields and bases, 161–164. *See also* Bellows Field; Hickam Field;
        Wheeler Field
    forts, 164–166
Oglala, USS, XIII, XIV, 142, 201–202, 203
oil embargo, against Japan, 18–19, 70, 137, 186, 199, 204, 206–207, 217
Oklahoma, USS, 166–167
    Battleship Row position, 11, 216
    capsized, 138, 167, 179, 202, 216
    casualties, 166, 167
    commissioning of, 166
    destruction of, XIII, 166, 167
    factors increasing loss of life, 167
    heroism aboard, 40
    post-World War I service, 166
    protecting USS *Maryland*, 138
    salvage operation, 167, 203
    sinking of, 167
    survivors, 167
Okumiya, Masatake, 144
OP-20-G, 97
Operation Matador, 23, 27
"Operation Olympic," 80–81

P

Pacific Fleet (U.S.), 169–174
    aftermath of Pearl attack and, 170
    airpower and, 170
    Asiatic Fleet and. *See* Asiatic Fleet
    casualties on December 7, 169, 201
    color-coded contingency plans, 170
    commander in chief. *See* Kimmel, Husband; Nimitz, Chester

destruction statistics from attack, VII
growing, after Pear attack, 173–174
moved to Pearl Harbor, 192, 205–206, 235
Nimitz assuming command, 158, 170
Nimitz inspirational speech to, 171
organization/command structure, 172–173
personnel growth, 173
Plan Orange (Japanese attack) contingency, 170, 182
post-World War I status, 169–170
vessels, on December 7, 1941, 169, 173
    See also aircraft carriers; destroyers; *specific vessels*
Pacific theater, 248–249, 254–255. *See also specific countries*
Pacific War Memorial Commission, 15
Pact of Steel, 151, 237
Panay, USS
    Japanese attack on, 174–176
    Yangtze Patrol and, 174–175
panic, after Pearl attack, 176–177
Panter-Downes, Mollie, 68–69
Patterson, Cissy, 105
Patterson, Joseph, 104–105
Pearl Harbor attack
    action report, 177–180
    aircraft flight direction, 51
    casualties, IX, 169, 201
    controversies surrounding, X–XI
    decision for, 110–111, 241
    fuel stocks unharmed, 114, 169, 179
    Honolulu perspective, 91–92
    immediately before, VII, IX
    lack of preparedness for, XI
    overview, VII–VIII, IX–XI
    Pacific Fleet and. *See* Pacific Fleet (U.S.)
    as part of coordinated attack, 68
    pilot leading. *See* Fuchida, Mitsuo
    reactions to. *See* reactions to Pearl attack
    reasons for, X, 80
    ship damage summary, 202–204
    timeline, XIII–XV
    unifying Allies, 26
    weather report, 50
Pearl Harbor attack plan, 184–187
    adopted by Japanese, 110, 241
    aircraft carriers for, 5
    airplane tactics, 4–5
    chronology of Japanese activities, 81
    creation of, 112, 116, 163, 178, 184, 185, 258
    Hirohito involvement, 80
    inception of, 3
    Isoruku Yamamoto and, 163, 178, 184, 185
    Minoru Genda and, 112, 116, 258
    post-attack plan alternatives, 258
Pearl Harbor Survivors Association, 208
Pennsylvania, USS, 180–181
    during attack, 178, 181, 202
    avenging Pearl attack, 216
    casualties, 181
    commissioning of, 180
    cost of, 180
    in dry dock, 178, 181, 202
    nicknames, 180–181
    relegated to target duty, 181
    repaired/reactivated, 181, 203, 217
    scuttled, 181
    service record, 180
    specifications, 180

USS *Oglala* taking hit for, 202
World War II service, 181, 216
Percival, Arthur, 23–24, 27, 135
Perry, Matthew C., 107, 185, 186
Peterson, Louis, 141
P40 airplanes, 9, 161, 162, 163
Pharris, Jackson, 32, 40
Philippines
buildup of forces in, 182
forces present on December 7, 183
Japanese attacks on, VIII, 183–184
lost to Japan, 182
Plan Orange (Japanese attack) contingency and, 170, 182
preparation for attack, 182
strategic importance of, 183
U.S. granting independence, 183
See also MacArthur, Douglas
Phillips, Tom, 23, 24, 27, 28
Plan Orange (Japanese attack) contingency, 170, 182
Poland, Germany invading, 17, 65, 237, 238–239
Britain declaring war after, 17, 65, 90
events leading to, 65
France declaring war after, 17, 65, 90, 248
Italy response to, 151
New Zealand declaring war after, 90
starting World War II, 65, 130, 226, 237
U.S. response to, 65–66, 192, 195. *See also* Lend-Lease Act
Post-Arcadia Collaboration, 10
Prange, Gordon, 86–87
preparedness, 184–187
antitorpedo nets and, 4, 192
army/navy blaming each other, 24
C.C. Bloch and, 21–22
command structure for, 21
disarmament agreements and, 186–187
documentary film questioning, 128
George C. Marshall and, 24, 137–138, 207
historian views, 82–87
isolationism impacting, 185, 186
Plan Orange (Japanese attack) contingency, 170, 182
Roosevelt cabinet meeting on December 5, 195–196
underestimating Japanese, 185, 187
U.S. military strategy (pre-attack), 187
See also blame, for Pearl Harbor attack
press, isolationist, 104–105
prisoner of war, first, 146, 164
Public Works Administration, 195
Punchbowl Cemetery, 92, 245
PURPLE, 37–38, 95, 96

R
radar
detecting incoming Japanese planes, VII, 84, 137, 165, 167, 178
limited use of, 208, 232
reports handled ineffectively, XV, 84–85, 137, 167, 178
Radford, Arthur, 141
radio (1941), 45, 47
Raleigh, USS, XIII, 203
Rankin, Jeannette, 189–191
blaming British for manipulating U.S. to war, 191
Eleanor Roosevelt courting war support, 189–190
first woman in Congress, 189
isolationist platform, 189
as pacifist, 189, 190
sole opponent to war declaration, 41, 189, 191, 193
Rayburn, Sam, 191

reactions to Pearl attack
Adolf Hitler, 88
American public, IX, X, 8–9
Benito Mussolini, XV
Britain, 24–26, 68–69
Charles de Gaulle, 52
Chester Nimitz, 158, 212
Congress, 40–41
Franklin D. Roosevelt, 9
isolationist press, 104
Joseph Grew, X
Los Angeles blackouts, 176
Los Angeles Times, X
memoirs (American), 140–143
memoirs (Japanese), 144–147
New York Mayor (La Guardia), 8
panic in America, 176–177
USS *Washington*, 8
Winston Churchill, VIII, 26, 28, 34–35
Yosuke Matsuoka, 140
readiness for attack, VII
recruiting
in Australia, 29
code analysts, 36
"Remember Pearl Harbor" encouraging, X, 181
women, 229, 230–231
Reeves, Thomas, 32, 40
Reuben James, USS, 48, 154
revisionist historians, 82, 84, 85, 99
Rhee, Syngman, 245
Ribbentrop, Joachim von, 63, 64, 66–68, 238, 239
Richardson, James O., 191–193
blaming Roosevelt for Pearl disaster, 192
as CINCUS, 191
declining Pearl investigation lead, 100
Kimmel replacing, 121
opposing fleet transfer to Pearl Harbor, 192
relieved of command, 85
replacing C.C. Bloch, 21, 191
retirement of, 192
on Stark negligence, 193
vetoing antitorpedo nets, 192
warning of Pearl vulnerability, 85
Robalo, USS, 121
Roberts Commission, 86, 98
Rochefort, Joseph, 36–37, 97, 149, 150
Rogers, Edith Nourse, 190, 229, 230
Rommel, Erwin, 7, 18, 22, 251, 253
Roosevelt, Eleanor, 194
false reports of San Francisco attacks and, X, 177
Jeannette Rankin and, 189–190
marriage to Franklin, 194
Nomura and, 159
perspective entering World War II, 190
Roosevelt, Franklin D., 193–196, 194
amending December 8 speech, 9, 193
Arcadia conference and, 9–10
asking for war declaration, 9, 41, 190
assassination attempt on, 194
as assistant secretary of navy, 194
"Big Three" conference attendance, 196
birth of, 193
blame for Pearl Harbor and, 82, 85, 86, 95–96, 101, 192
Cabinet meeting after attack, 9
Churchill and, 9–10, 35
contentious press relations, 105

death of, 196
December 5 cabinet meeting on Japan war preparations, 195–196
final appeal to Hirohito, 71, 96
"Four Freedoms" speech, 48, 195
Henry A. Wallace and, 232–233
historical term length, 193
isolationism and, 103
memorial to, 196
on neutrality vs. national security, 65
New Deal, 44, 103, 194–195
polio paralysis, 194
political career, 194–195
proclaiming state of emergency, 48
public works successes, 194, 195
receiving message of attack, 193
response to *Panay* incident, 175
speech to nation, 9, 193
vice presidents of, 232–233. *See also* Truman, Harry
view of inevitable war involvement, 190
Ross, Donald Kirby, 39, 156–157
Rowlett, Frank, 36, 37
rumors, of further attacks, 176, 177
Russia. *See* Soviet Union
Russo-Japanese War, 70, 185, 197

S

Sakamaki, Ensign Kazuo, XIV, XV, 145–146, 164
salvage operations, 201–204
    ammunition usable after, 204
    delays in, 203
    diving operations, 203
    financial value of, 204
    organization and implementation, 203
    summary of damaged ships, 202–204
    USS *Arizona*, 13–14, 203, 204
    USS *Oklahoma*, 167, 203
sanctions against Japan, 204–207
    America First opposition, 103
    China invasion triggering, 70, 109, 110, 204
    failure of, 204, 207
    freezing assets, 54, 213, 219
    French Indochina seizure and, 206–207
    Henry Stimson pushing, 205, 206
    Japanese alliances and. *See* Tripartite Pact
    Japanese response to, 217, 218
    Neutrality Acts and, 103, 153–154
    1941 embargo, 18–19, 54, 83, 137, 199
    oil embargo, 18–19, 70, 137, 186, 199, 204, 206–207, 217
    Panay incident and, 205
    Roosevelt planning, 83
    steel embargo, 70, 83, 137, 204, 205
    U.S. opposing (1937), 225
    voluntary embargo, 109
Saratoga, USS, 169, 179
Sazanami, 114, 115
Scanland, Francis W., 202
Schofield Barracks, X, 50, 51, 129, 162, 164
Scott, Robert, 32, 40
scouting force ship, Japanese, 115
Senn, Thomas J., 234
Shaw, USS, XIII, 203
Shimazaki, Shigekazu, 113
ships
    airplanes vs., 3–6
    Axis, seized by U.S. Coast Guard, 155

1922 treaty limiting, 5, 70, 183, 186
See also aircraft carriers; battleships; cruisers; destroyers; Pacific Fleet
    (U.S.); submarines
Shiranui, 115
Shokaku, VII, 5, 111, 114, 115, 150
Short, Walter C., 207–209
    accepting military command of Hawai'i, 92, 207
    anticipating sabotage attack, 208
    on December 7, 166
    denied legal counsel, 98
    exoneration of, 101, 208
    honored by Pearl Harbor Survivors Association, 208
    not using radar effectively, 208
    not warned about attack, XI
    opinion on attack responsibility, 22
    parking airplanes wing tip to wing tip, 207
    receiving message of failed negotiations, XV
    relieved of command, 123, 166
    responsibility for attack and, 22, 96, 97, 98–99, 207, 208
    as scapegoat, 207, 208
    testifying at investigation, 101
Short biplanes, 1
Signal Intelligence Service (SIS), 36, 37, 38, 39, 61, 62, 95, 137
Singapore, 134–135
    British defensive system, 134–135
    expected attack on, 24
    Japanese attacks on, XIV, XV, 6, 25, 26, 28, 35
    Japanese takeover of, 135
    weaknesses of, 134–135
Sino-Japanese conflict, 108–109, 219
Sino-Japanese War (1894–95), 70, 108
Sino-Japanese War (1937), 16
Smith, Margaret Chase, 190
Social Security, 117, 195
Sorge, Richard, 199
Soryu, VII, 5, 111, 114, 115
Soviet Union
    after World War II, 243–244
    Anti-Comintern Pact and, 66, 99, 197, 198, 225
    arms race with U.S., 243–244
    benefiting from U.S. in World War II, VIII
    Britain forwarding U.S. equipment to, 199, 210
    Cold War, 14–15, 127, 220, 243–244
    declaring war on Japan, 255
    Five Year Plan, 209–210
    Germany attacking, X, 6–7, 210, 251
    Japan relations, 109, 110, 111, 197–199, 206
    military buildup, 197
    nonaggression pact with Japan, 110, 111, 206
    nonaggression pact with Nazi Germany, 17, 18–19, 66, 198, 210, 239,
        249, 251
    reparation demands to Japan, 246
    repelling Germany, 251–252, 253
    rise to power, 197
    war with Finland, 249
Speer, Albert, 243
Spruance, Raymond, 150, 172–173
Stalin, Josef, 209–210
    "Big Three" conference attendance, 196
    destroying domestic rivals, 210
    disdain for Nazis, 17
    feelings of Allies toward, 17
    Five Year Plan, 209–210
    Hitler assurances of alliance, 239
    knowledge of Pearl Harbor attack plan, 210
    misplaced trust in Hitler, 210

political/military career, 209–210
revolutionary life of, 209
surprise at German attack, 18
threatening separate German peace, 254
See also Soviet Union
Stark, Harold R., 211–212
censuring of, 22
failure to alert forces, 22, 62, 211–212
James Richardson accusation of negligence, 193
keeping Fleet at Pearl, 192
memo giving attack warning, 86
questions about December 6 whereabouts, 211
receiving message of attack, XIII
reporting attack, XIII, 122
responsibility for attack and, 22, 62, 123, 193, 211–212
steel embargo, against Japan, 70, 83, 137, 204, 205
Stimson, Henry L., 212–213
birth of, 212
education of, 212
investigations of responsibility, 100
on maneuvering Japan to attack, 83
named secretary of war, 212
pushing Japan sanctions, 205, 206
refusing recognition of Japanese conquests, 206, 225
as secretary of state, 212
supporting Lend-Lease Act, 127
Stimson Doctrine, 206, 212
stock market
1929 crash, 194, 225
response to Pearl attack, 177
Stratton, Donald Gay, 12
submarines
Chester Nimitz and, 158, 170
heroism aboard, 174
Kimmel son lost in, 121
off Caroline Islands, 33
Pacific Fleet (U.S.), 172, 173, 174
positioned to destroy escaping ships, 185
sinking USS *Cynthia*, 8
submarines, at Pearl Harbor
blocking harbor, XIII
captured, 163–164, 202
chart taken from, 202
damaged/disabled, XIV, XV, 51, 116, 163–164, 201
deployment of, 116
Kimmel hearing about, 121, 178
Kimmel not responding to, 178
lack of communication/response to, 22, 85, 178
pilot memoirs, 145–146
salvaged in 2002, 204
spotted, 85
Stark failing to notify navy of, 22
sunk before attack, 12, 130, 178, 204
two-man midget, 114, 116, 147–148, 202, 204
submarines, German
disrupting British supply lines, 212, 226
early air power demonstration, 4
firing on USS *Reuben James*, 48, 154
initiating undeclared naval war, 155
Nimitz researching, 158
post-war reduction requirement, 236
precipitating U.S. to fire on all German ships, 48, 154
in World War I, 224
sugar plantations, 78
Sweden, 155
Switzerland, 155

T
Tanaka, Giichi, 185–186
"Tanaka Memorial," 185–186
Tanikaze, 115
tanks
British, 7
German, 7, 18
Japanese, 34, 135
Soviet, 104, 251
Tansill, Charles, 82–83, 85
Taylor, Delia, 38
Taylor, Ken, 161
Tennessee, USS, 215–217
attack of, 216–217
avenging Pearl attack, 216
Battleship Row position, 11, 215–216
burning, 179
commissioning of, 215
crew casualties, 216
deactivated, 217
keeping *West Virginia* afloat, 202
post-attack service, 216, 217
pre-attack service, 215
repaired/reactivated, 203, 217
sheltered from torpedo attack, 216–217
sold for scrap, 217
specifications, 215
Tennessee Valley Authority, 195
Thailand, 59
Thomas, Francis J., XIV, 179
Thomas, Richard, 74
Thomas, Sir Shenton, 23–24
timeline, XIII–XV
Togo, Shigenori, XIV, 53, 54–55
Tojo, Hideki, 217–218
attack plans and, 217
as both minister of war/prime minister, 217
decision to attack United States, 110–111, 241
declaration of war, 53–54, 218
defending attack decision, 218
diplomatic relations, 54–55
10-point proposal from Hull, 217, 241
viewing attack as shameful, 217
Tomich, Peter, 40
Tone, 114, 115
"*Tora! Tora! Tora!*" (message), 13, 144, 177
Tora! Tora! Tora! (movie), 130–131, 165
torpedo planes, 4–5
account of USS *Oglala* strike, 201–202
antitorpedo nets and, 4, 192
attack of, VI, XIII, 111–112, 144, 179–180
history of, 1, 3
ordnance, 113
shallow-water torpedoes for, 5, 130
Toyoda, Teijiro, 218–219
Tripartite Pact, VIII, 66–68
creating Axis power alignment, 17, 53, 110, 186, 206, 213
Matsuoka negotiating, 139, 140
message to U.S., 17, 186
mutual war with U.S. and, 68
participating countries, 17
renewal of, 198
Yugoslavia forced to sign, 18
Truman, Harry, 219–221
becoming president, 196, 220
birth of, 220

death of, 220
deciding to use atomic bomb, 81, 221, 252
offering military training services, 219–220
political career, 220
as vice president, 220
Truman Doctrine, 220
Turner, Richmond K., 21, 170, 174, 211
Tyler, Kermit, 84, 165, 178

U

United Nations
    Atlantic Charter and, 83
    charter of, 93, 246
    Cordell Hull and, 92, 93
    founding of, 246
    four freedoms and, 48
    Korean conflict and, 245
    Relief and Rehabilitation Organization, 243
    Security Council, 246
United Nations founding, 93
United States, 223–227
    arms race with Soviet Union, 243–244
    Cold War, 14–15, 127, 220, 243–244
    decision to enter World War II, VIII, IX–X, 226
    end of war for, 254–255,
    forced into World War II, VIII, IX–X, 226
    internment camps, 35, 117
    interwar period, 225–226
    life in 1941. *See* culture (1941); daily life
    providing supplies after war, 243
    public reaction to attack, IX, X, 8–9
    rebuilding Japan, 246–247
    results of World War II, 242
    taking offensive in World War II, 253
    in World War I, 223–225
Urakaze, 115
Ushio, 114, 115
Utah, USS, 11
    attack of, XIII
    beyond repair, 180, 203
    capsized, 40, 202
    heroism aboard, 40
    remaining on harbor floor, 204

V

Val (Japanese aircraft), 111, 113, 114
Van Valkenburgh, Franklin, 11, 13, 39, 119
Van Valkenburgh, Franklin, Jr., 120
Versailles Treaty
    ceding German land to Poland, 65
    Germany forced to accept, 236
    Germany opposed to, 237
    Hitler violating, 16, 237–238
    Italians walking out of negotiations, 237
    Japan feeling cheated by, 237
    Russia not included in, 237
    United States rejecting, 102, 225
Vestal, USS, 11, 12, 40, 50, 119, 203, 216
Vietnam. *See* French Indochina
von Hindenburg, Marshal, 237
von Neurath, Konstantin, 243

W

WAC (Women's Army Corps), 229–231
    African American, 230
    arguments for, 229
    as auxiliary to army, 229–230
    excluded from combat training, 230
    first assignments, 229–230
    made permanent, then eliminated, 231
    as part of army, 230–231
Wagner, Frank D., 4
Wake Island, 231–232
    casualties, 232
    Japanese attacks on, VIII, XV, 6, 227, 231–232
    lacking resources, 232
    location of, 231
    ranking officer on, 231
    strategic importance of, 231
    surrender of, 231–232
    taken by Japan, 149
Wallace, Henry A., 232–233
Wallin, Homer N., 203
War and Remembrance, 130
war criminals, 243, 247
Ward, James, 40
Ward, USS
    firing first Pearl Harbor attack shot, 178
    notified of midget sub presence, 85
    reporting sighting of sub, 121
    sinking midget submarine, 12, 148, 178, 204
    survivor, 12
Washington, USS, 8
Washington Naval Conference, 70, 225
Washington Naval Treaty, 5, 70, 183, 186
Wasp, USS, 174
WAVES (Women Accepted for Voluntary Emergency Service), 233–234
weather report, 50
Welch, George, 51, 161
Welles, Roger, 166
West Virginia, USS, 216, 234–236
    after-action report of attack, 236
    attack of, XIII, 235–236
    avenging Pearl attack, 216
    Battleship Row position, 11, 215–216, 235
    casualties, 235
    commissioning of, 234
    explosion of, 216
    as flagship (after attack), 236
    heroism aboard, 40, 216, 235
    listing after attack, 202, 203, 216
    pre-war service, 234–235
    repaired/reactivated, 203, 236
    sinking of, 179
    specifications, 234
Wheeler Field
    attack of, 161–162, 178
    casualties, 162
    damage/destruction at, 114, 145, 162
    first attack bomb landing at, 112
    perspective from, 161
    planes taking off from, 114, 163
Whitaker, F.H., 203
White, Commander William, 236
White, William Allen, 191
Wichita, 154
Wilkinson, Theodore, 211
Wilson, Woodrow, 10, 93, 102, 151, 166, 223–224
Winds of War, 130
Wohlstetter, Roberta, 83–86, 96
women
    in army. *See* WAC (Women's Army Corps)

in Congress, 189, 190
cryptanalysts, 38
fashion trends (1941), 49
first in Congress, 189
first in Senate, 190
recruiting of, 229, 230–231
right to vote, 190
WAVES, 233–234
World War I
    affecting Germany, 236, 237
    effects of, causing World War II, 236–237
    United States in, 223–225
    See also Versailles Treaty
World War II, 247–255
    American reluctance to enter, 18, 65–66, 102–103
    Axis powers, 16–20
    causes of, 236–241
    countries entering. *See* declarations of war
    end of, 254–255
    European theater, 248, 254. *See also specific countries*
    German victories, 249–251
    impacting Pacific ships before December 7, 7–8
    interwar period after, 225–226
    Japanese decline during, 80
    neutral European countries, 155
    Pacific theater, 248–249, 254–255
    resource requirement projections for, 226
    retreat of Germany, 253–254
    start of, 65, 130, 185, 226, 237
    turning around, 251–253
    U.S. forced into, VIII, IX–X, 226
    U.S. offensive, 253
    WAC (Women's Army Corps), 229–231
    WAVES served in, 233–234
World War II results, 242–247
    Europe, 242–243

France, 244
Germany, 242–243
Great Britain, 244
Israel, 245
Marshall Plan and, 220, 243
Nuremberg trials, 243
Soviet Union, 243–244
Wouk, Herman, 130–131

Y
Yamamoto, Isoruku, 257–259
    attack plan, 3, 114, 163, 178, 184, 185
    attack plan adopted, 110, 241
    birth of, 257
    as carrier captain, 5
    explaining plan importance, 144
    midget submarine plan, 147–148
    plane shot down, 187, 259
    retreating from Midway, 150
    signaling attack, 55, 116
    six-month promise, 148–149, 184–185
    targeting aircraft carriers, 163
Yamashiro, 216
Yangtze Patrol, 174, 175
Yorktown, USS, 149
    in Battle of Coral Sea, 150, 253
    Japanese ship damage from, 115
    sinking of, 150, 174
Young, Cassin, 40

Z
Zangara, Giuseppe, 194
Zeroes, 27, 111, 113, 114, 141, 257
Zuikaku, VII, 5, 114, 115, 150